American Justice
in Taiwan

AMERICAN JUSTICE IN TAIWAN

The 1957 Riots and Cold War Foreign Policy

STEPHEN G. CRAFT

UNIVERSITY PRESS OF KENTUCKY

Scholarly publisher for the Commonwealth,
serving Bellarmine University, Berea College, Centre College of Kentucky,
Eastern Kentucky University, The Filson Historical Society, Georgetown
College, Kentucky Historical Society, Kentucky State University, Morehead
State University, Murray State University, Northern Kentucky University,
Transylvania University, University of Kentucky, University of Louisville, and
Western Kentucky University.

Editorial and Sales Offices: The University Press of Kentucky
663 South Limestone Street, Lexington, Kentucky 40508-4008
www.kentuckypress.com

Library of Congress Cataloging-in-Publication Data

Names: Craft, Stephen G., 1963- author.
Title: American justice in Taiwan : the 1957 riots and cold war foreign
   policy / Stephen G. Craft.
Description: Lexington : University Press of Kentucky, [2016] | Series:
   Studies in conflict, diplomacy, and peace | Includes bibliographical
   references and index.
Identifiers: LCCN 2015037944| ISBN 9780813166353 (hardcover : alk. paper)
   | ISBN 9780813166360 (pdf) | ISBN 9780813166377 (epub)
Subjects: LCSH: Reynolds, Robert—Trials, litigation, etc. | Courts-martial
   and courts of inquiry—United States—History. | Trials
   (Homicide)—Taiwan. | United States. Uniform Code of Military Justice. |
   United States—Armed Forces—Taiwan. | United States—Foreign
   relations—Taiwan | Taiwan—Foreign relations—United States. |
   Taiwan—Politics and government—1945- | Riots—Taiwan—History.
Classification: LCC KF7642.R49 C73 2016 | DDC 343.73/014—dc23
LC record available at http://lccn.loc.gov/2015037944

This book is printed on acid-free paper meeting
the requirements of the American National Standard
for Permanence in Paper for Printed Library Materials.

∞

Manufactured in the United States of America.

Member of the Association of
American University Presses

In memory of Lloyd E. Eastman

Contents

Photographs follow page 130

Technical Note

For this work, I have used *pinyin* to romanize most Chinese names and terms. The exceptions are individuals and Taiwan's major cities more well-known in the 1950s by the Wade-Giles usage. In addition to aborigines and the Hakka people, Taiwan's population consisted mostly of Han Chinese whose ancestors emigrated to Taiwan after the fall of the Ming dynasty in the 1600s and speak a dialect from Fujian Province. After 1945, Taiwan came under the control of the Republic of China (or Nationalist) government, bringing about an influx of people who originated from every Chinese province. Both groups shared Chinese surnames and ultimately used Mandarin Chinese. To distinguish between the two, I use the term mainlander(s) to refer to the 2 million Chinese refugees who came to Taiwan after 1945 and the term Taiwanese to signify those born and raised in Taiwan. In those situations where it is impossible to distinguish between the two, I have simply used the term Chinese.

Abbreviations

BCC	Broadcasting Corporation of China
BE	Bureau of Far Eastern Affairs
CA	Records of the Office of Chinese Affairs
CAT	Civil Air Transport
CIA	Central Intelligence Agency
CID	Alien Criminal Investigation Division
CINCPAC	Commander in Chief Pacific Command
ECA	Economic Cooperation Administration
FAP	Foreign Affairs Police
GRC	Government of the Republic of China
ICA	International Cooperation Administration
IRP	Institute for Revolutionary Practice
JCS	Joint Chiefs of Staff
MAAG	U.S. Military Advisory and Assistance Group
MDAP	Mutual Defense Assistance Program
MDT	U.S.-ROC Mutual Defense Treaty
MSP	Mutual Security Program
NA	National Archives and Records Administration, College Park, Maryland
NACC	Naval Auxiliary Communication Center
NATO	North Atlantic Treaty Organization
NSB	National Security Bureau
NSC	National Security Council
OCB	Operations Coordinating Board
PPC	Peace Preservation Corps
PRC	People's Republic of China
ROC	Republic of China
SOFA	Status of Forces Agreement
TDC	U.S.-Taiwan Defense Command
UCMJ	Uniform Code of Military Justice
U.N.	United Nations
USARPAC	U.S. Army Pacific Command
USIA	United States Information Agency
USIS	United States Information Service
WEI	Western Enterprise, Inc.
WJDA	Waijiao Dangan, Institute of Modern History, Academia Sinica, Nangang, Taiwan

Preface and Acknowledgments

My first encounter with the story of Sergeant Robert Reynolds, the shooting of Liu Ziran, and the subsequent riots occurred in 1987 when I was a graduate student at Ohio University. Months before, I lived in Luodong, Taiwan, for a year as part of a college internship in which I taught English and worked at a children's orphanage. Initially, my interest in graduate school was solely to get a better grasp of East Asian history and politics before returning there to pursue a career.

My first year in Taiwan represented almost total cultural immersion. Few foreigners lived in Luodong at the time. One could go for days and not see or speak to another foreigner. It was before the economic boom that brought the 7-Eleven stores that operate twenty-four hours a day, the plethora of American fast food chains (there were only three McDonald's fast-food restaurants on the entire island in 1985), and all the other great changes that I would not witness until 1991 when I returned to live in Taichung for a summer to begin doctoral research and teach English. Although I learned to speak Chinese and some Taiwanese, if there ever was an innocent abroad, I was it. I knew little about the culture or the people, and experienced a number of cultural misunderstandings. Learning the language was frustrating. Being constantly stared at and feeling the intense scrutiny from people could at times be unbearable. (Unable to learn the language and deal with the culture shock, my roommate from Oklahoma cut short his internship after only four months.) Nevertheless, I made friends and experienced a considerable number of personal changes. My belief in American exceptionalism diminished considerably. Leaving Reagan's America for a year certainly modified my perception of the United States' place in the world as a superpower and made me rather critical of the manner in which America sometimes wielded power.

Cold War Taiwan was very different from the one that exists today. During the Iran-Contra Hearings of 1987, not only was Taiwan identified as one of the countries that gave support to the Contras fighting communist Sandinistas in Nicaragua, but a U.S. congressman insisted on referring to it as a democracy. Although Taiwan had the trappings of a democracy in the mid-1980s, the fact remained that the island was under the one-party rule of the Kuomintang or Nationalist Party, with Chiang Ching-kuo, son of Chiang Kai-shek, as president. Television news broadcasts showed him from time to time talking to folks on the street, often wearing a two-piece jogging suit.

Taiwan remained under martial law. There was a strong military presence, with soldiers guarding bridges and manning pillboxes while military policemen roamed the streets in their black and white cars with flashing red lights. There were beaches where one could walk but not take photographs for security reasons. Pirated copies of books on Chinese history often did not include chapters critical of Nationalist rule in China and Taiwan. Books that had a picture of Mao Zedong, leader of the People's Republic of China, on the cover had the character for bandit (*fei*) written on his face. There was relative freedom, and yet there were events in Taiwan's recent history that were too sensitive to discuss even in private with locals. Just a few years before, the government had cracked down on an effort by Taiwanese in Kaohsiung who gathered to express their discontent.

As a graduate student, I was very interested in learning more about Taiwan's history, the background behind the Republic of China's control of Taiwan since 1945, and the origins of the Taiwanese independence movement. In those days, the opposition party, or *dangwai*, evolved into what became known as the Democratic Progressive Party (*Minjingdang*). The *dangwai* seemed quite popular in Luodong, if not Yilan County in general. Having witnessed the election campaigns and celebrations that occurred in 1985 that brought a *dangwai* candidate to power in Taiwan's provincial legislature, my interest led me to write a paper on the origins of the *dangwai* for a course on Chinese politics taught by Dr. Willard Ellsbree. Although there was no direct relationship between the proponents of independence and the Reynolds case, I acquired a cursory knowledge of the shooting and riots that remained with me.

My subsequent research interests took me elsewhere in Chinese history and I lived in Taiwan from 1993 until 1998. As a resident alien, I was well aware that I fell under the legal jurisdiction of the ROC. Fortunately, despite being involved in traffic accidents in which I was spilled off my bicycle or motorbike by Taiwanese drivers, interrogated by an employer who wanted to know if I had been involved in a brawl involving foreigners and Chinese (the answer was no), and falsely accused by a neighbor for destruction of property, I never found myself under arrest or even investigated (that I know of). I entered a Taiwan civil courtroom just once, and only to affirm that a bank check had been lost, not stolen. The five male and female judges of the court were quite friendly and patient as I answered their questions in Chinese. Granted, I sensed that I had a higher status and received better treatment compared to other internationals because of the fact that I was a U.S. citizen, and can think of numerous occasions in which U.S. citizenship saved me from one annoyance or bureaucratic obstacle after another. For example, when my wife and I were married there in 1993, I was issued an Alien Registration Card without any questions, whereas other foreign nationals, including those from the United Kingdom with Taiwanese wives, were discriminated against, leading to protests in the mid-1990s. Nevertheless, in the times that I have lived outside of the American legal system in Taiwan, Hong Kong, and China over the last thirty years, I understood that, U.S. citizen or not, I was not beyond Chinese law.

Living in East Asia also gave me an understanding of how Chinese and Taiwanese deal with burglaries, traffic accidents, and domestic violence. Most Chinese and Taiwanese that I knew never kept a pistol in the home. A knife and/or superior numbers were generally preferred for offensive and defensive purposes. Gun violence did occur from time to time in the 1990s, but nothing on the scale seen or experienced in the United States. There is violence that occurs in Taiwan and China, but the manner in which people defuse or escalate conflict is different. This insight is reflected in my analysis of the events of 1957.

My experiences in Asia partly explain why I remained intrigued by the Reynolds incident. Between 2002 and 2009, I made trips to several archives in the United States, the United Kingdom, and Taiwan. Usually I was doing research for another project, but I took the time to dig up any documents pertaining to Black Friday and related issues. The incident remained a sensitive topic politically in Taiwan, as I discovered when asked why I was so interested in the riots and Liu Ziran. One of the positive aspects of the election of President Chen Shuibian, of the DPP, in 2000 was the opening of diplomatic archives that had been sealed for years by the Nationalists, including those pertaining to this case.

After reading the primary documents that I discovered and doing some tentative writing over ten years ago, the issue of GIs, diplomatic immunity, and status of forces agreements seemed relevant to the present. Not only did the United States continue to maintain troops in Okinawa and South Korea, where incidents involving U.S. soldiers that resulted in rape or death occurred, but thousands of men and women were deployed in Afghanistan and Iraq as part of what the Bush administration called the "War on Terror." Under the Obama administration, the increase in troop levels in Afghanistan and the use of unmanned aerial vehicles, commonly and erroneously known as drones, to carry out air strikes has led, not by design, to numerous incidents. Innocent civilians have been killed either by GIs on the ground who were subsequently tried in the United States by court-martial or by UAV pilots stationed in Nevada and elsewhere who ostensibly cannot be held accountable for any crimes. Then, in 2012, George Zimmerman, an armed Neighborhood

Watch volunteer, followed a young African American by the name of Trayvon Martin in the mistaken belief that Martin was a gang member who had carried out crimes in Zimmerman's neighborhood. The result was a scuffle in which Zimmerman shot and killed Martin, and claimed self-defense under Florida's Stand Your Ground law. In 2013, Zimmerman, in a situation in which there were no witnesses, was found not guilty by a jury of six women, leading to protests. If my analysis of the events of 1957 is influenced by presentism, these matters (plus the Amanda Knox case in Italy) were probably uppermost on my mind.

In the many years that I have devoted to this project, I have accumulated numerous debts to many who provided assistance of one type or another. I should begin by thanking administrators and colleagues at Embry-Riddle Aeronautical University. Former university presidents George Ebbs and John Johnson graciously provided research funding. William Grams, dean of the College of Arts and Sciences, Donna Barbie, chair of the Humanities/Communication Department, James Ramsay, chair of the Department of Security Studies and International Affairs, and Michael Hickey, dean of Research and Graduate Studies, provided travel funds and other support critical to the project's completion. James Libbey and M. B. McLatchey, colleagues at the Daytona Beach campus, took the time to read the manuscript in its entirety: Yang Li, formerly with ERAU's Prescott campus, provided feedback on my translations of Chinese sources and assisted in other ways. A special debt is also owed to Sue Burkhart and Liz Sterthaus, of ERAU's Interlibrary Loan Department, for their tireless efforts in fulfilling my numerous requests.

Outside of ERAU, I must thank several scholars in Taiwan: Peter Wang Chen-main for assistance in tracking down sources; Lin Zhengzhen for helping me gain access to online databases as well as to the library at National Zhongxing University in Taichung; Zhang Juide for assistance while doing research in the diplomatic archives housed at the Institute of Modern History in Nangang. In the United Kingdom, a debt is owed to Simon Fowler for following up with research at the Public Records Office in Kew, London. In the United States, I need to thank: George Herring, Noel Pugach, and Stephen MacKinnon for reading the manuscript and providing helpful suggestions; Lin Hsiao-tung and Kang Jiashen for converting Chiang Kai-shek's diary entries from "grass writing" into a word-processing format; Rebecca Livingston for making copies of photographs located at the National Archives and Records Administration in College Park, Maryland; and William Dawson, Glenn Jones, Vincent Kramer, Robert Sheeks, Karen Brady Smith, and John Thomson for sharing photographs, newspapers, and insights from life in Taiwan in the 1950s. I need to also thank Don Wiggins for putting out a call on my behalf to Taiwan expatriates from the 1950s on his U.S.-Taiwan Defense Command blog.

I dedicate this book to Lloyd E. Eastman, whom I only had the pleasure of knowing for just a few years. My interest in learning more about the Nationalists and Chiang Kai-shek naturally led me to his work, which I greatly admired, and Lloyd's expertise in modern Chinese history was the primary reason why I entered the doctoral program at the University of Illinois at Urbana-Champaign. Sadly, it was during my first year there that Lloyd learned, while doing research in Taiwan on a proposed biography of Chiang Kai-shek, that he had brain cancer. In the last months of his life, Lloyd remained a caring adviser and teacher, never wanting to impose on his advisees because of his illness unless absolutely necessary. Without Lloyd's support at critical moments, I would never have completed the doctorate and achieved a relatively successful academic career. This simple dedication comes nowhere close to repaying the debt that I owe him.

Finally, I am grateful to my wife, Demi Wen-ling Lin, my son, Robert, and my daughter, Brittney, who will be happy to see her name in print a third time. Without their love and support this book would not be possible.

Introduction

Shortly after World War II, the United States possessed Leased Base Agreements with only three countries: the United Kingdom, the Philippines, and Cuba. Although its troops still occupied Germany and Japan, it otherwise was in the process of demobilizing what had been, for U.S. standards, a huge military machine. With the advent of the Korean War in 1950, U.S. policy shifted back toward deploying large numbers of forces and possessing base rights throughout the world. Troop levels in the 1950s never approached those of the Second World War, but were still rather high compared to former peacetime standards. By 1957, nearly 1 million U.S. military personnel were stationed in thirty-six countries on 250 bases that utilized four thousand square miles of foreign soil, comparable to the state of Connecticut. In addition to the soldiers, there were twenty-three thousand civilian employees and four hundred thousand dependents, bringing the total number of Americans abroad to nearly 1.5 million. The cost to construct all of these facilities totaled billions of dollars, while an estimated $2.2 billion was invested in local economies, where 350,000 locals were employed by the U.S. military.[1]

The presence of so many Americans throughout the world eventually led to misunderstandings, cultural clashes, criminal behavior, and incidents on foreign soil. In 1951, the North Atlantic Treaty Organization (NATO) powers signed the Status of Forces Agreement (SOFA) in which Article VII declared that in cases in which a member of the military had violated laws of both the sending and receiving states, the sending state had the primary right to exercise jurisdiction over offenses: solely against the property or security of the United States; solely against a member of the U.S. armed forces, or its civilian component or of one of their dependents; arising out of any act or omission done in the performance of official duty. The receiving state had primary right to exercise jurisdiction in all other cases. To use an example provided by the State Department, if a U.S. soldier killed a Frenchman, the soldier would be tried in French courts unless France agreed to waive jurisdiction. If a U.S. soldier killed another U.S. soldier, damaged American property, or ran down a Frenchman while driving a jeep on duty, the soldier would face a U.S. court-martial.[2]

Then and later, the NATO SOFA became a matter of controversy. The treaty did not go into effect for the United States until August 23, 1953, after considerable debate in Congress. The Department of Defense demanded exclusive jurisdiction, but the State Department insisted on the NATO formula when engaged in base negotiations with NATO and non-NATO countries. Both departments remained at odds over the issue throughout the 1950s. Meanwhile, some U.S. congressmen opposed allowing GIs to be tried under foreign law, arguing that the U.S. Constitution should follow the troops wherever they were deployed. These politicians pushed for amendments that gave the United States exclusive jurisdiction over GIs. Moreover, the United States possessed bilateral administrative agreements with a number of nations, many in Asia, that denied those countries jurisdiction regardless of the severity of the crimes. Generally, SOFAs and these other bilateral agreements were signed with nations where the United States had either ground forces and/or naval and air bases. Although American troops were not engaged in major fighting around the world after 1953, the Pentagon justified its demand for exclusive jurisdiction on the grounds that its military personnel were located near Cold War front lines or potential hot spots.

Another aspect of the U.S. military component to containment during the Cold War was the use of Military Assistance and Advisory Groups (MAAGs), in which army, navy, and air force personnel were deployed around the world. They often operated where the United States had no bases working with America's allied armed forces. The alliances, bases, and MAAGs served the overarching goal of containing communist expansion. Unlike U.S. personnel stationed in a country that signed a SOFA with the United States, the advisors enjoyed diplomatic immunity. They received this protection on the grounds that they were part of the local U.S. embassy.

For hundreds of years, various nations offered protections to the representatives of foreign thrones and heads of state before the practice was codified by European powers at the Congress of Vienna in 1815. The concept of diplomatic immunity evolved throughout the twentieth century, but the intent was always to provide protection to a limited number of ranking diplomats and their administrative and technical staff. The United States, though, abused the practice of diplomatic immunity. Although small in number when compared to the forces stationed at bases and installations that fell under the SOFA umbrella, MAAG advisors still represented several thousand personnel in uniform who answered only to the U.S. Uniform Code of Military Justice (UCMJ). The situation only worsened when the Department of Defense demanded that MAAG dependents receive diplomatic immunity. Even if a host nation had a SOFA with the United States, MAAG forces and their dependents were immune to host nation justice. In recent years, SOFAs have been criticized for being "not quite full-blown extraterritoriality."[3] On the other hand, diplomatic immunity was indeed extraterritoriality.

For host nations, especially those that had only recently emerged from colonialism, agreeing to give MAAG units diplomatic immunity placed them in a considerable political bind. As allies, they wanted U.S. support to defend themselves against aggression, if not to expand their power to roll back communism, but they also sought to protect their sovereignty. Accidents or intentional acts by MAAG advisors had the potential of leading to outbreaks of anti-American protest that could lead to a break in relations with the United States or even topple a government. Many U.S. allies possessed a mentality much like that of NATO member Iceland in the 1950s. As a study of overseas bases written in 1957 explained, Icelanders "dislike the presence of foreign forces stationed on their soil, yet they welcome the protection which they know this provides them."[4] As much as a SOFA seemed to be "not quite full-blown extraterritoriality," it was preferable to diplomatic immunity, a status that a soldier carried whether on duty or not.

Similarly, the United States walked its own political tightrope. Policymakers believed that the bases and troops were essential to the country's security, the growth of its power and systems, and the maintenance of world peace. Nazi and Japanese expansion in Europe, the Middle East, and Asia and the technology that emerged from World War II, including atomic weapons, called into disrepute the old isolationist notion that the United States was secure behind two oceans. To acquire those bases and to operate on foreign soil, it had to compromise by allowing some of its troops to be tried by foreign law while assuaging U.S. domestic opposition with data that showed that the overwhelming majority of U.S. troops accused of some criminal offense would be tried under the UCMJ.

The SOFAs, bilateral treaties, and similar agreements that allowed MAAG units to operate under diplomatic immunity became the glue that held the American containment structure in place. Without them, the United States could not have maintained and expanded containment beyond the end of the Cold War into the twenty-first century, such as making former Soviet-occupied countries members of NATO. In areas of the world where the United States engaged in and continues to see combat, such as Iraq and Afghanistan, the agreements signed with those countries are quite different. In the case of Iraq, the United States has a Security Agreement that contains language often found in a SOFA but which allows Iraqis jurisdiction over American forces. By contrast, the SOFA with Afghanistan provides American troops immunity from Afghan laws and gives full jurisdiction to U.S. authorities.[5] In an environment in which the host has no jurisdiction, an incident or series of incidents involving U.S. GIs engaging in criminal activities or committing murder and rape could make the U.S. position untenable.

The rape of an Okinawan girl by three U.S. servicemen in 1995 led to a fire-storm of protests there. Several years later, the deaths of two South Korean girls in an accident involving U.S. soldiers led to a similar outburst in anger against SOFAs.[6] Then and now, anti-American protests and riots only give host nations a reason to rescind their invitation to empire or hegemony.[7]

No one was more sensitive to this problem in the 1950s than President Dwight D. Eisenhower. As a man who once defended the American empire in Panama and the Philippines, commanded allied forces in Europe during World War II, and served as the first NATO commander, who better than he understood the potential for strained relations between the United States and its allies and former foes caused by a vast American presence in the form of an occupation force? As Supreme Commander in Europe during the Second World War, he proved fairly adept in dealing with western European allies and overcoming the problems and challenges of having a vast army in the United Kingdom that became part of what one British historian has described, in nostalgic terms, as the "American occupation of Britain."[8]

As president, Eisenhower understood the stakes if Americans were forced to abandon their bases or withdraw their advisors because incidents involving U.S. soldiers stirred up local nationalism. Indeed, in October 1956 he asked Frank C. Nash, former assistant secretary of defense for international security affairs under both Truman's administration and his own, to do a study of U.S. overseas military bases. Eisenhower viewed such bases as vital for "deterring aggression" and to the security of the United States and its allies, but international communism worked for their removal. Moreover, he recognized that "the natural frictions which arise from stationing substantial numbers of troops in a foreign country, and above all the intense spirit of nationalism of our times, have combined to sharpen local opposition to vitally important U.S. bases and facilities even on the part of non-Communist elements." Eisenhower insisted, "We must develop the feeling that the U.S. military facilities, far from being derogation of local sovereignty, are a part of the security system of the host countries."[9]

Despite Eisenhower's genuine intentions and concerns, diplomatic immunity and (to a lesser extent) SOFAs did undermine sovereignty. The Department of Defense sent MAAG advisors and their families around the world to live and work beyond local law. One of those places was Taiwan, controlled by the Republic of China (ROC). As long as the two allies prevented any major incidents from occurring, such as rape or murder, the alliance, which weathered a number of crises in the 1950s, stayed intact. Unfortunately for the Eisenhower administration, a shooting incident in 1957 led to a controversial court-martial and a contentious verdict that spawned protests by

ROC nationals. The protests highlighted the problem of armed advisors living in foreign lands protected by diplomatic immunity, the U.S. conceptions of "standing your ground" and "defending your castle," and a U.S. military justice system that appeared to be biased and racist. Anger spawned by all of these issues resulted in riots that not only led to an alliance crisis but afforded other Asian allies an opportunity to demand either jurisdiction in specific cases involving GIs in which Asians were killed or a SOFA that gave allies, including those in Europe, more jurisdictional power. If not managed well, these events had the potential to not only severely damage relations with a key Cold War ally in a manner that opened up Asia to communist aggression, but also to undermine America's entire containment structure.

1

A Shooting on Grass Mountain

On March 20, 1957, Master Sergeant Robert G. Reynolds and his wife, Clara, returned to their home after spending the evening playing pinochle with some American friends. A forty-one-year-old native of Maryland, Reynolds had served in Taiwan for just over two years as a member of MAAG-Taiwan. Clara, who came from Coatsville, Pennsylvania, and was Reynolds's second wife, worked in the local Post Exchange, or PX.

Reynolds was now at the end of his tour and preparing to move his family back to the United States to await reassignment. He had served in the U.S. Army for many years, almost exclusively in Asia. Born in 1915 and having two brothers and three sisters, he graduated from high school in 1932, four years after his father passed away. Reynolds spent several years working as a farmhand before taking a job as a plumber's helper in 1941 and working as a labor foreman from 1942. He enlisted in the army in February 1945. His first tour of duty was in the Philippines as a medical supply specialist. After being discharged, he worked at Veterans Administration hospitals in both Pennsylvania and Maryland before reenlisting in the army, which posted him to Camp Zama, Japan. During the Korean War, Reynolds served with the 8603rd Mobile Surgical Unit in Korea, which operated near the front lines from July 1950 to May 1951, handling thirteen thousand patients. His unit was thirty miles south of the Yalu River supporting the 1st Cavalry and 25th Infantry Divisions in November 1950 when Chinese Communist troops attacked the Eighth Army and routed it back across the 38th Parallel into South Korea. During his stint Reynolds earned a Bronze Star, a Good Conduct Medal, and six Combat Stars. He left Korea in July 1951 for Fort Sam Houston in Texas before being transferred to Taiwan in February 1955, where he worked at a medical depot warehouse. Since 1950, his superiors had rated his efficiency consistently as Excellent and his character as Excellent or Superior, except for his first year in Taiwan, in which he was rated as Good in both aspects.[1]

According to Reynolds's statements to U.S. criminal investigators, the couple arrived at their home on Grass Mountain around 11:30 P.M. Located north of Taipei, capital for the ROC, Grass Mountain was both home and workplace for hundreds of ROC officials and troops, including their leader,

Chiang Kai-shek. Just a few years before, Chiang renamed the area Yang-mingshan in memory of a Ming dynasty scholar, but to the Americans and the locals it was still Grass Mountain. The area hosted numerous military installations and hundreds of Americans. The Reynolds family lived in an American-style home built exclusively for MAAG personnel. After parking their car, they found their seven-year-old daughter, Shirley, and their *amah*, or housegirl (a young Chinese woman named Yao Limei), asleep.

Before going to bed, Reynolds used the toilet while his wife took a shower in a stall that lacked doors and shower curtains. Reynolds left the bathroom through a side door to go to their bedroom, where he lit a cigarette, and then stepped out into the living room to turn out the light. Suddenly his wife called out in an excited voice, "Hey, hon." Thinking that she had seen a spider (large, but harmless house spiders are common in Taiwan), Reynolds checked on his wife. Through the side door his wife exclaimed, "Someone is looking in through the window at me!" Reynolds told his wife to remain in the bathroom and to act normal. He went to a cabinet, pulled out a .22 revolver, and loaded it with nine bullets—a process he later estimated took three minutes.

The bathroom window, with a curtain that covered only half of the tall and wide window, faced the front of the house, so Reynolds walked through the living room, dining room, and kitchen to the back door. Unlocking it, he opened that door and a screen door to get to the back porch and the walkway that led to the front. The house was actually a duplex, and Reynolds went to his neighbors' front porch and looked around the corner to his right. Clearly outlined by his neighbor's porch light was a Chinese man wearing a khaki uniform. The man had climbed up on the window perch and was peering through the bathroom window at Reynolds's naked wife. After waiting about thirty seconds, Reynolds called out, "*Ni deng I deng*," or "Wait a minute." Reacting to the voice, the man jumped down from the window perch, which sat four feet off the ground, and stood up. Reynolds noticed that the Chinese man had a four-foot-long stick or pipe in his left hand. The man slowly advanced on the American soldier, ducking under a clothesline before raising the weapon high. Reynolds again called out, "*Ni deng I deng*, or I'll shoot." The man now took a long stride, the object in his hand hitting the side of the house. Reynolds jumped back, then fired one shot, hitting the alleged assailant. Grasping his chest, the Chinese man crossed the lawn and tripped on the neighbors' front porch steps before falling down into a bamboo grove.

Reynolds now rushed into his driveway, calling out, "MP, MP, MP, MP!" He hoped to hail one of the Chinese military policemen who patrolled the streets and whom he often encountered even after midnight. Getting no response, Reynolds went back to his house and told his wife to call the Foreign

Affairs Police (FAP), the Chinese bureau that dealt with issues involving for-eigners, and the MAAG provost marshal's office. He then turned and walked to where the wounded man lay on the ground. As Reynolds approached, he was surprised to watch the man jump up to his feet and shuffle sideways toward him. Again, the Chinese man failed to heed a verbal warning to stop. Thinking the man had a knife or a gun, Reynolds fired a second time. He did not know if he hit the man again or not, but his alleged attacker reeled, and then made his way into a side street toward a nearby park. During this entire altercation the man never uttered "a sound or spoke a word" other than a groan before collapsing in the park across the street. The MAAG ser-geant turned and went back into his house. Once inside, Reynolds placed the revolver on a living room table, and there he sat and waited for the arrival of Chinese and American policemen.[2]

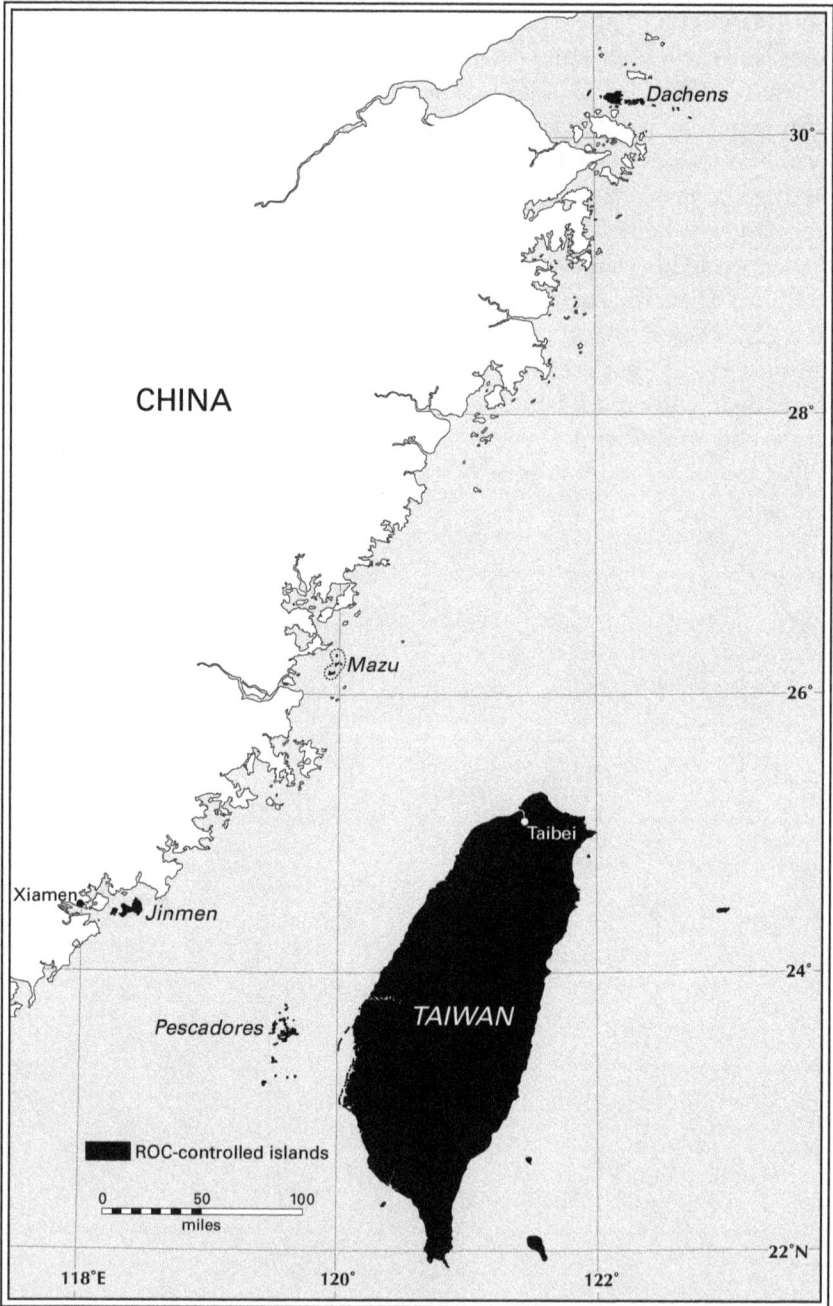

ROC-controlled Taiwan and neighboring islands. (Map by Dick Gilbreath, University of Kentucky cartography lab)

2

Islands against the Red Tide

Sergeant Robert G. Reynolds, a member of the U.S. Army, shot a Chinese man, presumably a soldier in the military of the ROC. On the surface, those facts alone would have astounded anyone who understood U.S.-ROC relations in the context of the Cold War. The two countries were supposed to be staunch allies, united in their opposition to the communist People's Republic of China (PRC). In the United States it was known as Red China, while Taiwan, more commonly known among Westerners as Formosa, represented Free China, the true China that needed to be defended. It was this alliance that brought Reynolds and the unidentified Chinese man into close proximity with one another and that ironically led to a soldier ostensibly shooting an ally.

Irony seems to have no bounds. The alliance and U.S. support for the ROC in and of itself represented a historical paradox. Just a few years before, top U.S. leaders despised Chiang Kai-shek, head of the ROC, whose stature in America declined from the hero of China and a close World War II ally to leader of a regime marked by disunity, military defeat, inflation, and charges of corruption. With defeat certain, Chiang retreated to Taiwan with 2 million loyal followers in 1949. The Truman administration absolved itself of any responsibility for Chiang's political collapse, pointing out that the ROC had received $2 billion in U.S. aid since 1945 and that much of the millions of dollars worth of U.S. military hardware it bought fell into communist hands. Despite Taiwan's strategic importance, President Harry Truman and Secretary of State Dean Acheson distanced the United States from Chiang to avoid antagonizing the PRC and waited for the "dust to settle" on the Chinese civil war before making any significant policy changes toward China. On January 5, 1950, Truman ruled out U.S. military intervention, aid, or advice to save Chiang Kai-shek from communist attack.[1]

The situation for the generalissimo and his followers on Taiwan seemed bleak. Those who stood fast when all others abandoned him recalled that on several occasions Chiang considered committing suicide. Without American aid, his demise seemed certain.[2] His weak military forces retained a precarious hold on Taiwan, the Penghus, and the offshore islands of Jinmen, Mazu, and the Dachens. A PRC attack against Jinmen in 1949 was just beaten off.

Great Britain and India accorded the PRC diplomatic recognition soon after Truman's announcement, and there was the threat of the U.N. removing the ROC from the Security Council and turning Taiwan into a U.N. Trusteeship. Internally, the 2 million Chinese refugees were a minority compared to the nearly 8 million Taiwanese—with whom there were already tensions. After the ROC liberated the island from fifty years of Japanese colonial rule in 1945, Nationalist policies led to Taiwanese discontent. The February 28th Incident of 1947 occurred after Nationalist police, trying to arrest a woman selling cigarettes illegally, fired on angry bystanders, killing one. The next day, protests against government monopoly and corruption led to a riot that resulted in Nationalist troops killing an estimated ten thousand Taiwanese, though there have been claims that the numbers were actually much higher.[3] One factor in the ROC's favor was that Japan had instilled anti-communism on the island. This and the anti-communist campaign implemented by the Nationalists prevented Taiwan from becoming fertile ground for PRC subversion.[4] Otherwise, Chiang's only hope of salvation was World War III breaking out between the superpowers and their allies, leading to U.S. aid, much as Pearl Harbor had done nearly ten years before.[5]

Salvation, of a sort, arrived in the form of the Korean War. North Korea's invasion of South Korea in June 1950 prompted Truman to embark on a global policy of defending European and Asian governments against communist encroachment and to reevaluate the United States' relationship with Chiang Kai-shek. PRC intervention in November moved Truman in 1951 to approve a plan to provide Chiang, a man he once called a crook, with political and economic aid. The administration sought to give Chiang over $237 million, 40 percent of the money allotted to the Mutual Defense Assistance Program (MDAP). In May, Truman inaugurated the Mutual Security Program (MSP), in which he asked Congress to appropriate $555 million for the defense of Asia, "a vast area stretching from Afghanistan to Korea," where "free countries are struggling to meet communist aggression in all its many forms." Later in the year Congress approved the Mutual Security Appropriations Act and earmarked $300 million for Taiwan in 1952.[6]

Truman further ordered the U.S. 7th Fleet to patrol and "neutralize" the Taiwan Strait to prevent either side from expanding the Chinese civil war. On August 5, the United States and the ROC agreed to the stationing of the 13th Air Force (Provisional), a fighter-bomber squadron, in Taiwan. The United States also sent a team of thirty-seven American officers from Tokyo to Taiwan to determine what military assistance would be required to prevent Taiwan's capture by Chinese Communists. The survey team limited itself to assessing the needs for Taiwan proper and the Penghus; it did not inspect the tiny offshore islands.[7] The Americans found an army infiltrated by communists and not capable of prolonged battle. Too many units were understrength, the types of troops varied greatly, and the many types of rifles used by ROC soldiers prevented standardization.[8]

Recognizing that Chiang's troops could carry out raids along the PRC's coastline, the Department of Defense decided in April to send a MAAG unit to assist Taiwan with its defense. Numbering about five hundred personnel, MAAG would not only train Nationalist troops, but would distribute aid provided under the MSP and MDAP.[9] The first man to head MAAG-Taiwan was Major General William C. Chase, who commanded a brigade of the 1st Cavalry Division in the Pacific in General Douglas MacArthur's theater before becoming division commander and participating in the occupation of Japan. Chase, who headed MAAG-Taiwan from May 1, 1951, until June 27, 1955, reported to the Commander in Chief Pacific Command (CINCPAC).[10] MAAG-Taiwan was divided into army, navy, and air sections, each having a separate commander. Besides working with the ROC's Ministry of Defense on war plans, MAAG was supposed to reorganize, reequip, and retrain the ROC's military. MAAG personnel, however, were involved in neither the direct training of ROC forces nor (in theory) the issuing of orders to the Chinese military. They worked, or so one MAAG advisor wrote, with an opposite Chinese number in a "*frank and friendly manner*" (italics in the original).[11]

The top political component or umbrella of what became known as the "country team" was the U.S. ambassador. In 1953, the post was filled by Karl Lott Rankin, a longtime Foreign Service officer described by Alexander Hermann, the British consul to Taiwan, as the "ideal man for the post . . . shrewd, diplomatic, dignified and unassuming," a man who maintained excellent relations with the ROC while "not blind to the Nationalists' faults." Hermann's successor, Andrew Franklin, appraised Rankin as "firmly anti-communist," a man who viewed Asian neutralism as being just as dangerous to U.S. interests as communism, and who had "meticulous respect for Chinese sovereignty."[12]

The third component to the country team was the director of the U.S. economic mission. Between 1954 and 1957, Joseph L. Brent, a Foreign Service officer whose career stretched back to the 1920s with experience in the Middle East, took charge of the International Cooperation Administration-Taiwan (ICA). Originally, the economic mission oversaw the dispersal of aid under the Economic Cooperation Administration (ECA) before being renamed the ICA. The ECA's Far Eastern Division had operated in China since 1948, but imminent Nationalist collapse had led the ECA to do an economic survey of Taiwan. The ECA concluded that Taiwan's existing agricultural and economic infrastructure provided the basis for successful economic rehabilitation that would make Taiwan a model for Asia. After the Truman administration's decision to provide the ROC with economic assistance, ECA experts played the role of economic advisors to many ROC government and industrial branches in the quest to bring about economic stabilization, much as MAAG sought military stabilization.[13] Rankin claimed that between 1951 and 1957 the ROC needed an average of $90 million in economic aid, some of which paid for rural development and land reform.[14]

Finally, the country team was rounded out by the head of the U.S. Information Service (USIS) in Taiwan. USIS directors posted there possessed Foreign Service and/or military backgrounds and always had a China connection. From 1956 to 1958, USIS-Taiwan was headed by Ralph Powell, a former U.S. Marine Corps intelligence officer during World War II who served in China in 1946 and 1947 before becoming a lecturer at Princeton University and the National War College as a Chinese military expert. As part of the U.S. Information Agency (USIA), which was created in 1953, USIS represented the propaganda arm of the U.S. government, having the task of "selling the American way" of life in order to counter Soviet propaganda and promoting educational and cultural exchanges. To that end, USIS established a reading room to provide propaganda and world news to a Taiwanese public starving for information after years of Imperial Japanese censorship, and it sent mobile units into the countryside to show films and provide other entertainment. It also sold subscriptions to *Free China,* which published articles written by liberal Chinese that were, at times, critical of Chiang Kai-shek. Over the next few years USIS added offices beyond Taipei, including one in Kaohsiung, a major port city in southern Taiwan, where Foreign Service officers studied Chinese.[15] According to Rankin, USIS-Taiwan carried out its mission at a total cost of "a few hundred thousand dollars yearly." If true, this still represented a significant amount of money, considering that USIA's Far East budget in the mid-1950s totaled $2.7 million.[16]

In the early 1950s, political, military, and economic aid to Taiwan seemed imperative, especially after the PRC entered the Korean War. The Truman administration feared that a communist takeover of Taiwan would directly threaten the U.S. defense of Japan, Okinawa, the Philippines, and indirectly Southeast Asia. Weaknesses undermined the ROC's overall qualitative military strength. Although possessing high morale, ROC infantrymen lacked shoes, uniforms, antitank guns, and heavy automatic weapons. Political commissars penalized "initiative" and undermined "the authority of commanders of all echelons." Military hospitals were overcrowded. Field sanitation was "neither practiced nor understood." Men trained while swarmed by flies and mosquitoes with no protection. The ROC military had a "highly developed spy system," including "plain clothes agents with all units," but could not carry out tactical reconnaissance or combat intelligence. Overall, there was a "lack of real leadership" that Chase and others blamed as the primary reason why the ROC lost China.[17]

Meanwhile, MAAG found the air force less than 25 percent effective across the board and observed that a PRC air attack would eliminate it in two days without intervention by the U.S. 5th and 13th Air Forces that operated out of Japan and the Philippines. It had little air-to-air combat or ground support experience. With a total strength of 524 officers and 247 enlisted men, it needed highly trained air crews and mechanics. The navy, which possessed little sea experience or grasp of amphibious operations, faced a shortage in trained, professional officers as well as ships. The largest ship in the ROC fleet, a cruiser acquired from the British, defected to the communists. According to a secret U.S. study, "In brief, the Chinese Nationalists do not have an efficient, modern fighting force."[18]

To ensure that Taiwan and the nearby Penghus were viable "counterweights," the Truman administration provided millions in aid to rebuild the ROC military and help Taiwan "attain a self-supporting status." In terms of priority for MDAP aid, Taiwan followed Indochina, where the French were fighting Vietnamese communists, but received aid equal to that of NATO countries.[19] Between 1945 and 1965, Taiwan received over $2.2 billion in economic assistance, making it the sixth largest recipient of U.S. aid to developing countries. Between 1950 and 1966, the United States provided the ROC with over $2.4 billion in military assistance, putting it third behind France and Turkey but slightly ahead of South Korea. Washington also helped rebuild the ROC air force. The ROC's twenty-four propeller-driven fighters were no match for Soviet-supplied MiG-15 jet fighters that attacked ROC aircraft in the Taiwan Strait and ROC ships and U.S. reconnaissance flights around the Dachen Islands.[20] Between 1953 and 1957, America sent Taiwan 214 F-84 Thunderjets (straight-winged jet used by the ROC either as fighter-bombers or for tactical reconnaissance) and 269 F-86 Sabres (sweptwing jet fighters) to counter the MiG-15s. The ROC also possessed two jet-powered Martin RB-57 reconnaissance aircraft.[21]

The reversal in policy toward Taiwan quickly evolved into deeper ties between the United States and the ROC. This was not by total design. When Dwight Eisenhower became president in 1953, he had no intention of discontinuing the policies of the previous administration, but he rejected ROC requests for a mutual defense pact. During the presidential campaign he threatened to unleash Chiang Kai-shek on the PRC, but after the election he only went as far as to announce that the U.S. 7th Fleet would deneutralize, meaning it would not stop Chiang Kai-shek from attacking the PRC. The First Taiwan Strait Crisis, in which PRC artillery fired on the islands of Jinmen and Mazu, changed all of that. The crisis led Washington in December 1954 to sign the U.S.-ROC Mutual Defense Treaty (MDT), which committed the United States to militarily preventing the communist takeover of Taiwan and the Penghus. On January 29, 1955, both houses of Congress voted overwhelmingly in support of the Formosa Resolution, which authorized the president to "employ the Armed Forces of the United States" to protect and secure Taiwan and the Penghus "against armed attack" as well as "related positions and territories of that area now in friendly hands." Those "related positions" were Jinmen and Mazu. (The U.S. evacuated ROC forces from the Dachens.)

Like Truman, Dwight Eisenhower believed in the domino theory, the idea that if a nation fell to communism, its neighbors would follow in its wake. In fact, he coined the phrase "'falling domino' principle" in 1954 just weeks before French airborne troops surrendered at Dien Bien Phu and before France agreed at Geneva in July to pull out of North Vietnam. Even if he did not intend to defend Jinmen and Mazu with all-out military force and preferred that Chiang Kai-shek reduce his forces on the tiny islands, Eisenhower worried about the psychological impact of the loss of those islands on the ROC and overseas Chinese.[22] During the offshore crisis, the question of the island's strategic importance brought him into disagreement with British prime minister Winston Churchill, an old friend who scoffed at the idea that a Communist Chinese takeover of Taiwan would threaten security in the Pacific. Eisenhower explained that since the French were out of Vietnam, Chiang Kai-shek remained the only force to contain communism in Southeast Asia: "We cannot afford the loss of Chiang unless all of us are to get completely out of that corner of the globe. This is unthinkable to us."[23] Ike insisted that Taiwan and the offshore islands be defended, and that the morale, vigor, training, and equipping of Chiang Kai-shek and his soldiers be sustained. If Chiang and the ROC disappeared, the millions of overseas Chinese living throughout Southeast Asia, who were dual citizens of China, would "deem themselves as subjects" of the PRC. In Eisenhower's judgment, the "communist sweep of the world" proved "faster and much more relentless" than the swift expansion of Adolf Hitler, Benito Mussolini, and the Japanese warlords. As the president told another friend, the loss of Taiwan to "ruthless peoples who are for aggression and for capturing the minds and bodies of additional millions" would be "catastrophic" for Southeast Asia.[24]

The American commitment to defend Taiwan in the early Cold War years established a de facto Two China policy that persisted into the twenty-first century, long after Washington dropped official recognition of Taiwan in favor of the PRC. From the perspective of allies, as well as both the administration's supporters and critics, this commitment to Taiwan seemed disproportionate to its importance or value as a Cold War ally. Indeed, the 1957 study of overseas bases commissioned by Eisenhower noted that compared with Japan, South Korea, and the Philippines, "Our political stake in Taiwan outweighs its strategic value as a link in the Far East defensive perimeter."[25] For Eisenhower, Taiwan's political and strategic values were intertwined. The fall of the offshore islands meant the collapse of Taiwan; the collapse of Taiwan would undercut the morale of the Philippines, South Vietnam, Thailand, Cambodia, and Laos. In 1955, he was prepared to expand the size of the U.S. Air Force squadron there to a wing and send a division of marines as a way of demonstrating America's commitment to defending Taiwan. A National Intelligence Estimate suggested that U.S. refusal to defend the islands would cause Southeast Asian countries, where America had no bases, to doubt its commitment to defend them from communist expansion.[26]

Yet, Eisenhower never intended for the United States to lead an ROC invasion of the PRC. This was a position he maintained long before he became president. As president of Columbia University in the late 1940s, he told Hollington Tong, an alumnus who later served as the ROC ambassador to Washington, that Taiwan should become independent. When Tong demurred, saying it could be used to recover mainland China, Eisenhower responded negatively: "But that would mean war with the Soviet Union."[27] As president, his views had not changed, and he wanted to avoid involving the United States in any local fighting over those islands. Four months after passage of the Formosa Resolution, Ike decided not to defend the offshore islands with American troops, putting the onus instead on the ROC army. From a practical military view, he never saw the value of putting a large number of ground forces on those islands. In 1955, General Matthew B. Ridgway, then army chief of staff, argued that Jinmen and Mazu could not be held without U.S. troops. Infuriated, Eisenhower told Admiral Arthur Radford, head of the Joint Chiefs of Staff (JCS), "If you have to put foot soldiers in there (considering the Chinese troops already there) then we can't hold anything in the world. I have no intention of putting American foot soldiers on Quemoy. A division of soldiers would not make any difference."[28]

Instead of ground forces, Ike relied on MAAG advisors and stationed nuclear-capable missiles on Taiwan. In January 1956, Admiral Felix Stump, CINCPAC, with the support of the State Department, proposed that such missiles be sent to Taiwan in order to boost ROC morale and strengthen the U.S. commitment to defend Taiwan. A secondary purpose was to keep the number of U.S. military personnel there to a minimum.[29] In March 1957, the United States and the ROC signed a joint communiqué formalizing the decision to install Martin TM-61C Matadors on Taiwan. The Matador was a surface-to-surface tactical cruise missile, developed by the Glenn Martin Company in the late 1940s, capable of carrying either a three-thousand-pound conventional warhead or a nuclear warhead for a range of six hundred miles. A leak by an ROC diplomat in May 1957, a day before the ROC planned to make an official announcement, led to descriptions of Taiwan as an "atomic base." Around the same time, Wilber Brucker, secretary of the army, and Admiral Arleigh Burke, chief of naval operations, announced that the U.S. 7th Fleet already possessed a nuclear capability. Although the Matador unit began moving immediately into Tainan, located in southwest Taiwan, not until the following year would the missiles be armed with atomic warheads.[30] Naturally, the announcement that the missiles were to be installed within a short range of the PRC angered Beijing, which had its ambassador in Geneva protest this "act of aggression."[31]

The alliance with Taiwan, the advisors, and the missiles were in line with Eisenhower's policies. In addition to Taiwan forming a crucial link in the U.S. defensive perimeter strategy, the administration's New Look strategy focused, in part, on reducing U.S. troop strength and keeping down costs through reliance on nuclear weapons.[32] In 1954, Admiral Radford had argued that the United States needed to draft 1 million replacements every year in order sustain its large overseas presence, as America was "spread-eagled" in Korea, Europe, and other areas of the world. By 1957, in an effort to maintain the national economy, the administration needed to reduce the number of soldiers in the entire military to less than 3 million. To achieve the goals of protecting the economy and providing flexibility in dealing with threats, the United States needed to rely more on nuclear weapons and mobile forces and less on overseas troops. Radford added that "as we make further reductions in our overseas deployments, we must make it clear to our Allies that the power of the U.S. Armed Forces, with their atomic weapons capability, is an ever-ready threat of devastation to be used against any Red aggression."[33] MAAG and the Matadors fit well into the New Look scheme, especially since Ike had long concluded that tactical nuclear weapons were necessary for the defense of the offshore islands.[34] The advisors and the Matadors would hopefully prove to be a more effective and cheaper deterrent in holding back the communist red tide.

3

Advice and Dissent

In the 1950s, Americans and Chinese usually did not shoot one another as Sergeant Robert Reynolds did, but U.S. and ROC officials certainly experienced their share of frustration and anger as allies. Alliance friction was practically guaranteed. Besides cultural differences and resentments that stretched back to World War II, the relationship was not one of equals. The United States was a hegemonic superpower, while the ROC government, which once nominally ruled a country of considerable demographic and geographic proportions, now only controlled a group of islands with a population of less than 10 million. Washington did not intend to make Taiwan a colony, but its efforts to ensure that the ROC effectively contained the PRC and became a showcase for Asia revealed the extent and limitations of its hegemonic power in Asia in the 1950s.[1] Americans were paternalistic, impatient, and demanding in giving their advice. Although U.S. support and protection prevented defeat by the communists, the ROC had its pride and wanted to limit its dependency on America. While it tried to secure more aid and other political goals through manipulation of the U.S. government, the ROC allowed a secret unit of Japanese military advisors to operate in Taiwan to counterbalance MAAG's attempts to exert influence at all levels of ROC policymaking. Chiang Kai-shek never accused the Americans of being imperialists, but the meaning may have been implied when he spoke of "interference" with his internal administration.[2] The complex story of the tensions that existed in the alliance prior to the Reynolds shooting needs to be explained. It provides a background for Chinese reactions to the shooting and subsequent events; some at the time believed it was *the* context for Chinese frustration with Americans.

In the years prior to and after signing the MDT, the United States and the ROC worked at cross purposes. Politically, the fundamental hope that Chiang Kai-shek held out to Chinese everywhere was restoration of Nationalist control over mainland China. All ROC policies were, in theory, geared toward fulfilling that goal. This overarching policy carried certain assumptions: Chiang Kai-shek would remain leader of the ROC; he and his officials would decide what form of government would rule over ROC territory; and the ROC would determine the size, extent, and nature of its military and use it to defend that territory and carry out guerilla raids against the PRC as a precursor to invasion. Although a new cabinet was formed in 1954 around a number of men who were Western-educated and possessed expertise that could have proven attractive to U.S. policymakers, the Yui Cabinet, named after Premier O. K. Yui (Yu Hongjun), a graduate of an American missionary school in Shanghai and later the mayor of the city, did not represent Western-style liberalism and wielded little power. Chiang Kai-shek remained firmly in control. Vice President Chen Cheng, along with his younger brother, headed the C. C. Clique, an ultraconservative faction that had existed since the 1920s. The Legislative Yuan consisted of Nationalist politicians who claimed to represent China's provinces, many of whom were conservatives loyal to Chiang Kai-shek.

By contrast, the United States wanted the ROC to pursue a Taiwan-centered policy in which it became a democratic and economic showcase for Asia that maintained the vital link in containment while strengthening ties with other Asian nations in a manner that halted communist expansion. Just after signing the MDT, the National Security Council (NSC) issued NSC-5503, which laid out a policy for Taiwan that reflected continuity with the Truman administration. One of the top objectives was to make the ROC "increasingly efficient . . . evolving toward responsible representative government."[3] To help secure this objective, Americans wanted to see new blood at the top. Many no longer held Chiang in high regard; some now called him "Chancre Jack." Since the late 1940s, U.S. officials had inquired about the possibility of one Chinese general or another becoming a successor.[4] Much to Chiang's annoyance, Americans of different political stripes hoped that a Third Force, a liberal alternative to both Chiang Kai-shek and Mao Zedong, could emerge from the shadows. In 1953, Chiang complained to Admiral Radford, then CINCPAC, about contradictory U.S. efforts to train, subsidize, and encourage a "Third Force" while it simultaneously supported and sought to strengthen his own government.[5]

Besides wanting Chiang out of power, Americans were displeased that one of Chiang Kai-shek's two sons, Chiang Ching-kuo (Jiang Jingguo), was an imminent successor. Chiang Ching-kuo spent many years in the Soviet Union, including twelve under house arrest at the order of Joseph Stalin. He also married a Russian woman in the process. After the retreat to Taiwan, his father appointed him to important positions responsible for preventing communist infiltration, such as heading the Peace Preservation Corps (PPC), which by 1954 numbered seventy-five hundred, not including "a considerable number of spies and agents."[6] In 1950, Chiang Ching-kuo instituted political and psychological indoctrination of ROC troops using the political commissar system borrowed from the communists. In 1952, he revived the former San Min Zhuyi Youth Corps as the Chinese Youth Anti-Communist National Salvation Corps in an effort to extend political indoctrination and military training into the educational system to prevent student demonstrations and seditious behavior. It represented both a significant part of the Nationalist Party's membership and Chiang Ching-kuo's base for building political power.[7] In 1955, his father put him in charge of the National Defense Council, which oversaw all security agencies, including those for the Nationalist Party, the Ministries of Defense and Foreign Affairs, the Taiwan Garrison Command, and the military police.[8]

Yet, in the eyes of many Americans, Chiang Ching-kuo was anathema. He represented repression: a sinister force behind what critics called a police state. The years Chiang Ching-kuo spent in the Soviet Union made him suspect and led to accusations that he used Soviet techniques to control Taiwan.[9] His secret police carried out the White Terror in Taiwan, arresting an estimated ninety thousand, accusing them of being communists, trying them before a military court, and executing half of them. In 1954, ROC officials learned there were fourteen thousand people locked away on Green Island who had been convicted or were awaiting trial before undergoing reeducation.[10] In early 1955, around the time the Nationalists were evacuating the Dachens, Madame Chiang Kai-shek and the wife of Claire Chennault, the former U.S. general with ties to Civil Air Transport (CAT), sponsored a fashion show to raise money for charity. A number of "bullies" led by one of Chiang Ching-kuo's associates disrupted the fashion show and overturned diplomats' cars. Although the real target may have been Madame Chiang, who had a contentious relationship with her stepson, some Americans perceived the event as an anti-American protest.[11]

Instead, Americans favored General Sun Liren, a graduate of the Virginia Military Institute who served with distinction during World War II. For a number of U.S. government officials, congressmen, and military leaders, Sun personified both U.S. military doctrine in China and "American-style political liberalism." Alexander Hermann called him the "White hope of the Americans."[12] In conversations with U.S. officials in the early 1950s, Sun condemned the political commissars while MAAG leaders openly criticized Chiang Kai-shek. As early as 1951, Chiang allegedly had evidence that Sun and a top ROC air force general were sharing government secrets with the United States in order to curry favor and overthrow the government. In 1954, Chiang appointed Sun to be his personal military advisor, but stripped him of power and authority in an apparent effort to limit Sun's influence.[13]

After MAAG advisors arrived in Taiwan, the State Department, the

Department of Defense, and the JCS pressured the ROC to democratize. Republican congressmen and State Department officials complained about how Chiang Ching-kuo's secret police endangered the "civil rights of the people." In 1952, the State Department and the Department of Defense demanded that Chiang Kai-shek end the political commissar system and introduce democracy into the ROC military.[14] The Americans wanted advisors to work in sensitive areas of the government, especially the PPC. Not only did Chase discover that the PPC was carrying out espionage work against MAAG, leading to a swift protest, but two Chinese nationals were arrested by the PPC and sentenced to ten years in prison for merely communicating with a Chinese professor at the University of California.[15] ROC officials refused Chase's request that an advisor be assigned to the PPC, saying the PPC had nothing to do with Taiwan's defense and that his request exceeded his orders.[16] When Chase persisted, Foreign Minister George K. C. Yeh (Ye Gongchao), a graduate of Amherst and Cambridge, countered that the PPC was "part of our internal administration." Surely the United States did not "wish to interfere in our internal administration." Meanwhile, the State Department requested files on a Chinese gentleman who immigrated to the United States and was subsequently arrested during a 1951 business trip to Taiwan. The ROC promised the Americans a seat at the trial, only to have the PPC sentence the man to life imprisonment without informing U.S. authorities of the hearing.[17]

The nature of ROC control over Taiwan and Chiang Ching-kuo's role continued to trouble leaders in Washington after Eisenhower came into office. In 1953, Admiral Radford himself warned Chiang Kai-shek not only about the political control over ROC officers, but the perception of Taiwan as a police state where, overseas Chinese complained, a person was guilty until proven innocent, undercutting U.S. progress there. He spoke of how overseas Chinese had to prove they were not communists before they could do business in Taiwan, which in many cases was impossible. Chinese summoned by the PPC refused to return to Taiwan, fearing arrest. Radford claimed that Taiwan could become "a show window of democracy in Asia as well as a bastion of anti-Communist forces," but U.S. public opinion mattered and Eisenhower's policy toward Taiwan could be "affected by any unfavorable turn in public opinion" against Chiang and his regime. Although impressed by Chiang Ching-kuo's competence and diligence, Radford believed that he needed to live in the United States to understand the American point of view.[18]

Since the United States spent millions in aid and felt obligated to look to the future, the Department of Defense and the State Department brought Chiang Ching-kuo to the States in 1953 for two weeks so that he could "get

Advice and Dissent   23

interested in the American democratic way" and win U.S. support when he took power. Chiang met with high government officials, including Eisenhower, and with Americans of different backgrounds across the country. (He refused to meet with former president Truman.) He told some Americans that he had seen "real freedom in this country" and that it was "a land of plenty." From time to time, Chinese and Americans asked blunt questions about his Soviet background or the secret police nature of Taiwan. When he departed, Radford wished that he had stayed two years, not two weeks.[19]

This attempt to teach Chiang Ching-kuo democracy did not have its intended effects. The son and father resisted American efforts to bring about political change. When MAAG pressed the ROC to abolish the political commissar system, Chiang Kai-shek privately accused the Americans of "interference."[20] After a six-day military conference in 1953 between top Chinese and American officers, Chiang Kai-shek lashed out at his commanders, telling them that all criticisms of the party and the political commissar system carried out in "private" showed disloyalty to him and the country. The political commissars would remain in place, and from that point forward his generals were not to discuss with U.S. advisors matters involving the government or the party that were indirectly related to military affairs.[21]

Chiang Kai-shek also moved against anyone who complained about the power and activities of his son. In 1954, K. C. Wu (Wu Guozhen), the former governor of Taiwan, was forced to leave for the United States after an alleged assassination attempt. Wu later claimed that he refused an order from Chiang Ching-kuo to have a Chinese businessman executed because of communist connections and that he complained to Chiang Kai-shek about the secret police and the military courts.[22] There were also rumors that Wu received strong backing from the United States and angered Chiang Kai-shek by complaining to Americans about his regime.[23] Much to Chiang Kai-shek's annoyance, Wu used his exile to criticize Chiang's regime as "undemocratic," and for its "one-party rule." In particular, Wu published an article in *Look* magazine entitled "Your Money Is Building a Police State in Taiwan."[24]

The next year, to the shock of the Americans, Sun Liren and approximately three hundred ROC officers loyal to him were arrested because of an alleged plot to overthrow the government. General Peng Mengji, the chief of general staff, leaked information to a *Time* correspondent that Sun allegedly tried to carry out two plots against Chiang Kai-shek's life.[25] State Department officials rejected such claims, believing that Chiang Ching-kuo moved against a potential successor to his father. The generalissimo apparently feared that Sun would lead a coup or take power after his death.[26] Americans were outraged by what they called a "frame up" by Chiang Ching-kuo.[27]

Because Sun supported the "establishment of a more democratic system," State Department officials viewed his detention as "yet another sign of the steady degeneration of the political respectability of the Nationalist regime." All of this paralleled an ROC trend to reject American advice.[28] Sun's arrest posed a danger to U.S. efforts because he was greatly admired by the overseas Chinese community. Admiral Radford called Sun one of the "ablest officers" in the Chinese army, condemned the political commissar system for hampering rather than helping Chinese army morale, and described the termination of Sun's career and service as a "great loss."[29] In October, an enquiry found Sun guilty, but Chiang Kai-shek ordered that the general not be punished further and be given the opportunity to redeem himself.[30] Sun spent much of the rest of his life under house arrest, and the Americans were helpless to do anything to assist him. British naval officials considered the case a "slap to the American face." The Americans had been overeager in pushing for Sun to become chief of the general staff (Peng Mengji's job) and too outspoken in describing him as the "only really worthwhile high-ranking general" in the ROC.[31] The case certainly threw a cold chill on U.S.-ROC relations. It was a warning that anyone close to or favored by the Americans could quickly find themselves in disfavor with Chiang's regime.[32]

In the meantime, Chiang's government became even more repressive toward those who espoused liberal ideas. In October 1956, on the occasion of his seventieth birthday, Chiang Kai-shek called for constructive criticism of the ROC, similar to Mao Zedong's Hundred Flowers Campaign that same year. Such criticisms were portrayed as a "most acceptable" birthday gift. Intellectuals in Taiwan took Chiang up on his offer and demanded more freedom of the press, more freedom to travel, and less political control—less Nationalist Party and more democracy. Although no one dared to criticize Chiang Ching-kuo, Lei Zhen, editor of *Free China* and a critic of the Youth Corps, described Chiang Kai-shek as another Empress Dowager Cixi, a reference to the woman that dominated the Qing dynasty in its final years, and suggested that he abide by the Chinese constitution and step down when his term ended in 1960. Within a few months there was a backlash. In January 1957, the Youth Corps issued a three-thousand-word manifesto calling for "ideological armament" against "camouflaged Liberalism" at a meeting of all university and middle school chancellors and principals, with Chiang Ching-kuo in attendance. Youths were warned to be on guard for "ideological smuggling" and that all should rally around Chiang Kai-shek.[33]

Besides disagreement over Taiwan's political leadership and development, the two allies since 1950 differed on military strategy and the size of the ROC army. After Truman announced that the U.S. 7th Fleet would neutralize the

Taiwan Strait, he rejected Chiang's proposal to launch air strikes against PRC airfields and to confine communist warships. Chiang Kai-shek chafed at the restraints imposed upon him and criticized what he called the United States' Eurocentric Cold War policy.[34] In terms of the ROC military itself, Americans complained about how the Defense Ministry centralized too much power.[35] On occasion, they threatened to cut off aid if the Chinese did not comply with their demands for reform or retain certain Chinese officers in authority.

One of the most contentious issues between the two allies in the 1950s pertained to the size of Chinese divisions. During the last months of the Korean War, Chase not only sought to reduce the number of ROC divisions to twenty-one, composed of nearly twelve thousand men apiece, but did not want MDAP funding to go to any division at less than 95 percent of full strength. Reorganization would reduce overhead, increase the firepower of Chinese divisions, and allow the ROC to defend Taiwan and/or possibly send elements to Korea. Chase's proposal convinced Chiang Kai-shek of a U.S. conspiracy to prevent him from attacking China. Reorganization, the Chinese said, would put ten thousand officers out of a job and undermine the prestige of the regime and military morale.[36] General Zhou Zhirou, then chief of the general staff, declared that reorganization would only occur *after* the arrival of U.S. aid. To reorganize beforehand meant "no material improvement to counterbalance the psychological impact."[37] When Chase persisted, Chiang Kai-shek ordered George Yeh to take the matter straight to Admiral Radford. Yeh explained that the government had to remind people that it intended to recover the mainland: "That, in short, is not only our most effective morale builder, but also our whole *raison d'etre*." Since coming to Taiwan, the ROC army had shrunk from thirty-eight divisions to twenty-eight, and was prepared to go to twenty-four. Any further reductions suggested that the ROC had lost "sight of our ultimate objective of recovering the mainland." Radford, however, refused to override General Chase. Chiang resisted what he described as MAAG interference with ROC internal administration, but there was little he could do. He knew that without the United States the ROC could not maintain its independence.[38]

Although NSC-5503 declared that the United States would continue to provide military assistance, American attitudes toward recovery of the mainland obviously did not change in 1955. Not only did neither the MDT nor the Formosa Resolution mention Jinmen and Mazu by name, but Eisenhower essentially "leashed" Chiang Kai-shek. Washington approved ROC military operations against the PRC only as long as they were limited in scope, were not costly, and did not drag the United States into a war. American refusal to specifically commit itself to the defense of the offshore islands, potential springboards into China, angered Chiang Kai-shek. This is not to say that the U.S. military saw no value in the islands. MAAG thought their real significance lay in their use to gather intelligence, launch raids, and be of political and psychological value against the PRC. For his part, Eisenhower would defend Jinmen and Mazu to protect the morale of ROC troops, whom he knew did not want to become permanent "prisoners" on Taiwan.[39]

Yet, Ike preferred that Chiang focus on making Taiwan a strong anticommunist position from which he could use his forces in Korea or Vietnam. The president thought it a mistake for Chiang to become fixated and pinned down by the offshore islands. He explained to Roy Howard, of the Howard-Scripps newspaper chain, that Chiang should not "center the whole question of the morale of his people on those two islands," or else their loss would have the same impact that Dien Bien Phu had on the French.[40] In June 1955, Secretary of State John Foster Dulles expressed to British foreign minister Harold MacMillan the hope that Taiwan would stabilize within a few years once the mainlanders gave up hope of returning to China and merged with the Taiwanese to form a "kind of self-government in Formosa."[41] Just months after passage of the Formosa Resolution, Ike offered Chiang a choice of either making the offshore islands into outposts with scaled-down forces or evacuating them in exchange for U.S. naval interdiction of the Taiwan Strait. The proposal stunned Chiang Kai-shek, leaving him visibly shaken.[42] The generalissimo had already abandoned the Dachens as part of the deal to get the MDT. To give up more territory would only further damage morale. He warned Washington that they would have to find another Chiang Kai-shek, because no one would follow him if he ceded those islands to the PRC. Ike did not press the issue, as doing so would have meant damaging or destroying the alliance. In this respect, Ike leashed the United States to Chiang Kai-shek. In a 1956 meeting with British prime minister Anthony Eden, Eisenhower made it clear that he would not "desert Chiang Kai-shek." He accepted Chiang's rationale that to be driven off the islands in battle was one thing, but to simply walk away without a fight would only harm morale in Taiwan and Southeast Asia.[43]

Diplomatic efforts by the administration to reduce conflict in the Taiwan Strait, though, led to ROC backlashes. When Eisenhower and Dulles pushed for establishing two Chinas (much like the two Germanies, two Koreas, and two Vietnams), in which both Chinese governments would be sovereign and have representation in the United Nations, Chiang Kai-shek rejected the formula. It denied him the political claim to represent all of China and undercut the hope of going back home. U.S. pursuit of a Two China policy only enhanced his fear that the United States would sell him out.[44]

In August 1955, the United States and the PRC held ambassadorial talks in Geneva, Switzerland, after the latter announced an interest in resolving tensions over Taiwan. Dulles pushed for the "principle of the nonrecourse to force" over Taiwan, whereas the PRC called on the United States to withdraw its military assets from Taiwan and the offshore islands and end the trade embargo against the PRC. Angry and suspicious, Chiang feared another "Yalta 'sell-out,'" referring to the Yalta Agreement of 1945 when the United States, behind China's back, agreed to cede Chinese territory to the Soviet Union in return for the latter attacking Japan. The ROC called on the Chinese press to condemn the talks, sparking what both the U.S. embassy and the British consulate called a "savage, anti-American press campaign."[45] Although the talks deadlocked, they lowered ROC morale. In November 1955, George Yeh told Rankin, who along with top U.S. Army and Navy officers in Taiwan opposed the talks, that a recent trip to the United States left him discouraged and concerned that "Americans were losing interest in Free China, and that there was a definite trend toward the eventual recognition of the [PRC.]" Most Chinese had not forgotten that the United States wrote the ROC off to a certain extent after 1949, and they were convinced, in Rankin's words, that the "isolationists, Europe-firsters, fellow-travelers and others who . . . continue to hate the guts of Chiang Kai-shek" would sell it out.[46]

The political and military tensions in the alliance impacted economic policies as well. Although the Korean War, neutralization of the Taiwan Strait, and dispatch of aid saved Chiang Kai-shek from defeat, Washington did not immediately flood Taiwan with money. In 1951, the State Department refused to even allow Taiwan to purchase oil from the United States, leading Chiang Kai-shek to write bitterly that because of Dean Acheson's opposition to his government, "Our air force cannot wage war, it cannot train pilots . . . it cannot take off and it cannot bomb the mainland."[47] To his exasperation, Washington announced that the ROC could no longer use U.S. aid to balance its budget and American economic advisors insisted that the ROC lower defense expenditures.[48] State Department officials complained that taxes were not high enough, demanded strict supervision of how U.S. aid was dispersed and control of the government's cash flow, and even asked for a five-year plan.[49] Essentially, the Americans wanted the ROC to develop an import-export economy that could make Taiwan financially independent. ROC officials reacted negatively to all of this. Chiang Kaishek believed that allowing MAAG advisors to supervise ROC finances constituted "interference." By the end of 1951, Chiang complained that since the arrival of MAAG, the government had received "not one gun and not one bullet." Instead, the Americans tried to control the ROC's economy and military affairs.[50]

The tensions involving MAAG and economic policies worsened under Eisenhower. NSC-5503 placed heavy emphasis on strengthening Taiwan's economy, including establishing "well-balanced trade" with noncommunist countries, especially Japan and the Philippines, encouraging overseas Chinese investment in Taiwan, and promoting fiscal responsibility and the "revision of programs which run counter to prudent U.S. advice."[51] Each year, the ROC ran a $40 million deficit due largely to military expenditures, of which Taiwan paid only 20–25 percent. Although the ROC army saw qualitative improvement and became the second largest noncommunist army in Asia by 1959, Taiwan lacked arsenals to build heavy weapons, depended on the United States for weapons and equipment, and required U.S. air, naval, and logistical support to sustain a defense.[52] The Americans also rejected attempts to secure more aid. In 1954, the ROC proposed the Kai Plan, designed to build and train nearly 350,000 men in Taiwan to launch limited counterattacks against the PRC at a cost of $135 million. The cool reception from the Americans forced the ROC to revise what it called a year later the Xie Plan, in which 162,000 men were to be trained and supplied at a cost of $106 million. Again the Americans balked, but the Chinese insisted they needed the aid to offset the decline in exports.[53]

While U.S. officials pressured the ROC to balance its budget and raise taxes, Defense Minister Yu Dawei, holder of a Ph.D. from Harvard, countered that in the battle for the salvation of the free world, money was of no consequence. Newspapers in Taiwan proudly declared that it had one of the lowest tax rates in the world, and there seemed to be no impetus to either lower expenditures or raise revenue. Instead, the American-educated finance minister, P. Y. Hsu (Xu Baiyuan), allowed the situation to worsen until, in the words of William P. Cochran, the U.S. chargé d'affaires, "we all have a crisis on our hands, then turn to the US and say, 'You have to rescue us from economic collapse.'" According to Cochran, Hsu took "the short-range view: in a few years they'll be back on the mainland, the stay here is temporary, so why bother about expanding the island's economy?"[54] Just as likely, ROC authorities understood that a Taiwan-centered economy sent the message that there would be no return anytime soon. At any rate, Rankin encouraged Hsu to raise taxes, operate the government-monopolized power and sugar corporations more efficiently to increase revenue, and pursue a true balanced budget rather than one balanced only after massive U.S. contributions. Vice President Chen Cheng retorted that raising electric power rates would lead to fierce opposition in the Legislative Yuan.[55]

The added costs and continued requests for more aid only strengthened American resolve to reduce the ROC's military expenditures. The United States tried to take a firm approach. In the summer of 1955, the Pentagon removed both Chase and General John C. McDonald, MAAG deputy chief, from command, and replaced them with Major General George W. Smythe and General Edwin Walker. Presumably, the Pentagon was unhappy with Chase, who seemed ineffective in restraining the Chinese. For example, because the United States refused to introduce ground forces on the offshore islands, Chiang Kai-shek, over the opposition of Chase, sent another division to Jinmen to support the five already there. Admiral Alfred M. Pride, who commanded the U.S. 7th Fleet, thought that Chase spoiled the Chinese and shrugged everything off by saying, "Oh, you know how the Chinese are."[56] Cochran believed that the Pentagon was impatient with Chase's inability to insist that the "Chinese do as we wanted and do it our way." In particular, the Pentagon became annoyed when the ROC diverted large amounts of MDAP equipment to certain units that were supposed to be deactivated while leaving others unsupported. The Pentagon sent Smythe and Walker to Taiwan to "get tough" with the ROC.[57]

Almost immediately the allies clashed. Earlier in the year the ROC had announced a plan to create nine reserve divisions, bringing their total to thirty. For the ROC it was a matter of saving face. Prior to 1949, the United States supported thirty divisions on the mainland, which was the same number maintained in South Korea. Chase and McDonald got into heated arguments with ROC generals, including Sun Liren, over the scheme to the extent that the ROC demanded that McDonald be recalled. CINCPAC and the JCS agreed to a reserve pool, but turned down the plan for nine divisions because it meant more hardware for ROC soldiers. The Chinese, who had already created the nine divisions, refused to break them up. The result was an impasse that lasted through the summer.[58] Then, in early August, in the middle of the Geneva talks and the atmosphere of Sun's detention, Smythe and Walker in almost blunt terms conveyed the JCS's decision to reject the nine-division plan. The decision deeply angered ROC officials, who believed that a deal had been made and now felt betrayed.[59]

On top of this, the ROC had seventy thousand "ineffectives," soldiers who were semi-retired or about to retire. Yu Dawei wanted a $48 million ICA fund to cover their salaries and pensions. When the United States balked, Chiang Kai-shek called Joseph Brent into his office to ask that the ineffectives be placed on the ICA payroll immediately. Yu Dawei then called a meeting of Chinese officials as well as Brent and General Smythe to say that if the money was not paid, the generalissimo would "lose face." It was a clear attempt to call out and coerce the Americans. Brent fired back that Washington wanted the money used to "reestablish the ineffectives in civilian life," not to pay their salaries. The United States already covered eight thousand and could handle another twenty thousand to twenty-two thousand, most of whom were in hospitals, but not all seventy thousand. This refusal angered Yu Dawei, who had brought about the "showdown" and lost face, and the ICA and embassy officials saw this as one more example of the "new atmosphere" in which the Chinese tried to force an issue against U.S. advice.[60]

Matters only got worse. In late July, Chiang Kai-shek held a conference of eight hundred senior officers. There, he read out the names of specific officers, who were required to stand up while he read "critical comments concerning—their ability, faults, errors and omissions." Chiang added that he was reading from MAAG reports. Regardless of whether the generalissimo agreed with the assessments, his "public immolation of his officers" put the onus on MAAG and created a rift between the officers and the advisors.[61]

It was in this atmosphere that the ROC spent U.S. aid with or without MAAG support, and assigned officers who spoke no English or who were ordered not to use the language when working with the advisors. The Ministry of Finance insisted on a budget guaranteed to lead to a deficit because it refused to increase taxes. In September, when the ROC sent more troops to Jinmen than could be supported, Smythe protested and warned that the lack of harmony reduced "the general effectiveness of our Sino-American team."[62] Shortly thereafter, Smythe left Taiwan because of a heart attack. Walker, an ultraconservative who proved controversial in the 1960s for his attempted right-wing indoctrination of U.S. troops, carried out his "get-tough" orders so well that he created an episode with the Chinese, and was removed from command by CINCPAC.[63]

These confrontations with MAAG led Chiang Kai-shek to request that the Americans appoint a commander, preferably a navy officer, for all U.S. forces in Taiwan. After signing the MDT, the Americans established the U.S.-Taiwan Defense Command (TDC). Initially, its head simultaneously wore the hat of commander of the U.S. 7th Fleet patrolling the Taiwan Strait. On February 28, 1956, Admiral Stuart Ingersoll, who replaced Pride, notified the ROC that he was now senior commander of all U.S. forces on Taiwan and the main point of contact for the Defense Ministry. Nevertheless, the chief of MAAG reported directly to CINCPAC and still oversaw all military aid.[64]

The U.S. policy of getting tough clearly failed. In 1956, an assessment of the ROC military suggested that the army could defend Taiwan and the Penghus, but not the offshore islands. Neither the navy nor the air force possessed the strength necessary to defend ROC territory. The ROC ran 40 percent deficits that were covered by foreign aid, without which the entire military could not function at its current strength. Americans claimed that Taiwan had the second-best economy in Asia, and wanted to showcase it to those millions of overseas Chinese that Eisenhower did not want swept away by the communist red tide. By May 1957, the ROC army totaled nearly 460,000 men. The NSC and the State Department both viewed the ROC's huge military as inimical to economic growth. It was too large, in MAAG's opinion, to be sustained by the population of nearly 10 million. Deficits could reach what MAAG called "dangerous proportions."[65]

Thus, the MDT did not usher in an era of improved U.S.-ROC relations. Instead, the U.S. refusal to recover the mainland, interest in evacuating the offshore islands, diplomacy in the form of the Two China policy and ambassadorial talks in Geneva with the PRC, and insistence on troop reduction and establishing a Taiwan-focused economy took a toll on ROC morale. The net result was an increasing ROC sense of despair that troubled Rankin because "their morale is our first line of defense."[66] He told a U.S. senator that the erosion of ROC morale went back to 1953, when the Korean War ended. As long as that conflict continued, it gave the ROC hope that international events would turn in its favor. They never did to the extent that the ROC would have liked. By 1957, the PRC was perceived as a major military power with growing prestige and influence in Asia, its entrance into the U.N. seemed inevitable, and the interest of U.S. allies in supporting the embargo against the PRC was waning.[67] One U.S. official noted that the slogan "Return to the Mainland" was used less in 1956 than it had been the year before. General Benjamin Davis, head of the 13th Air Force (Provisional), observed that mainlanders in the military were "slowly and reluctantly becoming reconciled to the idea that they would not be returning to China" and that their "propaganda is quite unrealistic."[68] Yu Dawei admitted that the ROC had no hope of returning without U.S. assistance. At times, the defense minister traveled to Washington in an effort to go over MAAG's head to get what he wanted, only to find that the Eisenhower administration refused to order MAAG along desired lines.[69]

In 1956, ROC morale plummeted further when an opportunity arose to roll back communism in Europe. The previous year, MAAG and the CIA had ceased supporting commando raids into the PRC because they were ineffective. For months, Chiang Kai-shek urged that the United States provide logistical support for a campaign against the PRC. He argued that U.S. aid accompanied by limited military operations would give hope to people behind the Iron Curtain and lead to liberation in Asia and Europe while avoiding a major war.[70] Otherwise, the generalissimo worried that a U.S. troop drawdown in the Pacific without a liberation policy would only lead Asia to believe the United States would abandon its overseas bases.[71] Then, in October and November, the Hungarian Revolution against Soviet domination occurred, capturing world attention. Chiang declared that, like Abraham Lincoln, who emancipated the slaves, Eisenhower had the opportunity to free the millions struggling for freedom. He begged Eisenhower "to help the people of Hungary who are still fighting and dying for a cause of which the free world is proud, but which the free world has not yet seen fit to give sufficient help."[72] Ike's decision not to liberate Hungary disheartened homesick Chinese. Months later, Stanway Cheng, editor of the *China Daily News,* told State Department and USIA officials that the mood of the Chinese on Taiwan was "ugly" because they were impatient to return home. Unfulfilled promises from Chiang Kai-shek and the American refusals to liberate Eastern Europe during the Hungarian crisis and support freedom fighters when they rose up in communist countries left Chinese disappointed and discouraged. Likewise, Payne Templeton, an ICA-Taiwan official, observed, "The mainlanders are particularly irritated, feel disappointed and frustrated toward American policy and their fading hope of ever returning to the Mainland."[73]

U.S. changes to the military structure it had established in East Asia did nothing to encourage hopes of recovering the mainland. In March 1957, Admiral Stump transferred his post as CINCPAC from Tokyo to Hawaii. Admiral Ingersoll no longer continued in his dual role as commander of the U.S. 7th Fleet and the TDC, but instead retained only the latter title. The Matador missiles and an air base under construction near Taichung were publicly described by one U.S. official as "gifts to keep the Nationalists happy." Worse, Washington showed little interest in a demand by the Philippine government to turn the Southeast Asia Treaty Organization, created in 1955, into another NATO by guaranteeing automatic assistance if any member nation was ever attacked by the PRC. Taiwan was not a member of SEATO, but American disinterest suggested that its Cold War policy would remain on the defensive. An editorial in the *Commercial Times,* a Hong Kong newspaper, noted that Chinese were skeptical of American intentions. The U.S. provided aid, but it restrained the ROC from attacking the PRC. It was imperative that Chinese not allow another's policy to sacrifice their "self-respect" and "freedom."[74]

In January 1957, Chiang Kai-shek asked Rankin point-blank whether the United States would support an ROC counterattack against the PRC. The ambassador answered that although Americans sympathized with the

ROC's desire to liberate China, counterattack "brought visions of bullets flying through the air and the danger of involving the United States in war." In response, Chiang made it a point to state three times that the ROC would honor its commitments to the United States and would do nothing "to harm American interests."[75] Two months later, during a secret session of the Nationalist Party's Central Committee, the generalissimo announced that an attack against the mainland was better "later rather than earlier." The decision to hold off such an attack for another five years reportedly deflated Chinese morale even further.[76] Yu Dawei had already told ROC officials for over a year that the military's strength would peak in 1957, and that the best time to counterattack would be mid-1957.[77] In Chinese minds, the window of opportunity was closing fast, especially since Taiwanese, who had no desire to "return," made up over 30 percent of the ROC army.

All of these frustrations and tensions did not signal the alliance's demise. British consul Andrew Franklin noted that "every week if not day, Admirals, Generals, Pentagon and State Department officials, not to mention Congressmen, Senators, and other camp followers and cheerleaders pass through" in an effort to build broader ties with Taiwan or between Taiwan and other nations. Pilots from South Vietnam were trained there, and South Korea and Taiwan carried out an "air mobility exercise." In 1956 alone, Vice President Richard Nixon, Dulles, Radford, and Allen Dulles, head of the CIA, visited Taiwan, as did Boeing B-47 Stratojets and a plethora of U.S. generals for celebration of Double Ten Day, the anniversary of the 1911 Revolution that overthrew the Qing dynasty. The Americans that Franklin encountered were often staunch anti-communists who agreed with Admiral Pride's statement that "Red China is on the march with logic, patience and determination. Its rulers are cruel. They are determined to dominate Asia to rule as much of the rest of the world as they can get their hands on."[78]

Below the surface, though, there were other tensions in U.S.-ROC relations that had less to do with disagreements over high politics. What began as a modest American presence mushroomed into a considerable U.S. footprint on the island. Although American officials opposed introducing a large number of ground forces into Taiwan or the offshore islands, the growing ties between the United States and Taiwan brought thousands of Americans to the island nation anyway. Among them was a certain Sergeant Robert G. Reynolds and his family, who were soon at the center of a storm of controversy between ROC nationals and U.S. authorities, one that would cast the bright light of scrutiny on the lifestyles of Americans living in Taiwan.

4

Little America on Taiwan

Despite Eisenhower's genuine concern about the number of U.S. bases and troops stationed around the world, a kind of global military sprawl with its inherent costs and potential harm to America's world image, he had no idea of the scale by which MAAG and numerous U.S. government agencies had multiplied on Taiwan. The escalation of U.S. advisors and agency employees had begun before Eisenhower became president. In 1951, there were five hundred MAAG officers and enlisted men, double the group's original intended size. The next year, General Chase recommended an increase to a total complement of 777 advisors. (This was far short of the three thousand that the secretary of the navy wanted to see in Taiwan.[1]) Ambassador Rankin agreed, as long as they were posted throughout the island and not concentrated in Taipei. He feared that a large U.S. military presence in the ROC capital would give the impression of an "'occupied' town." By February there were 760 MAAG advisors out of a total of nearly 1,000 U.S. military and civilian personnel, along with 118 dependents. As more Americans arrived, Rankin wanted to keep the influx from "looking too much like a military occupation or . . . neo-imperialism of American origin."[2]

Then, in May 1952, Chase proposed that the dependents of MAAG advisors be permitted to reside in Taiwan in order to boost MAAG morale, which was suffering from a shortage of good recreational facilities and housing. By the end of the year, plans were made to construct housing in preparation for the influx of nine hundred MAAG dependents expected in Taiwan by 1954. The U.S. government allocated money to construct homes on Grass Mountain in an area known as Shanzhihou, or "rear of the mountain." There, the U.S. government built a large housing complex for MAAG and other military personnel. The 217 homes formed a neighborhood similar to that found in a typical American community or suburb. The one-story duplexes came with American-style roofs and chimneys and considerable yard space that provided privacy and plenty of room for children to play.[3] It was in one of these homes that Sergeant Reynolds lived with his wife and daughter.

From the outset, U.S. State Department officials frowned on expanding the number of MAAG advisors who were joined by their families. Only six years had passed since U.S. troops were prevalent in the ROC's World War

II capital of Chongqing. In the final months of the war, U.S. agencies there detected a level of anti-foreignism not seen since 1939. In particular, there was "organized hooliganism" against American soldiers, especially if seen driving their jeeps with Chinese girls inside. Locals referred to this phenomenon as the "jeep-girl business." It was believed that the hooligans, who threw sticks and stones at the jeeps, were organized by none other than the Youth Corps, sponsored and controlled by the ROC. In some cases, Chinese policemen hauled the women to jail while onlookers jeered at the hapless GIs. There were claims that the Chinese despised Americans, and Americans retaliated with "bitter hatred." Reportedly, GI truck drivers and Chinese chauffeurs vied to drive each other off the road. The so-called wartime cooperation between Chinese and Americans was a myth. Cooperation, it was said, was "piss poor," and the Americans were "pissed off."⁴

Although these portrayals were judged by other U.S. officials to be exaggerated, they nevertheless held grains of truth. The bringing together of large numbers of Americans with Chinese could potentially lead to conflict. Director of Far Eastern Affairs Walter McConaughy and Assistant Secretary of State for Far Eastern Affairs John Moore Allison were staunch anti-communists and supporters of Chiang Kai-shek. Yet, both agreed that while allowing dependents to live in Taiwan would boost MAAG morale, the "development of a large dependents' colony in Formosa will have strong political overtones." Increasingly in Europe and Asia, there was "criticism of 'overly large' U.S. official families abroad." Such criticism provided the communist propaganda mill with grist to win "sympathy among Asians who decry the building of 'little Americas' in underdeveloped countries receiving U.S. aid." In the United States, critics pointed to the "'wasting' of tax dollars abroad to maintain U.S. official families 'in luxury.'" McConaughy and Allison warned, "There is little doubt that creation of an 'American zone' or an 'American village' on Formosa (replete with 'Americans only' shopping center, recreation halls and collective diplomatic immunity) would stimulate anti-Americanism among the Chinese and make more difficult the accomplishment of some of our major objectives."⁵

These concerns were ignored. The number of MAAG advisors and dependents increased in 1955 to seven thousand in reaction to the shelling of Jinmen and Mazu and growing PRC military strength in the area. The U.S. presence led Alexander Hermann to describe Taiwan as a place where Americans "flamboyantly dominate."⁶ Two years later, expansion continued because of both construction of the large air base near Taichung that could accommodate American strategic bombers and the introduction of the Matador missiles. By January 1957, there were 10,475 Americans in Taiwan, an increase of nearly three thousand since the previous January, though down slightly since the summer. The number of military personnel and their dependents climbed nearly 45 percent in one year, from 5,655 to 8,157. By the end of 1957, MAAG advisors composed 61 percent of that number, with nearly 1,930 advisors and 3,060 family members, far exceeding the original plan for only 250 personnel. No other civilian government agency or military entity and their dependents could claim to represent 10 percent or more of the total American presence. For example, fifty-two Americans with seventy-seven dependents worked for the embassy; fourteen Americans with twenty dependents worked for USIS. The ICA was represented by 153 Americans with 154 dependents; the Naval Auxiliary Communication Center (NACC), a CIA front, employed 196 with 307 dependents. The strength of the 13th Air Force (Provisional) stood at 497 with 316 dependents; the U.S.-Taiwan Defense Command at 200 with 170 dependents; the 176th Army Security Agency at 376 with 25 dependents.[7]

In addition to the military, the Nash Mission, commissioned by Eisenhower to study the overseas bases, found that twenty-six government agencies had personnel on the island. Ambassador Rankin also noted the multitude of U.S. organizations and the "complex chain of command." He saw "15 lines of authority from agencies in Washington" flowing to subordinates in Taiwan who engaged in the "building of separate little empires, and some not so little." Half of the noncombat personnel in Taiwan simply did housekeeping work. Rankin preferred to rely on "indigenous" personnel because of their linguistic skills and lower turnover rate. Many agencies simply duplicated one another. Rankin opined that these agencies believed the solution to every problem was to send more Americans. Around one thousand Americans were engaged in intelligence work, with ten channels of higher authority.[8]

The cost of maintaining over four thousand military and civilian personnel was $50 million annually. The U.S. government footed 90 percent of the bill.[9] Rankin's biggest fear was that the large number of Americans abroad would damage the U.S. image. He complained to Admiral Radford that, along with the Americans, "We have imported a Little America, and one need only to observe the street traffic and the new housing developments, etc., built for American personnel by the Chinese."[10] Little America segregated Americans from the "local people for whom they are supposed to work. All of this in the unhappy tradition of colonialism."[11] Too many aid projects that required large staffs reminded "Asians of colonial days."[12] Americans also patronizingly referred to other countries as "underdeveloped."[13] Rankin wanted to "confront the communist menace firmly and successfully without alienating our friends abroad by what now appears to many of them as neo-colonialism." Indeed, in 1957 the Nash Mission found that the U.S. presence in Taiwan was an affront not only to the Chinese, but to foreign diplomats as well, such as the Japanese ambassador, who stayed at an American military installation in the middle of Taipei that was identified on large billboards as "Freedom Village."[14]

Although Eisenhower's New Look strategy called for a reduction in the size of the military, this did not stop the Defense Department or other U.S. agencies from dispatching large numbers of personnel overseas. People like Rankin, who opposed the trend, wondered what lay at the bottom of this bureaucratic empire building. In 1955, he thought he found the answer when he read an article in the *Economist* written by a former British civil servant named Cyril Parkinson. Parkinson argued that civil officials expand their workload "so as to fill the time available for its completion." Paperwork that could be completed within minutes or a couple hours now requires a full day. Burdened by increasing paperwork, they insist they need a colleague to share half of the load. Then a request is made to hire subordinates, fulfilling what Parkinson called two axioms: "An official wants to multiply subordinates, not rivals" and "Officials make work for each other." Soon, seven are doing the work of one. To support his case, Parkinson pointed to how the number of colonial officials, just over three hundred in 1932, when the British empire was at its greatest extent, increased five times by 1954, despite considerable shrinkage of the empire.[15]

Although there may have been some truth behind Rankin's observation, the reality was more complicated. The propaganda, economic, and intelligence missions could not all be performed by MAAG, and there was impetus to send more civilians to take up the burden. For example, in March 1955, after a visit to Taiwan, John Foster Dulles observed that U.S. intelligence gathering in the area was "not too good." MAAG personnel were too few and overtaxed by other responsibilities, and he wanted to augment intelligence collection. In addition to growth in intelligence agencies, U.S. officials claimed in 1955 that low-ranking aircraft mechanics were needed in the aftermath of the First Taiwan Strait Crisis to supervise repairs and maintenance of the ROC's jet-powered aircraft.[16]

None of this, though, explains why the Pentagon sent so many MAAG advisors to Taiwan. The U.S. military, like Eisenhower, had been sensitive to the need to keep soldiers out for fear of alienating locals. In 1955, when Dulles suggested sending a U.S. Marine division to Taiwan, Admiral Radford countered that the move needed Chiang Kai-shek's permission, would be expensive since housing needed to be constructed, and would create problems by introducing thousands of soldiers who would be "paid far in excess of Chinese

Nationalist troops and would take away all the girls." Chiang Kai-shek made the point moot by turning down the offer.[17] That same year, though, General Ridgway, who disliked the New Look's emphasis on nuclear weapons over the ground forces as a deterrent and publicly declared that troop reductions jeopardized national security, proposed sending antiaircraft batteries, supported by twelve thousand U.S. troops, to aid Taiwan's air defense.[18] Both General Chase and Admiral Pride countered that the "political and administrative disadvantages of stationing sizable US tactical forces would outweigh possible military advantages." By 1956, Rankin, Radford, Pride, and Stump believed there were already too many Americans in Taiwan. "The high standard of living of low level American military families," argued Stump, "is in marked contrast to the low living standards of many high level Chinese." Although not alarming, there was evidence of growing resentment.[19]

To reduce the American presence on ROC soil, the United States pushed to withdraw advisors from the offshore islands. In July 1956, Rankin explained to Chiang Kai-shek that the eighty-five hundred Americans and dependents connected with official U.S. operations created friction with the Chinese and Taiwanese. The ambassador wanted the Chinese to become more independent, citing American colonels who did not want to issue orders to an ROC general and felt that they were not advisors but rather a "crutch." Withdrawing advisors made sense because the Chinese did not need any further instruction and it would reduce the costs for MAAG. Chiang Kai-shek nixed the idea. He could tolerate a reduction in the number of Americans on Taiwan, but opposed the withdrawal of advisors from the offshore islands for fear it would damage Chinese morale. Ultimately, Radford retained a small number of advisors, in part to mollify Chiang Kai-shek.[20]

Even so, removing advisors from the offshore islands made little impact on the number of Americans still in Taiwan. Compared to other countries where MAAG had personnel, the U.S. presence remained considerable. Taiwan possibly had the largest concentration of MAAG personnel in the world at that time, which from the British consul's point of view showed the deepening U.S. commitment to the ROC. In 1957 there were only 724 advisors in South Vietnam (more than double the number allowed by the Geneva Accords of 1954), accompanied by a high number of dependents, 1,800. In Thailand there were roughly 430 MAAG personnel with 318 dependents.[21] The arguments made for withdrawing MAAG from Jinmen and Mazu should have been valid for Taiwan.

In 1956, Rankin shared his concerns about the huge American population and the overlapping U.S. agencies with Richard Nixon, who visited the Philippines to celebrate the country's tenth year of independence before touring Taiwan, South Vietnam, Thailand, Pakistan, and Turkey. Nixon saw a similar situation in those countries. Sharing his findings with Eisenhower and his cabinet, Nixon argued that all government agencies needed to report to the local ambassador, as Rankin suggested, and there had to be an effort to reduce the number of Americans going overseas, including MAAG units that "were too big." "All of these oriental countries have their pride," Nixon advised. "It was probably better to let them do things their own way, even if they were done less effectively than we Americans would do them." The dilemma for Eisenhower was that no one had any real solutions to deal with an ongoing issue. As Treasury Secretary George Humphrey pointed out, "the Administration had been talking about this problem for nearly three years and as yet had not done a damn thing about it."[22] Although they pinpointed some agencies as being the worst offenders, especially the ICA, and knew from their directors that they, too, saw the problem, there was no bureaucratic mechanism to deal with it, or, if one existed, to make it more effective in overcoming the inertia.

Meanwhile, Americans remained in Taiwan by the thousands, where they enjoyed considerable privileges—especially if they were military or civilian government employees. Besides living in American-style homes or a compound of only Westerners, each family had an *amah*, or maid (some as young as thirteen), who cooked, washed clothes, cleaned house, and cared for any children. There were also houseboys and yardboys who did particular chores. Glenn Jones, eleven years old at the time, remembered living in Taipei with a maid, cook, and houseboy despite his father earning only a warrant officer's pay. Many families owned an automobile, with some having a Chinese chauffeur. The local PX provided items from home not generally sold in Taiwan. American kids went to their own schools, such as the Taipei American School, which Robert Reynolds's daughter attended, in their own buses. Reacting negatively to the claim that Americans had a lower standard of living in underdeveloped countries, John Hart, who spoke Chinese and previously worked for ICA-Taiwan, said that the nursemaids and chauffeurs allowed Americans the freedom to pursue their own pleasures, day or night, "a luxury denied most Americans" in the United States.[23]

In rural southern Taiwan, the U.S. military established separate compounds for each service branch. Vincent Kramer, whose father was a lieutenant colonel in the U.S. Marine Corps, remembered that their compound contained roughly seventy to eighty families living possibly in the quarters of former Japanese naval officers constructed before 1945. Each home was provided with two maids and a cook, and the entire compound was protected by Chinese military policemen trying to keep "dirt poor" locals from stealing

American property. The automobiles on the roads were predominantly either military or owned by Americans. Kramer's family had their vehicle shipped from San Francisco. Locals "walked, rode bikes or, if they were lucky, had motor bikes" or took pedicart taxis. Lacking potable water and fresh food, the families ate mostly canned U.S. goods unless their cook purchased pork or red snapper in the nearby town of Zuoying. The children of marine and army personnel (the latter were bused) attended the school established in the compound. While Kramer's parents attended social gatherings with Chinese to promote goodwill, he and his brother rarely encountered Chinese and Taiwanese children. Although kids played Little League Baseball or participated in the Boy Scouts, life in rural Taiwan was austere compared to Taipei. According to Kramer, "There was no TV, no ice cream, no radio, no phones, no comic books." There were also no vacations except that once a year, Americans traveled as a group to a resort constructed at Sun Moon Lake near Taichung. Because of the rural conditions in the south, Kramer's mother had to fly to Taipei to deliver his baby brother. Yet, Kramer admitted years later that Americans enjoyed a "standard of living . . . greater than that of the inhabitants of the island."[24]

Like their counterparts in Europe, many Americans could be unofficial ambassadors who did good works and did not despise people on Taiwan. After local disasters, such as typhoons, MAAG and other military or civilian personnel rebuilt homes for locals.[25] Like on the offshore islands, they also contributed to the "GI Joe" business that supported the local economy, giving Taiwanese and Chinese workers opportunities at employment in service industries, such as barbering and laundry cleaning.[26] Not all locals looked upon such a symbiotic economic relationship in a negative light. Of course, there also was the seedier side that included bar girls and brothels that most would have frowned upon, if not resented.

Still, some encounters between locals and Americans could be unpleasant. William Dawson remembered that, as a young boy, he and other bored American kids would throw mudballs at Chinese buses, hitting passengers who sat behind open windows, and were chased by the Chinese driver of a fuel tanker that nearly wrecked because of their antics. Once, while he was waiting for a bus, a young Chinese or Taiwanese man riding by on a bike spat on him. Years later, Dawson asked rhetorically, "Now why do you suppose he would feel that way about these outsiders?"[27]

Of course, these were minor annoyances involving kids that fortunately did not lead to any major incidents. Nevertheless, there were certain American actions and attitudes that had the potential to alienate allies and stain the U.S. image. One in particular was American participation in the black market. In 1957, Fred Sparks, a writer for Scripps-Howard, blasted the black market in American goods in Taiwan as a "blight on United States prestige." He described the PXs as "international chain stores which import state-side commodities with diplomatic immunity." Americans stocked up on certain goods and items and then dumped them on the black market. He insisted that every day there was "a parade of cooks and Amahs and houseboys heading for the black market with poorly wrapped packets, middlemen for their American bosses." Reaping profits, Americans became "multi-millionaires by native comparison," and in the process they undid all the good that came from the presence of American military personnel and economic aid because such a "minor crime" branded the United States as "a nation of petty pilferers."[28]

Although Sparks engaged in journalistic sensationalism, the issue of the black market had indeed existed for several years. Initially, it involved U.S. intelligence agents operating in Taiwan. In February 1951, the United States established Western Enterprise, Inc. (WEI). WEI consisted of six hundred CIA operatives who carried out clandestine operations using ROC guerillas against the PRC. When it handed over its responsibilities to MAAG it was renamed NACC.[29] The "secret agents" sent to Taiwan by Washington were described by Chinese officials as "crude, if not rude, men." Their attitudes and behavior forced the ROC to demand that some be recalled to the United States. Chinese who worked closely with WEI noticed friction not only between the agents and the local population, but between the agents and MAAG as well. Some agents engaged in smuggling activities and sold cars on the black market. MAAG found it difficult to control this activity since the agents moved freely through customs. Meanwhile, the increased value of gold on the black market led to fluctuations in commodity prices, forcing the ROC to impose restrictions to prevent individuals from engaging in currency exchange of gold and U.S. dollars.[30]

The problem only worsened with the growth in the American population. In 1953, ROC officials were described as "greatly perturbed," presumably with MAAG personnel, that Americans were selling duty-free items, such as cars, refrigerators, and household appliances, on the black market.[31] Chase promised to crack down, but the practice persisted. In November 1956, MAAG issued a directive that all U.S. military personnel, U.S. citizen employees of the armed forces, and their dependents were to refrain from reselling items purchased from the PX to ROC citizens or Americans who lacked commissary privileges or else they would face disciplinary action.[32]

Such directives were useless when the U.S. military and overall community ignored them. Beginning in April 1957, the U.S. Navy Commissary became the predominant seller of goods to American citizens in Taiwan, but the officer in charge believed that his job was only to ensure that food got to the shelves and asserted that "he was no policeman." Americans with commissary privileges (one thousand Americans lacked such privileges) were able to take full advantage while Admiral Ingersoll and others turned a blind eye, undercutting efforts to restrict U.S. goods from hitting the streets.[33] One embassy official discovered that the navy commissary sold three times as many goods as the embassy commissary, and that the most popular items that appeared on the black market, such as yeast, were constantly out of stock.[34] U.S. authorities ultimately could exert little pressure on the ROC since the Americans were only "guests." On the other hand, the ROC refused to crack down on the black market because most government officials were the prime customers and complicit in its existence. As Howard Chaille, a U.S. embassy official observed, "a great number of the members of the Chinese Government have spent many years in the States and they, and their families, have acquired American tastes."[35]

Then there was the local demand for U.S. currency. William Dawson remembered the power of the U.S. dollar, and recalled that the ROC's New Taiwan dollars were "like play money."[36] Although private trading of foreign currency was prohibited, some Chinese shops and peddlers sold their wares only for U.S. dollars. A Chinese American operated a clothier shop across the street from MAAG headquarters. He purchased his goods direct from Hong Kong with U.S. currency and advertised his products in U.S. dollars. In the process, he drove out of business another clothier whom the ROC denied the same privileges. Employees of CAT, the cargo and commercial airline subsidized by the CIA that operated out of Taiwan, paid their rents and servants in U.S. dollars. Chinese shopkeepers listed prices in both New Taiwan and U.S. dollars, but offered to reduce the price of their products if customers paid in American money.[37]

The black market and the power of the American dollar were only further evidence of the economic disparity between the Chinese and the Americans. Worse, they suggested that Taiwan had become an American colony. In 1957, Fred Sparks called Taiwan the "49th state." He argued that since 1951 the United States had pumped so much economic and military aid into the island that it had "militarily and economically been little more than an American colony." The advisors were not the problem: it was their families. American homes in Taiwan possessed "almost all the whizzing electrical gadgetry of stateside living, imported at stratospheric cost." By contrast, Chinese who once lived in "oriental splendor" now resided "in a hovel, counting rice grains, without the semblance of sanitary comfort." Sparks claimed that

Americans acted very similar to the British Raj of India: "They have their own tight social sets, and while they might have a few pet English speaking Chinese friends, usually the only native seen is the 'boy' who slip-slips across the floor." He did not blame "American wives" for trying to maintain U.S. standards in Taiwan, but warned that there could be blowback.[38] Sparks later described Americans in Asia as: "cellophane-wrapped, aloof, disinterested in all things Oriental. They are the snobs of snobs." He criticized them for their "endless . . . lavish parties they could not afford back home." They seldom invited natives into their homes, refused to buy local goods, showed no interest in the local language or culture, ate at restaurants that catered only to foreigners, segregated their children from those of the natives, and wasted U.S. taxpayer money on first-class accommodations.[39]

Without doubt, Sparks engaged in hyperbole. For example, Vincent Kramer, who had little contact with local children, learned, at his father's insistence, both Chinese and how to use an abacus from a Chinese navy officer.[40] Language schools offered courses in Mandarin Chinese to U.S. civilian and military personnel, though this limited interaction with Taiwanese who were either not part of the officer corps or spoke only the local dialect or Japanese.[41] Sparks certainly incensed people like Karl Rankin, who defended those who spent nearly two years on a tour in Asia doing a job that did not require learning the local history, language, and customs and brought them into contact with only a small number of Chinese.[42]

Nevertheless, there was no denying that many Americans lived in isolation from the natives. As early as 1955, journalists commented on how Americans in the Philippines and Taiwan showed little interest in the customs and language of the people. In Taiwan, they only entertained each other or Chinese they knew professionally.[43] They also looked upon the Chinese with a sense of racial and cultural superiority. One notorious example was the wife of General Smythe, who succeeded Chase in 1955. She constantly insulted the Chinese and made jokes about "niggers" even though General Benjamin Davis (of Tuskegee airmen fame) and a number of other blacks were stationed in Taiwan as part of the 13th Air Force (Provisional). Only Smythe's heart attack salvaged the situation by forcing his wife out of Taiwan, to the relief of Americans and Chinese alike.[44]

Unfortunately, similar attitudes were found among other U.S. officers. Foreign newspaper reporters were appalled by the "condescending" attitude of MAAG advisors toward the Chinese, while Japanese living in Taiwan noted that many Americans maintained little "social contact" with the Chinese.[45] Some Americans generally viewed the Chinese as dishonest, saying they "spoke three forms of official truth: modified truth which they tell their superiors, barely recognizable truth, which they sometimes tell to the Americans, and the untruth, which they tell to the press and everyone else."[46]

There were U.S. advisors who admitted to journalists that they did not like living in Taiwan, complaining of "bad roads, the water, the fluctuating electric current, and the graft of Chinese servants." They also "missed TV" and other American amenities and felt that the Chinese "were not grateful enough for U.S. aid."[47] Some apparently held the Chinese in contempt precisely because Taiwan relied heavily upon U.S. aid. In 1957, an American colonel told a member of the British consulate that U.S. officers found it difficult to take Taiwan and Korea "quite seriously as 'fully sovereign countries' in the same way as . . . Japan." They recalled the latter's "fighting qualities" from World War II, but those that fought in China during the war and in the Korean War had "grave doubts of the Chinese and Korean capacity to 'fight a war.'" According to the colonel, these attitudes, which were "too widespread and deep-seated" to deal with, were exhibited to Nationalist officers. Moreover, Chinese on Taiwan were envious of the Japanese and believed that the ROC got only "second-class treatment from the Americans in the way of military aid."[48] A Chinese source added that in a situation where the United States provides economic aid, the recipient develops an inferiority complex and the donor acquires a "superiority complex, despises the recipient and assumes a lordly attitude which makes things worse."[49]

The economic disparity certainly did not diminish any sense of Chinese inferiority. In 1957, Ardith Miller, a secretary at the U.S. embassy, learned from Chinese friends that there was a "rising resentment against Americans because of our preferred status—that is we come over, then bring our 'Little America' to make us comfortable; have our own PX and Commissary where we can get almost anything we need or want while the Chinese cannot get much of anything unless they buy on the black market."[50] Most Chinese did not live in luxury. Even those that were rich, explained an informant, were "reserved in their show of a higher standard of living (no flashy cars or house—at least outside—no display in public of their comforts or luxuries.)" The informant added that a number of acquaintances showed displeasure when he purchased an air conditioner.[51]

The acute disparity in income between U.S. advisors and their counterparts ensured a certain level of resentment on the part of the Chinese. Although Chiang Kai-shek maintained a large military, this did not translate into high salaries for his officers and men. In 1951, some lower-echelon officers were paid as little as US$9 a month.[52] In 1957, the salary of an ROC colonel was reportedly less than US$30 a month—but if married with children, he needed to make US$75 a month to care for his family. Many officers had to find second jobs and their wives had to work. Some colonels even resorted to knitting at home. An air force wing commander collected spent cartridge casings that he melted down and sold to feed his hungry enlisted men, who made less than US$5 a month. There was also a feeling that U.S. embassy and MAAG officials were unaware of Taiwan's true economic conditions because they only associated with upper-class Chinese.[53] Meanwhile, Fred Sparks claimed that there were Chinese women who vowed not to marry until "The Return."[54] Lower-ranking soldiers, who were single and poor, struggled to find a wife in a culture that expected the man to pay a dowry. Naturally, some soldiers resented GI competition for women and GI relative wealth.[55] There were reports of numerous jilted Chinese lovers and husbands, and an alleged incident in which a Chinese man threw acid into his girlfriend's face "for being seen with an American."[56] In 1956, stones were thrown at an American sergeant walking with a Chinese woman.[57] In a related incident, a U.S. sergeant and his Chinese wife got into an argument with a Chinese officer and a pedicab driver. The argument drew a crowd, who thought it was dispute over a girlfriend. Swift action by the police prevented it from escalating.[58]

Although Rankin may have disagreed with aspects of Sparks's argument that Americans were the "snobs of snobs," he actually blamed them for what he later described as a rising tide of anti-Americanism in Taiwan. In 1957, the ambassador observed that the now eleven thousand Americans in Taiwan "ride about in new cars, enjoy various special privileges and living standards which seem very high to the Chinese." They occupied themselves "with almost every phase of Chinese life on a scale scarcely less extensive than colonial powers in their colonies." In fact, Rankin thought the Americans in Taiwan exceeded the number that lived in the Philippines when it was a U.S. colony.[59] Andrew Franklin did not observe growing anti-Americanism, nor did he think of Taiwan as being either U.S. occupied or an American satellite. Nevertheless, he could see friction because Chinese saw themselves as superior to the "green-back rich and PX-privileged American." He was amazed that the Chinese were not subservient to the Americans and that the two allies maintained a "sense of equality."[60]

The fact that there was friction between Americans and Chinese was not an unusual phenomenon. During World War II, the U.S. presence in the United Kingdom created problems for the Anglo-American allies despite the similarity in language and culture. Britons who experienced rationing and bombings developed similar resentments against Americans, who were perceived as "oversexed, overpaid, overfed, and over here." Likewise, many Americans that arrived in Britain were ignorant and arrogant, experienced culture shock, and never acquired more than a shallow understanding of the people and place, especially if they already possessed an anti-British out-look.[61] One major difference between the U.S. occupation of Britain and the perceived American colonization of Taiwan, besides the fact that millions were stationed in the former, was that the United States and its ally used the United Kingdom as a platform to attack the enemy. Welcomed or not, the Chinese had to suffer the U.S. presence for the duration. Another difference was that the Chinese and Americans were not equals. The GIs and the thousands of dependents enjoyed the trappings of an occupying army or a colonial power, including diplomatic immunity. Nevertheless, the Chinese were not about to totally bend their backs to placate the Americans or to allow Taiwan to be totally dominated by the United States. On February 21, 1957, two U.S. Air Force generals arrived in Taiwan on a "familiarisation trip." The next day they asked a Chinese colonel why locals did not celebrate George Washington's birthday. The colonel answered, "We are not a colony yet."[62]

5

A Law unto Themselves

The fact that American military personnel and their families enjoyed diplomatic immunity convinced some critics that Taiwan was indeed a U.S. colony. The rationale for extending such protection to its advisors was that MAAG forces were members of the embassy. In 1951, the United States and the ROC signed the Mutual Defense Assistance Agreement, which contained the following clause: "such personnel, including personnel temporarily assigned, will, in their relations with the Chinese government, operate as a part of the United States Embassy, under the direction and control of the Chief of the United States Diplomatic Mission."[1] More to the point, as a Defense Department official explained to a House committee in 1955, "We have thought, as far as our military-assistance advisory groups are concerned . . . they are doing the same sort of work as the traditional diplomat and that they should have the same status."[2] Not all nations accepted such an interpretation, but Spain, Turkey, Iran, Greece, Japan, and now the ROC did. An amendment to the 1951 agreement granted diplomatic immunity to MAAG dependents. By 1955, two-thirds of U.S. military personnel and their dependents on Taiwan served under MAAG. MAAG also allowed its advisors to possess weapons in their homes as long as they were registered.[3]

The U.S. demand for immunity from Chinese criminal prosecution reflected principle, precedent, and prejudice. The principle—or rationale—can be gleaned from the debate that occurred between the Departments of State and Defense when discussing the matter of a SOFA with NATO and non-NATO powers such as Japan. In August 1950, Frank Pace, secretary of the army, introduced a SOFA that demanded exclusive jurisdiction. Defense Secretary George C. Marshall opposed exclusive jurisdiction for U.S. troops during peacetime, so Pace resubmitted a jurisdiction article similar to Article VII of the NATO SOFA. Neither State nor Defense Department officials were totally satisfied with Article VII, but William Draper, a former army general and now the U.S. ambassador to NATO, and General Thomas Handy, commander in chief of the U.S. European Command, agreed that the NATO SOFA represented the "lowest common denominator." The State Department nevertheless insisted that when negotiating for base rights with NATO and non-NATO countries, the United States should only "request," not demand, additional privileges or benefits. Its requests should not "interfere with our obtaining the base rights we need and must not cause local political repercussions." Despite the Draper-Handy Agreement, the Defense Department continued to insist on exclusive jurisdiction when negotiating base rights with nations like Italy, Spain, and Morocco, whereas the State Department preferred the NATO formula. Base negotiations were delayed for months because the two departments disagreed on the matter of jurisdiction.[4]

When the question of a SOFA for Japan arose, the two departments remained at odds. In 1952, Dean Acheson argued that ever since the Declaration of Independence "U.S. public policy has been opposed to the immunity of the military from the criminal jurisdiction of the civilian authority." Indeed, a cursory look at the document reveals that two of the facts Thomas Jefferson listed as proof of the tyranny of the king of England against the colonies were: "He has affected to render the Military independent of and superior to the Civil power" and "For protecting them [armed troops], by a mock Trial, from punishment for any Murders which they should commit on the Inhabitants of these States." Moreover, the Japanese represented the vanguard in Asia's opposition to extraterritoriality, and to deny them any type of jurisdiction would be viewed by them as a "gross discrimination" that signaled that they were: "1) not sovereign; 2) a defeated enemy; 3) racially inferior." Maintaining good relations with the Japanese was difficult, but would be made "impossible if U.S. forces are looked upon as a symbol of western discrimination and arrogance toward Asiatics." Furthermore, "the entire non-white world will be watching closely . . . to determine if we are willing to work with a non-white country on the basis of equality and partnership." Acheson contended that "the one great issue which will be decisive in setting the basis of our future relations with Asia will be questions of equal treatment." Discrimination at home practiced abroad would only make U.S.-Asian relations "intolerable."

The Department of Defense, now led by Robert Lovett, was influenced by the views of the JCS and General Ridgway, who at the time was Supreme United Nations Commander in Korea. They countered that placing U.S. forces under Japanese criminal jurisdiction opened them to "harassment," including trumped-up charges, from Japanese officials and nationals to the point that it hampered their mission and lowered morale. Americans would be subject to "strange laws" and procedures "administered by a people who have different standards and a different outlook from our own and who were not so long ago our bitter enemies." During World War II, American GIs were not subject to other nations' laws, including those of allies, especially when in forward areas.[5] One could extend the military's reasoning to the

ROC: although an ally, it had "strange laws"; it was more a Cold War front line than Japan; and MAAG advisors could be falsely accused.

It was true that during the Second World War the United States demanded exclusive jurisdiction over its forces fighting in Europe, China, and elsewhere. Even in the United Kingdom, where GIs shared closer linguistic, judicial, and cultural ties, the U.S. military wanted exclusive jurisdiction because the American people opposed their boys, many drafted against their will, being tried in a foreign court. So it was no surprise that the United States expected the same for its troops in China, where the culture and legal system stood as a polar opposite to its own. On October 1, 1943, the United States and the ROC signed the "Regulations Governing the Handling of Criminal Offenses Committed by the Armed Forces of the United States in China." The United States retained exclusive jurisdiction unless it consented to allow a soldier to be tried in Chinese courts. Chinese authorities could question, arrest, search, and detain U.S. soldiers who allegedly committed a criminal offense, but they were obligated to hand over suspected offenders to American authorities.[6]

After World War II, the precedent of according diplomatic immunity to military advisors was established when the United States created a military advisory group to China. The difference was that dependents did not receive that protection. In 1946, General Marshall argued that extending diplomatic immunity to family members was justified in "a country as unstable and politically corrupt as China." Acheson, then acting secretary of state, sympathized with Marshall's position, saying there would be serious repercussions if U.S. civilians, including dependents, "were subjected to some of the procedures existing in Chinese judicial and penal institutions." Nevertheless, he could not see how the United States could ask the ROC to relinquish jurisdiction. As a result, he modified the agreement and removed dependents from the article pertaining to jurisdiction.[7] Yet, several years later, Acheson and the Defense Department placed dependents beyond Chinese law. To do so was astounding because the same arguments that Acheson used to defend giving Japan criminal jurisdiction applied equally to the ROC.

How could Americans ignore their own history of fighting what they perceived as tyranny only to export it in the form of diplomatic immunity for their soldiers? It was one thing for the United States to expect the ROC to accord protection to Ambassador Rankin and the rest of the embassy staff and their families. This was a longstanding practice in international relations, not only between European powers but even between China and its neighbors. However, it was never intended for such a custom to be applied to thousands of military personnel and their dependents, who were thus subject to only U.S. military justice. Such a demand can only be described as a gross abuse of a fairly sacred principle in international relations. One could make a case for giving diplomatic immunity to select American personnel, such as MAAG advisors on Jinmen or Mazu, where they were not only exposed to artillery fire (two were killed in 1954), but could be captured by the PRC. Otherwise, there was no reason to provide so many members of MAAG with diplomatic immunity. The U.N.'s International Law Commission spent much of the 1950s establishing a new convention for diplomatic immunities and intercourse in part because of past abuses by Nazi Germany and the Soviet Union. Ironically, it was the United States that encouraged the ILC's work, including sharing evidence of Soviet abuses.[8]

It is also ironic that the United States demanded that an Asian government, especially a Chinese one, allow so many of its military personnel and their dependents to enjoy diplomatic immunity. It is an understatement to say that a major sore point in China's relations with the Western powers was extraterritoriality, one of the most hated vestiges of what the Chinese called the unequal treaties. For one hundred years, starting in 1844 with the signing of such a treaty, Americans did not have to fear punishment from the Chinese legal system, and there were many expatriates, including missionaries and merchants, that opposed the efforts of Chinese nationalists who agitated for removal of this protection. Americans had no faith in Chinese justice, especially after the Terranova Incident of 1821, in which a naturalized American sailor, who deliberately tossed a pot at a boatwoman below that struck and killed her, was tried and executed under Chinese law. In those one hundred years, only one American was ever executed by the U.S. Court for China for killing another human being, a foreigner; another committed suicide before facing execution for killing several Chinese. In the 1920s, an American army deserter received a life sentence for killing a Chinese policeman. Most cases involving involuntary manslaughter ended with not guilty verdicts or sentences of one to three years in prison.[9] These relatively light punishments in cases in which Americans killed Chinese nationals did not endear the Chinese to American justice. In 1943, the U.S. government officially agreed to abrogate its extraterritorial privilege after Chiang Kai-shek demanded a new treaty in order to give China greater equality in international affairs. To repackage extraterritoriality into diplomatic immunity undermined that equality. Did diplomatic immunity not represent a form of discrimination and racism against the Chinese?

This raises another question: why did the ROC agree in 1951 to what just a few years before would have been described as an "unequal treaty"? The Foreign Ministry later admitted that the agreement reflected the exigency of the moment. The ROC desperately needed military aid and paid the political price of granting diplomatic immunity to American advisors, who were relatively few in number. As a Foreign Ministry official later asserted, given the circumstances of the time, the ROC could not "express any dissent." In 1954, Premier O. K. Yui claimed that he would pursue a realistic policy of "frank cooperation" with the United States. The ROC needed so much assistance that it was "academic to talk about sovereignty and interference."[10]

By 1955, though, ROC officials had changed their minds. They wanted a SOFA with the United States. Under Article VII of the MDT, "The Government of the Republic of China grants, and the Government of the United States accepts, the right to dispose such land, air, and sea forces in and about Taiwan and the Pescadores as may be required for their defense, as determined by mutual agreement." The United States proposed that all U.S. forces sent to Taiwan be granted diplomatic immunity pending ratification of the MDT by both countries and the signing of a separate military agreement. The ROC reply only agreed to accord diplomatic immunity on a provisional basis pending the MDT coming into full effect, as it did on March 3, 1955. As a legal advisor for the State Department acknowledged, the Chinese could interpret the exchange of notes to mean that "MAAG privileges to all United States military personnel" expired on that date.[11]

In the meantime, the United States and the ROC signed provisional measures that gave diplomatic immunity to units supporting U.S. Navy medical research, electronic countermeasures, and radio communications. In May 1955, when both sides sat down to discuss coordinated planning, including American use of airfields and dispatch of military units to Taiwan, the ROC demanded base rights and a SOFA to cover all units outside of MAAG. Based on his discussions with Defense Minister Yu Dawei, Admiral Pride commented that until there was a SOFA, "it seems doubtful that U.S. plans for the defense of Taiwan can be fully implemented."[12]

The model that the U.S. *could* have had in mind was the agreement it reached with the Netherlands in 1954. The SOFA contained the NATO-Netherlands formula, as it became known, which actually limited jurisdiction by not specifying any particular crimes: "The Netherlands authorities, recognizing that it is the primary responsibility of the United States authorities to maintain good order and discipline where persons subject to United States military law are concerned, will, upon the request of the United States authorities, waive their primary right to exercise jurisdiction under Article VII . . . except where they determine that it is of particular importance that jurisdiction be exercised by the Netherlands authorities."

Instead, in August 1955, the State Department gave the ROC Foreign

Ministry a draft that granted the United States "exclusive jurisdiction" over its soldiers in Taiwan. This was done at the insistence of John Foster Dulles, who, with the Defense Department's full support, wanted U.S. military personnel, their dependents, and defense contractors to be exempt from Chinese customs and taxes and for the ROC to waive jurisdiction in all criminal cases. The rationale underpinning the request was the potential for war over Taiwan, or so the Americans claimed. The chances for hostilities to extend to Taiwan were remote, but not impossible. It was the same rationale used by the United States when it refused to grant South Korea a SOFA. Nevertheless, the fact remained that Americans had no faith in Chinese justice. For much of the history of Chinese-American relations, the United States traditionally opposed allowing its citizens to be tried in Chinese courts. In particular, U.S. authorities pointed to how the Chinese system could place a person in double jeopardy, trying an individual more than once for the same crime.[13]

The United States could have requested that the ROC agree to certain provisions and safeguards that were found in the NATO SOFA. It specified that the sending and receiving states would cooperate in criminal investigations, including sharing of collected evidence; the accused had the right to confront witnesses against him or her; the accused had a right to legal counsel; a government representative was allowed to sit in on the trial and communicate with the accused; and the accused would never face double jeopardy.[14] These provisions should have been enough to satisfy U.S. authorities that any American soldier would enjoy some protections if the ROC insisted on trying him or her for murder or rape, but they did not.

Given China's history in which unequal treaties robbed it of judicial sovereignty over foreigners, it was impossible for the ROC to sign an agreement that surrendered jurisdiction in every case. Government officials in Taipei already possessed copies of SOFAs that the United States had signed with European states. Those agreements established a baseline minimum for the legal authority that the ROC expected to possess, and it wanted more. In January 1956, the ROC countered with a proposal for a SOFA that not only imposed taxes and reduced some of the privileges enjoyed by MAAG, but demanded criminal jurisdiction based on what can be called the Japan formula.[15]

On September 29, 1953, the United States and Japan agreed to amend the Administrative Agreement of 1952 and bring it more in line with the NATO SOFA. Under Article XVII, Japan was accorded exclusive jurisdiction over U.S. troops in cases involving treason, sabotage, or espionage against Japan. Jurisdiction went to the United States in cases where GIs committed crimes against U.S. property, against other members of the U.S. armed forces, or while on duty. The language gave Japan more jurisdictional authority than the Netherlands formula would have and listed specific offenses that might land a GI in a Japanese court.[16] In this respect, Acheson was correct when he said that other nations watched what the United States did in Japan. The ROC not only wanted such jurisdiction, but wanted the cases of "particular importance" to specifically include murder and rape.

The ROC government saw the necessity of pursuing a precedent-setting agreement for a couple of reasons. Over the last century or more, the Chinese had suffered at one time or another from foreigners who often escaped Chinese justice. Also, just a few years previously an infamous case of alleged rape had occurred in China. In 1946, two U.S. Marines were accused of raping a Beijing University student in what became known as the Shen Ch'ung Incident, an affair that is still discussed in schools on both sides of the Taiwan Strait. The event spawned a nationwide anti-American movement. The presence of twelve thousand Americans troops and the people's opposition to a civil war that they believed the United States perpetuated with its aid to Chiang Kai-shek contributed to Chinese anger over the incident. Prior to the alleged rape, there were numerous claims that undisciplined U.S. soldiers engaged in reckless driving, robberies, and drunkenness, as well as cases of Chinese nationals being beaten or pushed to their deaths by U.S. troops. One of the two marines was court-martialed and convicted, but U.S. Navy authorities overturned the ten-year sentence and set the man free. Although both the Chinese Communists and Nationalists tried to exploit the movement to their own advantages, neither was able to control it.[17]

Similar incidents would only undermine stability in Taiwan, and the government needed to satisfy the demands of its people. As early as 1952, the ROC government became concerned with the behavior of MAAG advisors. Fifty advisors committed unspecified crimes in the first eight months of that year. In such an environment, Chiang Kai-shek wanted to establish some precautions or safeguards.[18]

Besides domestic considerations, the government also had to protect the ROC's international prestige. To ask for an agreement that placed Taiwan at a status below Japan and Europe would cause the government to lose face. According to Stephen Comiskey, of the State Department's Chinese Affairs Division, the Chinese wanted a "mutually agreeable 'face-saving' device and that they are not required to concede more than other US—and particularly Asian—allies." This phenomenon of nations wanting similar, if not better, agreements than those reached between the United States and other nations was not unique to the Chinese. In the course of doing his study of overseas bases for President Eisenhower, Frank Nash discovered that around the world the United States faced the difficulty of signing new agreements on its terms because host nations wanted treaties similar to those reached elsewhere. "It is remarkable how closely one country follows the arrangements reached with another," Nash observed. Compromises made with one country because of the exigencies of the moment "are being reflected more and more in the demands of other countries with whom we are negotiating." He concluded, "The time has long since passed . . . where the United States, as a government, can make arrangements with one nation without regard for possible repercussions with another."[19]

Naturally, U.S.-ROC negotiations hit an impasse. The extent to which the ROC rewrote the original U.S. draft surprised the American embassy. Rankin wondered if this was the ROC's way to "vent annoyance over numerous misunderstandings and disagreements with US military on administrative matters which have occurred in proportion to increase of US forces here." The ROC's position was "so far from current US policies" that agreement was "almost impossible."[20] The United States rejected the ROC's counterproposals on several grounds. Giving the ROC jurisdiction over cases involving murder or rape superseded the language found in other SOFAs. Washington wanted to "establish a desirable precedent" should it ever have to negotiate a SOFA with, say, South Korea.

Moreover, the Americans had their own domestic political considerations. When the NATO SOFA went before the U.S. Senate for ratification, there were politicians who opposed granting host nations, even if they were allies, such broad jurisdiction. In particular, John Bricker (R-OH) introduced his famous Bricker Amendment in 1953, which called for a constitutional amendment that would limit presidential power to conclude executive agreements (which did not require Senate approval) and treaties. Bricker also became an outspoken critic of the NATO SOFA, calling it "one of the worst [treaties] I have ever seen." He introduced a reservation to the treaty that would have essentially provided for exclusive jurisdiction over U.S. troops. The reservation failed by a vote of 53–27.[21] To overcome opposition, the Eisenhower administration targeted key senators, telling them that if the treaty went down to defeat or was impaired by reservations like that of Bricker's, "our whole policy with respect to NATO would be jeopardized." Although the NATO SOFA and the agreement with Japan obtained Senate approval, this did not prevent politicians from introducing resolutions, such as one in 1956 by Senator William Jenner (R-IN) calling on the Senate Committee on Foreign Relations to rescind the NATO SOFA in the name of protecting the constitutional rights of GIs who had been tried in European courts.[22]

Finally, what ROC officials did not know was that in October 1953 the Japanese government agreed to a secret minute, or modification of the original agreement, that stated that "as a matter of policy the Japanese authorities do not normally intend to exercise the primary right of jurisdiction . . . other than in cases considered to be of material importance to Japan." Essentially, Japan secretly conceded that it would not seek a wider jurisdiction than was already spelled out in the Netherlands formula. State Department officials made it clear that the secret minute could not "be revealed" to the ROC.[23] In fact, this minute was so sensitive that for years they insisted that it only be shared on a need-to-know basis within U.S. embassies, for fear of a leak and subsequent public outcry in Japan.[24] Regardless, Japan remained unique in that it was the only Asian country in the 1950s that had a NATO-type SOFA with the United States.[25]

The ROC did compromise by suggesting that it would grant the United States broad jurisdiction except in cases involving assassination or treason. Again, the U.S. government refused to grant the ROC any specific jurisdiction over U.S. troops. Admiral Stump, CINCPAC, disagreed with his own government's rigid stance. He argued that the United States should give Taiwan what it wanted, with the ROC's assurance that it would demand jurisdiction only in cases involving treason. CINCPAC criticized U.S. negotiators for humiliating an ally, and believed that Congress should be told point-blank that the United States could not afford to impose terms worse than those given to Japan, a former enemy. Stump added, "No national pride should be callously crushed by singling out 1 country as inferior to the others."[26] He warned against making the ROC appear as a "puppet" and exposing the United States "to strong emotional reaction of all of Asia against 'imperialism,' 'white domination,' and 'extraterritoriality.'" Stump believed the ROC would honor an oral gentlemen's agreement that promised the United States exclusive jurisdiction, saving Chinese face and assuaging the U.S. Congress.[27]

William P. Cochran concurred, saying that the chances of U.S. troops committing acts of treason and assassination were "negligible." He urged the State Department to "strike while the iron was hot" and accept the ROC compromise. Instead, fearful of Congress's wrath, it refused. Cochran acknowledged that while the State Department might have to appease Congress, it had to consider the views of Taiwan's "Legislative Yuan which will find it difficult to swallow an arrangement less favorable to allied China than we granted to ex-enemy Japan."[28]

Complicating the SOFA talks were negotiations for base rights in Taiwan. Admiral Ingersoll blamed the failed SOFA talks on the Chinese, who tried to win concessions from the United States, and worried the ROC would use the base talks to seek greater jurisdiction over U.S. troops. CINCPAC preferred that base discussions be separated from SOFA, but still maintained that the United States should give the ROC the same rights as Japan as long as the ROC provided verbal assurances that it would seek jurisdiction only in cases of treason. The Defense Department sided with Ingersoll, who wanted exclusive jurisdiction, as did others in the State Department who believed that CINCPAC discounted the power of Congress. The ROC countered that agreeing to exclusive jurisdiction only played into the hands of Chinese Communist propaganda, would anger its politicians, made the government look inferior, and marked the return of extraterritoriality. Members of the Office of Chinese Affairs disagreed, arguing internally that the ROC could accept exclusive jurisdiction in a secret annex, similar to that of Japan and other countries. Beijing would not know of the secret annex and thus there would be no propaganda issue. Moreover, the ROC would still have jurisdiction over any Americans not serving in the government or military, undercutting the extraterritoriality argument.[29]

The overarching concern for the State Department and Pentagon remained that of Congress. Defense Secretary Charles Wilson worried about the Bow Amendment, introduced by Representative Frank T. Bow (R-OH), which demanded that all SOFAs be modified to give the United States "exclusive jurisdiction" over GIs. In 1956, Bow traveled to Japan to study its prisons, and then wrote an article for *American Legion Magazine* that negatively portrayed Japan's criminal justice system in a manner described by U.S. military officials as "fallacious."[30] Nevertheless, Bow's amendment forced Eisenhower to fight hard against what he called "the protagonists of worldwide U.S. exclusive jurisdiction within bounds."[31] Besides domestic opposition, U.S. officials remained concerned about the impact of a U.S.-ROC SOFA on negotiations with South Korea and the Philippines.[32] If the United States gave the ROC a Japan-type SOFA, other Asian countries would certainly demand the same.

From October 1956 through March 19, 1957, U.S. and ROC negotiators met several times, still unable to reach an agreement. The Americans were instructed that if the ROC continued to oppose waiving the right of jurisdiction because of domestic reaction that it represented extraterritoriality, and that the ROC expected equal treatment, the Chinese were to be given a warning: negative U.S. congressional reaction would make the defense of Taiwan difficult and could threaten SOFAs and other bilateral arrangements all over the world. The United States could make the waiver for everything but security offenses secret, much as it had done with many other countries

that experienced less tension than Taiwan, placing the ROC on equal footing. The ROC, though, again demanded jurisdiction in cases involving murder and rape. Washington refused.[33]

Meanwhile, since the ROC did not have access to the secret minute, it
continued to demand the Japan formula because it went beyond the Netherlands formula, not knowing "that the Netherlands and the Japanese formulas
are virtually identical in substance" thanks to the secret minute.[34] U.S. officials acknowledged that the ROC should at least be given a SOFA that contained the Netherlands formula in order to give it "equal treatment with our
other allies."[35] Pentagon officials, though, still expected the ROC to orally
assure the United States that it would waive jurisdiction in all cases. They still
worried that giving the ROC any jurisdiction would place the United States
in a difficult negotiating position with South Korea and remained concerned
about the reaction of U.S. congressional leaders to anything less than exclusive jurisdiction that "would probably come as the result of some controversial
case on the Island."[36]

For the ROC, to agree on anything less than the Japan formula represented a total humiliation. It would have reduced the ROC's status to below
that of not only Japan, but other U.S. allies. The ROC had already made a
major concession to grant diplomatic immunity to MAAG personnel and
dependents as well all other U.S. military personnel. In March 1957, it
made another concession when it agreed to accord the same to Matador missile personnel "pending completion of the status of forces and military facilities agreement now under negotiation."[37] As a result of signing both the
MDT and the Matador Agreement, Robert Dechert, a Defense Department
general counsel, believed that the United States stood "on very sound ground
. . . in maintaining that all of our forces in Taiwan are presently entitled to the
same privileges and jurisdictional immunity as members of the MAAG."[38]
The ROC needed a SOFA to show that it possessed at least some level of
independence and jurisdiction over U.S. troops operating on its soil.

Meanwhile, diplomatic immunity undercut U.S. propaganda about itself
and provided copy for the communist propaganda machine. Early in 1956,
PRC propaganda claimed that the U.S. dominated or controlled Taiwan. In
order to save face and avoid looking like a U.S. colony, the ROC tried to
portray an image of independence. "As an independent nation," George Yeh
observed in 1958, "we don't like to have foreign troops in our country. As a
matter of fact, the Americans who are here in Taiwan are military advisors
and there are no American military bases here." Yeh added that the ROC
could pull out of the MDT with a year's notice.[39] The odds of the ROC exercising its option were nil. Moreover, regardless of their actual role, the pres-

ence of so many American advisors and agencies did not imply strength. It reflected that internal weakness needed external shoring up.

Nevertheless, the ROC wanted jurisdiction of some kind. For America's allies to demand protection of their sovereignty was not extraordinary. In 1956, even the Soviets were forced to sign bilateral agreements similar to a SOFA with several East European countries.[40] Even if people on Taiwan benefited from the U.S. defensive umbrella, it was a humiliation to have thousands of Americans residing on Taiwan, living in their own Little America, some of them armed, and out of reach of Chinese law.

Fortunately, there had been no serious incidents in Taiwan, or at least none reported by U.S. officials. Between January 1956 and August 1957, MAAG-Taiwan carried out thirty-four courts-martial. All of those tried were enlisted men, and fourteen were found guilty. There were also summary courts-martial, involving one officer and the charged enlisted man, that found twenty-eight GIs guilty. Thirteen were convicted of drunkenness and disorderly conduct, but the rest were found guilty of unlawful cohabitation, smuggling, black market activities, traffic accidents or violations, and various petty cases. In no case was any Chinese injured even though most drunk and disorderly crimes were committed in Chinese bars or "houses of ill-fame which cater to American enlisted men."[41] Rape allegations were made from time to time, but no MAAG men were ever tried for rape in the 1950s, though it was possible to avoid prosecution by paying off the victim's family. For example, a barmaid filed a NT$6,000 claim against a MAAG sergeant for an alleged rape, torn clothing, and a broken watch, but the man paid only NT$1,000 to settle the matter.[42]

Such incidents never compelled the U.S. State Department to compromise and acquiesce to ROC demands for a SOFA. Several more years passed with no agreement seeming possible. It is unfortunate that the U.S. government did not sign a SOFA with the ROC. Despite the warnings and concerns raised by U.S. military and diplomatic personnel, inertia or willful refusal prevented bureaucrats from taking problems seriously and head-on. If Taiwan was so vital to U.S. containment policy, the United States should have been willing to give the ROC a SOFA, base or no base, with the NATO-Netherlands formula rather than humiliate its ally and demand exclusive jurisdiction. Congressional opposition was not insurmountable and in many respects became a convenient excuse to not make any concessions. Although the United States had an obligation to uphold its judicial system for its troops stationed abroad, it needed to meet the demands of its allies as near to halfway as possible. Regardless of how Washington felt about Chiang Kai-shek, his son, or the Nationalist Party, it still had an obligation to the people of Taiwan. It had helped to liberate them from the Japanese during World War II, and it wanted to protect them from communism. The United States should have worked to establish safeguards, due process, and justice if an American brought harm to any of them—not as colonial subjects, but as equals before the law. Until a SOFA was signed and as long as MAAG personnel enjoyed immunity, all the ROC could hope was that no U.S. soldier committed a major crime, such as murder. Unfortunately, just such a case occurred. Sergeant Robert Reynolds shot and killed an ROC national. Chinese and American authorities now had to decide whether it was self-defense or cold-blooded murder.

6

A Tale of Two
Criminal Investigations

On March 20, 1957, Chinese and American policemen received calls that a U.S. soldier had just shot another man outside of his home on Grass Mountain. Within minutes, Major Han Jiali, a ten-year veteran of the police force and chief of the Yangmingshan Foreign Affairs Police (FAP) section, arrived at the home of Sergeant Reynolds. Han went by the English name of Charley and apparently had good English-speaking skills.

Reynolds explained what had transpired, motioned toward where he thought the wounded man might be, and expressed concern that he would die if not provided medical attention soon.

The next policeman to arrive on the scene was Sergeant Eugene R. McJunkins, a member of the U.S. Marine Corps who had twelve years' experience as a criminal investigator and had dealt with 150 homicides. McJunkins could see that Reynolds was "emotionally upset . . . crying, very disturbed," and that his wife, who was wearing a housecoat or bathrobe, "was nervous and disturbed." Before McJunkins could even read Reynolds his rights, the MAAG sergeant admitted that he had shot a man. When told that he needed to know his rights, Reynolds responded, "I have nothing to hide."[1]

Han, McJunkins, and Reynolds joined the search already in progress in the park for the injured man. A heavy fog covered Grass Mountain that night. After twenty minutes of searching, Reynolds found the lifeless body first. U.S. investigators determined that Liu ran seventeen feet east away from Reynolds to a side street and then turned south, traveling another 192 feet before collapsing. McJunkins told Reynolds to stay put while he investigated. Liu's body lay face down, with his hands thrown above his head, as if he had been running, tripped, and fell. Liu's head pointed north, in the direction of Reynolds's home. Reynolds became "remorseful," so McJunkins walked him back to the house and advised him to get some sleep. It was already 1:00 A.M., and he decided not to question Reynolds until later in the day. Going back to the body, McJunkins found a man wearing a khaki uniform with two bullet wounds: one in the stomach and the other in the left breast. He found no exit wounds. Major Han identified the dead man as Liu Ziran, whom he had known for three years.[2]

At this point, the cooperation exhibited so far in the investigation by the Chinese and Americans began to break down. McJunkins and Han went back to the bathroom windowsill where Liu allegedly stood, peeping in at Clara Reynolds over the top of the plastic curtain. They found dirt and scuff marks on the wall, dirt on the window ledge, and evidence that someone had recently tampered with one of the hooks that held the window open. In the area where Reynolds claimed to have shot the man the first time, investigators found a spot where someone had recently slipped and fallen, leaving a shirtsleeve impression on the ground.

While Chinese authorities examined the body, the two policemen then searched for the three- or four-foot-long object that Reynolds claimed to have seen in Liu's left hand. McJunkins became concerned by the manner in which Chinese investigators dealt with the body, because his training taught him to investigate—not contaminate—the crime scene. At the spot where Liu supposedly laid after being shot the first time, the damp ground looked disturbed. Expanding the search pattern, McJunkins found a small stick lying eight feet from the window ledge, but around fifty-four steps—or 162 feet—from Liu's body. (McJunkins clearly walked in a straight line from the object to the body.) The stick was only two feet long and "as big around as a man's thumb." It seemed foreign in an area where bamboo and azaleas grew several feet tall. Major Han did not believe it was the weapon. Not only was it four feet from where the deceased fell the first time, but that night, clouds and mist covered everything on Grass Mountain. When McJunkins picked up the stick, dew drops fell from it. In fact, Han expressly told McJunkins, who had been trained by the Federal Bureau of Investigation and apparently ignored his experience about noncontamination, to not touch the stick so that it could be checked for partial fingerprints. Instead, McJunkins picked up the stick because he believed Han and another policeman had no intention of doing anything with it. Holding the stick with two fingers, McJunkins went to Reynolds's home and asked, "Is this the stick?" Reynolds answered: "It could be but I thought it was bigger than this."[3]

Shortly thereafter, a Chinese colonel from the Alien Criminal Investigation Division (CID) took over the investigation from Major Han. The colonel demanded permission to interrogate Reynolds. McJunkins refused, saying that he had already done so (which was not entirely true) and would get a statement from the American later in the day. When the CID colonel insisted, McJunkins responded that Reynolds had diplomatic immunity. Under the agreement signed in 1943, the Chinese only had jurisdiction when the United States gave its consent (which was also not entirely true).[4] McJunkins did have Reynolds send his *amah*, or housegirl, to the police station for questioning and handed Reynolds's revolver over to the Chinese CID. When McJunkins later learned that the CID man interrogated Reynolds anyway, he told one of his superiors that the CID men "were unfair because they have no jurisdiction over him."[5]

Later that morning, Lieutenant Colonel Joseph L. Salonick, of the provost marshal's headquarters, took the director of the FAP and his staff to the Reynolds home to reenact the events of the previous night. What Salonick did not know was that Reynolds had reenacted the shooting several hours earlier at Chinese insistence. To Salonick's dismay, Chinese photographers were already on the scene despite repeated requests that no one be allowed in the area while they conducted their investigation. After Reynolds rehearsed the incident several times, he gave a statement. An official from the procurator's office wanted to question Reynolds. Salonick refused. All questions would come through him. The answers provided by Reynolds were taken down by a Chinese official who often disagreed over how a word or phrase should be interpreted. After Reynolds answered questions through Salonick, the Chinese official then asked that Reynolds sign a statement written in Chinese. Again, Salonick not only objected, but repeatedly told the Chinese that their statement was wrong.

Increasingly, the Americans recognized an unusual reticence in Chinese behavior. In years past, both sides generally cooperated unless the case involved someone of great importance on the Chinese side, such as smuggling cases. Otherwise, each shared information and worked together. In the Reynolds case, Chinese authorities proved to be very uncooperative. Despite promises, Chinese authorities were not forthcoming in providing statements given by Reynolds's *amah* and Major Han just hours before Salonick brought Reynolds to the Chinese police station for interrogation. Later, when the Chinese performed both an autopsy and a ballistics test, they stonewalled in sharing their results. On several occasions the provost marshal attempted to meet with the director of the FAP, only to be told that the appointment had been cancelled because the director was "ill." When documents were released to the Americans, they were always in Chinese and without English translations. The excuses for not providing translations became comical. On one occasion, an FAP official said that he had the translations in his desk, but the drawer was locked and he did not have a key. Eventually, U.S. authorities were told that all information related to the case would come from the Ministry of Foreign Affairs, only further convincing the Americans that ROC officials were obstructing the investigation. On April 3, the

Americans tried to interview Yao Limei, the *amah,* only to learn that she had been ordered to meet with Major Han. U.S. investigators considered the possibility that Han was under orders to coach her before she could be interrogated by them.[6]

In particular, ROC officials refused to say who Liu Ziran was or what he did for a living. As one American investigator summed up the situation, "A veil of secrecy has been drawn around Liu's official military branch of the Republic of China."[7] What little that U.S. investigators learned suggested that Liu worked for the government. The night before he was killed, Liu had attended a party and been introduced to Americans as a major in the Ministry of the Interior's secret police.[8] Yet, ROC officials claimed that all records pertaining to Liu "were retained personally by the Vice-President of Nationalist China." One official denied that Liu was a military officer of any kind, but someone who liked to wear uniforms to impress the women in the dance halls. When Salonick asked the chief of the CID point-blank for the dead man's name and whether he served in the military or had a police record, he received only silence for an answer. Salonick heard from other CID men that Liu worked as a typist in the Institute for Revolutionary Practice (IRP), located on Grass Mountain and directly controlled by Chiang Ching-kuo. The Americans viewed Liu's job description as "typist" as a Chinese ruse to hide his real identity. U.S. officials learned from informants that Liu was either an instructor at the IRP or an intelligence officer with the rank of major or colonel. As one investigator observed, "It is quite obvious that Liu was no ordinary, run of the mill, citizen."[9]

The IRP was no ordinary school. It was formed by Chiang Kai-shek himself on July 26, 1949.[10] The philosophy behind the training and education revolved around the ideas of Wang Yangming, the same Ming dynasty scholar after whom Grass Mountain had been renamed, and Sun Yat-sen, founder of the Nationalist Party: "Knowledge and action go hand in hand" (*zhixing heyi*) and "It is easier to do a thing than to know the why" (*zhinan xingyi*). Chiang Kai-shek tried to instill these ideas into a party that, in his judgment, had lost both its revolutionary spirit and China. He wanted party members to get closer to the people and understand their conditions in order to help them solve their problems. The school's connection to clandestine work may have been the fact that the party financially backed underground activities in the PRC that were carried out by either party members or military officers, who were school trainees, or civilians still in the PRC who were unable to escape but understood the party and its policies as well as the local conditions.[11] The goal, of course, would have been to undermine the PRC regime and enable the ROC to recover the mainland. By 1952, the institute had graduated over three thousand cadres that took positions inside the party and the government.[12]

The Americans had their own descriptions for the institute. Colonel Walter E. Barker, the embassy army attaché, bluntly called the IRP a Nationalist "brainwashing school for senior officials."[13] Paul Meyer, the embassy's political affairs officer, described it as a "supersecret organization whose existence was not to be mentioned in public." Ambassador Rankin noted that the IRP received no money from the United States and that IRP officials deemed "US policy toward China as woefully inadequate."[14]

Claims that Liu Ziran was in fact a security or intelligence agent seemed plausible. The secret headquarters for the National Security Bureau (NSB), Taiwan's version of the Soviet Union's KGB, was also located on Yangmingshan.[15] The U.S. Army Pacific Command (USARPAC) observed that civilians were prohibited from entering U.S. Army residence areas with the exception of ROC military personnel and secret police agents, implying that Liu was one or the other or both. Although a younger brother who also worked at the IRP said Liu Ziran had been employed there since 1949, a Taiwanese wrote a letter to a Japanese newspaper editor claiming both to know Liu personally and that he worked for the NSB. All of this was of course sheer speculation and unfounded rumors. The most that the ROC initially admitted about Liu's background was that he was married with one child. His wife's father, who was deceased, was once an intelligence agent, and his brother-in-law was an instructor at the IRP.[16]

Lack of cooperation on both sides foreshadowed that this case would be fraught with tension and controversy. U.S. investigators tended to believe Reynolds's claim that he initially acted to defend his home and family. He had been warned to be alert for burglars in the last two or three months of his tour. Since his tour would soon end and he had money in his home, Reynolds thought the intruder looked through the only open window with the intent to steal. By contrast, Chinese perceived more sinister motives. In fact, two days after Liu's death, his widow, Ao Tehua, sent a letter to Major General Frank S. Bowen, who had become head of MAAG in 1956, that accused Reynolds of killing her husband in a "barbaric, cold blooded manner." The letter added: "In our grief we raise our voice of protest against such barbaric behavior and trust that appropriate action befitting the crime will be taken." Looking at the "grammatical structure of the letter," one American investigator concluded it had been written by ROC officials and that she "merely signed her name."[17]

True or not, the Chinese press began discussing what became known as the Liu Ziran Incident. The Americans observed that Chinese newspapers played on readers' sympathies by noting that Liu left behind a twenty-nine-year-old widow and a sixteen-month-old baby and was a poor yet "genial, amiable individual."[18] Eventually, Chinese newspapers became more critical of Liu Ziran's character, but of greater importance, writers and readers raised a number of questions about Liu's shooting in a manner U.S. investigators described as displaying "a very rabid anti-American emotional attitude."[19] In reality, the opinions expressed were not anti-American, but actually simple questions. As one Chinese in Taipei noted, "clouds of suspicion" surrounded the case. Information about the crime scene released by the ROC suggested that Liu's body laid a considerable distance from Reynolds's home and that he had been shot in the back. Liu had no weapon and no wooden object was found at the crime scene. Chinese investigators reported that the bathtub in the Reynolds duplex was dry, raising the question of whether Clara Reynolds did indeed take a shower that night, tempting Liu to peep through the window. The *United Daily* reported that Reynolds had recently been involved in an incident in which he punched a Taiwanese postman in the face.[20] Other newspapers accused Reynolds of being guilty of manslaughter if not murder, questioning why a so-called peeping tom would not simply have run away but rather charged an armed man twice, including once after being shot.

If this was murder or manslaughter, what was the motive? There was the claim that Reynolds and Liu Ziran, who allegedly spoke broken English, were friends and partners in the black market, selling military ordnance. Liu lived beyond his means in luxury through introducing Chinese women to foreign men while selling the latter's goods on the black market. Supposedly, Liu was notorious for borrowing money, and possibly in debt to Reynolds. Although Yao Limei claimed to have met Liu Ziran the night prior to the shooting for the first time when returning to the Reynolds home after watching a movie, there was speculation that Liu and Yao had tickets to a party but she stood him up.[21] In the process of confronting her, Liu got into an argument with Reynolds over their alleged business dealings. Then there were claims that both men were infatuated with the same Chinese woman, and when Liu refused to stop his advances, Reynolds killed him. It was further conjectured that since the two were partners on the black market, Liu stopped giving the American his share when he heard that Reynolds would be transferred out of Taiwan. When Liu visited Yao Limei, with whom he had been intimate for some time, Reynolds surprised him and killed him. Reynolds not only shot Liu once in anger but chased him down and shot him once more as the man lay wounded.[22]

Although the veracity of such theories remained to be seen, Taiwan readers tended to believe them rather than Reynolds's claim that he shot a peeping tom who tried to attack him. One journalist opined that Americans, "who are open-minded on relations between men and women," would not have "viewed a man peeping at a bathing woman" as constituting "a motive for murder." In a letter to the editor of the *United Daily*, a reader rejected Reynolds's claim that he fired only in self-defense because it was "impossible" for Liu to possess a firearm of his own, and believed Reynolds fired to kill. The reader claimed that many Chinese thought that U.S. soldiers were "scum," and that similar incidents had occurred in the past.[23]

There was also outrage over the fact that U.S. authorities did not even detain Reynolds but rather allowed him to go freely about his business. A newspaper in southern Taiwan published a political cartoon of Karl Rankin in a robe holding a scepter over his head while Reynolds stands beside him, a smoking gun in his hand, and Liu Ziran lies on the ground in a pool of blood. Because of the rising anger over the case, ROC authorities asked nearly a week after the shooting that Reynolds be placed in detention pending a court-martial because they feared they could not adequately protect him from mob attacks.[24]

In time, the Chinese press, particularly the *United Daily*, a major privately owned paper known as the true voice of the Nationalist people, honed onto the fact that U.S. military personnel had diplomatic immunity because of the 1951 agreement.[25] It described the shooting as the second of its kind since U.S. military personnel were stationed in Taiwan. The newspaper claimed that the previous year a GI had shot and killed a Chinese man accused of being a thief. Since the man had diplomatic immunity, the incident had been handled by U.S. authorities, who transferred the soldier back to the United States.[26] Neither the U.S. government nor military officials ever spoke of such an incident, which either did not occur or was covered up by the American military. Regardless, with several thousand GIs in Taiwan, there were demands for a SOFA similar to the one signed between Japan and the United States. Many insisted that the Americans hold an open court-martial in Taiwan, setting an important precedent.[27]

Naturally, the Americans were incensed by the newspaper coverage. In General Bowen's eyes, the Chinese press had created a cause célèbre out of Liu Ziran even though that same press excoriated his alleged bad character, forcing his widow to defend his name. To Bowen's anger, the Chinese press described the two-foot-long stick as a "twig" and insisted that it could never have been used as a weapon, claimed that Reynolds was drunk and got into a quarrel with Liu Ziran even though he was not known as a drinker and consumed only coffee that evening, and suggested that both men were engaged in black market activities, a notion proven false by ROC investigators. Indeed, despite many rumors that both men had a business relationship selling goods on the black market, the Taiwan Provincial Public Security Bureau found no evidence that Reynolds had a relationship with either Liu Ziran or his wife.[28] Bowen was also irritated that a few weeks before, a Chinese burglar broke into a U.S. Foreign Service officer's home, where the two fought before the burglar stabbed the American in the neck with a sharp instrument, just missing an artery. The man had yet to be captured by the police and the Chinese newspapers said nothing about the incident, but for the Reynolds case there was "a great hue and cry" and a "great deal of publicity—all of it unfavorable to Sgt. Reynolds." Bowen exerted pressure on the ROC government to force the press "to live up to an agreement . . . that only the bare facts would be announced and no further comment be made until the completion of the investigation."[29]

The American general apparently succeeded. From early April on, the U.S. embassy noted that stories about the case "abruptly ceased" and remained that way through the end of the month.[30] Even when another GI went AWOL, got drunk, trashed a Chinese bar in Taipei, and beat up an ROC national, the Chinese press laid low. Even if the United States succeeded in forcing the ROC to impose a gag order on the press, one newspaper editorial noted that the Chinese people themselves were not gagged. They talked about the case, and rumors abounded. The local English-language newspaper, the *China News,* insisted that in the name of U.S.-ROC cooperation, it was imperative to explain to the people why Reynolds enjoyed diplomatic immunity and was not subject to Chinese law.[31]

By March 26, ROC authorities realized that MAAG-Taiwan had concluded that Reynolds fired in self-defense and therefore did not intend to prosecute him. They also learned that Reynolds would return to the United States as planned. The head of the Police Commission's Foreign Affairs Office explained to the provost marshal that he been confronted with a serious situation: public opinion believed that a man who had just killed a Chinese citizen was about to "flee" the law. Two Chinese newspapers had already called for a "reasonable, legal resolution" of the Liu Ziran case.[32] The Foreign Ministry made repeated requests of the U.S. embassy to have Reynolds court-martialed, and insisted that there was sufficient evidence to suggest that the killing of Liu Ziran "exceeded the proper limits of self-defense." It further asked that MAAG detain Reynolds and take the role of cop and prosecutor, not of defense counsel. MAAG, though, had no reason to arrest him because it had no evidence that Reynolds committed murder or manslaughter.[33] On March 29, Sergeant Billie Chaney, an investigator, declared that cooperation by U.S. and ROC officials had been "nullified" by the latter's attitude and that Liu Ziran unlawfully entered Reynolds yard for "illegal purposes." Reynolds's wife, maid, and daughter were dependent upon him for protection, and with retreat impossible because of Liu's sudden attack, he acted in self-defense.[34]

On April 3, the autopsy report and ballistic analysis performed by the CID finally reached the hands of U.S. authorities. The autopsy, performed by a pathologist from National Taiwan University in the presence of two U.S. Army colonels, described Liu as Mongolian, around thirty years of age, weighing 170 pounds, and standing about six feet tall, making him taller than the average Chinese. Examination of the stomach contents revealed that Liu had not only eaten rice, meat, and vegetables, but also had been drinking the night he was killed. Recent abrasions to the knees and left ankle were noticeable. The first bullet passed through the abdomen and liver, and 150 cc of blood collected in a nearby body cavity. The second bullet entered the left chest and pierced a lung, which partially collapsed under the weight of 2,250 cc of blood. Shock, resulting from massive internal bleeding, was listed as the cause of death. Ballistic analysis showed a perfect match between the two bullets extracted from Liu's body and those fired from Reynolds's gun in the laboratory. More damning for Reynolds was the analysis of Liu's uniform, which showed evidence of nitrates (gunpowder residue) around the bullet holes, suggesting that he had been shot at very close range, not more than thirty centimeters (about one foot).[35]

On April 8, the Procurator's Office for the Taipei District Court issued its report to the ROC Foreign Ministry. Reynolds admitted to Major Han that he had shot a "Chinese soldier because he was peeking at my wife taking a bath." He told his wife to remain in the bathroom and pretend to manicure her nails. When he confronted the man, he fired in self-defense when Liu allegedly attacked him. Procurator Lo Bida declared that common sense would suggest that Liu would have run away as fast as possible either after Clara Reynolds informed her husband of Liu's presence, showing some "fright in expression," or when confronted by Reynolds. The dew drops on the alleged weapon suggested that the stick had never been handled until Sergeant McJunkins picked it up. Yao Limei and a Chinese MP reported hearing two shots in quick succession, less than thirty seconds apart, contradicting Reynolds's claim that he fired two shots two minutes apart. When the procurator arrived at the crime scene, he discovered that the body was lying with the head pointing toward the Reynolds home. This implied that Liu Ziran was not shot in the act of running away when he died. According to the report, the angles of the bullet wounds, the powder residue, and witness statements to the quick succession of shots suggested that Reynolds fired at point-blank range on Liu, who fell to the ground after being hit in vital organs, then stood over Liu, who was too weak to resist, and fired a second time. (The report did not explain how Reynolds could stand three or four feet over the victim and fire a bullet only one foot away.) Thus, Reynolds's statements were not truthful, and he "killed willfully and maliciously and not properly in self-defense." Since he had the status of a diplomatic official, the chief procurator recommended that Reynolds be tried by U.S. authorities.[36]

The report incensed U.S. investigators. Reynolds claimed that he did not know Liu Ziran: a statement supported by both Yao Limei (who denied knowing Liu or that Reynolds had any business dealings with the dead man) and Liu Ziran's wife.[37] Reynolds confronted a man he believed intended to rob him, and did not seek to shoot. If he had, he could have shot Liu through the bathroom window or simply shot him as he perched on the windowsill. After the first shot, he sought only to hold the man until MPs arrived. The American also passed a voluntary lie detector test given to him on May 2.

As for the pathologist's report, U.S. experts expressed "curiosity" that the report spoke of the distance at which Reynolds fired his weapon: "The fact that the shots were fired from *any* distance is entirely unrelated to the subject of an autopsy." They noted the "black matter" around the bullet holes, but saw "no visible powder or powder burns at either point of entrance." For some time, the Chinese refused to hand over Liu's clothing and return Reynolds's revolver, making it impossible for the Americans to do their own tests to prove or refute Chinese allegations. Once the weapon and jacket were in their possession, forensic analysis performed by a U.S. military police laboratory in Japan detected no nitrates around the bullet holes. The procurator's report spoke of three separate statements taken from Reynolds, and implied that he had lied because each was different. U.S. investigators denied that Reynolds even submitted statements to the Chinese, and called one statement an "outright fabrication." As a result, the Americans branded the Chinese accusation of murder "a theory evolving from conjectures without sufficient evidence."

Overall, the Americans were angry with the lack of Chinese cooperation, and stung by Chinese newspaper accounts in which the "character and reputation of local American servicemen in general have been publicly maligned." U.S. investigators concluded that Reynolds killed Liu Ziran in self-defense, protecting himself and the lives of his family against a man who intended to use a dangerous weapon, such as a knife or gun, to inflict "great bodily harm." The use of force was justified because "retreat was not reasonably possible because of the spontaneity of the ensuing action and the fact that Reynolds was at his own home."[38]

In the judgment of Lieutenant Colonel James Fewster, the first investigating officer who had to decide whether to file charges, Reynolds's version of events best fit the evidence found at the scene. When Clara Reynolds informed her husband that someone was looking at her while she bathed, Reynolds, fearing that the intruder could attack her, told her to do nothing that "would let the intruder know he had been observed." Because she was between him and the intruder, Robert Reynolds's actions were consistent with those "expected of an average man in his right mind seeking to protect the security and privacy of his home and family." Reynolds confronted the intruder with his nine-shot .22 revolver with the intent of defending himself, capturing the intruder, or causing him to flee. Instead, the man attacked, forcing Reynolds to fire at close range. Testimony from Major Han showed that the stick found there could have both been construed as an iron bar and inflicted serious injury or death. After the first shot, Reynolds called for military policemen. Getting no reply, he sought out the intruder for "humanitarian reasons" and intended to provide medical care, only to be attacked again, forcing him to fire a second shot. The Chinese autopsy report stated that Liu was shot at close range. In Fewster's judgment, this substantiated Reynolds's statement that he fired "as a final resort." Witness testimony that Reynolds drank coffee that night meant that he was in possession of his mental faculties. A chemical test showed that Liu Ziran drank alcohol, but because the test did not indicate how much, Fewster assumed that Liu was not drunk and "in full possession of all his mental faculties." In addition, Reynolds's superiors described him as mature, stable, conscientious, serious, and by all accounts "a dedicated family man of high moral character." He had "many Chinese friends," and participated in "Sino-American civilian community activities which include Free and Accepted Masons, Scottish Rite and the Ali Shan Shrine Club."[39] Fewster concluded that Reynolds had committed justifiable homicide, should not be charged, and should be sent back to the United States immediately "to assure a minimum of discussion and prevent him from being subjected to further criticism of the indigenous population."[40]

U.S. military authorities also refused to provide any compensation to Ao Tehua. The day after the shooting, James Pilcher, the embassy chargé, met with Salonick and Captain Hugh R. McKibbin, the MAAG chief of staff, to see if a fund already existed for the purpose of paying money to victims in cases where "buddies" were accused. Salonick admitted that the practice existed in Germany and elsewhere, but no such fund had been established in Taiwan. In April, Ao Tehua wrote a letter to General Bowen asking for compensation, and she filed a suit seeking NT$638,800 (over US$25,000) to cover funeral costs, "spiritual consolation," and her child's education expenses.[41] Although a legal precedent existed in which the U.S. Congress had previously made reparation to victims without admitting liability, MAAG commanders refused to budge for fear that compensation implied that Reynolds was guilty.

Military officials preferred to neither prosecute Reynolds nor make an ex gratia payment (a gift without acknowledgment of liability) to Ao Tehua, but they came under pressure from ROC officials, who insisted that all of the evidence pointed to cold-blooded murder, not self-defense. The embassy called the accusations "unwarranted and gratuitous." In particular, one piece of information allegedly shared with U.S. investigators by the Chinese, but never to the general public, was that Reynolds allegedly had made threats against Chinese nationals. After the break-in of his car, he supposedly had threatened to kill the next person that tried to steal from him.[42] In official documents, neither U.S. investigators, MAAG commanders, nor anyone in the U.S. embassy ever mentioned that Reynolds had made such a threat.

Despite Fewster's decision to not charge Reynolds, CINCPAC presumably chose to assign Lieutenant Colonel Ross R. Condit as the new investigating officer to the Reynolds case. Born in 1917, Condit was a veteran of World War II who would go on to serve in Vietnam before becoming a brigadier general commanding forces in Japan.[43] In late April and early May, Condit held three hearings to determine if Reynolds should be court-martialed under Article 118 for murder. He cross-examined witnesses even though he was an investigator, not a lawyer, by training. Reynolds was represented by a defense counsel, Captain Charles Steele.[44]

Condit and Steele elicited a number of salient points from investigators through their cross-examinations. Reynolds's revolver did indeed fire the bullets that killed Liu Ziran. A test for nitrates on Liu's clothing came up negative, but it had rained while Liu Ziran's body laid on the ground that night and a full month had elapsed since the shooting before the Americans could perform their own tests. Sergeant Chaney described the weapon that Liu supposedly wielded as capable of puncturing the eyes, ears, or throat, making it a dangerous, if not lethal, weapon. The investigator added that for the first time in his experience in Taiwan, his Chinese police liaison, who had worked with him on numerous cases, was ordered not to cooperate with the Americans. Lieutenant Colonel Samuel McClatchie, a physician who attended the autopsy, believed that Liu might have survived the first shot had he received medical treatment. Sergeant McJunkins acknowledged that Liu Ziran could have entered the front door where Reynolds's wife was standing if Reynolds had retreated after Liu made his first alleged advance toward him. Salonick testified not only that Chinese authorities refused to cooperate during the investigation, but that a number of Americans kept weapons in their home because of "peepers," to protect their homes, or for self-defense.

As part of the investigation, Condit called Chinese police officials to the proceeding, including Major Han. The Chinese policeman's statements, not sworn because of Chinese custom, provided a variation on the events described by the Americans and shed more light on Reynolds's previous altercation with a Taiwanese. According to Han's testimony, which was corroborated by the acting chief of the FAP, Reynolds said that after he shot Liu, the wounded man ran and dropped by the roadside. Reynolds walked ten steps toward his house in order to call the police before he realized that Liu was again on his feet. Reynolds called out for the MPs. Getting no reply and with Liu running across the street toward the park, Reynolds fired a second shot, not knowing if he scored a hit. In other words, the second shot was not fired on a man advancing for the second time, as Reynolds had told McJunkins, but rather at a wounded man trying to escape. (Yet, Han's testimony was odd because Liu Ziran was not shot in the back and it contradicted the key Chinese point that Reynolds fired at point-blank range at a wounded man.) As for the deceased, Han said that Liu Ziran was a former officer in the ROC military, had worked at the IRP for over six years, and was known to drink "a little." He added under cross-examination that Liu was right-handed—a statement that by its nature called into question Reynolds's claim that his attacker brandished a stick in his left hand. Although Condit claimed the stick might have appeared as a "steel bar" and "a very dangerous weapon" at night, Han did not believe that it was the weapon that Liu allegedly wielded.

Han also testified that he knew Reynolds not only socially but officially because of two incidents. On one occasion someone had stolen some clothing from Reynolds's car. On the second, Reynolds had gotten into a physical altercation with a Taiwanese postman, who was interviewed by Chinese police after the shooting. The man claimed that Reynolds's daughter grabbed his mail bag and threw it on the ground. The postman scolded her, but as she ran away, she fell. Upon being told that the postman had beaten her, Reynolds confronted the man, using Yao Limei as an interpreter. Despite the postman's explanation of what had happened, Reynolds slapped the man's face several times, leaving him with a bloody nose. After investigating the incident, Han met with Reynolds, who wanted to file a complaint with the postman's superiors. When told that he should have reported the incident to the police rather than take actions into his own hands, Reynolds dropped the matter.[45] Nevertheless, Chinese authorities obviously saw significance in the incident. This combined with the alleged threat to shoot the next person that tried to steal from him showed that Reynolds was predisposed to use violence against someone that angered him.

When Reynolds faced questioning, Condit immediately asked why the sergeant did not simply yell through the window or throw something at the window rather than retrieve his revolver. Reynolds responded that he did not see anyone, though he believed his wife when she said a man was outside looking in. Condit then asked what exactly did Reynolds see in Liu Ziran's hand. Because he had built a barbeque pit in that area, the sergeant thought it was one of the half-inch steel pipes used to hold the grates. When asked why he did not immediately retreat or yell for the MPs after firing the first shot, Reynolds claimed he wanted to see what was in the man's hands. He called for an MP and, getting no response, walked back to the front door to tell his wife to call for the police. It was then that Liu Ziran "jumped up just like a rabbit or deer" and came toward him. Condit asked again why Reynolds did not retreat. The sergeant answered, "I was more scared of the man the second time than I was the first. . . . Common sense would tell anybody that a man who has been shot one time is not going to come up on you unless he has some kind of weapon. He's bound to have a gun or knife in his hand." Under cross-examination, Reynolds insisted that he fired only because he feared for his life.[46]

After hearing the testimony and considering the evidence, Condit concluded that Reynolds fired the first shot in fear: one that Liu Ziran might have survived. However, Reynolds could have retreated before Liu made a second attempt. Condit recommended that Reynolds be tried, not for murder, but for voluntary manslaughter: "homicide caused by an act likely to result in death, intentionally committed in the heat of sudden passion brought about by provocation."[47] The charge carried a maximum punishment of a dishonorable discharge, forfeiture of all benefits, and ten years of hard labor. Although Lieutenant Colonel George M. Thorpe, the MAAG judge advocate, concurred with Condit's finding, General Bowen did not. He opposed putting Reynolds on trial. If such an event had occurred in the United States, Bowen personally would not have filed charges: "It is felt, however, that in the interests of the individual himself and in view of the conditions existing out here and the relationship that the best interests not only of justice but also of Sino-American relationships, the man should be brought to trial."[48]

The question now was where to hold the court-martial. With the backing of the ROC's Ministries of Justice and Foreign Affairs, Defense Minister Yu Dawei wanted it held in Taiwan. U.S. officials met with their counterparts from the Foreign Ministry, Defense Ministry, and the Government Information Office and reached the consensus that the trial should be held in Taiwan and be open to the press and public. Legal experts from Okinawa and Hawaii were flown to Taiwan to participate in the court-martial.[49] U.S. authorities also held two briefings with the Chinese press to discuss the Uniform Code of Military Justice in preparation for the trial. The first went badly because it consisted of MAAG personnel telling the press what it could and could not do, while the reporters demanded to know if Liu's widow would be compensated. Only the second briefing focused on military court proceedings.[50]

Both sides now looked to the trial to resolve the case. More than Sergeant Reynolds, U.S. military justice, if not the basis for the U.S. criminal justice system, was on trial. On the eve of the court-martial, a Chinese newspaper editor commented that Americans should be allowed to handle the case, not just because of the 1951 agreement involving MAAG, but because "we Chinese . . . have implicit confidence in American justice and do not fear that a U.S. Army court-martial will be especially indulgent" toward a soldier who shot and killed a Chinese citizen. The editor added that "strict justice will be done in this case not only because it involves the honor and integrity of the American judiciary," but also because of the close relations between the ROC and the United States.[51]

7

The Court-Martial of
Sergeant Robert Reynolds

On May 20, 1957, the general court-martial of Sergeant Robert G. Reynolds commenced at 9:00 A.M. in the Sugar Building, the headquarters for MAAG-Taiwan.[1] The building's chapel served as a courtroom. Reynolds was one of 5,586 U.S. soldiers to be tried before a general court-martial that year alone.[2] The U.S. military's history of meting out justice and punishment to its own goes back to the American Revolution. Over time, the Articles of War have experienced reforms that have brought it more in line with the civilian judiciary. Reynolds benefited from recent reforms stipulated by the Alston Act, or Selective Service Act of 1948, and the U.S. Uniform Code of Military Justice of 1950. For the first time, the accused would be tried by a law officer who operated much like a civilian judge, defended by a lawyer appointed by the judge advocate general, and tried, at request, by a military jury of which one-third of the jurors were enlisted men.[3]

The twelve jurors were initially composed of six colonels and six master sergeants. Of the twelve, all but one had read newspaper stories about the case. Captain James S. Talbot, the prosecutor, peremptorily challenged one of the sergeants, asking that juror to be excused because of a perceived bias. The juror was subsequently dismissed. Another juror, a sergeant, asked to be excused because he had known Reynolds for a year and could not be impartial. Afterward, Captain Steele, who continued to defend Reynolds, asked the jury several questions: Do you know the meaning and effect of the word self-defense? Do you believe that if the law permits a man to maintain weapons in his home for defense that the law also permits the use of those weapons should the circumstances require it? Do you believe that a man has not only the moral obligation but also the duty to protect not only himself but his loved ones against attack? During voir dire, in which the lawyers questioned the jurors to determine their competence, another sergeant admitted to the defense counsel that he would not abide by the court's definition of self-defense if it conflicted with his own views. The prosecution challenged, and the juror was subsequently excused. Steele also peremptorily challenged a colonel, who left the room.

As a result, only eight jurors remained: five colonels and three sergeants. Since the Fifth Amendment of the U.S. Constitution does not apply to those in the military, a court-martial, unlike a criminal trial, does not require a full jury of twelve peers. In fact, the Alston Act stipulated that a jury be composed of no less than five. Although there was a provision within the new code to add new members,[4] no effort was made to find four other jurors inside or outside of Taiwan. In the end, it might have been wiser, from a political perspective, if such efforts had been made, to avoid accusations from the Chinese that the trial was a sham.

After completing voir dire, Colonel Burton F. Ellis, the law officer or judge, read the charge against Reynolds: that he had committed voluntary manslaughter by willfully and unlawfully killing Liu Ziran with a revolver. When asked for a plea, Reynolds responded, "Not guilty."

In his opening statement, Captain Talbot informed the jury that voluntary manslaughter was "an unlawful homicide resulting from an intention to kill or inflict grievous bodily harm." Reynolds was not being charged with murder because the government recognized that there were extenuating circumstances.

After presenting the bare facts of the case, Talbot called Sergeant McJunkins to the stand. McJunkins recalled warning Reynolds that although they were friends, Reynolds was under no obligation to say anything. Reynolds pointed to the .22 caliber Harrison & Richardson revolver, for which he had a weapons permit, lying on the table and confessed that he had just shot a man. He added, "I don't know whether he was killed or not." Reynolds admitted that he fired without aiming, at point-blank range, when Liu Ziran allegedly attacked him. If he had reached out his hand, the gun would have touched Liu's body. While Reynolds asked his wife to call the police, Liu stood up at a distance of fifteen to twenty feet and advanced. Reynolds claimed he fired at point-blank range but did not know if he hit the man or not. McJunkins noted that there was dirt on the windowsill and scuff marks of rubber and dirt below the window ledge and that a neighboring apartment's porch light provided enough lighting to differentiate between a man and an animal. Under redirect and recross, McJunkins testified that the stick he discovered looked as if it had been handled recently, and that it was not as damp as the foliage that lay beneath it.

The next witness for the prosecution was Yao Limei, Reynolds's *amah*, or housegirl. Captain Steele immediately questioned her qualification to be a witness by asking her if she had made any statements to anyone else about the case, and whether she had given a statement to a police official. Speaking softly, she admitted giving two statements to the Chinese police, but denied that her testimony had been coached. The defense did not object to her being a witness, but Steele declared that she had not truthfully answered all of his questions. Under the prosecution's redirect, Yao Limei testified that she had worked for two years for the Reynolds family, living in their home at Quarters B-1, generally staying overnight. Her bedroom was located near the front door. On the night of the shooting she was awakened by gunfire. She distinctly heard two shots. After the second shot, Yao said that Clara Reynolds asked her to call Major Han Jiali, and that she heard Reynolds calling for MPs. Under defense cross-examination, she testified that she put Reynolds's daughter to bed around 7:00 P.M., and that she read a book until 10:30 P.M., at which time she went to bed herself. Yao recalled that the time between both shots was "three to four seconds," suggesting that the shots were fired in quick succession. She denied making previous statements that the shots were separated by forty-five to sixty seconds, and that she saw Reynolds right away after the shooting. After calling Major Han, Yao never saw Reynolds from the doorway. When she stepped outside the house, she could not see him for the heavy mist.

Major Han then took the stand for the prosecution. He restated what he said during the earlier hearings. When Talbot asked if Liu Ziran was left- or right-handed, Han answered, "When I usually observed him playing ball, he used his right hand." Han left the stand, but was recalled later by Talbot, who raised questions about the stick recovered at the scene. Han said that Reynolds initially saw a stick, but when Liu grabbed his abdomen after the first shot, Reynolds admitted seeing no stick or weapon. No stick was found at the spot where Liu first fell, and the stick McJunkins recovered was four steps from where Liu went down. He saw dew on the stick, and believed a partial fingerprint could have been taken from the stick before McJunkins grabbed one end. When McJunkins initially showed the stick to Reynolds, the latter answered, "No, that isn't. That was bigger than this." Han never found an object matching the length and diameter that Reynolds described. Colonel Ellis, though, asked Captain Steele if he objected to Han's testimony that Reynolds denied that the stick found was the weapon. Steele answered, "I certainly do," and the testimony was stricken.

Under cross-examination, Han testified that at the first spot where Reynolds claimed that Liu fell there was a shirtsleeve imprint and a "sliding footprint." Steele pressed Han on his testimony that Reynolds claimed that Liu Ziran tried to flee. When Steele suggested that what Reynolds meant was "move," Han claimed that the exact word Reynolds used was "run away," suggesting that Liu Ziran was shot a second time in the act of fleeing. Han also contradicted U.S. investigators, who testified that Liu wore the uniform of a Nationalist officer. Although he had previously seen Liu wear a uniform with a major's insignia, Liu wore no such insignia the night he was killed. The police major testified that Liu wore a Sun Yat-sen uniform (attire named after the Nationalist Party's first leader) worn by government officials, including those at the IRP, where Liu Ziran worked.

The trial continued to the next day, when in the afternoon Captain Steele began his defense by trying to impeach Yao Limei's statements. He called to the stand Captain Patsy M. Potalivo, a fourteen-year veteran who spoke Chinese. Potalivo insisted that Yao claimed that there was nearly a forty-five-second gap between the shots.

In a move to suggest that Reynolds had good reason to fear for his family's safety, Steele asked Colonel Salonick if there had been an increase in break-ins involving the homes of U.S. military personnel. Salonick testified that since his arrival in June 1956 there had been a 20 percent increase in burglaries and break-ins in the Taipei area, and U.S. personnel were periodically warned to be on alert. After the prosecution objected to the questioning, Steele argued during a sidebar with Colonel Ellis that Reynolds had been given an order "to be especially watchful." The order, Steele added, explained why Reynolds went outside his home and confronted Liu Ziran. The defense also tried to use the testimony of Reynolds's neighbor, who experienced a near break-in, but after another sidebar discussion Colonel Ellis ruled the testimony irrelevant. Interestingly, Steele never mentioned the actual break-in of Reynolds's vehicle, possibly because he knew of rumors that Reynolds made threats afterward.

In an effort to impress the jury with Reynolds's good character, Steele called two Chinese officers to the stand. Since the U.S. military court lacked subpoena authority in Taiwan, both men volunteered to testify as private citizens. The first was Colonel C. C. Kung, who was in charge of the medical depot warehouse where Reynolds worked. Kung described Reynolds as "diligent," "very hard working," and truthful. When asked by Captain Talbot if he had ever seen Reynolds angry, Kung answered no. The second character witness, Major General Yang Wenda, also appeared in the capacity of a civilian. Yang had known Reynolds for a year, and he portrayed Reynolds as hard working and effective, a man that had improved one of the Chinese medical warehouses. Two American colonels who supervised Reynolds as part of the MAAG medical corps in Taiwan corroborated the two Chinese officers' testimony. All declared that Reynolds's performance in duty was excellent.

Steele then called Reynolds's wife, Clara, to the stand. On this day, she wore a black dress, leading a Chinese reporter to describe her as "not very attractive." She brushed aside Chinese journalists, saying, "I don't talk to nobody." Accompanying her were two nurses, giving the impression that she was ill.[5] She described taking a shower after she and her husband arrived home from a night of playing pinochle. Although the bathroom window glass was frosted and covered with a long plastic curtain, she noticed while drying off "a man in the window." Immediately she broke down on the witness stand, leading Colonel Ellis to call a short recess. After resuming her testimony, Clara Reynolds recalled seeing a man's eyes in the window. Scared, she called for her husband. After he took his revolver and she heard the back door slam shut, Clara Reynolds went into their bedroom. She heard her husband call out "Stop" in Chinese. Then she heard someone jump to the ground, followed by what sounded like a "fire cracker." She put on a housecoat and waited in the living room. Her husband came to the front door. After she unlocked and opened it, he told her to have Yao Limei call the FAP and that she should call the provost marshal. While the *amah* called the FAP, Clara Reynolds heard a second shot. This testimony suggested some time passed before Reynolds fired a second time at Liu Ziran. Her testimony was supported by a MAAG sergeant who lived just seventy-five yards away from the Reynolds duplex. He recalled hearing two sharp reports that were thirty-five seconds to one minute apart.

Then Steele called his final witness: Robert Reynolds. Sergeant Reynolds answered questions about his family and his military career, including about letters of commendation written by his superiors. Steele asked Reynolds if he had ever been punished for a minor offense under Article 15, court-martialed, charged or convicted of any offense in his civilian life, or convicted of a traffic offense. To all of these questions the sergeant answered no. Reynolds told the court that the previous year he had bought a revolver from another MAAG soldier who served on one of the offshore islands. He received permission to keep it in his home, and had never fired it before the night of March 20. After his wife told him that a man was outside the bathroom window, he told her "not to get excited" and that he would see what the man wanted. Thinking the intruder to be a burglar wanting to steal his money, he unlocked the drawer where he kept the revolver, unwrapped and removed it from a cellophane bag, and loaded nine rounds. Reynolds testified that he took the revolver because there might have been more than one person outside in the night. He admitted making a lot of noise, including stepping on pieces of coal on the sidewalk spilt by the coal delivery man that day. His steps sounded as if he was walking on ice particles. When he confronted Liu, he intended to hold the man until the FAP arrived. Instead, after Reynolds said "Wait a minute" in Chinese, Liu jumped down from the window ledge. Reynolds saw something flash that looked like a steel rod or pipe. When Liu was eight to ten feet away, Reynolds warned Liu to stop again or he would shoot. When less than six feet away, Liu raised his left hand and made a long stride. Reynolds pulled out the gun, took one step back, and fired. Liu Ziran tripped and fell under bamboo trees. Reynolds could only see his feet, so he went to the road and called four or five times for the Chinese MPs.

Getting no response, Reynolds went to the front door of his home and told his wife through the front screen door to have their *amah* call the police. Hearing movement in the bamboo grove where Liu Ziran fell, Reynolds walked back toward that area. When he was twenty feet away, Liu began to advance toward Reynolds in a slouching position with his hands by his side. Yelling "stop" and believing Liu had a gun or knife, he fired a second time when Liu was allegedly only twelve feet away (not point-blank as McJunkins had testified). Reynolds declared that Liu could have run anywhere else after being shot once, but since he ran at him, he assumed that Liu had a weapon. He denied that Liu was simply trying to run away, as Major Han claimed. Liu allegedly changed his direction of movement when Reynolds told him to stop and had the side of his body facing Reynolds. It appeared to the sergeant that Liu "was going to kill me or harm me in some way."

Under cross-examination, the prosecution suggested that Reynolds had "calmly loaded [his revolver] with nine shells" after his wife informed him of Liu's presence. Reynolds admitted that he did nothing to scare the man away and that he had left his wife "standing in the bathroom" despite knowing that someone was peeping at her through the window. He denied using his wife to keep Liu transfixed in the window, and stated that he never told her to remain there. He only told her to act normal because she was easily frightened. He acknowledged that the back screen door did slam on his way out and confirmed that he thought the man had a pipe or rod in his hand that made a scraping sound. Once Reynolds called out, he had neither time to fire a warning shot nor to aim at Liu's arms or legs. After firing one shot, he knew that he had scored a hit because a flame appeared over the part of Liu's jacket that covered the stomach. During the second alleged attack, he fired no warning shot because, again, he had no time. Reynolds denied firing his gun twice before going to the door, but admitted that if he had to do it all over again, he would have fired a second time because he believed Liu could have gotten to his front door faster than, or as fast as, himself.

Reynolds also conceded that he had had a previous altercation with a postman, but insisted, when Talbot referred to the man as a "Chinese National," that the man was Taiwanese. Apparently, by trying to draw an ethnic distinction, Reynolds was disassociating the earlier altercation from the shooting, undercutting any suggestion either that his action against Liu

Ziran was premeditated or that he was predisposed to shoot a Chinese person. Talbot, though, did not ask any further questions about the incident and let the matter drop. He did observe that Reynolds was willing to fire to seriously injure or kill a man that he speculated was armed, and asked if he would have fired the second shot despite not knowing for sure the man was armed and that he would be court-martialed. Reynolds answered, "I believe I would, sir." Under redirect, he said that he could have shot Liu nine times during the first encounter whether standing or laying down, implying that he did not use overwhelming force against Liu.

On May 22, both the prosecution and defense rested. That evening, the court and jury went to the Reynolds home to observe the scene at night. The next day, the court convened for closing arguments. Captain Talbot elected to allow Steele to present his arguments first, but he asked the jury to consider one question: "Under the same circumstances, would you . . . have fired that second shot?"

Steele began by declaring that all of the testimony supplied by U.S. investigators supported his client's statements. Steele pointed to the contradictions in Yao Limei's statements to Chinese and U.S. investigators and declared her to be an unreliable witness.

Steele then turned on Major Han, whom he called the "prosecution's star witness." He reminded the jury that not only had Han testified under direct and cross-examination, but he volunteered to go to the stand once more to discuss why he did not believe that the stick McJunkins discovered was the object that Liu Ziran allegedly held in his hand. Steele argued that Reynolds was too busy concentrating on his attacker's face to focus on the object in his hand. Given the situation and the conditions under which the alleged attack occurred, the stick may have looked like a baseball bat. Steele also took Han to task for using the word "flee" instead of the less sensational word "move." Even though Han could speak English, he refused to explain the different meanings of the two words, and Steele claimed that Han purposely interpreted Reynolds as saying that he shot Liu Ziran as he tried to "flee." The defense counsel described Han's testimony as "so loaded with venom and prejudice to the accused that the court should give full consideration to Major Han's knowingly twisting his testimony in an attempt to persuade this court that Sergeant Reynolds intentionally murdered" the victim.

After going over all of the testimony provided by character witnesses, investigators, Reynolds's wife, and then Reynolds himself, Steele argued that the prosecution had not proved beyond a reasonable doubt that Reynolds willfully and unlawfully killed Liu Ziran. He told the jury to put themselves in Reynolds's position, mentally and physically, and in the same circumstances. Steele noted that, "Unfortunately, this case has had undue and great publicity because of the fact that it is an international incident—the nationals of two sovereign states." He observed as well that the press had criticized the prosecution's conduct with "speculation, falsehoods, entire misconceptions." Steele declared that he did not want to "castigate" or "indict the entire press," but he did blame "some irresponsible persons" who had twisted the facts.

Turning back to the case, Steele questioned what legal right Liu Ziran had to be outside of Reynolds's house that night. A thirty-three-year-old married man was "crouched in a woman's bathroom window looking at her naked body staring at her. Who knows what kind of thoughts was going through his mind." Rejecting the prosecution's description of Liu as a peeping tom, Steele suggested that he was worse: a man who could have easily knocked down the "flimsy window," implying that Liu Ziran lusted for the woman and potentially could have raped her. Clara Reynolds was scared, by her own testimony, to the point that she could not move. Steele declared that Liu Ziran did not want to steal money as long as he looked at her. A peeping tom or a thief would have simply run away. Instead, Liu, six feet tall and 170 pounds, "wanted something in that house and if he had to kill a man that was in his way, he would have done it and he tried to." He told the jury to put themselves in Reynolds's position that night, faced with a man that held a stick that could have been used to gouge the eyes or throat. Under the circumstances, Steele believed that the jury could do nothing but vote for acquittal: "To find this man guilty of the crime charged will blast forever his Army career, label Clara Reynolds a convict's wife and the little daughter a convict's daughter."

After a short recess, Talbot began his closing arguments by observing that Captain Steele was both a "good speaker" and a "good actor," and that he preferred to appeal to the jury's reason, not emotions. This was why he allowed Steele to present his closing argument first. He described the jury as a "blue ribbon court." Its members had an average of two years of college, and some had attended Command and General Staff College, the Army War College, and the Air Force Staff College.

Talbot argued there was reason to believe that Reynolds had indeed committed voluntary manslaughter. The stick Liu Ziran supposedly handled was more of a toy for a seven-year-old girl than a lethal weapon. Did Reynolds act out of fear or anger, and if anger, why? Talbot questioned if it was "reasonable for an American woman" to shout out to her husband and remain in her bathroom while a man looked in. Reynolds did nothing to move his wife out of the bathroom, but simply grabbed his weapon and noisily exited the back door. Talbot suggested that the scuff marks could have been placed there by the Reynolds child or children in the neighborhood. There was no other evidence that a man had jumped from the window, and why would a right-handed man pick up a stick with his left? Talbot asked what would motivate Liu to attack Reynolds, especially after being shot? With Reynolds as the only witness, there was little evidence to prove or disprove Reynolds's account of that night.

Talbot further argued that there was little reason to believe that Reynolds's life was ever in danger. He wondered why Reynolds, after shooting a man, did not go into the house to call the police rather than going back out if he was so afraid for his life. After firing that first shot, did Reynolds have good reason to still believe that his life was in danger, and would the jurors have pulled the trigger a second time when a man is twelve to fifteen feet away? The laws of the United States allowed a man "in his own yard, in his own house, to stand his ground. He is not forced to retreat." Yet, Reynolds had eight rounds left. He could have fired a warning shot, or fired into the ground, into Liu's leg, or over his head. Building on Major Han's testimony, Reynolds suggested that he had to capture a burglar. Talbot disputed what he called a "wild tale." Reynolds did not have to capture Liu Ziran, an ROC national, whom he knew to be wounded. Talbot also rejected the notion that Liu Ziran was either a burglar or a "pervert." If a man was going to steal from Reynolds, why would he peep into the family's bathroom window? Reynolds did not shoot with premeditation, but he killed "out of anger or heat of passion or fear."

After Talbot finished his closing remarks, Colonel Ellis gave instructions regarding voluntary manslaughter. In addition to killing "in the heat of sudden passion by adequate provocation," Ellis added it could have been produced "by fear as well as by rage." He further explained that for an individual to be excused for killing out of self-defense, that person had to believe that they and/or their family were in danger. Moreover, since they were guarding their home, they were not required to retreat but could stand their ground to repel an attack, including inflicting death. Self-defense and defense of a wife and child were excuses for killing an assailant. Finally, Ellis told the jury that the defense had introduced evidence of Reynolds's good character: "Considered and weighed alone or in connection with the presumption of innocence and all the other evidence in the case, this evidence of the accused's good character may be sufficient to cause a reasonable doubt as to his guilt thereby warranting acquittal." Ultimately, it was up to the jury to decide how much weight to give such evidence versus other evidence presented in the trial.[6]

The court closed at 11:25 A.M. The jurors deliberated for more than an hour. At 12:55 P.M., the court went back into session to read the verdict.

After a secret ballot, the jury found Sergeant Reynolds "not guilty." Despite instructions to the contrary from Colonel Ellis, Americans in the courtroom broke out in a loud cheer, and some walked over to shake Reynolds's hand. The applause died only after Ellis called multiple times for order in the court. The Chinese spectators quietly filed out of the chapel.[7]

8

Justice of a Different Culture

The acquittal stunned and angered the Chinese. A fifteen-year-old girl from Chiayi, a city in southwest Taiwan, wrote a letter to the ROC Foreign Ministry asking the question uppermost on Chinese minds: how was an individual who admitted to shooting another person found not guilty? The verdict left many who were appreciative of American aid, such as twelve Chinese who signed a letter to the editor of the *Central Daily News,* feeling a sense of "disappointment." Newspaper reports claimed that the ROC government considered launching a formal protest, and quoted an ROC official as saying that top government officials were "just as angry about this (the trial) as the man in the street." This certainly was true. Internally, the ROC Foreign Ministry declared the trial and verdict, from a legal standpoint, to be flawed.[1] To reporters, George Yeh asserted that the verdict was unfair. A trial observer from the Ministry of Justice called the trial "biased."[2] Within hours, a Ministry of Justice spokesman issued a statement that the "application of law codes and the adoption and rejection of evidences were not all fair." He also suggested that the ROC should remove diplomatic immunity from American GIs.[3]

Hours after the verdict, hostility toward Americans became palpable. Americans on Grass Mountain were cursed at by small groups of Chinese, forcing the ROC to double the security for those living there. People in the city of Keelung, a major port near Taipei, immediately expressed anger against the verdict.[4] In Washington, D.C., Chinese reporters boycotted a press conference given by the undersecretary of the army. Angry overseas Chinese students at a school in Banqiao, not far from Taipei, held a protest that very afternoon that involved "heated and bitter" discussion of the verdict. At Tunghai University, a U.S.-supported Christian school near Taichung, a student protest became so overwrought with anger that the university's president confronted them "'with tears in his eyes' in order to calm them down." Students also refused to attend a dinner reception given by a faculty member because Americans were invited. In Hsinchu, also southwest of Taipei, an ICA-Taipei educational specialist had his car vandalized outside of a secretarial school. A few MAAG advisors were spat upon.[5]

The polar opposite reaction to the "not guilty" verdict on the part of

Americans and Chinese is not difficult to comprehend. Chinese understanding of the case was based predominantly on the trial testimony and exhibits reported in Chinese newspapers, including the rumors and speculations. Trial observers raised several questions and made statements that all suggested that Reynolds deliberately shot Liu Ziran. If Clara Reynolds knew that someone was looking at her, why did she not just walk out of the bathroom? Why did she just stand there and call loudly to her husband? Why did Liu Ziran not just run away when she called for her husband? Why did Reynolds not fire warning shots? Two witnesses said that they heard two shots fired in succession rather than minutes apart. Reynolds claimed that he shot Liu Ziran once at several feet when the Chinese autopsy suggested that he fired twice at point-blank range. Somehow, Liu Ziran managed to run a great distance despite being shot twice, and even though he allegedly collapsed running downhill away from Reynolds, his head faced toward the Reynolds home. There was no blood at the two locations where Reynolds claimed that Liu fell after being shot, nor a blood trail, suggesting that he was shot twice in the same location. Major Han allegedly found the American sergeant sitting in his living room, panting as if he had been running or even in a fight. Reynolds was the first person to find the body, implying that he knew exactly where Liu Ziran had been shot dead.[6] Thus, Reynolds's testimony was perceived as contradictory, and his answer that he punched a "Taiwanese, not Chinese" postman did not resonate well with the Chinese people.[7]

Moreover, the U.S. and Chinese legal systems were quite different. Americans believed in the notion of a trial by your peers, presumption of innocence, and a good defense lawyer to challenge the prosecution's evidence. Under Chinese law, there was no jury system. Instead, evidence was presented by the prosecution and defense without cross-examination of witnesses or the legal banter between lawyers commonplace in the American judicial system. The accused could not confront witnesses unless allowed to do so by the judge. Hearsay testimony and evidence obtained illegally by investigators could be used in court. Investigations were not public knowledge, and the accused could not hire a lawyer until the procurator issued an indictment. Since 1935, the ROC legal system had allowed for presumption of innocence. However, the tradition still prevailed that, once arrested, one was guilty until proven innocent. There were no protections against self-incrimination. The judge listened to the evidence and made a ruling (*ziyou xinzheng*). Once judgment was passed, the accused could appeal to a higher court for a reduction in the sentence.[8]

Furthermore, under U.S. jurisprudence, there are varying degrees of murder as well as voluntary and involuntary manslaughter. There was no legal precept in Chinese law similar to "voluntary manslaughter." The traditional Chinese concept of justice always expected some type of punishment for a homicide, and it could be a life for a life.[9] An ROC report stated that the Chinese believe in the concept that "human life is beyond value" (*renming guantian*), while U.N. ambassador Tsiang Tingfu, holder of a Ph.D. in history from Columbia University, told Americans that the Chinese perception of justice demanded punishment even in cases involving self-defense.[10] According to Andrew Franklin, in a case like the Reynolds shooting, "any person killing another, whether accidentally or not, is automatically considered guilty of a crime." This explained why British diplomats in China were never permitted to drive their own car, "since accidents became incidents." It also shed light on why ROC officials admitted that while Liu Ziran had a sordid background, that fact did not justify his "murder in cold blood by an American." Of course, ROC officials' speaking of murder did not mean that Chinese judges would have passed a harsh sentence against Reynolds. Chinese criminal law did allow individuals to defend themselves and others against an attacker without punishment, but if the self-defense was "excessive" the individual could receive a remitted sentence. In the opinion of many Chinese, including lawyers and law professors at the time and later, Reynolds's so-called act of self-defense was more than excessive.[11]

There was no expectation of the death penalty, but there was expectation of some type of acknowledgment of wrongdoing or punishment. Calling the trial unfair, Justice Minister Gu Fengxiang told legislators that under Chinese law a judge could commute or not pass a sentence against someone who acted out of self-defense, but the person would still be found guilty.[12] Weeks after the trial, the ROC issued a pamphlet that stated that after Liu Ziran was killed, every Chinese hoped that "the guilty one would be duly punished. . . . Because we Chinese have the concept and custom, not that a killer must die but that he at least bears some guilt, could it be just or fair for Reynolds in the end to be beyond reach of the law?"[13] Along the same lines, Franklin observed that for Chinese, "their whole history made it impossible for them to understand an acquittal without even a rebuke or a reprimand."[14]

As a result, the Chinese public concluded that U.S. military justice was flawed. The headline of one paper declared that a "Killer's 'friends'" had set him free. One writer called the trial a "Hollywood court-martial."[15] Others described the jury as "absurd" (*huangtang*) and Captain Steele as "insolent" (*kuangtai*).[16] The *Independence Evening Post* declared that allowing Reynolds to be tried by a U.S. military court was a mistake; finding him not guilty was an even bigger one. The court-martial was not only illegal but unjust. The *United Daily* expressed outrage at the fact that Reynolds remained "beyond the law" in a matter "dripping wet with blood," and described the trial as "one-sided."[17] Reynolds admitted to shooting and killing another human being, but was found not guilty on the basis of self-defense, proving that Americans in Taiwan enjoyed extraterritoriality.[18] Twelve Chinese signed a letter to various newspaper editors demanding that Reynolds be deported and that compatriots mobilize to raise money for Liu Ziran's wife and child.[19]

In addition to the verdict, the Chinese were particularly incensed by American cheers when it was read. A letter of protest signed by fifteen National Taiwan University students appeared in the *New Life* under the headline "The Horrible Victory Applause." Even in the United States, such a reaction violated courtroom decorum. The Taiwan-based British journalist Spencer Moosa, who had covered China since the 1930s, wrote that the celebration represented an "indecent gloating, an outrage to the dead man and his widow." For some Chinese, the cheers implied that Americans had taken an "us" versus "them" mentality. As one newspaper editorial put it, "The court room is not a ball field."[20]

Ultimately, the Chinese believed the jurors to be biased. Instead of a jury of twelve, four were excused. One reader called it "a jury of 'one-color' U.S. servicemen," and demanded that the ROC either pursue a SOFA like that between the United States and Japan, or modify the 1951 agreement so that Chinese nationals could serve on the jury. With the Chinese legal system clearly in mind, a lawyer argued that the jurors lacked the legal knowledge of an expert and were easily biased by just one juror. If the determination of guilt had been left in the hands of the American judge, as it would have been in a Chinese court of law, the verdict would have been different. Gu Fengxiang told legislators that the jury did not focus on whether Reynolds was guilty or not, but rather on whether his act of self-defense was proper. Some educated Chinese believed that the judge and jury in the case were, in the words of an unnamed Chinese informant, "very much prejudiced (racial and otherwise) in favor of Reynolds." He added: "Personally, I think the statesman way—which may not be the legal way—to settle the shooting was to pronounce Reynolds guilty of some charge, pass a sentence, ship him to the States, suspend the sentence."[21]

Of course, most people living on Taiwan simply did not understand how the U.S. legal system operated. General Peng Mengji faulted both the ROC and the United States for not explaining to the Chinese people that this was not a return to extraterritoriality but simply how a U.S. military court-martial operated. An internal investigation by the ROC actually blamed the Chinese press for the failure to educate and inform citizens about the differences in U.S. and Chinese laws. Only one newspaper, *New Life*, published such an article, entitled "An Introduction to U.S. Court-Martial Trial Procedures." Chinese law prevented the press from discussing a criminal investigation, but editors and journalists had ample time and space to provide readers a preview of the trial to come. The ROC report concluded that if all newspapers had discussed why Reynolds had diplomatic immunity, the differences in Chinese and U.S. trial systems, and the fact that in Britain, France, and the United States a jury decided the outcome of a trial, the people would have been better prepared for the not guilty verdict.[22]

The press alone should not shoulder the blame. The government had the responsibility of keeping its people apprised of the trial process by issuing statements at least to those newspapers and broadcast companies controlled by the ROC. The United States and ROC were allies during World War II, and there were many Chinese legal experts who had studied law in America and Britain whose knowledge could have been better utilized. A thorough understanding of how the U.S. system worked, rightly or wrongly, might have dissuaded the ROC from seeking a court-martial. If the ROC wanted a military trial on its soil rather than allowing Reynolds to be tried elsewhere, it was incumbent on the government to make some effort—in an atmosphere where the U.S. authorities tried to educate journalists, only to be ignored— to lower expectations of a guilty verdict. Yet, the ROC's own angry reaction reflected either an ignorance of the Western legal system or an unwavering conviction that the evidence overwhelmingly tilted the scale of justice toward guilt. Both statements are not mutually exclusive, but the root of the issue was the fact that most people on Taiwan presumed Reynolds to be guilty. This presumption of guilt might have made any attempts to educate the Chinese about the trial process futile. As an educated Chinese explained to an American officer, the Chinese people generally lacked "juridical sense." Unlike in the United States, lawyers did not hold an important status in Chinese society. Morality superseded justice in the Chinese mind.[23] Similarly, and presumably referring to Liu Ziran, Chiang Kai-shek told an American official that to understand East Asians, "you must realize that if they believe that an individual is a good person, regardless of what legal proof is used to show that that person has committed a crime, they will still see that individual as a good person doing good work."[24]

In the face of this weltering criticism of U.S. military justice or lack thereof, the Americans were put on the defensive. General Bowen upheld the court-martial proceedings, saying that it had been an open court with members of the ROC Ministry of Justice and select journalists attending. The journalists were even briefed on the UCMJ so that they could understand procedures. Bowen defended the verdict, and quoted Colonel Ellis, who called the trial "the fairest . . . that he had ever heard of." Despite Chinese cries of partiality and that the prosecutor did nothing "except trying to whitewash Sergeant Reynolds," he thought the prosecutor had "worked very diligently to see that the Chinese version of the case . . . was presented to the court."[25]

Rankin also denied the ROC charge that the trial process and verdict were unfair. He consulted with the ROC when constituting the court, brought in experts, and briefed the press before the trial commenced. He accused the Chinese of not cooperating in the investigation, "except in a perfunctory fashion, which led to the inescapable conclusion that they did not want the record of Liu . . . to see the light of day." Because Reynolds was the only living witness and because no prior relationship could be established, "an acquittal on grounds of self-defense was all but inevitable."[26] In a meeting with Chiang Kai-shek four days after the trial, Rankin defended Bowen's handling of the court-martial and praised him for the care he took to seek the advice of experts and to open the trial to the press. The diplomat believed the court had no choice but to hand down an acquittal. Becoming quite agitated, Chiang countered that he had not been consulted and "that an American court martial should not be held on Chinese soil; that it reminded everyone of extraterritoriality."[27]

It is no surprise that both the Chinese and American communities on Taiwan were polarized by the shooting, the trial, and their conceptions of right and wrong. The Americans came to Taiwan with notions that one had the right to bear arms. Bob Pierpoint, a Japan-based journalist with CBS, argued that in U.S. society it was not unusual for an American to have a weapon in their home, and use it if anyone tried to break in.[28]

They also brought their concept of the right to stand your ground. After the trial, James Pilcher explained to a Foreign Ministry official that under U.S. law, when individuals are attacked in their own homes, "the law imposes no duty to retreat upon one who, free from fault in bringing on difficulty, is attacked *at* or *in* his own dwelling. Upon the theory that a man's house is his castle . . . he has a right to protect it and those within it from intrusion or attack . . . he may stand at bay and turn on and kill his assailant if this is apparently necessary to save his own life." According to the U.S. Court of Military Appeals, the same rule applied to U.S. military personnel:

His home is the particular place where the necessities of the services force him to live. This may be a barracks, a tent, or even a foxhole. Whatever the name of his place of abode, it is his sanctuary against unlawful intrusion; it is his "castle" and he is there entitled to stand his ground against a trespasser to the same extent that a civilian is entitled to stand fast in his civilian home. No reason in law, logic or military necessity justified depriving the men and women in the armed forces of a fundamental right to which they would be entitled as civilians.[29]

None of this reassured the Chinese, who were now confronted with a situation in which armed U.S. soldiers, on duty or off, were not only protected by diplomatic immunity, but could claim "self-defense." Chinese nationals found the American conception or interpretation of what constituted "self-defense" even more frightening than diplomatic immunity. Chen Guyuan, a law professor at National Taiwan University, argued that once Reynolds fired more than one shot, he crossed the line beyond what is appropriate for self-defense. Liu's actions were nonthreatening, and Reynolds had no reason to shoot the man. Chen also thought that most nations would call Reynolds a murderer. If everyone claimed self-defense in similar situations, there would be a breakdown in law and social order.[30]

Some Chinese agreed. Thirteen National Taiwan University students declared that Chinese lives were now in danger. If a U.S. soldier could kill an empty-handed Chinese person and claim self-defense, no one was safe.[31] Although Taiwan received economic and military aid from the United States, one writer was not sure that a Chinese life was of equal value to an American one.[32] Another reader suggested that the United States had developed a five-point plan to provide aid to weak nations, and now the Chinese could see that there was a sixth one: "shoot people from the countries receiving U.S. aid." The reader warned that if Chinese citizens wanted to enjoy the freedom of not being shot, they should stay away from all U.S. soldiers.[33]

It is not difficult to understand why the Chinese viewed Reynolds's actions as excessive. In Taiwan, most people did not own guns, though many could use knives or bamboo sticks. People dealt with burglars or intruders, but the use of force did not have to be a first option. They usually defused such situations in a less violent manner, such as calling out "thief" from within the home, trying to attract the attention of neighbors or even a nearby policeman. Such shouts would be enough to scare a would-be thief away. In this environment, Reynolds's use of force came as a shock for the Chinese.[34]

This raises the question of why Reynolds did not take the same approach. It was the very question that Condit put to Reynolds, but which went unanswered during the pretrial hearing. Assuming that Liu Ziran was a peeping tom and that Reynolds believed that someone might be breaking in, he could have taken a number of steps that might have led to a different outcome. He could have told his wife to simply put on her clothes, turn out the light, and step into the bedroom. If Liu Ziran had merely been tempted to gaze upon a naked woman, he would have walked away once Clara Reynolds disappeared from sight. If he were a burglar or a sexual pervert bent on rape, as portrayed by Reynolds's defense attorney, he would have had to either break down a door or somehow come through the window. Reynolds or his wife could have immediately phoned the FAP or shouted for an MP from within the home. The shouts alone perhaps would have scared Liu Ziran away regardless of his intentions. Instead, as the prosecution argued, Reynolds asked his wife to remain in the bathroom, naked, to keep the man's attention while he took three minutes to load a revolver and then maneuvered to outflank whoever was standing outside the home. Although Reynolds claimed that he armed himself because there may have been more than one person outside, and assuming that his version of events was the most truthful, he seemed bent on confronting whoever was outside his home even though this put him, and ultimately his family, at unnecessary risk.

Of course, many Chinese believed that Reynolds wanted a confrontation. ROC government officials knew of the alleged verbal threats and informed U.S. authorities. In fact, the day after the jury reached its verdict, a MAAG sergeant who lived near the Reynolds home told the U.S. assistant air attaché that Liu Ziran was known among the American community as "the man who bought black market items from Americans and their servants." He also suggested that Reynolds had a predisposition to kill. After the incident with the Taiwanese postman, Reynolds allegedly developed a "dislike" for Chinese and supposedly "stated on a number of occasions that he would get one before he left."[35] Whether the man told the truth is unclear. He may have been the source for Chinese investigators or he might merely have corroborated the stories already floating around Grass Mountain. He may have held a grudge or disliked Reynolds enough to spread such damaging rumors. If he was lying, he took a risk, since such conduct could have turned many in MAAG against him if the word got out. If true, did he assume that Reynolds would be found guilty, only to be shocked by the acquittal and feel a need to express what he heard to higher authorities? Or was he so intimidated by the American community, including his fellow soldiers, that he came forward only after the trial? Being a star witness for the prosecution would likely have made his continued stay in Taiwan untenable, making him a pariah.

For its part, the U.S. military failed to take measures that would have provided some safeguards against such shootings. Attacks on foreigners were rare. U.S. military personnel should never have been allowed to have weapons in their homes while off duty. They should have been trained in how to defuse situations, such as a peeping tom or even a burglar, with use of force as the last resort. Taiwan and any other Asian country was no place for American frontier justice, in which one confronted another only to find themselves resorting to a "stand your ground" defense. Although Americans made much of Liu Ziran's character and the secretive nature of his background, information about Reynolds's disposition in the weeks or months prior to the shooting should have come to the attention of MAAG commanders. There should have been mechanisms that allowed for other soldiers to inform their superiors anonymously of his alleged activities. The incident involving the Taiwanese postman and the alleged threats should have been brought to the attention of his superiors even if charges were not pressed. It is difficult to say whether Reynolds suffered from post-traumatic stress disorder from his time in Korea and whether this phenomenon, which had yet to be fully addressed by the U.S. military, impacted his attitude toward citizens on Taiwan. Regardless, his superiors could have at least investigated rumors that he intended to bring harm to any Chinese. If true, there might have been enough evidence to rotate him and his family out of Taiwan immediately. If not, his superiors would have at least fulfilled their responsibility to the best of their ability.

Then there is Liu Ziran. Although the Chinese could believe that he engaged in black market dealings and was a womanizer, many could not believe that he was a peeping tom. The act of peeping, an accusation played up by the American and foreign press after the trial and events to follow, seemed so un-Chinese.[36] Most refused to believe or accept that a Chinese man desired to look upon a naked white woman. Why would Liu Ziran, who had a pretty wife and child, want to watch a foreign woman, older and seemingly less attractive, take a bath? In some cases, reporters went out of their way to describe Clara Reynolds as unattractive. One writer called the peeping tom accusation an insult to both Liu Ziran and the Chinese people. USARPAC likewise rejected the notion that Liu Ziran was a peeping tom, citing "the psychology of the Chinese people."[37]

Yet, there were reasons to suspect that Liu Ziran did indeed peep at Clara Reynolds. Anyone who has lived in Taiwan or China over the last fifty years knows that some Chinese, men and women both, can be innocently curious and inquisitive when it comes to gazing on and even physically touching Westerners. Many, especially the highly educated, would find such behavior embarrassing and inappropriate, but this does not preclude the possibility that Liu Ziran gazed, more out of innocence than perversion.

Moreover, there was a crucial piece of information about Liu Ziran that ROC authorities never released to the public. A prior accusation of peeping had been leveled at Liu Ziran. The incident occurred elsewhere. This information was shared with the Foreign Ministry, which may or may not have relayed it to the Americans.

Why was this information never brought out into the open? If not hearsay, it at least revealed a potential pattern of behavior on Liu's part. It would have undercut those who rejected the possibility of Liu being a peeping tom. Steele, of course, would have used it to bolster his argument that Liu was a potentially violent sexual deviant. From a Chinese perspective, though, engaging in peeping did not warrant an armed confrontation. As Tsiang Tingfu explained to an American audience, "Chinese regard peeping more as a sin than as a crime."[38] The Ministry of Justice official who told legislators about the previous incident added that whether Liu was a peeping tom or thief, he should not have been shot dead. In Chinese investigators' minds, punching a postman and making verbal threats revealed a violent temper and premeditation. Liu's behavior was irrelevant.[39]

Looking at the evidence as presented by the Americans, it is understandable that Chinese nationals had qualms about the case. It was Reynolds and American investigators who insisted that Liu Ziran was the belligerent and a serious threat. The only reason why the stick was introduced into evidence was because U.S. investigators claimed it was or could have been the weapon that Liu wielded, even though Reynolds himself could not definitively identify it as such. The fact that no significant weapon was found anywhere near where Liu Ziran allegedly collapsed, twice, even troubled some Americans. Walter Robertson, assistant secretary of state for far eastern affairs, had enough concerns about the shooting to ask Karl Rankin, "Was it definitely established what the 'something' was that Reynolds claimed Liu had in his hand?"[40] It was the American forensic analysis that suggested that Liu had been shot at a close distance and not at point-blank range, and it was American witnesses who claimed that the shots were fired with a gap between them rather than almost successively.

In the end, though, it was up to the jury to decide, and probably an acquittal was a foregone conclusion. What they understood about the case and what they said among themselves was never made public, and one can only speculate what formed the basis of their verdict. Unlike Reynolds, no one stepped forward to be a character witness on Liu's behalf. During the trial, his widow described him to a reporter as a middle school graduate who went off to fight the Japanese during World War II, rising to the rank of major, and that he worked for the IRP. They met in Taipei, and while not rich, their marriage had its happy moments. Ultimately, she described him as someone who enjoyed making friends.[41] This type of information, which would have at least personalized the dead man, never came out in the trial. The ROC did nothing to provide more information about his background, including sharing the fact that he had been caught peeping before, even though Captain Steele petitioned twice that Liu's police dossier and personnel records, including those for the IRP, be provided to the defense.[42] The fact that the weapon was not what Reynolds described may have been immaterial. An unarmed man could have just as easily attacked Reynolds. The jury may have been predisposed to accept the testimony of American witnesses over that of Yao Limei and Han Jiali. Neither were sworn because of Chinese custom, and possibly the jury felt that this meant they could perjure themselves with impunity. In fact, the jurors were told by Colonel Ellis that Yao Limei's prior statement, in which she said the shots were fired nearly a minute apart, could be considered for purposes of impeaching her testimony on the stand.[43] Captain Steele may have succeeded in attacking their credibility. American witness testimony of hearing two shots fired nearly a minute apart and cries for an MP were consistent with Reynolds's statements. The lack of a blood trail was consistent with a man being shot twice without exit wounds and the blood draining into body cavities. There was no evidence that Reynolds shot Liu Ziran twice at point-blank range in a manner suggesting that Reynolds simply eliminated the wounded man. Without any other witnesses to describe the events of that night in a manner that corroborated the prosecution's theory or refuted Reynolds's testimony, the jury probably felt that there was enough "reasonable doubt" to acquit.

Did this mean that the trial was fair in accordance with American legal customs and did the process truly seek justice? A member of MAAG and an American journalist told one reporter that the trial was unfair. Another MAAG advisor questioned Reynolds's innocence, but still believed the process was fair. Sergeant C. L. Johnson tried to both commiserate with Ao Tehua and explain the jury's verdict in a letter to the widow written after the acquittal. Johnson expressed surprise at the verdict because he believed in his heart that Reynolds was guilty, but logically, he could understand why the jury acquitted. The lack of witnesses and the concept of "reasonable doubt" left the jury little choice. Johnson added that it was better for several guilty individuals to go free than for an innocent person to be punished. He hoped that Ao Tehua could understand the reasoning behind the verdict, and not look upon other Americans with the bitterness that she felt for Reynolds.[44]

From the point of view of the defense, Captain Steele and his client most likely believed the system worked. With the prosecution already handcuffed by weak evidence and the accused being the only witness to what transpired that night, the trial favored the defense, but that in itself did not make the trial unjust or unfair. Captain Talbot pushed Reynolds as far as he could with regard to motive, though he could have tried to elicit more information regarding the Taiwanese postman, his behavior in keeping his wife in the bathroom, or his preference to confront Liu Ziran. There were no character witnesses to challenge those who spoke of Reynolds as a solid, dependable worker. No one claimed that Reynolds was deeply involved in black market activity or opium smuggling, as some Chinese and USARPAC believed, nor did anyone come forward with personal knowledge that they heard the sergeant declare that he would "get one" before he left Taiwan. The only way to salvage the case would have been to accept the Chinese interpretations of the forensic evidence, but Talbot had no choice but to operate in accordance with the American evidentiary analysis.

For Chinese trial observers and in the opinion of Justice Minister Gu Fengxiang, though, Talbot simply did not make his best effort to prosecute the case. They were not alone. A *Time* magazine article portrayed Talbot and Steele as "comrades at law" because they shared the same office on Okinawa, had tried cases against one another before, and during the trial "conferred together amiably in whispers, continued their comradely discussions during recesses."[45] In other words, there was no adversarial relationship like that commonly found in U.S. courts, such as a state or federal prosecutor versus a defense lawyer hired by or assigned to a defendant. Instead, there was, for the Chinese, a lack of a vigorous prosecution, which reflected either incompetence or possibly even a willful effort to see that an American was found not guilty. Since Chinese officials told Americans about Reynolds's alleged verbal threats, it is obvious why they thought the process flawed, if not rigged.

For a trial so closely watched and one that affected what was supposed to be a close ally, more could have been done to create the impression that the court operated at its fullest legal potential. Although not obligated to do so, the judge advocate general's office could have made an effort to ensure that there were twelve jurors, not eight. If the U.S. military could fly a prosecutor and defense lawyer to Taiwan, surely it could have flown in an impartial (or less partial) jury from southern Taiwan, the Philippines, or somewhere else in the Pacific. Instead, the court limited itself to a jury composed of men who lived and worked in fairly close proximity to Reynolds, and probably were under considerable peer pressure to vote not guilty. Of course, expecting the 1950s U.S. Army, if not the Pentagon in general, to modify its rules to create a better impression of fairness may be asking too much. Still, it would have been a good faith effort. Otherwise, the use of a potentially partial jury left the trial open to criticism even from other Americans. Although the Reynolds case revealed the need for reform of the UCMJ, such reforms have been minimal and gradual, with little impact on the manner in which the military selects a jury.[46]

Both the ROC and the United States could have worked to reduce the nationalism and the "us vs. them" mentality that seeped into the investigation and the trial. If they could not work as a team, they could have allowed for an independent investigation by a group of respected international criminal investigators, with assurances that both sides would honor any recommendations. As two of the five permanent members of the United Nations, they could have even allowed for a U.N. commission to play the same role. Of course, this would have heightened publicity about the case and put both sides in an uncomfortable political corner at home and abroad. If there had been a SOFA similar to that with Japan, there would have been a Criminal Jurisdiction Subcommittee by which both sides could resolve disagreements over jurisdiction. Such a process might have helped to reduce some of the politics that came into play in this case.

Another potential solution would have been to revive the concept of the mixed court, composed of U.S. and Chinese jurists, which operated in China earlier in the century. Although controversial, this might have been a golden opportunity for both sides to work together in a manner that instilled greater trust in each other's judicial systems. Cooperation, full disclosure, and transparency in the cause of justice would have appealed to Asians, who had just emerged from colonialism, undercutting communist propaganda in the process. It might have worked to strengthen the adhesive qualities of SOFAs and similar agreements where the United States maintained troops. There is no evidence that anyone on either side thought along such lines, and it may have all been impossible. There were no formal agreements signed prior to the trial that afforded avenues of resolution, and each side viewed the evidence and one another's trial processes through their own cultural lenses. Besides, the ROC would have seen these options as a violation of its sovereignty much as the Americans would have if the shooting had occurred in the United States.

Ultimately, one measure to defuse a potential incident would have been to waive immunity and hand Reynolds over to ROC authorities for trial. The 1961 Vienna Convention on Diplomatic Relations provided sending states the option to waive immunity from jurisdiction, and it declared that members of the administrative and technical staff did not enjoy immunity "from acts performed outside the course of their duties."[47] To hand Reynolds over for trial would have been a step that reflected forward thinking and anticipation of changes in international norms. By 1957, Americans could see that the United Nation's International Law Commission was moving in that direction. Interestingly, the article that specifically mentioned that immunity did not apply for offenses committed outside one's duty was introduced just after the Reynolds case. There is no evidence that the case had a direct impact, but it is possible that the problem of according people, like MAAG, diplomatic immunity increasingly caught the attention of diplomats, international jurists, and foreign government officials. Of course, the decision to allow Reynolds be tried by the Chinese would have been extremely controversial in the United States, where politicians and their constituents opposed allowing U.S. soldiers to be tried in foreign courts.

Outside of Taiwan, though, there were Americans who were concerned with the verdict. General James Van Fleet, a World War II commander who once led the Eighth Army during the Korean War, remarked that Reynolds should have been punished and not acquitted. The *San Francisco News* called the army's exoneration of Reynolds a "blundering action."[48] William Ernest Hocking, a philosopher who formerly taught at Harvard, told John Foster Dulles that his acquaintances called the Reynolds case a "scandalous miscarriage." He had already written a letter to the editor of the *New York Times* calling for reinstitution of the mixed courts and opposing the reintroduction of extraterritoriality. Paul Denlinger, a professor at Yale University's Institute of Far Eastern Languages who asked the State Department to supply him with a trial transcript, thought that the distance of Liu's body from the Reynolds home made the peeping tom charge "suspect." Another American viewed the case as one of overkill, and suggested that it was Liu Ziran, when confronted by a man with a gun, who reacted in self-defense.[49]

In letters to the secretary of state and secretary of defense, a handful of Americans expressed outrage at the acquittal. A World War I veteran claimed that many Americans rejected Reynolds's claim that he merely protected his home, saying, "Peeping toms are not shot in this country. They are considered mal-adjusted and treated accordingly."[50] Carl Gamer, a professor of government at Monmouth College, shared the opinion of his students and Sunday school members that the shooting of a peeping tom, "despicable a creature he may be," would have been regarded in America, where college students engaged in peeping, "as extremely cold-blooded and disrespectful of life." This was not a case of self-defense, but rather an instance of "callousness toward Orientals which in a moment can undo the good our government and the American people are trying to do by spending hundreds of millions of dollars there." Mrs. E. Carpenter of Ann Arbor, Michigan, wrote, "'Window-peeping' is not deserving of *death*. I think something ought to be done to Sgt. Robert Reynolds. That was unjust to the Chinese." Likewise, Ival M. Crutcher, of Walla Walla, Washington, expressed the view, "I think it is a disgrace to the United States that the American soldier who took it upon himself to administer 'justice' in a foreign country should have been exonerated. . . . He has jeopardized the position of United States in the eyes of the world, for the sake of punishing—illegally—a 'peeping tom,' an offense which does not warrant such strong action here, much less abroad where it affects the welfare of all of the citizens of our country. I protest this, and strongly suggest that this soldier be punished for murder, as he deserves." In a postscript, Crutcher added: "What *wonderful* ammunition he has provided the Communists to use against us!"[51]

To each of these letter writers, the Defense Department answered that Reynolds had been tried and acquitted "after a careful consideration and evaluation of the evidence," and would not be retried because of the principle of double jeopardy. Eventually, the same message would be relayed to angry Chinese.[52]

U.S. military authorities might still have salvaged the situation and possibly averted a crisis if they had agreed to pay Ao Tehua compensation. The last day of the trial, Pilcher was meeting with General Bowen when an officer informed both men of Reynolds's acquittal. Not knowing about the applause by fellow Americans in reaction to the verdict, Pilcher observed that the trial had been open, fair, and "well handled." He recommended that MAAG consider pooling a fund to compensate Liu Ziran's family for his death. For over a minute Bowen was silent. Finally, he said, "Jim, I simply can't do that." The gesture would only make Reynolds look guilty.[53]

Thus, U.S. officials dug their heels too deep in their opposition to making an ex gratia payment to Ao Tehua. The payment, an apology, and maybe other measures to show concern for Liu's family prior to or after the trial might have gone a long way to mollify most Chinese. In fact, there may not have even been a request for a court-martial by the ROC if the United States had made such restitution. Instead, the level of distrust between the Chinese and Americans, which had existed for years, seemed insurmountable. Both rallied around their compatriot, whom they saw as the victim. Both viewed the evidence in such a way that drew foregone conclusions of guilt or innocence, and rejected the other's judgment as biased or engaged in deliberate attempts to deny one another information crucial to the investigation. By the time of the trial, both took an "us vs. them" mentality, possibly making justice as much a widow and orphan as Ao Tehua and her baby daughter.

Although there were already overt signs of hostility toward Americans, U.S. authorities went about business as usual. During and immediately after the trial, nothing extraordinary occurred to give them reason for concern. Embassy officials were well aware of past incidents in recent Chinese history in which ROC-led protests turned anti-foreign, and knew of the longstanding

Chinese hatred of extraterritoriality, but few incidences of anti-Americanism had occurred in Taiwan. On May 23, the embassy informed the State Department that the combination of the verdict, recent automobile accidents involving Americans, and a change in U.S. policy could lead to "an anti-American movement," but embassy and U.S.-Taiwan Defense Command officials believed that the ROC maintained such an "orderly government" that riots were unlikely—and that if they arose, they would be put down quickly.[54] Events soon proved them wrong on both counts.

9

Black Friday

On May 24, the day after Sergeant Robert Reynolds's acquittal for voluntary manslaughter, the staff for both the U.S. embassy and the USIS offices arrived at their respective workplaces around 9:30 A.M. The normal workday for personnel usually began two hours earlier, but the ROC announced the day before that it would hold three air-raid drills that morning from 7:30 to 9:15 A.M. During these drills, codenamed Operation Fist, paratroopers were to drop from planes as part of a mock invasion and the police would halt traffic.[1] Interestingly, the drill's script also called for Taiwan to come under an atomic attack by the PRC and for all major cities to be hit by simulated cruise missiles and air strikes, including one against the MAAG-Taiwan compound in Taipei.[2] In what proved to be a controversial decision, Ambassador Rankin had left Taiwan for Hong Kong four days earlier in order, or so he later claimed, to disassociate himself and the embassy from the Reynolds court-martial, with the intent of returning to Taiwan this day.[3]

At 10:00 A.M., Lieutenant Colonel George Chow, a MAAG political advisor, met with Lieutenant General Jiang Jianren, head of the General Political Warfare Department, to discuss ways of easing tensions caused by the Reynolds case. They considered publishing an article that explained the differences in U.S. and Chinese laws, the manner in which evidence is accepted or rejected during a trial, and the concept of proving guilt beyond a reasonable doubt. During the conversation, General Jiang conveyed that he had issued strict orders the previous evening prohibiting ROC soldiers from engaging in demonstrations or joining civilians protesting the Reynolds verdict.[4]

A half hour later, James Pilcher arrived at the ROC Foreign Ministry after being summoned by George Yeh. The foreign minister requested a retrial. Yeh warned that his people had been "aroused to boiling" by the verdict because many considered the trial to be a "miscarriage of justice." He added: "Enough words could not describe the U.S. legal process and the basis for the verdict as flawed." The defense counsel seemed more experienced and competent, whereas the prosecutor came off as "incompetent, meek and submissive," and worse, "brushed aside" his own evidence. Yeh worried that "popular feelings" might damage U.S.-ROC relations, and insisted that the

Americans reconsider the verdict. Pilcher responded that U.S. authorities agreed to allow Reynolds to be tried in Taiwan so that the Chinese could see justice done. The embassy never expected the trial to have the effect that it did at the moment. Pilcher did not believe that there was much chance of a retrial, but promised to look into the matter.[5]

Otherwise, nothing seemed out of the ordinary. No special precautions were taken to protect U.S. government and military personnel even though internal ROC documents show that the FAP warned Pilcher at 9:00 A.M. of the possibility of an incident and recommended that American businesses and schools close and embassy personnel leave the building.[6] For reasons never explained, the embassy ignored the warning and took no actions.

Around 10:00 A.M., Ao Tehua arrived at the embassy. She had already stood outside the Foreign Ministry an hour earlier, but now sat at the embassy's front gate. Accompanied by her cousin, who managed the Far Eastern Travel Service, she held in her hands a poster that said in English, "The Killer—Reynolds Is Innocent? Protest against US Court-Martial Unfair, Unjust Decision." Underneath the English words were Chinese characters that stated "Killer not guilty? I denounce. I protest." Ao Tehua chose the perfect place to express her anger. The embassy's location on Zhongzheng Road (named after Chiang Kai-shek) and Zhonghua Road placed it in a heavily populated area of Taipei, not far from the Central Market and a bus terminal. A small crowd mingled around her in curiosity before local police shooed them across the street. At 10:20 A.M., the chief of the Municipal Police arrived with twenty-two police officers and asked the woman to quietly leave. She refused.[7] By then there were approximately four hundred people outside the embassy.[8]

Meanwhile, Colonel Zhang Hanke, FAP chief for the Taiwan Provincial Police Administration, informed Karl Ackerman, the embassy security officer, that he had been instructed the night before to take "extra precautions against any incidents." Ackerman worried that an incident would occur now that Liu's widow had positioned herself outside the embassy. At Zhang's suggestion, Ackerman invited the woman into the building so that she could lodge a protest. She not only declined the offer, but demanded that Reynolds not leave Taiwan until she received "full compensation."[9]

The police hoped to peacefully resolve the situation by bringing the angry woman's sister to the embassy to persuade Ao Tehua to go home. In the meantime, Colonel Zhang first asked the woman to go into the embassy, but she answered: "I won't go in. Outside that gate is Chinese soil and on this spot I have my rights." Zhang then suggested that she take her protest to the Foreign Ministry. Again she refused, calling herself a lone protestor. Zhang

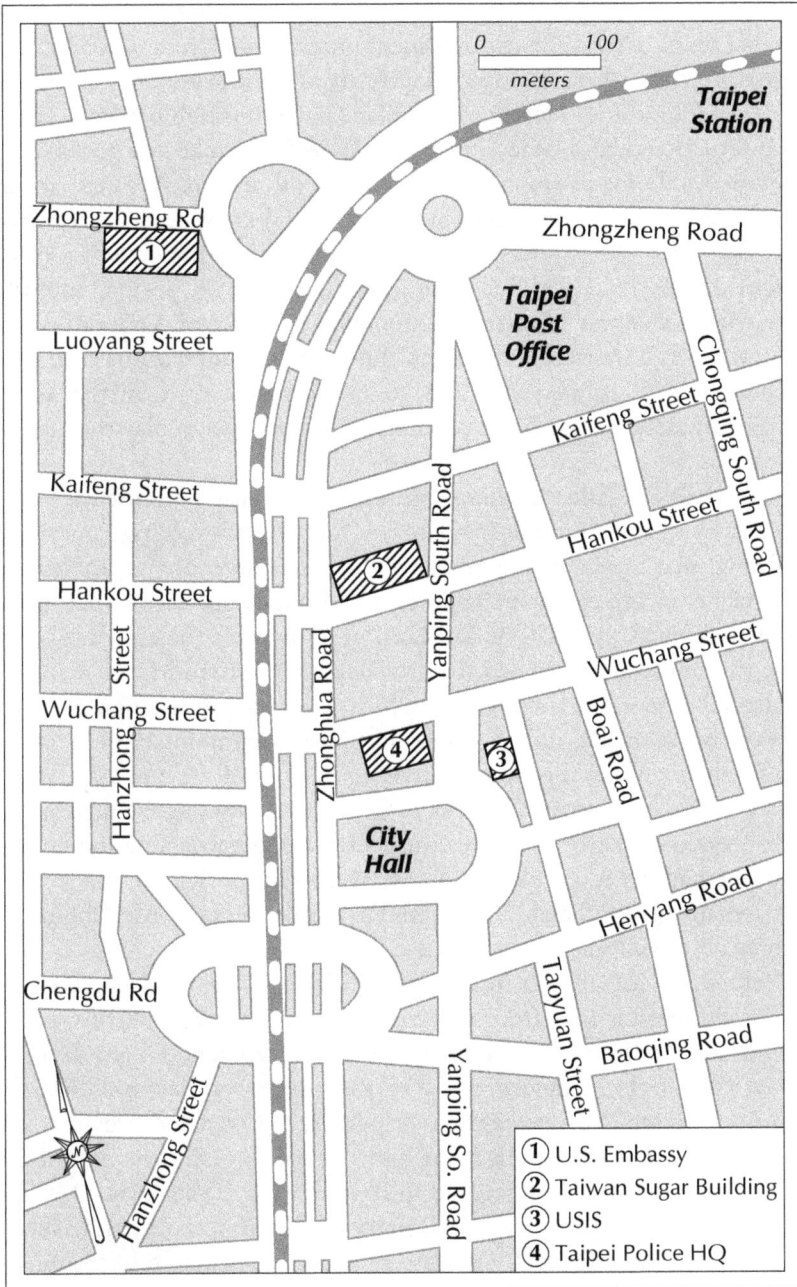

Detail of Taipei, area surrounding U.S. embassy. (Map by Dick Gilbreath, University of Kentucky cartography lab)

asked if she was trying to instigate an incident. She answered with a question of her own: "Could she not be a silent protestor on Chinese soil?"[10] In the background, the gathering crowd shouted insults at the policemen.

Several Chinese and foreign journalists, including Bob Brown, of United Press International, and Loren Fessler, of *Time-Life*, spoke and posed for pictures with Ao Tehua as she held her daughter on her lap. A female reporter for the Broadcasting Corporation of China (BCC) arrived on the scene with a tape recorder.[11] One embassy worker, who had had a previous run-in with the reporter, observed her "flouncing around, glowering, posing, and otherwise putting on a show of intense indignation in the small knot of people in the gateway." The woman interviewed the sobbing widow at the scene using the tape recorder, and played it back to an incensed crowd, further inflaming it. Fortunately for the Americans, the ROC refused to play the tape over the airwaves.[12]

Nevertheless, while the widow protested, the tension increased. Reports reached the embassy of minor incidents on the streets involving Americans.[13] Bob Brown met briefly in the embassy with Alexander Boase, the embassy press attaché, to see if anyone had requested police protection, because the FAP men claimed they had no jurisdiction to disperse the crowd. Shouting outside the embassy terminated the conversation.[14] Around 11:30 A.M., Captain McKibbin received a report that Chinese newspaper photographers were headed to Sergeant Reynolds's home on Grass Mountain. Expecting trouble and learning about the crowd gathering in front of the embassy, McKibbin went to see Lieutenant General T. C. Yu, vice chief of the general staff, and "expressed concern" over the situation developing outside the embassy. Because he had yet to speak with General Bowen, McKibbin made it clear that his visit was unofficial. As he left Yu's office, though, McKibbin could see worry on the Chinese general's face.[15]

There was good reason to worry. At 12:15 P.M. several hundred people were gathered across from the embassy. They were a mixture of Chinese and Taiwanese curiosity seekers, including women and children, who watched the spectacle before going to their intended destinations. There were also a number of students and soldiers.[16] Over the previous hour, a dozen armed Chinese policemen had arrived, a sufficient number, the embassy thought, and they seemed to have matters under control.[17] Colonel Zhang informed the Foreign Ministry of the large crowd and asked for instructions on how to deal with the protestors. He was told to reinforce the police already there, but not use force, so as to avoid precipitating incidents. Every so often a small group of individuals shouted slogans, but there seemed to be no apparent danger. The traffic in front of the embassy was not obstructed in any way. Most of the Americans and the embassy's Chinese staff left for lunch.[18]

The situation in front of the embassy, though, took a turn for the worse. The crowd grew angry. The BCC reporter tape recorded Ao Tehua as she continued her protest: "I thought that the United States was a democratic country, but I never would have thought . . ." Her sentence unfinished, she broke down in audible sobs before insisting that she would not leave.[19] In Chinese and Taiwanese, some in the crowd shouted that if Americans could kill Chinese and be set free by an unfair verdict, Chinese law needed to be changed to allow Chinese to shoot any Americans they encountered on the streets. Someone exclaimed in Taiwanese that if the government did not change its laws, there could be countless Liu Ziran incidents. Shouts of "Attack the embassy" and "Kill the Westerners," in Chinese and Taiwanese, could also be heard.[20]

By 12:30 P.M., hundreds of protestors (including students) surrounded the embassy, shouting anti-American slogans and carrying placards, suggesting that the "angry mob" had been organized.[21] A secretary to Taipei City's mayor, who was Taiwanese, told an embassy worker that "at one point . . . the rioters were mostly students and almost wholly Mainlanders."[22] However, a Chinese photographer, who had to make his escape after the mob tried to take his camera equipment, described it as "large numbers of Taiwanese and Mainlanders and many students from" National Taiwan University.[23]

Although the Taipei Municipal Police and the military police were supposedly ordered to "use all their power to disperse the mob, cut off the approaches to the Embassy and insure the Embassy's safety," the air-raid drills dispersed the police all over the city. Only a small number made it to the embassy, where some went inside while most remained outside "to grapple with the mob."[24] In reaction to the growing tension, the police quickly closed the gates and positioned themselves within the compound.

Shortly after 1:00 P.M. a Chinese merchant hung Ao Tehua's sign on the embassy wall. A Chinese shoeshine boy called out "attack."[25] The crowd moved toward the embassy gate. A stone thrown at the embassy building precipitated a "barrage" lasting forty-five minutes that shattered all of the windows facing the street. Several rioters tried to scale the embassy wall, only to be pushed back by policemen. "Whipped into a frenzy," the mob, now numbering about two thousand, unsuccessfully stormed the gate. Two men scaled the wall only to be driven out by the police. Hwang Zhenwu, head of the Taipei Garrison Command, now called for reinforcements, including cadets from a police academy.[26]

Only eight Americans and twenty-three Chinese employees were inside the embassy at the time. Those not on the premises were warned to stay away.

Around 1:00 P.M., a call for help went out to Pilcher to "get protection for the Embassy." Through an Associated Press reporter, Boase begged an ROC general to hold an air-raid drill in order to disperse the mob. Because the foreign minister was at lunch, Pilcher explained over the phone the situation to a Foreign Ministry official and demanded protection for embassy personnel. At 1:30 P.M., Pilcher learned of the serious turn of events at the embassy, and went straight to the Foreign Ministry, where he told ROC officials that police protection was "inadequate" and suggested that the Chinese use fire hoses and tear gas against the crowd.[27] At that moment, Chiang Ching-kuo was attending a luncheon with overseas Chinese students from the Philippines when he received a phone call from Le Gan, chief of the Taiwan Provincial Police Administration, explaining that protestors were about to enter the U.S. embassy. Chiang later claimed that he told Le Gan, "You must do all in your power to disperse the crowd. They must not be permitted to enter the embassy." He stayed abreast of events that went from bad to worse, issuing orders that the police do everything in their power to protect American lives.[28]

By 2:15 P.M. the mob had tripled in size, to six thousand. Awaiting reinforcements, the Chinese officers standing among the protestors and in the embassy grounds were "greatly outnumbered and anxious to avoid bloodshed." Lacking riot gear, the police could not stop the mob, which now used its weight in numbers to force open the embassy gate. Rioters rushed into the compound, overturning and smashing cars and ransacking the first floor while American and Chinese personnel gathered in an air-raid shelter on the second floor.[29]

Around the time that the protestors stormed the embassy, Foreign Minister Yeh returned from lunch. In Pilcher's words, "There were no niceties. I rose and stated this visit grieved me and that the U.S. Government demanded immediate assistance at the Embassy." Now that the protestors had penetrated the gate, he pleaded that the embassy faced a desperate situation and needed help immediately. Pilcher knew of the Americans trapped in the air-raid shelter, and he worried that a fire would turn the building into a "crematorium." Yeh agreed and saw no choice "but to call out the troops." Although American lives were in danger, the foreign minister then left for the Legislative Yuan for an hour to discuss the Reynolds verdict with lawmakers. Pilcher remained at the Foreign Ministry for another four hours, receiving reports from embassy personnel and supplying the Foreign Ministry "most of its intelligence on the situation." Yeh's decision to deal with Chinese lawmakers rather than the situation at the embassy incensed Americans, who viewed this as "Chinese indifference."[30]

Not knowing how long they would be trapped in the shelter, the Americans and Chinese huddled inside and stocked up on food. They eventually turned out the lights for fear of being discovered. There were two entrances, one of which was barred by a door that rioters pounded repeatedly. The other entrance originally had an iron door that had been removed. A U.S. Marine officer and one other American carried handguns and others armed themselves with fire extinguishers, with the intent of defending the open entrance. Howard Chaille, a survivor of an anti-American riot in Bogota, Colombia, convinced the men to hide all weapons and fire extinguishers. "Had we fired a shot," Chaille commented shortly after, "an international incident would have occurred and whatever chances we had at life would have been completely gone."[31]

Over the next two hours, nine waves of rioters forced their way into the embassy for durations of ten to fifteen minutes. Boase kept track of the surges. The crowd outside cheered as rioters hurled objects out the windows. A rioter cut down the U.S. flag, which was torn to shreds by the mob below. When an ROC flag took its place on the pole, "hysterical cheers" could be heard.[32] Rioters hung a second ROC flag from the embassy balcony. One cried out, "Long live the Republic of China." Another wrote in Chinese and English on the embassy wall, "Protest U.S. military's contempt for human rights!" Le Gan used a loudspeaker to demand that rioters cease and desist. One rioter, questioning his patriotism, asked, "Are you Chinese?" Another rioter, a Chinese cook, tried to instigate the crowd to attack Le Gan.[33]

Meanwhile, inside the embassy, filing and safe cabinets were smashed and their contents, including classified files, were strewn about on the ground. A group of forty youths gave speeches to the crowd, which applauded every time a piece of embassy furniture was thrown out. Approximately fifty students marched into the embassy compound every twenty to thirty minutes "shouting slogans and retiring in good order." Separate fires were set in the embassy, including in the Political Section. Down below in the embassy's motor pool, vehicles were overturned and a truck partially burned.[34]

A number of American personnel attempted to return to the embassy at the peak of the attack. Around 2:00 P.M., William H. Gleysteen tried to enter the compound, only to be told that rioters had entered the building and that Americans were trapped inside. The police blocked his way and told him to leave. A well-dressed Chinese man pushing a bicycle shouted repeatedly and angrily, "You're an American, get out." From Gleysteen's vantage point, he could see that the police allowed any Chinese to enter the area. He was the only person blocked off. Two hours later, he tried and failed to reach the embassy because he was "still in ignorance of the degree of the riot."

Eventually he decided to drive toward the Sugar Building, location of the TDC along Zhonghua Road, and the USIS buildings close to City Hall. Fire trucks and two trucks containing fake coffins made out of poles and covered with slogans about Liu Ziran drove past him toward the embassy.[35]

Two other Foreign Service officers, Henry Bonner and Jerry O'Grady, were returning from lunch. Along the way they ran into John Conroy. After parking their car two blocks from the embassy, the three walked to within fifty yards of the building, where they found "masses of people outside the motor pool, filling the driveway and perched on the walls." Bonner and O'Grady tried to work their way through the crowd into the motor pool. They were greeted with hissing and clapping, and forced to take cover in the garage after crawling over smashed vehicles. Although some angry demonstrators moved in their direction, a lone Chinese policeman stationed himself outside the garage. Fortunately for Bonner and O'Grady, no serious attempts were made to root them out of their hiding place. Nevertheless, they remained trapped for four hours. Conroy never made it to the embassy because pedestrians blocked his way, and he had no choice but to go back to the Sugar Building to call for help. He recounted afterward, "I was shoved and jostled, received hostile stares from the surrounding crowd, heard what I think were swear words in Chinese, and was spit at by one character."[36] It was possibly Conroy who had a Chinese peddler jump on him, hit him in the chest, and shout, "Don't let him get away."[37]

Despite the repeated surges into the embassy building, the Chinese police were successful in keeping the mob away from the air-raid shelter. The telephones were out of service and the Americans could not use their radio equipment to reach anyone on the outside. Although an exhaust fan continued to operate, the atmosphere within the shelter was stifling. Some feared they would suffocate to death should there be a power failure. The Americans prayed that the ROC would hold an air-raid drill to drive the people off the streets. When the sounds of a public address system became clearly audible, Howard Chaille hoped that someone would play the ROC national anthem, because the Chinese "took it so seriously they would have undoubtedly stood at attention."[38]

In fact, the sounds that the Americans heard were attempts by the police to save them. At approximately 3:00 P.M., Le Gan used a loudspeaker to ask the rioters to leave peacefully. Failing this, he ordered that shots be fired in the air, again to no avail. Reinforcements in the form of nearly eighty police cadets and forty MPs arrived and compelled the rioters to vacate the embassy. Twenty minutes later, over fifty students from Cheng Gong High School marched by the embassy but did not stop.[39]

Nearly a half hour earlier, Colonel Chow arrived on scene and learned that air-conditioning equipment had been ripped out and that protestors were scattering embassy documents all over the courtyard. At 3:05 P.M., he called General Jiang, with whom he had met earlier that morning, and told him that the mob was now "out of hand" and troops were needed to protect the embassy. At a nearby phone, Dr. Ernest Moy, a former Nationalist general who once served as Sun Yat-sen's secretary, spoke with Lieutenant General J. L. Huang, commander in chief of the Combined Services Forces. In scathing terms, berating him and the ROC, Moy demanded that soldiers be deployed to protect U.S. property. Chow noted that Moy and Huang were old friends, and "No less firmly established relationship could have survived that conversation." At 3:10 P.M., after receiving an update from Colonel Chow, General Bowen ordered that all U.S. personnel be warned to remain off the streets.[40]

Around 3:30 P.M., someone in the crowd shouted that Sergeant Reynolds had departed Taiwan. Indeed, Reynolds and his family had left the island two hours earlier on a routine flight before a couple of Chinese reporters could interview or photograph the family.[41] Two days later they arrived at Travis Air Force Base. There, Reynolds, flanked by USAF officers who limited reporters' questions and Reynolds's answers, insisted, "I'm sorry for what happened, but I was only doing what any man would do to protect his home and family."[42] He further stated that he had never been bothered by anyone before the Liu Ziran incident and that he initially intended to seek another tour in Taiwan. Now, he was on a twenty-day leave in preparation for taking up duties at Fort Benning before eventually becoming a MAAG advisor in South Vietnam.[43]

"Incensed to the boiling point," the mob launched successive charges into the embassy, overturning fourteen vehicles and wreaking further destruction. Despite the arrival of more security forces, the rioters continued to charge into the building, inflicting damage. Howard Jones walked from the ICA to the embassy entrance, where he observed not only a Chinese flag where the U.S. flag once flew, but other Chinese flags hanging from the building. One man stood on the balcony, speaking to the crowd of spectators. Jones could not enter the compound, and, not seeing any friendly faces, decided to return to the ICA offices.[44]

In the words of Joseph Brent, the ICA building, located five blocks from USIS, was a "sitting duck." Fortunately, most of the mob's fury was directed at the embassy. When some protestors began to shout "get ICA," about forty or fifty made their way toward the structure. However, the crowd dispersed when they saw that it was protected by MPs. At 3:00 P.M., Brent met with Taiwan's Governor C. K. Yen and Premier O. K. Yui. Only an hour before had George Yeh made Yen and Yui aware of the riots. Yen ordered security forces not to fire on the crowd, and had plainclothes policemen positioned in the ICA's neighborhood. Nevertheless, neither Brent nor Yen understood that the riot had turned uglier.[45]

At approximately 4:00 P.M. the rioters launched their ninth and final surge into the embassy. A few managed to get by the police and discovered the shelter. The rioters now battled the police in an attempt to storm it. Some of the Americans immediately ordered that the pistols be tossed under a bench to avoid bloodshed. Earlier, the husband of one Chinese embassy worker had entered the shelter and brought disheartening news about the events outside. When the rioters turned more violent, the man bravely walked out alone among the mob and declared that only Chinese were inside the shelter. Not believing him, the rioters demanded that the Chinese staff withdraw from the premises. Some of them pushed the Americans to the rear of the shelter before leaving the building. Although glad that their Chinese coworkers were safe, the Americans felt a sense of doom and understood that they "were in considerable jeopardy." According to Norma Platter, Colonel Zhang came into the shelter, apologized, and asked if there was a tunnel or exit, only to be told no. Without an escape route, the Americans believed that only a tank or armored car could save them. They also knew that no such vehicle was coming.[46]

Once the Chinese workers were out of the embassy, a few rioters made their way toward the air-raid shelter. Using matches, they discovered the eight foreigners. Shouting "Americans," they hurled lit cigarette lighters, thermos bottles full of hot water, metal wastebaskets, and telephones into the air-raid shelter. Talking to the rioters failed and seemed pointless. Standing in a confined, dark space, separated from the police and the general mob, the rioters could have easily committed an atrocity. Alexander Boase stepped toward the door first in a manner to show he was not armed. Immediately the rioters pummeled him. The Americans, men and women alike, ran a gauntlet of "clubs, stones, fists, etc." and vacated the shelter. The eight ran for blocks with the rioters on their heels, including one rioter who had already inflicted injury with a hammer. From time to time one of the Americans got in a good punch against a rioter, but they suffered more than they dished out from a mob that clubbed, kicked, spat upon, and stoned them.

With only a handful of policemen for protection, the embassy workers became separated as they made their escape. A police officer tried to put Boase, who already had a broken rib and blood draining into one eye, and Paul Meyer, chief of the embassy's political section, into a pedicab. Both men knew the pedicab was worse than useless for a quick getaway, so they moved on. Then another officer dragged the two men toward a black jeep. While Boase and Meyer struggled into the vehicle, the rioters surrounded and nearly overturned the jeep. Policemen, pressed up against the vehicle, tried to protect the Americans, but they could not stop the large stones that hit the windshield. Fortunately for Boase and Meyer, the jeep's shatterproof glass prevented more serious injury. A rioter stole the jeep's keys, seemingly dashing the Americans' hope of escape. The Chinese driver used pliers and a screwdriver to rip out the ignition and tried to hotwire the jeep using tin-foil from a pack of cigarettes. Police officers pushed the jeep through the streets at an excruciatingly slow one mile per hour while the driver tried to pop the clutch and start the engine. Rioters threw themselves into the jeep's path, hoping to prevent its escape. Finally, after traveling two blocks, the two Americans were overjoyed to see the arrival of three buses of security police armed with automatic weapons. The embattled Americans were transferred to a bus containing ten to twelve security guards and moved to a MAAG hospital. Meyer suffered numerous abrasions and bruises and needed stitches in his head as a result of being pelted with a wastepaper basket, stones, kicks, fists, clubs, and verbal slurs. The one that stuck out in his mind was "You killed Chinese; we kill you."[47]

The other Americans got away with minor injuries. Karl Ackerman was thrown into a jeep that sped away from the mob. Frank Nesci, a mail clerk, tried to escape with Ackerman. When someone in the mob threw a file cabinet at one of the women, Nesci went after the rioter, only to be surrounded and knocked unconscious. When he came to, he discovered that a policeman had pulled him to the street. He later credited the man for saving his life, because he felt he would "have been beaten or trampled to death" by the mob if left on the ground. The two then made their way to Ambassador Rankin's townhouse. While being beaten by the crowd, Howard Chaille and three others worked their way toward a car they wrongly thought was owned by a U.S. government agency. The four became momentarily lost, but a Chinese policeman grabbed one of the women by the hand and led the group into the Taiwan Provincial Hospital, where they received protection and medical care before being moved to the Marine Guards' House.[48]

Francis Prescott was inside the ambassador's townhouse when Frank Nesci was brought in "beaten and bloody." Earlier in the day, Prescott had tried to reach the embassy only to have his car surrounded by angry people shaking their fists "and cursing us in the vilest English." Prescott took Nesci to the MAAG hospital, where he found Meyer and Boas "badly beaten and mauled." Learning that the Americans at the Marine Guards' House needed further medical care, Prescott acquired a MAAG ambulance and a

Chinese bus with an armed guard and two Chinese policemen. After driving down Jinan Street and crossing to Canal, the little convoy spotted a large column of students heading their way. The Chinese policemen quickly told the Americans to lie down in the floor. When Prescott asked why, a policeman answered, "the Youth Corps." The trail of students, which was three blocks in length by Prescott's estimation, passed the ambulance without incident. Prescott picked up the injured Americans and drove them to the MAAG dispensary. He worried about Bonner and O'Grady, from whom nothing had been seen or heard other than that O'Grady's car had been smashed.[49]

While the wounded Americans received medical care and were taken to their homes, ROC authorities tried to convince U.S. officials that they had the situation under control. At 4:00 P.M., the Foreign Ministry issued alerts to Taipei County and the cities of Kaohsiung, Tainan, Taichung, and Hsinchu. The Ministry of Education notified school principals to send all students home once classes ended. Several hundred agitated students surrounded three Americans at the nearby Taipei train station, forcing them to seek shelter in the station manager's office, but all of the students returned to their homes after a Foreign Ministry official met with them to defuse the situation.[50]

Around 4:40 P.M., a previously scheduled air-raid alert sounded, and Foreign Ministry personnel made their way to the embassy and the local hospital to assess the situation and the condition of injured Americans. General Liu Wei, head of the military police, arrived with a company of MPs and joined Le Gan in asking the crowd to settle down and disperse. By now, the damage was done. The MPs were simply too slow to meet the crisis. The TDC notified the Pentagon that three thousand rioters had attacked the embassy, but that the Ministry of National Defense "assured" U.S. authorities that the riots "would be controlled 'immediately.'" Admiral Ingersoll likewise was informed by Defense Minister Yu Dawei that the troops were called out and that the "incident would not develop into anything more serious." By 5:00 P.M., the rioters inside the embassy were cleared out, but they would return shortly.[51]

Long before the destruction of the embassy, rioters were already attacking MAAG's communication facilities. Around 3:00 P.M., a crowd appeared outside the Sugar Building, three blocks from the U.S. embassy, and wrecked vehicles belonging to MAAG personnel. An American enlisted man drove up to the entrance just at that moment, and the mob descended on his car. Although he remained inside and managed to steer away from the rioters, the mob shattered his windshield, slightly injuring the soldier. Inside the Sugar Building, Captain McKibbin concluded that "the situation was dangerous." The mob outside was out of control. Fortunately, the steel gates at the entrance were closed. Standing inside the building were U.S. soldiers armed with Thompson submachine guns, with orders to protect cryptanalyst equipment at all costs.[52] If the rioters had entered the building, there might have been a bloodbath. Within a half hour the crowd numbered two thousand and was preparing to storm the building, but just at that moment two Chinese rifle companies and a squad of MP academy cadets arrived. They had been ordered there by Chiang Ching-kuo to protect the Sugar Building and MAAG homes and installations. By 6:00 P.M., more reinforcements were on the scene and all roads to the Sugar Building had been blocked off. Forty-five minutes later, TDC notified Washington that the building was secure, that a curfew was in effect, and that Chinese troops were protecting the compound.[53]

Once the situation around the Sugar Building stabilized, McKibbin and Colonel Chow drove to the ambassador's townhouse, where they found Howard Jones, James Pilcher's wife, and a number of embassy personnel, including one injured man, without any protection despite calls for help and a mob forming nearby. McKibbin asked if anyone wanted to be armed. Jones did and was handed a Colt .45 pistol from MAAG stock. McKibbin and Chow left the ambassador's townhouse only to find the mob a half block away in the process of attacking two Americans riding a pedicab to teach an English class. Although surrounded by several police officers, one was bleeding from the mouth, the other could not use his leg because a rock had struck his hip, and both had had their faces beaten. The MAAG officers put the two men in a car and drove them past the mob to the MAAG dispensary. Fearful that the mob could acquire weapons located in the dispensary, Chow asked Chinese authorities to provide more protection.[54]

Although the Sugar Building and the townhouse were spared, the same could not be said for the two USIS buildings. For most of the day, all had been quiet outside of the buildings, which remained open, and library patrons were well-behaved. At 3:00 P.M., female employees left for the day. Around 3:40 P.M., several groups of school youths arrived and attracted a small crowd. When an air-raid alert sounded an hour later, only a few Chinese staff remained in the building. At 4:55 P.M., some rioters broke out an office display window. Six policemen stationed themselves in front of the structure and moved the rioters forty feet from the buildings. American personnel were given time to evacuate. By 5:10 P.M., an estimated five thousand people were gathered outside. The policemen pleaded that the people destroy nothing. Instead, twenty to thirty demonstrators rushed the USIS buildings in five waves, sacking the library and destroying everything upstairs in an hour and a half. Radios, tape recorders, typewriters, and film projectors were smashed. The auditorium, the offices of Alexander Boase and Ralph Powell, the USIS director, and even the lavatories were all wrecked. Policemen and firemen were beaten in the process. Around 6:00 P.M., the protestors began burning books from the library, leading to the arrest of one. A half hour later, two companies of ROC troops arrived and assisted the police in clearing out the building and arresting some of the demonstrators. U.S. officials maintained afterward that the sacking of the USIS buildings did not stop until 7:00 P.M.[55]

By this time, Joseph Brent had returned home, where he learned the embassy and USIS buildings were in "shambles." He called Chiang Ching-kuo to "find out what the hell was going on." Brent demanded that protection be given to the Union Building, where the Mutual Security Agency, which provided economic aid to Taiwan, was located. Chiang and his wife later joined Brent for dinner, and for the next few hours information poured in that was mostly erroneous: "two students killed, two police killed, MAAG buildings are wrecked, MAAG buildings are not yet wrecked, the mob is here, the mob is there." Brent and others impressed upon Chiang Ching-kuo "that the only chance of salvaging even a shred of responsibility lay in squashing the riots before midnight."[56]

Long before then, the mob vented its fury elsewhere. Hearing that one of their compatriots had been arrested, the rioters rushed to the Municipal Police headquarters. The leader of the group was a mainlander, a real estate broker named Chen Zhengqiu, who demanded the fellow rioter's release and to be allowed to search the building for what were believed to be seven Americans taking refuge there (they were actually two Europeans). When his demands were rejected, Chen led the mob in attacking the police headquarters.[57] The police called on firemen to use their hoses against the crowd, prompting the mob to attack and overwhelm them. Some of the rioters set fire to the police garage, destroying four police motorcycles and wrecking several police jeeps and fire engines. A larger crowd attacked the main building, attempting to disarm policemen. When one officer was shot, the police opened fire on the crowd in self-defense, and to prevent the foreigners and weapons cache in the building from falling into the mob's hands. The weight of the crowd prevented the rioters in front from retreating. At 7:30 P.M., other rioters forced their way into the police headquarters and fought a pitched battle with policemen, who struggled to hold off the mob. Over an hour later three companies of ROC troops arrived and lifted the siege on the police headquarters. By that time, thirty-two policemen and eleven rioters were injured. An office boy, who worked at the Weather Bureau and had set the fire in the police garage, died of gunshot wounds at National Taiwan University hospital. Around midnight, the foreigners who had taken asylum in the police headquarters were escorted home.[58]

Hours earlier, at 5:30 P.M., Karl Rankin had arrived in Taipei on a CAT flight, completely ignorant of the day's events. Two ROC air force colonels met him at the airport and advised the ambassador to wait in the military terminal building so that he could avoid journalists waiting for him in the passenger terminal. Only then did he receive a vague reference to the "'trouble' over the verdict of the Reynolds court martial." One of the colonels "regretted, with diffidence, that there had been applause by Americans" when the court announced the not guilty verdict. With Rankin unable to reach the embassy, an American naval attaché picked the ambassador up at the airport and briefed him on the events known to that point. Rankin demanded to see the foreign minister, who dispatched Yu Dawei to escort the ambassador. On the way to the Foreign Ministry, Rankin watched as General Wang Shuming, commander of the ROC Air Force, jumped out of his car and ran into the middle of the street to Rankin's vehicle to express his regret over the day's events.

Rankin arrived at the Foreign Ministry at 7:00 P.M. He protested the damage inflicted on the embassy and the USIS buildings "with the strongest possible emphasis," and criticized "the slowness of the police in taking action." Rankin also "demanded full compensation and adequate apologies." He then asked George Yeh to accompany him to the embassy. Riding in the foreign minister's car, Rankin insisted on seeing the USIS buildings first. Passing through police lines, he saw hundreds of people still milling about and not fully controlled. Nevertheless, Rankin experienced no hostilities. One man even walked up to the car and blurted out to Yeh, "Mr. Minister, save us from this disgrace." The car approached to within one hundred yards of the two USIS buildings, which were clearly gutted, but the police were anxious and moved them along. As Rankin passed the Sugar Building, he saw that some of the windows were broken, but Chinese troops continued to keep the large crowd at bay.

The vehicle then made its way to the embassy. Stones pelted the car. When someone recognized Foreign Minister Yeh, they shouted, "Get him, he is to blame for everything." At 7:30 P.M., Rankin and Yeh arrived at the embassy, which had just been cleared of rioters, but a large crowd remained across the street. As the two emerged from the car, Rankin could hear people clapping their hands, and some rocks were thrown their direction. One struck the foreign minister but did not seriously injure him. Walking into the embassy compound, Rankin saw chairs, desks, typewriters, filing cabinets, small safes, and official documents scattered all over the ground. Among the debris he found pieces of the American flag and gathered up an armful. Rankin wanted to inspect the inside of the embassy, but the police urged him to leave before another incident occurred.[59]

Some Americans had already seen the destruction inside. At 6:30 P.M., Henry Bonner and Jerry O'Grady were finally able to leave the garage. Bonner went into the offices upstairs and found "absolute total destruction." Everything had been tossed outside with the exception of four safes. While Bonner and O'Grady sat on some broken filing cabinets, high-ranking police officers apologized and said they liked Americans. They offered Bonner and O'Grady water and cigarettes. One colonel remarked that "matters had gotten out of hand and they had not expected it." The two Americans were then placed in an ambulance that contained ten students who were bound and gagged. They had been arrested for fighting the police. All were taken to police headquarters, but the Americans received more Chinese hospitality and apologies. A deputy commander took both men home. Inside his jeep hung an eight-by-ten-inch photograph of Chiang Kai-shek shaking Ambassador Rankin's hand.[60]

At 8:00 P.M., the ROC announced that a state of emergency existed in Taipei. Earlier, Premier Yui had issued a statement deploring the riots and warning of severe retribution to those caught engaging in lawlessness. At the moment when the ROC announced that all was under control, one last attack was made against the U.S. embassy that led to further destruction, including to the code room. More fires were set, but they were quickly put out. Rankin and Admiral Ingersoll warned the ROC military that unless "sufficient troops" were brought into Taipei, "mob control of the city throughout the night would be truly disastrous." At 8:30 P.M., the commander of the U.S. 7th Fleet ordered certain vessels to set sail for Keelung.[61]

At 9:00 P.M., the ROC imposed martial law in Taipei as two Chinese divisions entered the city, but the city's mayor declared that the safety of Americans could not be guaranteed. Reports arrived that rioters were moving toward the Ministry of Defense. At 10:00 P.M., U.S. Armed Forces Radio-Taiwan advised all Americans to remain at home. An hour later, the home of Colonel Walter E. Barker, the embassy's military attaché, was stoned. Although General Peng Mengji informed Ingersoll at midnight that the situation was completely under control now that three and a half army divisions were in Taipei, with two deployed and authorized to shoot rioters, the crowds did not finally disperse until 1:30 A.M.[62]

Just before midnight, Donald Whittaker (another Foreign Service officer) and his cook rode their bicycles to the embassy to assess the damage. He counted two hundred to three hundred soldiers "in full battle gear" near the building. After identifying himself, Whittaker walked inside the compound. Using a flashlight, he found the door to the classified room intact, but a large hole now opened into the room. Several safes had been forced open, and he found documents classified as "SECRET" all over the floor. Fortunately, the Top Secret drawer remained locked and intact.[63]

Once the military truly had control of the city, ROC authorities removed fifteen cars from the embassy compound to do repairs and to prevent leaking gasoline from becoming a fire hazard. The cleanup was briefly halted so that the Americans could assess the damage. Before daybreak, ROC soldiers, under American supervision, walked into the embassy compound and filled one hundred large bags with the documents strewn on the ground.[64]

No amount of cleaning, though, could answer the questions that remained uppermost in American minds by the end of Black Friday. Were the riots spontaneous events or planned well in advance, and if planned, who instigated them? Why had ROC authorities failed to respond faster to prevent protests from spawning mob actions? Were the riots an expression of anti-Americanism or did they reflect an internal political struggle within the ROC government? What impact would the riots have on the status of U.S. forces in Taiwan, U.S. policy toward Taiwan and the PRC, and the U.S. alliance structure around the world?

10

Accusations

In the days that followed Black Friday, American nerves were rather raw and on edge. As a result of the riots, eleven American embassy and MAAG personnel, sixty-two police officers, and eleven rioters were injured. One rioter was dead. Another 111 individuals were under arrest. The U.S. embassy and the USIS buildings had suffered severe damage. Embassy personnel had been physically attacked and nearly killed. The American flag had been destroyed. These actions violated international law and other established diplomatic conventions, and could have been viewed as grounds for breaking diplomatic relations.

It is ironic that despite all of the U.S. intelligence work being done in Taiwan, the protests and riots caught the Americans completely by surprise. Although Americans knew of Chinese hatred of extraterritoriality, that Chinese were extremely angry with the Reynolds verdict, that students were discussing the case, and that demonstrations were possible, they were caught with their guard down.[1] Possibly they were lulled into a sense of complacency. The stability in Taiwan made such an occurrence seem impossible.[2] Whatever the reason, they were now incensed and felt betrayed. Andrew Franklin best captured the American mood in the riots' aftermath: "With the howls of an angry mob still in their ears, many Americans in the next few days were dazed, soured and disillusioned. In the uncertainty of the moment, there was also and not surprisingly, a strong element of fear and near-panic. Worst of all was a sense of wounded personal pride. The gallant ally had with painful suddenness turned into a snake in the grass. All the sentiment, as well as the aid, so generously and sometimes indiscriminately lavished, had overnight taken on the flavor of ashes."[3]

Meanwhile, the situation remained volatile. The day after the riots, university students marched toward the Ministry of Defense. Colonel Chow, the MAAG political advisor, wanted to speak with them but was warned away for fear of his safety. On May 26, lawmakers in the ROC's Legislative Yuan were reportedly doing everything possible to have martial law rescinded and were demanding an investigation of the Chinese military for "needless imposition of martial law, roughing up civilians by military and military preoccupation with placating Americans."[4] Many Chinese in Taiwan's major cities, including students, called on the ROC to prevent future U.S. courts-martial and eliminate diplomatic immunity for U.S. troops, and they demanded that Reynolds be returned to Taiwan to face a Chinese court. The Chinese officers that testified on Reynolds's behalf "received threatening phone calls," and one was forced to move after his house was stoned.[5]

On May 27, a crowd of two hundred gathered in front of an American home and tied a live rat to a bamboo pole, then shoved it under the gate in plain sight of Chinese policemen, who did nothing. Elsewhere, a large crowd shouted obscenities at another American home. Embassy staff suggested that Ambassador Rankin organize Americans for "self-protection." He refused. Instead, he advised George Yeh to tone down the press and take actions to defuse the situation. Rankin had already sent Ralph Powell to meet with American reporters in an effort to "kill rumors that were gaining currency." The U.S. military flew tear gas out of Okinawa to hand out to the Chinese police, and Rankin recommended that police be supplied with bamboo sticks to break up crowds.[6]

Americans, though, were in no trusting mood and took their own precautions. They organized a bus service that took people shopping, while tea houses and bars were declared off limits after 8:00 P.M. Those who owned cars were to keep their driving to a minimum. Some in the American community were already engaging in self-defense. Glenn Jones, a fifth grader at the time, remembered his mother being angry with his father for *not* owning a gun, while his father, a combat veteran of the Pacific War, laughed it off. On his own, the young boy stayed up at night protecting the family home with a BB gun and baseball bats. In southern Taiwan, where no riots occurred, Vincent Kramer remembered U.S. soldiers armed with submachine guns riding on school buses to protect American children trying to get to school.[7]

ROC authorities took measures to prevent further conflict. The Taiwan Provincial Government and the Taiwan Garrison Command issued decrees requiring all citizens to register weapons and ammunition, and threatened death to anyone convicted of being a "rumor agitator," starting a riot, engaging in work stoppage, inciting students, or illegally carrying firearms or explosives. When there was an attempt to give a funeral for the lone rioter killed, the Chinese military sent his body to a mortuary and locked up his home after sending the man's family "to 'a resort.'"[8]

A series of accidents and incidents involving Chinese and Americans occurred after the riots that could have thrown proverbial fuel on the fire. On May 25, Father Franco, an American priest, was riding his motorcycle in central Taiwan when a Chinese jeep crossed the center line and hit Franco head-on, killing him. Nearly fourteen hundred people, all but one hundred of whom were locals who admired the priest, walked in the funeral procession without incident. On May 29, a Chinese man was killed in Taoyuan when he lost control of his scooter in heavy rain and slammed into a five-ton tractor trailer driven by an American sergeant. The next day, a U.S. Air Force sergeant ran down a sixty-three-year-old woman in a Taipei suburb, killing her. At the request of the Foreign Ministry, the Americans held a court-martial on Okinawa and newspapers never publicized the event, including the man's acquittal in August.[9] That same day, a "minor riot" occurred at National Taiwan Normal University led by twelve tailors, twenty students, and a number of laborers and office workers wanting to demonstrate in order to keep the Reynolds case alive. The students were described by a Foreign Ministry official as "imbued with 'primitive nationalism,'" but other students opposed further protests.[10]

Although a number of Americans worried about a repeat of the Boxer Uprising of 1900, in which foreigners were surrounded in Beijing, none of these accidents and incidents blew up into new rounds of protests, but they kept Americans fearful and apprehensive. Nearly a week after Black Friday, Franklin found Americans to be "shocked and disillusioned" and their wounds deep.[11]

Early on the morning of May 25, U.S. embassy personnel arrived to assess the damage and to salvage what they could. Those who worked in the code room went around picking up rotors from cryptographic equipment as well as classified material. Remarkably, only six of the one hundred rotors were missing. There was no evidence that anything had been looted other than some New Taiwan and U.S. currency and some classified material including an emergency evacuation plan from Taiwan. The embassy staff were struck by how the "mobsters endeavored to avoid taking anything whatsoever." James Pilcher could not help but wonder whether the numerous "do not steal" signs nailed to the embassy walls had an effect. At 8:00 A.M., Rankin took Governor C. K. Yen to the embassy to show him "the systematic destruction, the slogans on the walls and the safes broken open." The Americans assessed the extent of the physical damage to both the embassy and USIS buildings as totaling around $500,000 (over $4 million in 2015 terms).[12]

The degree of American emotions roughly matched that of the damage. Franklin commented that the American "bitterness, as they surveyed the ruins of the Embassy and other buildings . . . had to be seen to be believed. This was precisely the kind of thing they had maintained could not happen in Formosa. And now it had happened."[13] Americans were left in an "emotional shock" equivalent to "having your teeth kicked out by your best friend."[14] U.S. officials did everything they could to convey to the ROC their anger and the potential ramifications of the riots. During the four hours that Pilcher begged the Foreign Ministry for help, he warned George Yeh and other officials that "the hundreds of thousands of U.S. dollars damage was insignificant to the damage to US/GRC relations and the prestige to GRC in the Free World." In Washington, Walter Robertson explained to Hollington Tong, the Chinese ambassador, that his government was "deeply disturbed and shocked" and that "no one could tell yet how far-reaching the consequences would be but it was an exceedingly unfortunate business which was bound to have harmful repercussions."[15]

In the White House, Congress, various government agencies, and the press in Washington, the mood was not much different from that of Americans in Taiwan. As Walter Robertson observed, "If the event had occurred in Moscow or Peiping [Beijing], it could hardly have exhibited a worse fury."[16] A Washington correspondent for the London-based *News Chronicle* declared that Americans "feel they have been kicked contemptuously by friends for whom they have risked and spent much."[17] No government wants to hear that its embassy has been nearly destroyed and its people hurt, but to have one's own ally inflict the damage and injury proved a major embarrassment. A State Department official tried to explain to the House Foreign Affairs Subcommittee why the riots occurred, saying there was "a deeply covered but definite element of xenophobia in the Chinese national make-up." Another found that some of the ROC's "staunchest supporters in Congress" now called for a review of the country's China policy.[18] Republicans in particular were furious. Senator Andrew F. Schoeppel (R-KS) told a member of the ROC embassy that the "conservative wing of the Senate displayed a chilly attitude toward the nationalist Government." Senator William F. Knowland (R-CA), known as the Senator from Formosa because of his strong support for Chiang Kai-shek, expressed shock, while Senator Styles Bridges (R-NH) insisted that "any further violence against the sovereignty of the United States absolutely will not be tolerated."[19]

The riots opened the door for Democrats, who had been blamed by Republicans for the fall of China to communism since 1949, to criticize U.S. policy toward Taiwan. Some, such as Senator Warren Magnuson (D-WA), wanted to end the trade embargo against the PRC, while others tried to get Representative Clement Zablocki (D-WI), chair of the House Foreign Affairs Far Eastern Subcommittee, to denounce Eisenhower and the ROC. Zablocki, who had been to Taiwan, refused. He did he suggest that U.S. policy toward Taiwan be reexamined, in the wake of several incidents involving U.S. troops, and questioned whether enough was being done to prevent such offenses.[20]

Although newspapers criticized Americans for their ostentatious life-styles and "contempt for the natives," the protests raised questions of how anti-American riots could occur in Taiwan, one of America's staunchest allies and a country that the United States provided millions of dollars in aid. Black Friday was a warning to Americans that friends could not be bought nor abandoned, leaving the United States essentially stuck.[21]

The riots allowed those who could influence U.S. public opinion to attack Chiang Kai-shek's regime and U.S. policy toward the ROC. *New York Times* columnist C. L. Sulzberger described the riots as a sign that the United States should consider recognizing the PRC and allowing Taiwan to become inde-pendent. Reporter Thomas Hamilton suggested that Taiwan be placed under United Nations trusteeship.[22] Outside of the *New York Times*, China experts like O. Edmund Clubb, a former Foreign Service officer who came under attack during the McCarthy era, called the riots "the most outrageous assault upon an American embassy, in any country, in this century," and insisted on a thorough review of U.S. policy toward Taiwan. The United States had to face the fact that the PRC was a world power and trying to get in the United Nations, while America spent millions on Taiwan, which would never recover the mainland. Nathaniel Peffer, professor of international relations at Colum-bia University, argued that the U.S. military presence in Taiwan made Chiang Kai-shek look like a "puppet in an American 'imperialist' show, and the island itself as a base for future military aggression." The riots were evidence of the U.S. military's unpopularity, making Taiwan a political liability, in which case the United States had to decide either to defend the island perpetually and eventually go to war or recognize the PRC and allow it to enter the United Nations. Then the United States, the two Chinas, and the United Nations could negotiate to allow Taiwan to become a U.N. trusteeship. The *Wheeling Intelligencer* editorialized, "Formosa is an embarrassment rather than an asset. Keeping Kai-shek and his cause and his followers alive not only has cost heav-ily in material outlay, but even more heavily in world prestige. Practically every other country has deserted the cause of Nationalist China."[23]

No one understood the potential ramifications of Black Friday for the U.S.-ROC relationship better than Chiang Kai-shek. On May 24, he was at his retreat on Sun Moon Lake in central Taiwan when he learned, after a mountain hike, of the riots. His immediate reaction was to order martial law to protect Taiwan from communist infiltration. Not all of the informa-tion reaching Chiang was accurate. When told of the attack on the police sta-tion, the number of dead was put at five as opposed to the actual one. Deeply unsettled by the day's events, he worried that the incident could lead to greater problems, including the Soviet Union using the riots to its advantage.[24]

Almost immediately the ROC engaged in damage control. Chiang Kai-shek fired Huang Zhenwu for failure to take the situation seriously; Liu Wei for failure to support the Taipei Garrison Command with his MPs, saying he could not intervene in a civilian matter; and Le Gan for failure to prevent the riot at the embassy. Calling Le Gan "stupid" (*hutu*), Chiang blasted him for refusing to order his men to fire on the crowd as a "disciplinary action," for fear of causing injuries. Chiang asked a rhetorical question: would the incident have been less severe if Le Gan had not shirked his responsibility?[25]

Next, the ROC extended apologies. Chiang Kai-shek personally expressed to Rankin the "great embarrassment and deep regret" for the events of May 24, and promised to punish those found responsible. In Washington, Hollington Tong verbally stated that his government "deplored the mob action" and delivered a note that expressed "profound regret." The note described the riots as arising "out of a public demonstration" against the Reynolds verdict, and said that the ROC would take all appropriate measures to protect American lives and property. George Yeh handed Rankin a note that said the ROC "accepts full responsibility for the losses caused." Yeh and Governor C. K. Yen both expressed "sincere shame and regret" to Rankin personally. In the meantime, the ROC provided a temporary location for the U.S. embassy and promised compensation.[26] Chiang Kai-shek met with Admiral Ingersoll and General Bowen to express "deep regret" for the incident, a desire to maintain good relations with the United States, and the need for the ROC to have the tools to control mobs.[27]

Then Chiang Kai-shek took personal responsibility for the riots. On June 1, he gave a radio speech in which he called Black Friday "one of the most shocking and most regrettable things" that had happened in the last fifty years. It was an unfortunate incident that "left on our national prestige and dignity a stigma not easily removed." He declared that his leadership was to blame. He understood why his people were angry with the Reynolds acquittal, but added: "No citizens of a modern and civilized nation should have sacked the Embassy of a foreign power and torn the flag representing that power," bringing "dishonor" to the nation. He insisted that his government and the United States remained close friends and declared that America had never committed aggression against China, always working to prevent its partition by foreign powers. Chiang held his security officials responsible for failure "to adopt precautionary measures at the outset" and for not taking "resolute steps" to deal with a situation that evolved from "peaceful demonstration into . . . mob violence."[28]

These efforts seemed to have little impact on the Americans. While they debated high policy at home, U.S. officials in Taiwan, in the heat of anger and sense of betrayal, were convinced that Black Friday represented an organized protest against Reynolds's acquittal. Rankin asked Chiang Kai-shek "why our Embassy had been left in the hands of an unarmed mob for several hours despite the large police and army resources available." Rankin suggested an answer: "that the organizers of the attack had sufficient influence to prevent effective action by the police." Chiang disagreed, blaming the riots on officials who were unwilling to accept responsibility. Otherwise, Chiang did not answer Rankin's question, and by his own admission in his diary he could not face Rankin's "stern rebuke."[29]

At a press conference held on May 27, George Yeh denied that either the ROC or any political organization was responsible for instigating the riots. Instead, the riots were an expression of "public resentment" against the verdict. Admiral Ingersoll retorted that the "verdict in Reynolds case is nothing more than an excuse to execute a plan already formulated." In a separate report, he observed, "It appears much more probable that the Reynolds case was exploited by someone or some group and that at least some advanced planning took place."[30]

There were several reasons to believe that the protests had been planned before the U.S. military court announced its verdict. Operation Fist kept military assets far from Taipei, and possibly allowed crowds to gather by the thousands in the area near the U.S. embassy because the numerous air-raid alerts held from 7:00 A.M. to nightfall disrupted their normal routine. (On the other hand, other reports suggested the purpose of the exercise was to divert people's attention from the Reynolds verdict and prevent violent incidents.[31])

Furthermore, newspaper articles appeared on Black Friday that both the Americans and British described as "inflammatory." According to Franklin, the articles suggested that the trial had been "rigged" and the verdict was "wrong and unjust." He added, "This view of the trial was shared by Chinese of all classes from the pedicab coolie at the bottom of the social ladder to Chiang Kai-shek at the top."[32] Particularly galling to many in the American community, including the TDC, were the articles written by Bob Brown of United Press International that allegedly "added fuel to the Reynolds' fire." Brown quoted unnamed sources that complained, for example, about how the prosecution sat on its hands, and wrote that Liu Ziran knew Reynolds. U.S. Navy sources observed that Brown was, "as were all Chinese pressmen, extremely biased in this case." Other foreign newsmen in Taipei told U.S. authorities that Brown's reporting verged on "libel and contempt of court."[33] Supposedly, Brown's "highly critical and inflammatory" articles gave the Chinese an opening to attack the Americans. It is true that Chinese journalists protected Brown from being beaten during the embassy riot, telling protestors that he was a friend and a man whose writings about the case were "impartial." However, a U.S. investigation later concluded that there was no evidence that Brown's pieces had any impact on the local Chinese press.[34]

Besides the inflammatory press, there was the presence of many key individuals that all pointed to careful choreography and orchestration. Ao Tehua's lone protest looked as if she "had been put up to it." Her protest sign allegedly "was literate and quite professionally done" and "indicated prior preparation." Information supplied to the U.S. embassy suggested that two Chinese reporters produced it and coached her.[35] The *San Francisco Chronicle,* known for being critical of Chiang Kai-shek, pointed to the reporter playing Ao Tehua's "vitriolic denunciation of the U.S." to the crowd, "well-dressed men" agitating the crowd, and slogans written in English on the embassy walls, such as "Chinese with blood in their veins want a few Americans lives." Colonel Barker, whose home was stoned the night before, noted that many of the rioters were students from three particular schools, suggesting that both the protests and riots were "well planned in advance." Several American journalists reported that Catholic priests were given advance warning not to go on the streets that day, though Catholic Missionary Fathers who taught at National Taiwan Normal University had no idea the riots had occurred. William Lederer, a former U.S. Navy officer and coauthor of the book *The Ugly American,* claimed that Chinese families admitted that their children had been lectured on "American imperialism" and instructed on where to assemble before marching to the embassy.[36] Rioters brought slogans that were posted on embassy property, and eyewitness accounts spoke of alleged "professional agitators" who organized the crowd and handed out money. Small groups of protestors were primarily responsible for the damage inflicted at the embassy and USIS, and none of it seemed random. Henry Bonner observed shortly after the embassy riot that it was "almost impossible to describe the extreme thoroughness of the destruction. It was so methodical that I cannot believe that it was not premeditated."[37]

Another sign of preplanning or collusion were reports that the ROC military and police simply stood by and did nothing. Several months after the riots, James P. Richards, special assistant to President Eisenhower for the Middle East, traveled to Taiwan to investigate the causes of Black Friday. There, he noted that the CIA had photographs that revealed that the "police made no real effort to control the mob."[38] Just before the wave that rooted out the Americans in the embassy shelter, Howard Jones, who tried and failed to enter the building during the riot, saw "a tank within one block of the Embassy with guns pointing into the air. The two or three men visible on the tank were smiling in the direction of the Embassy. A fire truck stood at the other side of the street but the personnel were passively watching the mob throwing furniture out the Embassy's windows. . . . I did not see any effort whatsoever to disperse the crowd." Jones said that the police acted like "spectators and seemed in most cases to be thoroughly enjoying the sight." The Philippine military attaché and other eyewitnesses also reported seeing soldiers and trucks idling near the embassy.[39] Some suggested that the police did not use force for fear of alienating the people. When Colonel Barker asked why during the embassy riot's peak the police and military did not take "positive action," he was told, "We must only take action we can explain to our people." In other words, if the police had used force as the Americans expected, Chinese protestors, legislators, and the press would have faulted the government for severely punishing people for expressing their outrage against what they and the government agreed to be an injustice. Indeed, when George Yeh met with lawmakers at the Legislative Yuan during the riots, "Emotions . . . were very much aroused" against the Reynolds verdict.[40]

One of the more revealing signs that the embassy riot had been planned occurred when Bonner and Jerry O'Grady were trapped in the embassy garage. A captain in the FAP sat down with them around 3:15 P.M. to assure them that they were safe. The officer launched into a long monologue of how Reynolds was guilty and "that this 'demonstration' was right" because the "Chinese people were very angry." Americans were wrong to demand diplomatic immunity for their military personnel. When Bonner asked if the protest had been planned, the officer answered in the affirmative, saying that his orders were to not use weapons or tear gas against the protestors and to ensure that no Americans were killed. The captain related that over the past year he had worked several cases involving rape and beatings by American soldiers that the U.S. government ignored. Bonner was struck by how pleased the captain was with the riot and the destruction of the embassy. Wearing no sidearm, the captain returned to say that a Chinese flag flew over the embassy and that the Americans in the air-raid shelter had been driven out with injuries. When Bonner asked him if the riot resulted from more than just the Reynolds verdict, the policeman answered yes: "this had been building up for some time."[41]

If planning had been made well in advance, who would have been responsible? At a June 5 press conference, Eisenhower suggested that although there were "signs of organization behind it, no one knows what."[42] Dulles sent Edwin Plitt, a career Foreign Service officer who once headed the international police force in Tangiers, to Taipei to convey Dulles's puzzlement as to why it took the ROC six hours to restore law and order despite all the police and military assets within a fifty-mile radius. Were the riots organized? Were they the result of a communist plot? What precisely was Liu Ziran's back-ground?[43] Representative Walter Judd (R-MN), a former missionary to China and a strong supporter of Chiang Kai-shek, believed that Americans wanted answers to the following questions: Who warned missionaries and other Americans to stay off the streets on May 24? Who wrote Ao Tehua's placard and told her to go to the U.S. embassy? Who led the waves of rioters into the U.S. embassy? Who tore down the U.S. flag?[44]

Outside of Taiwan, journalists suggested the protests were communist inspired. Conservative radio host Fulton Lewis claimed evidence of "very definite fingerprints of anti-American, probably communist incitation." George Sokolsky, an old China hand of fourteen years, wrote that the riots were not spontaneous, but communist orchestrated and timed to coincide with debates in the United States to end the trade embargo with the PRC. Sokolsky believed that Liu Ziran was a peeping tom: "all human beings enjoy the bizarre and Chinese of the lower classes do not regard nudity as a sin." However, a communist started a rumor that Chinese were fair game for armed U.S. soldiers, creating the riots. Since Chiang Ching-kuo provided security for Taiwan, Sokolsky demanded that Chiang Kai-shek either deport or "decapitate" all communists on the island, or fire his son "because Americans do not need to take this kind of thing from any country."[45]

Harold Hinton, a former U.S. military intelligence expert who worked for the RAND Corporation, believed that the protests were instigated by either the ROC or the PRC, or possibly both. He pointed to rumors, not denied by the ROC, that Chiang Ching-kuo had been in Beijing trying to make a deal with the communists. Two top American journalists had reported the previous February that Chiang Ching-kuo was negotiating to unify with the PRC but retain Taiwan as an autonomous province. (In fact, subordinates of both Chiang Ching-kuo and Chiang Kai-shek met with PRC foreign minister Zhou Enlai in July 1956 and April 1957, respectively, to discuss national unification and the idea of an autonomous Taiwan controlled by Chiang Kai-shek, but nothing came of the talks.[46]) In Hinton's mind, the Matador missile deployment was the real trigger of the protests, and the PRC and Chiang Ching-kuo's police state collaborated to drive the Americans out through riots because force was otherwise not an option.[47]

The view that communists were involved either as saboteurs or as ROC collaborators was a minority one. Most tended to blame elements of the ROC government. The day after the riots, Rankin told a Foreign Ministry official that three organizations in Taiwan were capable of using young people as tools in such instances: the Ministry of Defense's General Political Warfare Department, the IRP, and the Youth Corps. Rankin claimed that as a diplomat to the Soviet Union he had seen the same type of government mobilization get out of hand. There was reason to believe that Liu's colleagues at the IRP were behind the riots. According to Rankin, the IRP's purpose was to help individuals "develop national or 'revolutionary' spirit which is praiseworthy to a degree but can lead some people to excesses in crisis." Whoever they were, he concluded that, taking advantage of "differences in US-Chinese legal conceptions, and in anticipation of not guilty verdict, certain persons with some influence and connections prepared for demonstration at Embassy." When these protestors found only a few policemen, who had orders not to shoot on the crowd, they exploited the opportunity to attack the embassy. Yet Rankin had no hard evidence that Liu's colleagues instigated the riots.[48] Although U.S. officials could not entirely eliminate the IRP's involvement, they only had evidence that suggested that someone had organized the Youth Corps.[49]

While the Americans could not agree as to who would have given the order, two names that came to mind for many were of course Chiang Kai-shek and his son, Chiang Ching-kuo. The motivation would have been to send the message to the Americans and the ROC's neighbors that the Chiangs were not puppets of the United States. Mao Zedong, the leader of the PRC, certainly concluded that the Chiangs wanted to send such a message. Along similar lines, an unnamed liberal member of the Legislative Yuan, who blamed the one-man dictatorship in Taiwan, asserted that Chiang Kai-shek admired Syngman Rhee, president of South Korea, for his "talent for tweaking the American nose with impunity," and helped his son to engineer the demonstration in order to test U.S. resolve to back them. Xu Fuguan, editor of the *Democratic Review* and a professor at Tunghai University, told embassy officials that like the fashion show protest of 1955, "the May 24th riots [were] another slap at the American face and a further indication to President Chiang that he can flout the United States with impunity." One of Chiang Kai-shek's biographers has speculated that the generalissimo viewed the riots with satisfaction because they revealed he was no puppet of the United States.[50]

This left Chiang Ching-kuo, the man many Americans regarded with deep suspicion and viewed as the "sinister" master planner of Black Friday. In addition to being heir apparent, he certainly dominated the ROC's military and security apparatus. In fact, Chiang Ching-kuo headed each of the three organizations that Rankin believed capable of organizing the riots. Opponents of Chiang Kai-shek (including liberal Chinese politicians who supported a Third Force and Taiwanese demanding independence) naturally accused him of engineering them. James P. Richards learned from Chinese informants that Chiang Ching-kuo knew about the organized protest but never anticipated the attack on the embassy. When Richards personally reiterated to Chiang Kai-shek the accusation that Chiang Ching-kuo's Youth Corps was involved, the generalissimo made no comment.[51]

Some ROC officials claimed that Chiang Ching-kuo took advantage of the situation to attack the embassy and the USIS offices in order to embarrass the government's over-reliance on the United States. Ma Fuliang, a Western-educated former diplomat who now served as a Near East expert to Chiang Kai-shek, implicated Chiang Ching-kuo in the riots for that reason, saying Black Friday was planned at the IRP. Supposedly, Chiang Ching-kuo wanted to discredit the liberal ROC cabinet, who were described by Rankin as composed of "Western-educated Chinese who are ipso facto regarded with suspicion by many if not most of the old school." Several in the cabinet, especially Premier O. K. Yui and George Yeh, were criticized for backing the United States. Rankin believed that the Reynolds case simply gave someone the opportunity "to discredit them, and prepare [the] way for [a] cabinet along more traditional lines, possibly including old time military figures."[52] Finally, others suggested that Chiang Ching-kuo tried to carry out a coup d'état against his father. Even Mao Zedong later made such a claim.[53]

Another theory was that Black Friday was somehow connected to the drawn-out SOFA negotiations. Rankin observed that the Reynolds case and a similar one in Japan "contributed to public awareness here that US forces in Free China at present enjoy diplomatic immunity of unusual character." This and the "existent background of Chinese sensitivities, particularly lack of hope for the future and resentment against anything suggestive of extra-territoriality, provided ready base for popular reaction against Reynolds and the verdict of court martial." Rejecting the claim that the riots were a "spontaneous outburst," General Bowen blamed the Chinese press and members of the Legislative Yuan for denouncing the trial and railing against the "evils of diplomatic immunity" in a manner that inflamed "the man on the street."[54]

There was a consensus among many U.S. officials that the riots were a deliberate attempt to make an issue out of U.S. troops as a way of gaining leverage against the United States and forcing an agreement. Joseph Brent also thought the ROC wanted a "harmless show of popular sentiment" against both the verdict and the drawn-out status of forces agreement negotiations. ROC Foreign Ministry officials allegedly admitted to William Lederer that government officials hoped to establish that U.S. courts were unfair and that they used the protest to gain political advantage during the SOFA talks. CIA director Allen Dulles saw no evidence of communist influence, nor did he hold Chiang Ching-kuo responsible for instigating the protests. He did think that Ao Te-hua had "official backing" and that ROC officials reportedly viewed with "satisfaction" a series of events that had been "carefully planned" so as to put pressure on the United States, but then matters got out of hand. Dulles added that Reynolds's acquittal "touched Chinese National feeling at a very tender spot—namely, hatred of extraterritoriality." His brother, John Foster Dulles, did not rule out such a possibility: "We were even now negotiating a status-of-forces agreement with the Chinese National Government."[55]

Even if some Americans were convinced that elements of the government were behind the protests, no one could confirm that the events were indeed orchestrated. "A major difficulty in accepting the theory of deliberate instigations of the rioting by officially connected Chinese groups or individuals," a State Department official noted, "is the lack of clear evidence concerning possible motives for such action." Was this an effort to force the United States to give up "exclusive jurisdiction"? Were there individuals seeking classified documents to learn the direction of U.S. policy toward the ROC? Was it a "protest against U.S. curbs on Nationalist military activity"? Was it an effort to provoke an incident with the United States to force the ROC to negotiate with the PRC?[56] Americans could only speculate and theorize. They still had many questions, and they were not happy with the Chinese answers.

Chiang Kai-shek and Dwight D. Eisenhower greet one another in Taiwan during Eisenhower's 1960 Asian tour. (Photograph courtesy of the Dwight David Eisenhower Library)

Chiang Ching-kuo, son of Chiang Kai-shek, and his Russian wife, Fiana, prepare to fly to the United States in 1953 for their first American visit. During the 1950s, many Americans viewed Chiang Ching-kuo with suspicion and blamed him for outbreaks of anti-Americanism, including the May 24 protests. (Photograph courtesy of the Associated Press)

U.S. Ambassador Karl Rankin and Vice President Richard Nixon shake hands during Nixon's visit to Taiwan in 1956. In his five years as ambassador, Rankin persistently warned that the large number of American civilian and military personnel and agencies created the perception of Taiwan as an American colony. (Photograph courtesy of Princeton University Library)

In 1951, Major General William C. Chase arrives in Taiwan. During his four years as the first head of Military Advisory and Assistance Group-Taiwan, he not only oversaw the expansion of the number of MAAG advisors but proposed that their dependents be permitted to live in Taiwan with diplomatic immunity. (Photograph courtesy of the Central News Agency)

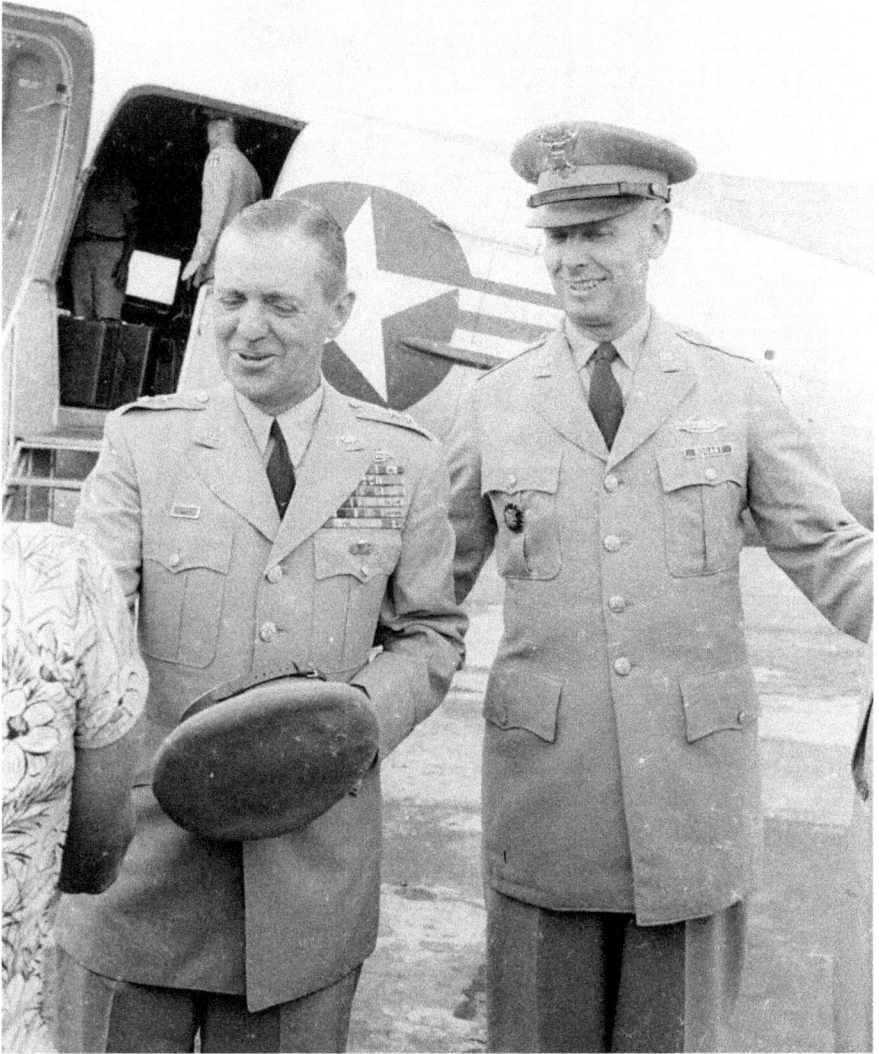

In 1956, Major General Frank S. Bowen (*left*) succeeded General Theodore F. Bogart as head of MAAG-Taiwan. Bowen opposed not only the court-martial of Sergeant Robert Reynolds, but giving any financial compensation to the family of Liu Ziran. (Photograph courtesy of the Central News Agency)

Sergeant Robert Reynolds, his wife, Clara, and daughter, Shirley, arrive at Travis Air Force Base on May 27, 1957, following his court-martial acquittal of voluntary manslaughter in the shooting death of Liu Ziran. (Photograph courtesy of the Associated Press)

Chinese and American investigators stand outside the duplex home of Sergeant Robert Reynolds, located on Grass Mountain, in the area where Reynolds claimed he confronted a peeping tom who approached him twice in a threatening manner, once after being shot. (Photograph courtesy of the National Archives and Records Administration)

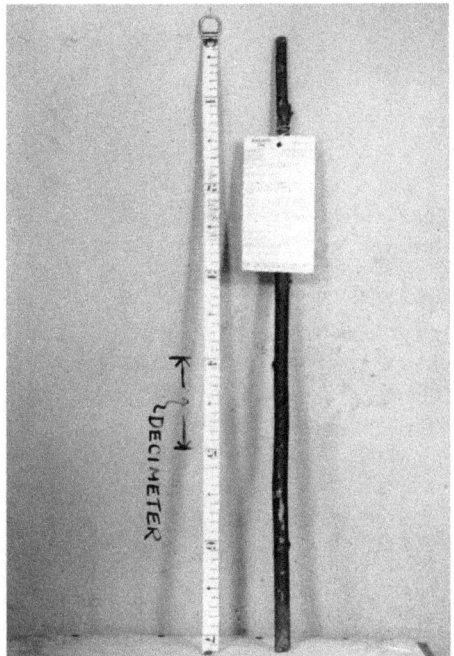

Sergeant Robert Reynolds claimed that his attacker initially wielded a three- to four-foot pipe. Only this two-foot-long stick was found in the area where Liu Ziran collapsed after being shot the first time. U.S. military investigators insisted that Liu Ziran wielded this as a weapon despite its not matching Reynolds's description. (Photograph courtesy of the National Archives and Records Administration)

Liu Ziran's body, after being turned over on its back by Chinese investigators, laid less than two hundred feet from Reynolds's front yard. Because Liu's head pointed toward Reynolds's duplex, the Chinese procurator argued that he had not collapsed while running away from a second mortal wound, but rather had been approached and eliminated at close range while facing his killer. (Photograph courtesy of the National Archives and Records Administration)

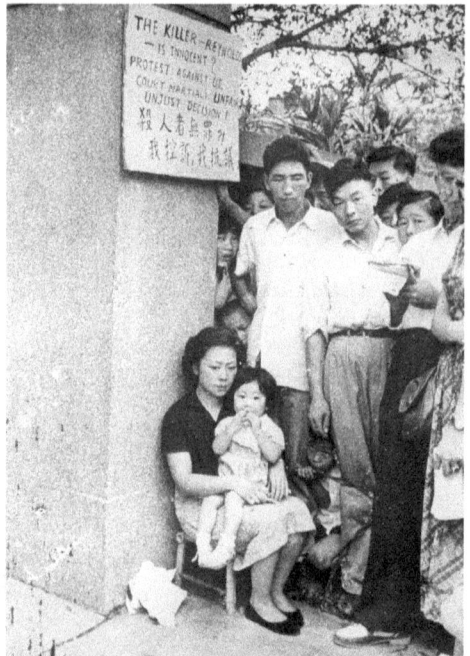

Liu Ziran's widow, Ao Tehua, and their daughter sit at the U.S. embassy while surrounded by reporters and bystanders. Ao Tehua refused to either enter the embassy or leave the gate, in order to protest Reynolds's acquittal. (Photograph courtesy of Princeton University Library)

Hundreds of onlookers watch as students from a nearby high school shout slogans and carry placards written in English and Chinese that condemn the Reynolds verdict and diplomatic immunity for U.S. advisors. The fact that the students were members of the Chinese Youth Anti-Communist National Salvation Corps (or Youth Corps) convinced Americans that the protest was staged by government officials. (Photograph courtesy of Princeton University Library)

Protestors stand on the U.S. embassy balcony after tearing down the American flag and replacing it with those of the Republic of China. The smaller sign, taken to the embassy by students, reads in Chinese "*Kangyi Meijun miaoshi renchuan*" (Protest American GI disregard for human rights) and in English "We Demand Fair Justice!" The Chinese on the white sheet reads "*Pengyo buxia ren! Xiaren changming! Meiguo buneng xue Edi*" (Friends don't kill. Killers pay with their life. America should not imitate Russian imperialism!) (Photograph courtesy of the Central News Agency)

Protestors do significant damage to the U.S. embassy while thousands, including police and military officials, look on. (Photograph courtesy of the Central News Agency)

ROC foreign minister George K. C. Yeh takes questions from reporters during a press conference held shortly after the May 24 riots. Yeh, who demanded that Reynolds be retried, incensed U.S. officials by choosing to meet with members of the Legislative Yuan rather than assist the Americans besieged at the embassy. (Photograph courtesy of the Central News Agency)

This Herb Block political cartoon depicts Senator William Knowland (R-CA), known as the "Senator from Formosa," lobbying the Eisenhower administration to provide Chiang Kai-shek with more U.S. aid before being hit by a brick that reads "Anti-American Riots in Formosa." Uncle Sam asks, "Oh. You were saying ____?" (A 1957 Herblock Cartoon, © The Herb Block Foundation)

In December 1957, Specialist Third Class William S. Girard and his wife, Haru "Candy" Sueyama, prepare to depart California for his hometown in Illinois. In January, he had killed Sakai Naka as she scavenged for spent shell casings. The Girard case and the Reynolds case became intermeshed to the extent that the May 24 riots led Eisenhower to make the controversial decision to allow Japan to try Girard in its court system. Although found guilty, he was given a three-year suspended sentence. (Photograph courtesy of the Associated Press)

11

To the Chinese Heart of the Matter

The accusations that a conspiracy involving elements of the ROC government led in whole or in part to Black Friday angered the Chinese, especially the generalissimo, who described U.S. officials in his diary as "irrational" and engaging in "unreasonable wild talk."[1] In particular, Chiang bristled when U.S. officials would not directly accuse his son of masterminding the riots. Instead, they made comments implicating Chiang Ching-kuo. Chiang Kai-shek believed that the United States took this approach to avoid a rupture in relations, but he described the Americans as pitifully "stupid, immature, suspicious" for not speaking directly, and he found it difficult to be on friendly terms with people unwilling to speak their mind. George Yeh explained to Rankin that Chiang Kai-shek could not understand why the Americans would even suspect his son. If the accusations were true, Chiang Ching-kuo "would have been acting against the interests of the State and against himself," i.e., Chiang Kai-shek.[2]

The criticisms leveled at the Chinese leader by the American media, particularly the *New York Times*, led him to write with bitterness in his diary that these people viewed him as unprofitable or useless. Meanwhile, it was difficult to control the anti-American sentiment prevalent throughout Taiwan after the Reynolds verdict. In reaction to claims that the protests were organized, Chiang noted that an "uncivilized demonstration" that destroys another nation's flag and embassy, violating international law, is an act that no government plans. Only communist countries engaged in such acts. The criticisms left Chiang Kai-shek rather depressed.[3]

Although the political stakes were high, ROC officials fired back with explanations and recriminations. The official Chinese version of what happened on Black Friday put the blame back on the United States and rejected claims that the protests were government organized. On June 14, Premier O. K. Yui's cabinet gave its report to the Legislative Yuan. The report described Liu Ziran's killing and presented what Chinese officials believed to be the events of that night in March. Then it provided a synopsis of efforts taken by the ROC to convince U.S. authorities to hold the trial "in a just and expeditious manner," implying delay on the part of U.S. authorities to hold a court-martial.[4] As for the trial itself, the report criticized the work of Captain Talbot, the prosecutor: "Throughout the trial, the manner in which the Trial Counsel questioned the defendant and handled evidence often left the people with the impression of being far from thorough." The verdict thus led to "widespread resentment among people of all walks of life."

The report pointed to evidence that the embassy riot was a spontaneous event. Only a few people were in front of the embassy when Liu's widow appeared to make her protest, but as the crowd grew larger, it attracted even more people, creating a snowball effect. As people gathered, they became incensed and let their "unreasoned emotion" get out of control. Indignation and resentment against the Reynolds verdict "developed unconsciously into a nationalistic sentiment." The report asked: if the riot was preplanned, why did it take three and half hours from the arrival of Liu's widow to the time that the first stones were thrown, and why another hour and twenty minutes before protestors entered the embassy? Why were the USIS buildings attacked so late in the day? Why were most American homes unmolested? None of this suggested prior planning.

As for the accusation that middle school students or the Youth Corps were the primary protestors, the report explained that the eleven injured protestors ranged in age from sixteen to forty-six, and hailed from several Chinese provinces: Taiwan, Fujian, Zhejiang, Liaobei, and Jilin. Their occupations varied from "office boys, salesclerks, pedicab drivers, printing shop workers, to editors, students and trades people." Of the 111 arrested, their ages also ranged from sixteen to forty-six. They too were natives of numerous Chinese provinces and consisted of "lower-level government employees, tailors, workers, drivers, farmers, trades people, office boys, peddlers, reporters, students and a number of unemployed." (In fact, two students, ages thirteen and fourteen, were arrested, but later released.[5]) The ROC could not see how it was possible that such a disparate group of individuals could organize and implement a prearranged plan.

The report acknowledged the presence of students, and admitted that they were "almost unanimously dissatisfied with the not-guilty verdict." However, students generally limited their protests to speeches and writings. Both the Ministry of Education and the Youth Corps advised students on the Reynolds case and tried to channel their feelings in order to prevent disturbances. Internal ROC documents show that the night before the riots, a warning went out to the Youth Corps that any protests could damage U.S.-ROC relations.[6] Nevertheless, fifty students from Cheng Gong High School left school premises without permission (purportedly their principal was ill) and marched by the embassy carrying placards, but they did not shout slogans, nor did they join the mob.[7] High school students who were unable to reach their respective campuses because of the air raid drill stopped at the embassy, as did students who left school to go home for lunch. These students, who wore uniforms and carried satchel bags, "out of curiosity at first and later under the spell of the mob psychology, followed the crowds into the Embassy and participated in their senseless acts of violence." In an attempt to counter the American accusation that the Youth Corps organized the embassy riot, the report asserted that all students in senior high school and above wore the Youth Corps insignia on their sleeves. It further argued that the facts presented "should serve to prove that the students' participation in the riots was not pre-arranged or organized."

Just prior to or after the fiftieth anniversary of Black Friday, those who protested or tried to control the protests wrote blogs or were interviewed by journalists for reminiscences about that day. A Cheng Gong High School student who spent the rest of his life in the United States as a university professor remembered that, as president of the student government association, he informed his classmates of the acquittal. They were all upset by what they deemed to be an unfair verdict and decided, with encouragement from their teachers, to "make a statement." A Chinese teacher who taught English helped them make up signs in English and picked out the route to march to the embassy. By then, of course, students and other protestors were already in front of the embassy. When a school administrator informed him that a Youth Corps meeting had been cancelled because of what was happening outside the embassy, he tried to stop the planned protest, but his classmates left on their own accord. In fact, the U.S. embassy managed to obtain an announcement made by the Youth Corps headquarters that went out at 4:00 P.M. on Black Friday informing all Youth Corps branches that "because of the illegal actions of a few unlawful elements, the sudden outburst is enlarging and changing its nature" and all parades and protests were "strictly prohibited."[8]

Another Cheng Gong High School graduate remembered having no interest in attending class after reading of the verdict in the newspaper. The student immediately bought paper to make posters to express his anger. He joined that group of students, accompanied by a teacher and school counselor, who marched to the embassy in the afternoon. Among them were individuals who made their names in a variety of careers: a diplomat, a professor of law at National Taiwan University, a novelist, a newspaper bureau chief, a deputy chief of the Ministry of Finance, and a famous doctor and legislator. They were joined by a future advocate for Taiwan independence who just happened to be at a nearby cram school preparing for the university entrance examination. Another helped the ROC in the 1970s to develop its Science and Technology Park and remembered the Liu Ziran Incident as instilling in him the idea that the ROC needed to become strong and powerful.[9]

Joining them were university students such as Chen Hanqiang, head of the student association at National Chengchi University, who blogged years later that rumors of Chiang Ching-kuo ordering students to carry out protests were untrue. No one gave him such an order. Chen insisted that he and fellow students spontaneously joined others from National Taiwan University and National Taiwan Normal University to oppose Americans having diplomatic immunity and the verdict.[10]

The report also explained why the police failed to control the crowd once it did become violent. It blamed a "lawless element" for inciting the crowd. Plainclothes policemen observed the ringleaders, but made no arrests for fear of inflaming the crowd against them. The FAP were told to protect the embassy but not use force. In the ten years since the February 28th Incident, the police had become complacent and were not proficient in using their assets to quell a mob. They reacted too slowly and the protest turned into a riot. Few policemen were on hand at the time. The Taipei police force numbered 1,321, but it was stretched thin by a heavy workload and by Operation Fist. Only a thirty-five-man mobile force was available, and it lacked training and equipment to deal effectively with a riot. At 6:30 P.M. on May 23, a message went out to all police stations in northern Taiwan to provide protection to foreigners after the Reynolds verdict, but otherwise no precautions were taken to prevent rioting. If the police had persuaded Liu's widow to leave the embassy, dispersed the crowd, or cordoned off the streets around the embassy, it is possible there would have been no incident. When the situation became desperate in the afternoon, the police were well outnumbered and in no position to stop the rioters. The day after the riots, one Chinese newspaper noted that the police were simply unable to suppress popular anger against perceived injustice.[11]

Then there was a breakdown in coordination between the civilian and military police that led to a crucial delay in which military policemen arrived only after the embassy had been thoroughly sacked. Troops were scattered by Operation Fist. Not until 2:00 P.M. did the Ministry of Defense learn that a mob was attempting to enter the U.S. embassy. The Peace Preservation Corps headquarters and the Taipei Garrison Command received orders to send forces to disperse the crowd and to protect Americans. At 2:30 P.M., General Peng Mengji ordered Liu Wei to allow Huang Zhenwu use of his MPs. Unfortunately, Huang hesitated to send in troops to put down the riot. Worse, both told Peng that all was under control at the embassy other than removal of the U.S. flag. When he learned the truth, Peng became extremely agitated with Huang, whom he described as "senile and insane," and with Liu Wei and Le Gan for their "totally ineffective" leadership. Two hours later, Peng ordered that three divisions be sent to Taipei.[12] By 5:00 p.m., Huang had two thousand men protecting U.S. military installations and homes, and a company of MPs had reached the embassy nearly a half hour before. Peng requested permission to use force, but not until after 6:00 p.m. did the cabinet finally relent. Even then, the cabinet refused to allow more Chinese troops to enter Taipei until nearly midnight. U.S. authorities in Taiwan believed that the cabinet delayed approval not only because it opposed the verdict and did not want to appear "too pro-American," but also because it feared that the use of troops might lead to a revolt by Taiwanese against the mainlanders.[13]

The report thus concluded that there was no evidence of a "planned or organized effort behind the incident," but rather it was an "unpremeditated emotional outburst." Without the preexisting anger against the Reynolds verdict, there would have been no riot. The report expressed regret for the mistakes, and acknowledged that the incident damaged ROC prestige. For obvious reasons, the report did not address specific accusations that internal elements, such as the IRP, were involved. Behind the scenes, the Foreign Ministry described the IRP as comparable to the U.S. National War College, and said that only senior military and civilian officials were eligible to take a "four-month long course on total mobilization against Communism." To say that IRP students were behind the riots was "uncalled for." Although the ROC refused to hand over official records regarding Liu Ziran or the IRP, George Yeh not only denied that the IRP was responsible for the riots, but insisted that Liu Ziran was merely a typist with the rank of captain, not major, and that he had an "all-round bad reputation."[14]

This nevertheless begs the question of whether there was a hidden hand—and if so, whose. Chiang Kai-shek certainly had his share of grievances with the U.S. government. He knew that many Americans wanted the "Chiang Clique" out of power, and that Washington would likely never wage a campaign to restore his government in China. The dependency on U.S. aid and the American attitude that came with it most certainly would have been galling. The riots could have been, at least at the highest levels of governments, simply another round in the long saga of tit-for-tat incidents that were part and parcel of alliance friction. Mao initially tolerated the unequal alliance relationship with the Soviet Union, including Soviet advisors who possessed diplomatic immunity, before throwing them out of China and ending the alliance.[15] Chiang Kai-shek could not do likewise: any potential payoff paled in comparison to the consequences. As an NSC assessment put it, "It seems highly improbable that any member of the highest echelons of the party and

government could have been privy to plans for violence for he would have recognized the damage to the GRC's vital interests which would result."[16]

There is no hard evidence that Chiang Kai-shek instigated the protest. If
anything, he seemed remote prior to the riots, leaving day-to-day matters in
others' hands. His diary says nothing about Liu Ziran or Sergeant Reynolds
until May 24. Although one of his biographers claims he looked upon the
riots with satisfaction, his diary reflects the concern of a leader who believes
that something had gone horribly wrong, anger that subordinates did not do
their jobs, and a genuine fear that the United States would change its policy
and use the riots as an excuse to oppose his leadership. Instead of a sense of
satisfaction, Chiang referred to the Taipei riots as a disgrace or humiliation
(*chiru*).[17] The protests did not enhance Chiang's standing as a world leader.
Indeed, Admiral Stump told him weeks later that Black Friday had severely
damaged his government's prestige.[18]

This leaves Chiang Ching-kuo, who obviously denied organizing the
riots. While having dinner at the home of Joseph Brent, he learned that the
embassy had already been gutted and the USIS buildings were under siege.
According to Brent, Chiang Ching-kuo was "genuinely perturbed" and left
shortly after 9:30 P.M. "with tears in his eyes." His wife remained behind, crying. Granted, Chiang's emotional outburst did not absolve him of complicity,
but to accuse him of trying to bring about a coup d'état raised the question
of why the son, who practically headed every security agency on Taiwan and
knew that he would eventually become a successor, would turn against his
father. To do so would have created a greater crisis for the alliance because
there was no guarantee the United States would recognize his leadership. In
the face of accusations that he engineered the riots, he later told Brent that
"anyone wanting to 'do something' would have been crazy to do it that way."[19]

Chiang Ching-kuo tried to fend off these accusations. He claimed that
the "inflammatory headlines" in Chinese newspapers following the verdict
led him to order the Information Bureau to stop further publication of such
articles. He told subordinates in the Youth Corps headquarters to prevent any
student strikes or demonstrations, to restrict protests to school campuses, and
to stay away from downtown Taipei. He insisted that approximately thirty
students, out of the thirty-three thousand Youth Corps members, had led a
silent parade to the embassy, but were led back to school by their teacher and
did no damage. (Alexander Boase, who saw Youth Corps students with his
own eyes in the afternoon, commented that Chiang's "statement requires a
'few grains of salt.'"[20]) Chiang denied that Liu Ziran was either a member of
the Youth Corps or an intelligence agent, and faulted the police for not taking action against Ao Tehua for fear of the journalists and public opinion.

He described the police as suffering from the mentality of the past, when mobs attacked policemen, and operating by the policy of "talk but do not take action" to avoid bloodshed and a psychology that "big affairs be transformed into small affairs, small affairs be transformed into no affair."[21]

If neither of the Chiangs was involved, could it have been the communists? In a conversation with Edwin Plitt, Chiang Kai-shek blamed Chinese authorities for allowing protests to get out of hand because they focused more on avoiding mistakes, were slow to act, feared taking responsibility, and saw no need to have the police open fire on the rioters. Yet, he faulted communist propaganda too.[22] The ROC embassy in Washington, D.C., pushed its government to find evidence of communist culpability. In a dispatch to George Yeh, Joseph Ku expressed concern that "so far our statements failed to give the satisfactory explanation" to the question, why did there occur a "sudden anti-American demonstration on an island supposed to be most friendly to the United States." Ku added: "It is important that we give the American people such an explanation. If we can attribute the riots to communist elements, people here would be more reassured." The ROC, though, never publicly accused communist instigators for Black Friday, and although Chiang Kai-shek initially claimed that several of those arrested were communists, he never raised the issue again. Three individuals with prior communist connections were arrested but ultimately were not blamed for hatching a communist plot. As time passed, Chiang faulted what he called "political opportunists," and only referred to communist propaganda or poison, not a specific communist conspiracy. The only instance of an ROC official blaming communists occurred when George Yeh commented that Ao Tehua came from a communist family who were active in the Chinese Communist Party. Otherwise, the issue was never raised again with the Americans. One suspects that if communists had been involved, Mao would have taken credit. The Americans never produced their own proof that communists tried to discredit the ROC. In fact, in December 1957 MAAG called Taiwan "the safest place in the orient today" in terms of susceptibility to communist subversion.[23]

In the weeks that followed Black Friday, ROC leaders (including Chiang Kai-shek) and government agencies held numerous meetings and did a postmortem of what happened, why it happened, and what could be done to prevent a similar occurrence. There was not necessarily soul-searching, because the government sympathized with the people. Still, the protests came as a total shock and there was an effort to be better prepared in the future. It is interesting that the government spent a good deal of time talking about the riots' root causes and future preventive measures that otherwise would have been superfluous if the protests and riots were orchestrated.

In particular, the Chinese press received blame for Black Friday. Of course, some believed the riots occurred because the press had otherwise been stifled by either the ROC or the United States. Greg MacGregor, a *New York Times* reporter stationed in Japan, blamed the ROC for not allowing its citizens to complain about wrongs perpetrated against them by U.S. soldiers or businessmen because the government wanted no trouble. MacGregor thought that five years of pent-up anger finally blew up over the Reynolds verdict. Bob Brown, who raised the ire of Americans with his critical reporting, likewise believed that anti-American feeling had been building, but because the press in Taiwan was so controlled and restricted by the ROC, there was "little criticism of the Americans." Thus, the court-martial and the ROC's displeasure with the verdict essentially opened the floodgates and allowed people to demonstrate without government interference until it blew up into rioting. Wang Dezhen, a member of the Legislative Yuan who held a graduate degree from the University of North Carolina–Chapel Hill and did translation work for USIS, faulted the United States's muzzling of the press as a factor behind the riots. She argued that if the newspapers had been allowed to publish all details and if citizens had been allowed to talk about the case on the streets, write letters to editors, and hold discussions, all of this would have released pent-up anger.[24]

ROC bureaus investigated the role of the press and discovered that after the Liu Ziran case occurred newspapers, including those that mentioned he was a typist, were ordered not to mention where he worked. They were also not to incite readers in a way that would harm U.S.-ROC relations and give the PRC's propaganda machine an opportunity to criticize the U.S. presence in Taiwan.[25] From early April to mid-May, articles related to the case were not inflammatory. After the verdict was read, many newspapers published stories with the large headline "Killer Is Not Guilty." The Nationalist Party's Central Committee issued instructions to three government papers, the *Central Daily News*, *China Daily News*, and *New Life*, to not write any editorials that would agitate readers. However, the government found it difficult to restrain privately owned newspapers in Taiwan and Hong Kong.[26]

Those responsible for trying to control the press never anticipated the reaction of citizens to what they perceived as an unfair verdict. At the time, there were two major stories being covered by the press: local elections and the China Ship Building Corporation's decision to rent out dock space to an American shipbuilding and dockyard firm. Readers ignored those stories and focused on the Reynolds case. No one anticipated that one or more reporters would record Ao Tehua and play back her anguished voice in a way that obviously touched people's hearts. The reporters by her side refused to leave as requested by the police. Eventually the people nearby reached an emotional state that made it impossible for the police to control them. After the riots, the government-controlled newspapers were instructed to not discuss ending martial law, the problem of the status of U.S. troops, and the Girard case in Japan, in which a U.S. soldier there had shot and killed a Japanese woman the previous January. Privately owned newspapers ignored government instructions to avoid inciting the people and instead emphasized the unfairness of the Liu Ziran case.[27]

The government did take some responsibility for the manner in which the protests were handled. The ROC leadership's chain of command did not allow subordinates the ability to take initiative. Chiang Kai-shek was miles away, apparently with little to no knowledge of the mood of the people or of any concerns that trouble could occur. Vice President Chen Cheng and Defense Minister Yu Dawei also were not in Taipei. When Richards explained that the CIA had photographs proving the "police made no real effort to control the mob," George Yeh remarked that the police could not fire without authorization from Chiang Kai-shek. In the end, Richards and other Americans faulted the centralization of power into the hands of Chiang Kai-shek for the slow response on the part of the ROC military and police to the events of May 24. Along similar lines, Chiang Kai-shek's self-analysis led him to believe that one of the great lessons of the riots was that the chain of command or line of authority was unclear.[28]

All of this, though, seems to be an excuse for failure to act. Although there is evidence of organization behind some of the protests, especially among the students, there is no proof that high officials ordered the people to engage in rioting. Some officials were just as genuinely surprised by the scale of the anger as the Americans. Nevertheless, the government was culpable. At the very least, the protests (if not the planning of the demonstrations) were tolerated because the gut reaction of most Chinese, regardless of where they lived, was to believe that the verdict was unjust.[29] This included government officials and military men, such as General Wang Shuming, whose diaries reflect the belief that U.S. advisors had extraterritoriality and that it was the unfair verdict that provoked the people.[30] As a result, those responsible for maintaining law and order sympathized with the people, and some were content to stand back and watch rather than intervene. High-level officials who remained in the capital preferred to be elsewhere during the critical moments when the protestors increased in number outside the embassy. George Yeh decided that dealing with angry legislators took precedence over any effort to assist the embassy. Premier O. K. Yui and other cabinet members kept their distance. Although Chiang Ching-kuo allegedly worried about rioting after the Reynolds verdict, he attended a social event at the embassy riot's peak and issued orders over the phone rather than moving to closer proximity to better assert command.

In sympathizing with their compatriots and tolerating (if not encouraging) the protests, the actions of ROC officials can only be described as reckless. They essentially allowed Pandora's box to open with almost no way to close it. ROC officials should never have allowed Operation Fist to go as planned and, as Chiang Kai-shek suggested in his diary, should have taken precautions. Instead, they did not fully appreciate the anger that many Chinese and Taiwanese felt about the verdict or the levels of frustration that existed among the people for one reason or another. Despite the assumption that Taiwan was a police state under the so-called iron hand of Chiang Ching-kuo, his grip on the people's mood or emotions was not that tight. Once the protests got out of control, the lack of assets, an inflexible chain of command, ineffective leadership, and a certain degree of complicity allowed the protests to spiral to the extent that the ROC was lucky that no American was killed. At times, policemen did take steps to prevent loss of life, including one who stopped rioters from setting fire to vehicles at the embassy.[31] Otherwise, the police were not prepared or equipped to take measures short of using lethal force.

Of course, some Americans would have preferred that they use lethal force. U.S. military officers suggested that the riots could have been prevented by a company of soldiers with orders to shoot. Although Chiang Ching-kuo claimed that he ordered those protecting the embassy to do everything necessary to stop the riot, one of his biographers argues that he ordered that the crowds not be fired upon. Years later, he allegedly told a subordinate that the Americans could always get a new embassy: "Better that than have the police in Ching-kuo's name shoot down citizens in the streets."[32] If true, this put him at odds with his own father while others took the blame and were relieved of command for failing to take initiative and use force. Not until the protestors became violent at the police station did force become an option. Otherwise, authorities were not about to use even minimal force, such as fire hoses, against their own people.

From the American point of view, this sympathy with the people was also evident in the treatment of those arrested. If the Chinese were unhappy with American justice, the shoe was now on the other foot. Of the 111 individuals arrested, seventy (half of whom were mainlanders) were released due to insufficient evidence. Besides fifteen middle school students ranging in age from thirteen to twenty-four, the occupations and interests of the rest consisted of car mechanics, tailors, barbers, a shop clerk, a waiter, a shoemaker, textile workers, law school students, etc. Forty-one were indicted, of which thirty-three were mainlanders. Their occupations varied if they had one. Some were merchants, office boys, peddlers, or pedicab drivers, and one was a Buddhist monk. Five were noted as having communist contacts at one time or another, including a newspaper editor who had joined the Communist Party and participated in an "anti-hunger and Anti-American movement" instigated by the communists before coming to Taiwan, where he wrote articles critical of the ROC. The ROC chose to try all of the defendants in a military court. Normally, military court trials were secret and closed to the public. Government authorities knew, though, that not only would U.S. embassy officials and journalists want to attend, but so would Chinese citizens.[33]

On June 18, trials for forty rioters commenced at the Taiwan Garrison Command's provost marshal's office. A three-judge panel was created for fourteen individuals arrested on more serious charges, while two courts with one judge apiece heard the rest. The newspaper editor suspected of being a communist agent was tried separately. Only three defendants hired civilian lawyers; all others were provided a court-appointed military legal counsel. Chen Zhengqiu, the real estate broker accused of leading the mob into the police station, defended himself and proved so eloquent in his cross-examination of witnesses against him that the court spent the entire day dealing only with his case. Unlike other defendants, Chen refused to stand before the court, but instead gave an hour-long speech from a table.[34]

The courts dropped the charge of rebellion and treason, while the U.S. embassy did not press any charges. Of the forty defendants, only Chen faced spending five years in prison for inciting mob violence. The rest were indicted for "insulting a foreign country" and destruction of property. A court spokesman announced that no one would receive the death penalty. On June 26, the judges passed their sentences. Of the forty, only twenty-eight were found guilty. Chen Zhengqiu and another individual were sentenced to one year in prison, the maximum penalty handed down against any of the defendants. The majority received a sentence of two to five months.[35] One newspaper editorial noted that while some wanted stiffer sentences, "it must be conceded that extenuating circumstances did seem to exist on May 24." There was no evidence that the riots were "preconceived," and the rioters were merely sucked into the "vortex of mob psychology."[36] In July, two others, both mainlanders and unemployed, were arrested for their involvement in the riots. To the chagrin of some in the U.S. embassy, the Foreign Ministry preferred not to hold another trial for fear it would "arouse the emotions of the people" and hinted that U.S. authorities should not press the ROC to make more arrests.[37]

None of this really answers the question of whether the protests were anti-American. Although the ROC officially referred to Black Friday as the "unfortunate incident," then and later, the protests and riots were labeled as "anti-American." On the American side, there was a conscious effort to publicly refer to events of that day as a "riot" and not "riots" to avoid "the bad psychological effect."[38] Internally, U.S. (and British) officials spoke in the plural when discussing Black Friday. Behind the scenes, Rankin found in Taiwan an "undercurrent of distrust and dislike of Western influences." Admiral Ingersoll agreed that anti-Americanism existed on Taiwan, though "not greater than expected in light of the numerous Americans obviously living on a much higher economic level than are the indigenous people." Although Chiang Kai-shek assured both Eisenhower and a U.S. senator that the riots were not a "case of anti-Americanism," the generalissimo privately viewed the actions of his people across the island as anti-American.[39] For both sides to publicly admit that the riots were inspired by anti-American protests put them in a political bind as allies and in terms of their global image. Such an acknowledgment would lend credence to communist propaganda of the U.S. domination of Taiwan and would have contradicted U.S. propaganda that it stood on the side of freedom.

Of course, there were manifestations of anti-foreignism along lines Americans could identify with historically. An attack against and near destruction of a U.S. embassy was fairly rare until the notion of taking hostages and launching terrorist attacks against U.S. embassies and consulates became more common later in the twentieth century. Besides the treatment meted out to embassy personnel, an ICA-Taiwan educational specialist was confronted that day by a menacing crowd that cursed his Chinese driver for "working for foreigners" and seemed "bent on some form of destruction" before the driver calmed them down. In another case, a mob gravitated to a hotel near the TDC's Sugar Building where Americans stayed. The crowd looked like it wanted to cause harm, but Ernest Moy confronted and persuaded the people to leave.[40] Then there were the physical attacks against embassy employees and English teachers and near attacks against other Americans, civilian and official alike. Even British subjects had to identify themselves as such to avoid the mob's fury, including Spencer Moosa, who was physically assaulted but not hurt after being mistaken for an American. The Western wife of a Filipino man riding in a pedicab escaped being attacked. Protestors went into the Luao Pub on Zhongshan North Road and attacked a bar girl who wore a Western hairstyle. Youth Corps members voluntarily skipped classes not only in Taipei, where they shouted "Drive Out the Americans," but also in Taichung and Tainan, where students demanded "U.S. GIs Get Out of Taiwan."[41]

From that perspective, it would seem that the riots were similar to anti-foreign movements that occurred in China in the nineteenth and early twentieth centuries, some of which were directed at Americans. The Boxer Uprising of 1900, in which foreigners were killed and the foreign legations in Beijing were attacked and put under siege until relieved by an international expeditionary force, came to mind fairly quickly. In addition, there were numerous other movements, including boycotts of U.S. goods, protests, and even incidents that led to the deaths of Americans. Such anti-foreignism, if it existed on Black Friday, would have naturally made the embassy a prime target.

It might also explain why the protestors gravitated to the USIS buildings. Not only did James Pilcher point to their geographic proximity to the embassy as well as City Hall Square, "a natural gathering place," but he acknowledged that Chinese connected USIS work with the embassy. In fact, the Chinese referred to it as "the Information Service of the American Embassy," using the term *xinwen zhu,* which carried "Chinese overtones of intelligence operations," to describe USIS. A few weeks before the riots, a Rotarian in Taichung came out against his chapter's support for the local USIS Reading Room, calling the USIS "an agent of 'cultural imperialism.'"[42]

Yet, not all Americans, even those at the center of the action, were physically attacked, including people who worked for U.S. agencies. Nor did the protestors try to destroy everything that represented America. Andrew Franklin noted that in Taipei "American goods and shops were unmolested." One shop still prominently displayed a photograph of President Eisenhower. Two days after the riots, U.S. flags flew over buildings without fear of destruction and two U.S. warships anchored in Kaohsiung, where sailors went ashore and were welcomed by locals.[43] Franklin spoke with numerous Chinese, including soldiers, who all thought he was an American and concluded that the protests were spontaneous and not anti-American. In June, the Taichung Municipal Council sent a communication to the U.S. Congress insisting that there was "no anti-American feeling among the Chinese people."[44]

Of course, it is quite possible that many were angry with U.S. policies in general, especially U.S. refusal to help the ROC attack the PRC. Many of those involved were indeed mainlanders, and less than one-third were Taiwanese. The verdict may have been a trigger to unleash pent-up frustration and anger that had brewed for years. James Pilcher certainly thought this also explained the attack on the USIS buildings. The Chinese wanted to recover the mainland, but USIS propaganda spoke of peace. The Chinese were frustrated with what they deemed to be "defensive policies" and turned the USIS into a "whipping boy." Government officials were already extremely frustrated with MAAG's policies and would have been angry if a representative of MAAG had killed one of their own and then was found not guilty. Then and later, it was suggested, mostly by Americans, that resentment against dependency on U.S. aid proved to be the main underlying factor for the riots.[45]

However, articles and editorials written by journalists, commentators, and learned Chinese and Taiwanese suggest that dependency was not the root cause of the protests. In fact, some Chinese felt a need to correct the record if Americans asserted otherwise. When Walter Judd suggested that Black Friday "reflected" smoldering anger against the American high standard of living, Ernest Moy made it clear that no such resentment caused the riots.[46]

What is clear is that the acquittal, not dependency, struck a raw nerve for the Chinese and Taiwanese.[47] The verdict created a sense of disillusionment. U.S. propaganda and Chinese perceptions of Americans were contradicted by American actions. In the words of one journalist in Bangkok, the Chinese now understood that Americans were "not so cute."[48] U.S. laws seemed barbaric in how they allowed killers like Reynolds to go free. One writer declared that while the United States was advanced scientifically, it remained behind other civilizations, philosophically speaking.[49] Another wrote that the Reynolds incident damaged the Chinese perception of the American spirit of democracy, freedom, and equality.[50] National Taiwan University students were compelled to write letters to the general public in which they protested the verdict and the American cheers that followed, cheers that one writer referred to as "uncivilized" behavior and "harm to justice."[51] People protested what they perceived as U.S. military injustice. The protests were portrayed as righting an American wrong, or they were anti-American in the sense that they expressed opposition to U.S. conduct or a human rights violation. People were angered by the partial jury and expected, in the interest of better U.S.-ROC relations, a retrial.[52] The Chinese appreciated U.S. aid, but they felt that as the leader of the Free World the U.S. should not damage the self-respect of the nations it helped through such verdicts.[53]

In many cases, those who participated in the rioting were reacting either to the verdict or to events as they unfolded, and were not part of any preplanned protest. Years later, a neighborhood chief in Banqiao remembered working as a cook at a small restaurant when he stepped outside and saw a large crowd moving toward the U.S. embassy, some shouting, "Drive out the Americans." He simply followed along with the crowd to the embassy, where much destruction had already occurred.[54] Chen Zhengqiu insisted that he only happened to be in the area after leaving a movie theater and joined the crowd outside the police station. He admitted to the court, "I was in the crowd. I was there talking and shouting simply because of my resentment over that American who killed a Chinese and was proclaimed not guilty." He added that he did not hate Americans nor was he anti-American. Another defendant claimed that he and three friends were near the U.S. embassy when they heard people say that the Reynolds verdict was unfair and that everyone should go to the embassy to protest. When he arrived, he watched students shout with emotion "Long live the Republic of China" and "Long live Chiang Kai-shek." A forty-three-year-old native of Shanxi who did temporary labor work for the U.S. 13th Air Force (Provisional) admitted that he entered the embassy and did some damage to express his anger against the verdict. The *United Daily* worker told Chinese judges that when he saw several women standing near the embassy crying and knowing about the verdict, he became angry and damaged embassy property. A man from Hunan acknowledged that the verdict moved him to go to the embassy to protest, though he never entered the grounds. An individual from Sichuan said that after he arrived at the USIS buildings he became angry when he heard someone say, "A foreigner killed a Chinese and is not guilty."[55]

Another issue very much on the minds of protestors and their supporters was diplomatic immunity, which only deepened the sense that the Americans perpetrated an injustice. Several Chinese and Americans told Ardith Miller that they agreed with a Chinese individual who said "it was not fair that the Armed Forces personnel could have diplomatic immunity enabling them to do practically anything and get away with it."[56] Besides setting an alleged killer free, diplomatic immunity essentially meant that Chinese and Taiwanese were second-class citizens on their own soil. One writer blamed diplomatic immunity for creating "unequal international relations."[57] The day of the riots, six hundred students and six professors from National Taiwan University's law school held a meeting to discuss the trial. In light of the Reynolds case and diplomatic immunity, students asked their professors if Taiwan was now a colony of the United States. The discussion led some students to yell, "Eliminate the unequal treaty."[58] Students at National Taiwan Normal University demanded their government do just that.[59]

In fact, ridding Taiwan of diplomatic immunity became a rallying cry of sorts. The editor of the *China Post,* who put so much trust in U.S. justice, wrote that that trust had been "misplaced." The not guilty verdict showed the need to revise the agreement with regard to diplomatic immunity. A Chinese lawmaker declared that the "No. 1 goal of the revolution was the elimination of extraterritoriality. . . . Just because someone is good to us does not mean we should casually give them extraterritoriality."[60] It was said that extraterritoriality was now a "historical relic" and the Reynolds case a "bloody lesson." To avoid another incident, the United States needed to surrender diplomatic immunity for its soldiers in Taiwan.[61] Newspaper writers and readers in Hong

Kong and Taiwan condemned diplomatic immunity as simply extraterritoriality, described the 1951 agreement as an "unequal treaty" that robbed the
ROC of the right to judge a killer, and demanded its cancellation.[62] It is no
surprise that the official Chinese report concluded that the Foreign Ministry should consider restricting diplomatic immunity and securing a SOFA.[63]

Even if the people were angered by the verdict, diplomatic immunity,
and the manner in which the United States meted out justice, not all Chinese
agreed with the behavior of their people. Many did feel shame and regret,
and a sense of doom for what had happened. Franklin spoke with Chinese
who thought the riots to be "suicidal," believing the "damage [to U.S.-ROC
relations] cannot be repaired." Opinion pieces in newspapers described the
unjust verdict or anger against diplomatic immunity as the root cause of the
protests, but called on people to calm down in the name of the U.S.-ROC
relationship.[64] On May 29, in what Joseph Brent described as "the tough-
est conversation" that he had with any ROC official, he listened as Defense
Minister Yu Dawei exclaimed, "once China was a great nation, with a great
culture and a great destiny, but then it started losing things—first territory,
then its unity, then its prestige, etc., until now. And now it has lost both its
self-respect and its great wisdom: 'The destruction of an Embassy cannot be
regarded as the act of a civilized nation.'"[65]

Not all Chinese felt that way. Overseas Chinese in Thailand were angry
that the ROC government even apologized. Did Chinese not have the right
to protest both the killing of another Chinese person by a U.S. soldier and
the acquittal? What right did the U.S. government have to lodge a protest?
Some who participated in the destruction of U.S. property might have been
embarrassed or remorseful, but they refused to apologize for the sentiment
behind the actions. The ROC expressed regret for the riots and the damage,
but that did not mean, in the words of an official document, "that the acquittal of Reynolds is no longer considered a miscarriage of justice."[66] Several
Chinese friends apologized to Ardith Miller for the riots, but also expressed
being "hurt by what they felt was an unfair verdict." In this respect, the people, like the government, blamed the United States for the riots because of
the not guilty verdict.[67]

Understanding the protests from this perspective helps explain why Taiwanese joined or led protests or participated in the rioting. In the case of
young Taiwanese students, one could argue they had been instilled or indoctrinated with a sense of nationalism by the Youth Corps. Those youths who
were arrested were few in number though. The rest were older with varied
occupations, and yet they too became angry and joined the protests. Possibly
this was a product not only of having been colonized by the Japanese for fifty

years before being liberated in 1945, but of what has been described as the assimilation, if not colonization, of Taiwan by the Nationalists.[68] Although some Taiwanese clearly identified with the Americans against the mainlanders for obvious reasons, others identified with mainlanders. They did so not because of pent-up frustration that they would not be able to recover the mainland, but rather because they shared that combination of resentment against American attitudes and a sense of injustice. A former embassy political officer who left Taiwan in 1956 certainly thought so. He argued that the Taiwanese now enjoyed a greater political freedom and economic status than they ever had before:

> But they still erupted into a furious rage against Americans who are their benefactors, their bankers and their protectors. Asians in general are convinced that they have a legitimate score to settle with the white man. In the case of Taiwan their anger was directed against the unending lines of flashy cars that push the plodding coolies off [the road], the American suburbs that sprouted on their rice paddies on [Grass Mountain], and against those Americans who never strayed from the paths connecting their compound, clubs and offices and whose attitudes towards "chinks" was obvious and humiliating. They were angry at the release of a white man who killed a Chinese. . . . The Formosa riot might have been organized, but the coolies would not have participated without a sense of hate and frustration.[69]

Of course, these comments were based on observations formed prior to the riots and may not be accurate. On the other hand, it is possible that the American presence had the effect of bringing some Chinese and Taiwanese closer together in terms of a shared nationalism or identity by standing up on behalf of Liu Ziran and Ao Tehua. Even if people knew of Liu's participation in the black market or that he was a womanizer, they still rallied to him and his family because the verdict was perceived as unjust. All of this suggests that if Chiang Kai-shek and the 2 million mainlanders were shipped off somewhere, leaving the Taiwanese with their American protectors, a similar incident could have occurred, possibly with similar results. Americans found it much more convenient to blame a communist or ROC conspiracy, dependency on U.S. aid, or ugly Americans than to accept the Chinese heart of the matter: that the U.S. military justice system and maybe the American conception of justice had been rejected.

12

Repercussions

While Washington and the ROC traded accusations and faced an alliance crisis, the acquittal of Sergeant Reynolds and the events that followed potentially had greater ramifications for the American position in Asia, where the riots gave the United States a black eye. In June, USIA reported that the riots became a "catalyst" for newspaper editors across Asia to criticize in "extensive and bitter tone" the U.S. military presence and make frequent use of the word "extraterritoriality."[1]

Black Friday could have negatively impacted the U.S. position in Asia in two respects. First, the United States could have been forced to remove the diplomatic immunity status of its MAAG advisors. There were fifteen hundred MAAG advisors in Southeast Asia, but host countries were, according to Frank Nash, "sensitive to charges that they are being controlled by the United States."[2] Washington faced the challenge of achieving the delicate balance between having enough advisors to defend allies against communist aggression and minimizing the number of advisors to avoid political problems. Second, the United States could have been pressured to grant further jurisdiction through existing or new SOFAs in the interest of keeping its troops and bases there. Black Friday proved to have greater repercussions for U.S. policy because it became intertwined with other cases involving U.S. GIs in Asia. Although the circumstances and the contexts behind these cases were very different, they exacerbated existing tensions where the question of jurisdiction was uppermost on Asian minds.

The most famous of these other cases occurred in Japan, a nation vital to America's Cold War containment policy. Frank Nash described Japan not only as the "northern anchor" of the United States' island chain of defense, but as a "great strategic prize" because it held "the most valuable US base complex in the Pacific area." In Japan alone, the United States used over 265,000 acres of land for naval bases, submarine sanctuaries, navy and USAF air bases, troop housing, and bomb and gunnery ranges. As of March 1957, there were nearly one hundred thousand military personnel, representing all military branches (half were air force), and over sixty-seven thousand dependents. These figures did not include personnel in Japan on rest and recuperation or who rotated through Japan to another assignment. On Okinawa, the United States had an additional twenty-five thousand military personnel and over eleven thousand dependents. Nash noted that Okinawa stood out as the "only place in the world where the United States is in control of a large foreign population and where the United States is therefore vulnerable to damaging charges of colonialism." Nash's base study did not detect any significant "irritations and points of friction" in Japan, and jurisdiction had never been a problem. On Okinawa, he claimed that "troop-community relations were good," though there were signs of resentment against colonialism, atomic weapons, and U.S. military installations. Nash nevertheless recommended treading lightly. While Japan was "essential to US security," what the United States did in Okinawa, the "very doorstep of Asia," had significant ramifications.[3]

Because of Japan's special place in America's containment policy in Asia, the United States needed to be sensitive to Japanese opinion. A study of U.S. troop withdrawal sentiments made by USIA in 1956 provided a slightly different picture of Japanese attitudes. In January 1956, USIA reported that 65 percent of 1,291 Japanese polled believed that the United States should withdraw from Japan. Of that number, 38 percent called for immediate withdrawal. When asked if they thought that U.S. bases were good for Japan, 51 percent responded that they were not good. Only 16 percent thought they were good. Of those taking a negative stance, 13 percent feared that Japan would be dragged into a war; 9 percent spoke of farming land being taken over or people living near U.S. bases having their land seized; 6 percent noted that morals near bases were lax; and 13 percent spoke of the noise made by bullets and shells, and incidents and accidents near bases. Unlike 39 percent of West Germans, who said the behavior of American soldiers was good (down from 54 percent in 1954), 49 percent of Japanese described GI behavior as fair and 14 percent as poor. On the other hand, only 2 percent thought that relations had worsened because of GI violence against Japanese or such behavior as throwing coins on the ground for children or pushing a woman into a river. Japanese who demanded immediate withdrawal tended to be better educated, male, aged 20–29, to live in a city of 200,000–600,000 on Hokkaido or to be from the Chugoku region of Japan's main island of Honshu, and to be members of the Socialist Party.[4]

The presence of so many American soldiers and dependents naturally led to tensions for different reasons. As in Taiwan, there was a gap in living standards between Americans and Japanese. Over twenty-five thousand Japanese women had married GIs since 1945, prostitution abounded around U.S. bases, and there were wage disputes involving either household servants or civilians working on the bases. Considerable resentment resulted from utilizing farmland for military purposes, and then there were the GI crimes. Since October 1953, American troops had committed approximately fourteen thousand offenses, but according to Douglas MacArthur II, the U.S. ambassador, Japan "ceded jurisdiction to us in all but four hundred and thirty. This is three percent compared to . . . the worldwide average in similar circumstances of twenty-eight percent."[5] The State Department credited the secret minute in the treaty with regard to waivers for that low percentage.[6] Nevertheless, the Japanese demanded jurisdiction in a particularly violent case that occurred in 1956. Japanese authorities arrested Private Orvis Boone of Galveston, Texas, for murder. Boone and his Japanese female companion lured U.S. soldiers into isolated areas, where he ambushed and robbed them. Boone killed a U.S. soldier in this manner, and later he and his female friend robbed and killed a Japanese woman. They burned down the woman's home to cover up their crimes. Boone received a fair trial in Japan and was sentenced to death.[7]

Around the same time, Japan demanded jurisdiction in a case that eventually captured world headlines and led to an alliance crisis with the United States. On January 30, 1957, almost two months prior to when Reynolds killed Liu Ziran, Specialist Third Class William Girard, a twenty-one-year-old native of Ottawa, Illinois, took part in a field exercise along with thirty other men belonging to Company F, 8th Cavalry Regiment. The five-foot-ten-inch, blue-eyed, brown-haired GI, who weighed only 160 pounds, had enlisted in the U.S. Army at age seventeen. Girard liked the army, wanted to reenlist, and enjoyed living in Japan, where he had developed a romantic relationship with a Japanese girl named Haru "Candy" Sueyama. The two had been together for nearly a year. Haru spoke little English, but she taught Girard Japanese phrases. Life in Japan seemed good for a young American who never completed a year of high school. Otherwise, Girard exhibited no exceptional qualities.[8]

On this particular day, Company F's field exercise occurred at what Americans called the Camp Weir range area. Eight square miles in size, the U.S. Army and Japan's Self-Defense Force shared the range, located near the village of Somagahara. When not in use, Japanese civilians were allowed to either farm the area or scavenge for brass shell casings. Girard and his squad members were to attack a hill defended by another squad. Although it was supposed to be a live-fire exercise, Colonel Herbert A. Jordon, the commanding officer, ordered his men to replace their live rounds with blank cartridges. Despite placing red boundary flags warning civilians to stay away, Jordon estimated there were over 150 men and women trying to gather spent shell casings. At one machine gun position, the gunner did not even have time to clear his weapon after he ceased firing before half a dozen civilians knocked him down in an effort to get the brass cartridges. The U.S. troops tried to shoo away the civilians, but to no avail, and no assistance from the local police was forthcoming.[9]

After Girard's squad played the role of both attacker and defender, his platoon leader, Second Lieutenant Billy Mahon, ordered Girard and Specialist Third Class Victor Nickel to guard a machine gun and field jackets left by some of the men in the company. Mahon noticed about thirty Japanese standing nearby, and worried they might steal something. Nickel thought they were harmless, and just collecting cartridges. Girard had a grenade launcher on his rifle. After he and Nickel took their position, Girard put a spent .30-caliber shell in the grenade launcher. Using his blank cartridge, he fired the empty shell casing from the launcher at a man in the act of scavenging empty cartridges. The shell passed harmlessly overhead. Then Girard spotted a woman named Sakai Naka also engaged in scavenging. He fired another .30-caliber shell, at a range of twenty to thirty yards, as she moved away from him. The shell hit the woman in the back, penetrating 3.5–4 inches into her body, killing her.[10]

During the subsequent interrogation, Nickel denied knowledge and involvement in the incident. As for Girard, he insisted that he only fired one round over the head of the Japanese. Over time, both men changed their stories. Nickel admitted that he had thrown some shell casings out toward the Japanese, one as close as ten yards, to lure them closer to the machine gun. He claimed that Girard told him to throw the cartridges on the ground, and then he would fire over their heads and scare them away. Girard even allegedly called for the Japanese to come closer. When six moved in to pick up the cartridges, Girard stood up with his gun and took two steps. Thinking they were being chased, the Japanese started to run, including Sakai. At first, Nickel said that Girard held the gun at the hip at a forty-five-degree angle to fire over their heads and pulled the trigger. Later, he claimed that Girard fired from the shoulder. When the woman fell, Girard supposedly tried to get the Japanese standing nearby to carry away her body, and told Nickel to tell authorities that he had fired from the waist and that "we did not throw any brass." Girard, who qualified as a sharpshooter on the M1 rifle, told U.S. investigators that he knew that his weapon, when fired in that manner, was accurate at short distances. He denied both knowing the grenade launcher's "striking power" and intending to hurt the woman. He also denied telling Nickel to throw out the cartridges. A lie detector test given by U.S. authorities, however, showed that Girard lied when he said he neither threw out cartridges nor aimed at the woman.[11]

A major question arose: which country would exercise jurisdiction in this case? If he was on duty, then U.S. authorities could prosecute Girard. If he was not on duty, Japanese authorities could rightfully claim jurisdiction. Despite Japan's strategic importance and the need to treat it lightly, the U.S. Army quickly claimed jurisdiction. On February 7, Girard's company commanding officer (CO) issued a certificate to the chief procurator of Masbashi District stating that Girard was on duty when he shot the victim. He had been instructed by his platoon leader to guard a machine gun and, in the course of his duty, fired a shell casing as a warning to Japanese civilians in the area. If a court-martial were to be held, the Japanese would be notified.[12]

The next day, Japanese newspapers turned the event into front-page news with sensational stories that in some cases claimed that Sakai Naka's death was no accident. Socialists used the shooting to launch anti-U.S. base diatribes, organized rallies, accused Girard of "deliberate murder," and demanded that the Japanese government claim jurisdiction. Although the local U.S. military commander issued a statement expressing regret for the shooting, the press was not mollified. Prime Minister Kishi Nobusuke warned a U.S. embassy official that the shooting could damage U.S.-Japanese relations and that leftists were exploiting the issue to score political points at his expense. Kishi added that "jurisdiction, fair compensation and prevention of recurrence" were key issues. The embassy, with U.S. public opinion in mind, advised Kishi not to demand jurisdiction even if the facts warranted otherwise.[13]

On February 9, however, the chief procurator sent Girard's CO his report. Japanese investigators stated that Girard threw out cartridges and shouted out "*Papa-san, daijobu*" and "*Mama-san, daijobu*," or "Old man, O.K., old lady, O.K." As Sakai and a man picked them up, Girard pointed to a hole and said "*Mama-san, Takusan-ne*," or "Old lady, plenty more." The man became suspicious and started to run. Girard shouted at the man, "*Ge-rou! Hey!*" and fired an expended cartridge. Then he turned to Sakai and said the same thing as she also tried to run. The cartridge hit a main artery and the woman bled to death. The chief procurator concluded that Girard's actions marked a "deviation" from his orders and thus he was not on duty.[14] Two days later, the Japanese announced they would try the GI for "infliction of injury and murder."[15]

Unlike the situation in Taiwan, the Administrative Agreement signed between the United States and Japan established a process for situations in which both sides were at an impasse. A Joint Committee composed of representatives from both countries would work together to resolve problems. On February 16, Japan's government asked that the Girard case be referred to the Criminal Jurisdiction Subcommittee of the Joint Committee. The subcommittee was composed of two representatives: a Japanese and an American admiral. The U.S. representative refused to allow the case to go to the subcommittee until there was further investigation. Although the provost marshal for Camp Weir found evidence supporting the Japanese contention that Girard's action did not arise out of performance of his duty, the Far East Command found no conclusive evidence that Girard exceeded his orders. Nevertheless, by March 7 the United States agreed to allow the case to go to the subcommittee.[16]

On March 12, Japan presented its evidence, which was, verbatim, the chief procurator's report of February 9. After listening to the summary, Admiral Miles H. Hubbard, the U.S. representative on the subcommittee, asked his Japanese counterpart if the incident occurred while Girard was on duty. The Japanese answered that Girard was indeed on duty, but that throwing out shell casings had nothing to do with guarding a machine gun. Hubbard retorted that Girard discharged his weapon in order to scare away the civilians and protect the machine gun, but the Japanese argued that the weapon was not in any danger. The civilians were indeed picking up brass, but in no way interfered with the machine gun. Nickel admitted as much. Moreover, Lieutenant Mahon stated that firing an empty shell from a grenade launcher was not authorized, and any officer seeing Girard discharge his weapon in such a manner would have stopped him. Hubbard suggested that Girard, in the act of trying to scare away the civilians, mistakenly believed that his action was necessary. The Japanese rejected that line of reasoning as pure supposition, and argued that the evidence pointed to a different conclusion.[17]

Over the next few weeks, the impasse remained, with neither side budging from their established positions. By late April, General Lyman Lemnitzer, the commander in chief, Far East (U.S. Army), demanded that the review process be expedited and that the U.S. claim of "primary right" to jurisdiction be affirmed. Ambassador MacArthur saw that not only did both sides have "strong legal arguments," but that there were "obviously important political considerations at stake, in Japan as well as elsewhere." Moreover, the case should have already gone to trial. MacArthur wanted to know the State Department's position on the definition of "official duty." Christian Herter, the assistant secretary of state, answered that the notion that Girard's actions were committed "in the performance of official duty" was "of dubious validity in light of facts . . . which are said to be undisputed."[18]

In Washington, Wilber Brucker told Lemnitzer that the United States had the right of jurisdiction even though he acknowledged that the evidence made it a close call. He wanted the Joint Committee to reach a decision, and viewed diplomatic channels as "unproductive and unwise." Brucker wanted a court-martial soon because he did not want the Girard case to enter the Japanese judicial system. Allowing the courts to try a soldier for actions committed while on "official duty" set a bad precedent, and the Girard case was "a poor one for initial judicial determination." So the Joint Committee tried to resolve the impasse, but Hubbard was informed that if the Japanese continued to insist on jurisdiction, he had authority to allow the Japanese to try Girard. If Japan did indeed put Girard on trial, the United States wanted him charged with the "least serious offense" possible. Brucker never informed the State Department of his decision to grant Japan jurisdiction if they persisted, and the Department of Defense had been led to believe that if a deadlock continued, the Japanese courts would decide if Girard shot Sakai Naka while on or off duty.[19]

By now, Japanese authorities believed that Girard never really intended to hurt anyone, but simply "acted only in a mischievous manner, perhaps, 'intending to have fun in a child-like way.'" After six weeks of negotiations, Admiral Hubbard decided to grant Japan jurisdiction. On May 16, the two sides reached a secret compromise. The United States maintained that Girard was on duty when he killed the woman, but would grant Japan jurisdiction as long as Japan indicted Girard for nothing more than "wounding resulting in death," which carried a maximum sentence of two to fifteen years. Japanese government officials also agreed to recommend that the court "mitigate the sentence to the maximum practicable extent." Brucker did this without consulting with the State Department even though it involved an interpretation of the Administrative Agreement. When the State Department issued a complaint, Brucker told Lemnitzer to ignore it. Nevertheless, the State Department believed that a deal had been made and that the United States should hold up its end of the bargain.[20]

The decision to hand Girard over to Japan sparked outrage in the United States. Congressmen demanded to see secret telegrams regarding the Girard case.[21] Angry veterans wrote letters to the State Department saying that Girard, while on duty, shot a woman committing a crime, and a GI could never get a fair trial in Japan. Americans, including Republican women's groups, assailed the State Department for signing agreements that "subject our boys to trial by aliens," and equated those agreements with the Genocide Treaty, which they interpreted as allowing Americans to be taken from their homes and tried in some foreign land. The state of Illinois passed resolutions both in the House and Senate declaring that if Girard were tried by Japan, a "great injustice" would be done in denying him his constitutional protections.[22] The *Cleveland Plain Dealer* described the decision "to sacrifice one American soldier in the interests of maintaining amicable relations with our former enemy" as "monstrous, morally wrong and wholly indefensible." Various newspapers in the Midwest vilified Admiral Hubbard for surrendering Girard to a country that the *State Journal* of Lansing, Michigan, described as "intensely anti-American." A *New York Daily News* editorial declared, "We thought the Status of Forces Treaty stank from the start. We think the stink is now so pronounced that Congress ought to jerk this Admiral Hubbard home and ask him who the hell he thinks he is and what he's up to."[23] Defense Secretary Wilson insisted that Girard remain in U.S. hands pending a review, and the Pentagon blamed the State Department for the Girard decision. Congressmen supported Wilson's position and called on the State Department to do all it could to protect a soldier who simply did his duty. On the defensive, Dulles fired back that the decision "to relinquish jurisdiction" was made by the Joint Committee under instructions sent by the army to the judge advocate general.[24]

In the meantime, Brucker decided that he wanted to unilaterally order General Lemnitzer to carry out the court-martial and inform the Joint Commission that the United States would not grant jurisdiction after all. Walter Robertson recommended that Brucker's message not be forwarded to the Japanese, "even if it required Presidential action to prevent it."[25] Dulles warned Brucker that an abrupt, unilateral reversal of the U.S. decision to grant Japan jurisdiction "would be understandably judged by the Japanese to be a repudiation of our international agreement with them," with profound and adverse impacts on U.S. relations with Japan "and our whole position in the Far East."[26] If Brucker did not live up to the agreement, "our whole relationship with Japan may be in jeopardy and it is pretty important."[27] In a conversation with Dulles, Eisenhower insisted that it was better "to pick up all our forces and hike out of there." He was even prepared to tell Prime Minister Kishi to "divide them by half" and "start a progressive withdrawal." Maybe such a move would calm the Girard situation down.[28]

Feeling the domestic political heat, Dulles told Brucker that he wanted to reverse the Joint Committee's decision and see if the Japanese would accept an immediate court-martial in which the minimum sentence would be three years. Because the Japanese, in "good faith," had already indicted Girard, set a trial date for June 21, and selected judges to oversee the trial, Dulles instructed MacArthur to explain to them that the United States preferred to resolve the matter diplomatically and not continue the judicial proceedings while both governments discussed the case. Essentially, Dulles wanted the Japanese to agree to put the matter back to the Joint Committee. Brucker backed down from taking unilateral action and would not seek a court-martial while both sides worked to resolve the issue diplomatically without prejudice to the issue of jurisdiction.[29]

On May 22, MacArthur met with Japan's Foreign Minister Ishii Mitsujiro. Ishii was sympathetic to the domestic problem facing Washington, but he had his own domestic issues. For the United States to change course after the Joint Committee made a decision would spark "very serious political repercussions."[30] The next day, Ishii notified MacArthur that he had already prepared a statement that presented evidence that Girard "fired toward" a Japanese national rather than "'at her' because otherwise he would then be accused of murder" and that stated that after weeks of deadlock the Joint Committee agreed to grant Japan jurisdiction. The statement noted the press reports emanating from the United States claiming that the Defense Department refused to hand Girard over and disseminating misinformation regarding the shooting. Japan saw "no constructive purpose" in withdrawing the arrangement made by the Joint Committee. Japanese officials were stung by U.S. press reports that a Japanese trial would be "unfair and prejudicial." If such attacks continued, they would be "unforgettable" for the Japanese people.[31] MacArthur warned Dulles that if the United States revoked its waiver "without reasonable and justifiable reasons pertinent to the case," the Joint Committee and ultimately the Administrative Agreement with Japan would "be seriously impaired." He saw the Girard case as having "the most grave and far-reaching implications not only for both Japan and the United States in terms of our vital interests in and future relations with Japan but also in terms of our entire posture throughout free Asia."[32]

It was at this critical moment that Black Friday occurred. In the aftermath of the Reynolds riot, Japanese citizens wrote letters to newspaper editors warning that similar rioting could occur in Japan or in other countries that had U.S. troops on their soil if the United States "ignores racial sentiments." A *Yomimuri Japan Times* editorial quoted General MacArthur, now retired, as saying that "even the best disciplined troops would become unpopular if they were stationed too long in a foreign country."[33] In a letter to a newspaper editor, a thirty-five-year-old Japanese clerk expressed that if the United States court-martialed Girard in Japan as it did Reynolds, there would be a similar reaction. Other newspapers warned that a misstep made in the Girard case would lead to riots that would do "tremendous harm" if American GIs got the impression from the Reynolds verdict that they could avoid paying the consequences for crimes. The *Asahi* noted that the United States had little appreciation for the fact that it stationed troops in foreign lands, and alienated locals by how it dealt with the Girards of the U.S. military. The *Hokkaido Shimbun* argued that the Reynolds riot and the Girard case both resulted from "American racial prejudice and superiority complex," while the *Tokyo Shimbun* observed that the stationing of GIs in Japan was not just for Japan's benefit, and that it was unwise for the United States to anger the Japanese people. Although an American consul found most newspaper discussions of the U.S. presence to be levelheaded, the articles nevertheless linked Reynolds with Girard. The shooting of Sakai Naka was viewed by Japanese as "a manifestation of a superior attitude toward Japanese by Americans and that the United States does not trust Japanese justice." To deny Japan jurisdiction would have "serious adverse repercussions on attitudes toward the US in this area."[34]

The U.S. diplomats were right that the Reynolds and Girard cases could have repercussions for the rest of Asia. In the Philippines, or what Nash called the "southern anchor of our defense perimeter in the Western Pacific," the United States possessed 542,000 acres of Filipino land to maintain several major facilities, including both Clark Air Force Base and Subic Bay. There were nearly ten thousand military personnel and almost twenty thousand dependents—far more than in Taiwan, where Rankin claimed the number of Americans exceeded that of the days when the United States colonized the Philippines. Although the Philippines achieved independence in 1946, Filipinos remained frustratingly dependent on the paternalistic United States. Filipino politicians used American bases to criticize the government and to stir up anti-Americanism or to lead some to support neutralism. In the ten years since gaining independence in 1946, over twenty Filipinos had been shot dead trying to scavenge for shell casings. In cases in which an American killed a Filipino on a base, the Philippines had no criminal jurisdiction. In 1956, troops at a U.S. military checkpoint stopped a truck full of manganese miners who supposedly had been mining on U.S. land in what became known as the Santamaria Incident, named after the truck driver. A prominent Filipino politician defended the man, and others demanded a new relationship with the United States. This and other incidents that involved U.S. bases occupying Filipino land led to what Ambassador Albert Nufer described as "a profound and sincere national reexamination" by Filipinos "of the entire fabric" of the U.S.-Philippines partnership.[35]

In the weeks prior to Black Friday, both governments held SOFA talks. The provisions for jurisdiction in both the NATO SOFA and the Japan SOFA significantly exceeded an agreement reached in 1947. Like the ROC, the Filipinos insisted on a treaty similar to Japan's, not NATO's.[36] When it came to seeking jurisdiction, Nufer observed that the Filipinos wanted "the same words and music as the record plays in NATO and Japan. Stating it another way and using universal language, a little semantic love play can get us what we need and, at the same time, make the Phils happy and self-dignified for the years ahead." Nufer added that to not give the Philippines similar jurisdiction "would be contrary to the interests of the United States in this important area, which is perhaps the keystone of US prestige in the Southeast Asia region." However, SOFA negotiations became strained, and the Americans could make no headway because the State Department opposed revealing the secret minute with Japan. It did not matter, because the Philippines would never have agreed to similar secret minutes or modifications of any agreement. President Ramon Magsaysay, who died in a plane crash in March 1957, feared that his own political enemies would use a SOFA with the Netherlands formula as a weapon against him.[37]

In the meantime, the Philippine government watched the Girard case in Japan. Its ambassador to Japan told MacArthur that "what happens in Girard case will vitally affect outcome of US-Philippine base negotiations." The press had little to say about the Girard case until the Reynolds riot, after which the press gave heavy coverage to both incidents. Because seventy thousand Chinese lived there and threatened demonstrations, the government not only heightened security for the U.S. embassy in Manila, but worried that protests would "trigger anti-Chinese feelings among pro-American Filipinos."[38] Meanwhile, editorials reflected concerns of "racial pride, national prestige, Asian solidarity, and resentment of the omnipresent power and presence of the US." Newspapers quoted Carlos P. Romulo, the Philippines ambassador to the United States, as saying that riots were likely to occur until jurisdiction was resolved to Asian satisfaction. According to Romulo, Asian countries were enjoying a postcolonial era in which "court jurisdiction is part and parcel of our national sovereignty and especially to peoples newly liberated, national sovereignty is sacrosanct. Anything that violates it arouses the deep resentment of the people."[39] Filipino politicians used the Girard and Reynolds cases to claim that the government was justified in demanding jurisdiction and that the courts should have authority to try offenses against Philippine laws.[40]

Repercussions were also felt in South Korea, where the United States maintained numerous air bases and port facilities that utilized seventy-one thousand acres and supported over sixty thousand military personnel.[41] Since 1949, the Korean Military Advisory Group had enjoyed the protection of diplomatic immunity even though there were Koreans who believed they should have jurisdiction, and since 1950 the United States had possessed exclusive jurisdiction over its troops. It refused to sign a SOFA, saying that Korea remained "on a virtual war footing," a point reaffirmed by the South Korean Supreme Court in 1957. Moreover, Frank Nash observed that "there are grave doubts concerning the adequacy of Korean legal procedures."[42]

Yet, South Korea saw its own share of incidents involving GIs. Some soldiers were known to be trigger happy, such as shooting women while they cut weeds near a U.S. air base or a boy that was swimming near a U.S. military area. In some cases, Koreans were shot dead for not halting when gate guards ordered them to do so. In 1956 there were 185 incidents involving Koreans and U.S. troops, including the wounding of sixty-one Koreans and the killing of thirty-nine by soldiers on guard duty. The number of incidents involving U.S. troops declined considerably in 1957, with only eight fatal shootings in the first nine months. This may have been thanks in part to the creation of nineteen Community Relations Advisory Councils involving the U.S. military and Korean authorities and a Committee Relations Advisory Group to work with the embassy, USIS, and the U.S. military. Nevertheless, the South Korean press provided plenty of publicity, which created a demand for, and a resentment against not having, a SOFA.[43]

Even if the South Korean press exaggerated events, more incidents followed that were concurrent with the Reynolds and Girard cases. In April 1957, there was the Paju Incident, in which four Korean boys got into an altercation with an American MP when he refused to return $5 given to him to purchase cigarettes. Allegedly, the MP assaulted one of the boys, only to be injured by a rock. In retaliation, his CO and the MP unit entered Yongju-dong village, searched over three hundred homes and establishments, seized over two thousand items from 185 properties, and then "illegally" arrested seventy Korean civilians. On the one hand, Yongju-dong became lawless and reliant upon thievery of U.S. military property and nearly half of the fifteen hundred villagers engaged in prostitution. On the other hand, the CO clearly exceeded his authority by seizing stolen property and was transferred out of the country. Nevertheless, a Korean lawmaker described the incident as "barbarous illegal acts" and questioned whether the United States' "arrogant attitude" encroached on South Korea's sovereignty. Korea's foreign minister demanded to know why Washington delayed signing a SOFA with Korea. In the days that followed, the Korean press claimed that a watch merchant in a village was robbed by Americans; another Korean was shot trying to break into the U.S. 7th Division's compound; two woodcutters were beaten by American sentries; and the body of a raped South Korean girl was found.[44]

That same month, an American MP named John W. Wilson stopped Korean black marketeers from robbing a military supply train. In the process, Wilson killed one of the Koreans. The eight gang members that were arrested claimed Wilson had been a confederate, but the Eighth Army later announced that Wilson had participated in a sting operation by pretending to be the gang's inside man. South Koreans rejected this explanation and argued that Korea needed a SOFA.[45]

After Black Friday, South Korean newspapers spoke of the "superior attitude of US forces abroad."[46] Some suggested this superiority in refusing to hand Reynolds over to ROC authorities led to the riots. Several supported the call by Syngman Rhee's government for a SOFA. The *Korean Republic* observed that the riots in Taiwan were "touched off by the problem of American nationals charged with criminal offenses. An Asian sore spot was touched, and violence erupted." Not providing other Asian countries with a SOFA like that with Japan was an "affront to other national dignities." The editorial added, "The United States must strive for equality—for the equality of its own nationals with those of the countries which it is helping, and for the equality of all Asians with the people of Japan who were—after all—our common enemy just a few years ago." While some criticized the Chinese for rioting, they demanded "clear-cut agreements on jurisdiction" and suggested that the U.S. military in Korea "should learn a lesson from the Taipei incident." Nearly all South Korean newspapers saw the Reynolds riot as a turning point in which the United States needed to review its relations with its allies as they related to jurisdiction over U.S. troops. The U.S. embassy noted that most South Koreans supported the United States and had been friendly toward Americans since the Korean War. Still, even though Syngman Rhee announced that the Paju Incident was closed, domestic politics and international prestige might affect how he handled future incidents. Moreover, the embassy advised against permitting more dependents to go to South Korea. Although dependents living in Seoul had not been a problem, "colonies of American women and children living in comparative luxury in the smaller cities are bound to generate envy and resentment among the local populace." Resentment of dependency on the United States made the matter of a SOFA sensitive, and Koreans would demand some jurisdiction.[47]

The Reynolds riot and the Girard case also affected Asian nations that, like Taiwan, had MAAG units but no bases. In Thailand, where the United States had less than one thousand MAAG advisors and dependents, all Bangkok papers condemned the Reynolds verdict as unjust. Thailand's foreign minister stated that only an occupying army had diplomatic immunity.[48] Stationing troops abroad with diplomatic immunity was like colonialism. How would Americans react if Chinese soldiers acted that way in the United States? American insistence on trying U.S. soldiers in their own courts only undermined the independence of the host nation, and Asian countries, especially Thailand, would not stand for this. One newspaper even warned the government not to allow too many Americans into Thailand.[49]

Making matters worse, a U.S. Marine driving a jeep struck and killed a Thai. Then a Thai servant claimed that she had been beaten by U.S. embassy personnel. The local papers quickly played up these incidents as being similar to the Reynolds and Girard cases. The USIS and local police immediately rebutted the woman's story, preventing further escalation in Thai sentiment. Nevertheless, a Thai newspaper claimed, "Americans can never be tried by court of country in which they commit offense." Fourteen editorials were written over a three-day period in late May that expressed sympathy for the Taiwan riots and argued that holding a U.S. court-martial on foreign soil only antagonized locals. One newspaper declared that the "incident which occurred in Taipei is the answer to question why Eastern Countries hate America." Another suggested that the Taiwan riots were a "lesson that ought make our government realize that putting foreigners on a pedestal will have bad results." A pro–United States newspaper asserted that the Taiwan rioters were heroes for refusing to become slaves. The incidents in Taiwan, Japan, and Korea were evidence that Americans "never respected independence of any Eastern country." Because of the large Chinese community in Thailand, Chinese newspapers used their entire front pages and most of their inside pages to run what one U.S. diplomat called "red ink headlines." Readers were incited by stories about how Americans cheered the verdict while Liu's widow wept. Even the *Hsin Bao,* described as anti-communist and pro–United States, called for Reynolds to be retried, for elimination of diplomatic immunity for Americans, and for the abandonment of the "warped idea" that the ROC should tolerate whatever the United States did "because of U.S. aid."[50]

In South Vietnam, where just over seven hundred MAAG advisors and eighteen hundred dependents lived, there might have been similar discussions. However, the government was already embroiled in a controversy with the ROC and the Chinese minority living in South Vietnam. The government led by Ngo Dinh Diem attempted to break Chinese nationals' hold over South Vietnam's economy and to force the assimilation of resident Chinese into the Vietnamese culture. The ROC asked the United States to get Diem to back off. It was during this moment of tension that Black Friday occurred. In a measure to keep the Chinese in South Vietnam from carrying out their own demonstrations, the South Vietnamese government cracked down. Coverage of the riots in Chinese newspapers in Saigon was censored, with the result that empty spaces were filled by photos pertaining to unrelated matters. Nevertheless, some newspapers in South Vietnam viewed the riots as anti-American, and one commented that "weak states have a basic inferiority [feeling]" and that the "overbearing attitude on the part of great powers nullified the value of the gifts extended by them."[51]

From Burma, Cambodia, and Ceylon to India and Indonesia, there was an outcry against the United States. Even in Malaya and Singapore, where there were large numbers of Chinese, there were calls for ending extraterritoriality and the U.S. troop presence. The English-language *Standard* went as

far as to describe, if not exaggerate, the effect of the riots on "American prestige and the sincerity of American foreign policy" as being as "disastrous as
the Hiroshima atom bomb." Thus, events in Taiwan, even if the United States
was not totally at fault, threatened to undermine the Eisenhower policy of
maintaining overseas Chinese morale and retaining their support for the
ROC. In 1957, nearly five thousand students in Taiwan were from Southeast
Asia and Hong Kong.[52] Many of them were angered by the verdict, and some
may have participated in the riots. Overseas Chinese newspapers became
conduits for Chinese to both vent their anger and feed on the arguments
directed against diplomatic immunity for U.S. soldiers. Ironically, by trying
to make Taiwan the locus for leadership of overseas Chinese, the Reynolds
riot potentially damaged the ROC's and the United States' image with the
very people that Eisenhower believed were key to containing communism.[53]

Unsurprisingly, the protests and riots gave the communists plenty of
political grist for the anticapitalist mill. In the PRC, state-run newspapers
ran articles for days detailing the riots and anti-American sentiment in Hong
Kong and Japan against "the 'brutality' of American treatment of Asians."
The PRC press portrayed the United States as a bully that felt neither sympathy nor sorrow for the death of Liu Ziran, and was bent on making Taiwan
into a dependency. Editorials described U.S. soldiers as raping, committing
murder, and making slaves of Taiwanese. The ROC, on the other hand, was
condemned for putting down the riots and apologizing to the United States.
The PRC called on Taiwanese to rise up and liberate themselves from the
American aggressors and the reactionary Chiang Kai-shek.[54] Radio Moscow claimed that the United States planned to establish a base in Taiwan,
while North Vietnam issued a statement that the U.S. presence in Taiwan
threatened peace in Asia through acts like those of Girard and Reynolds that
"unmasked the horrible faces of the American colonialists." In North Korea,
one newspaper predicted that the U.S. aggressor would be driven out of Taiwan and everywhere else it stretched its "aggressive claws" and committed
"bestial outrages," while a communist paper in Hong Kong demanded that
the United States "withdraw from our Taiwan."[55]

In this international political climate, the Eisenhower administration
now needed to take steps to reduce the tensions in Asia caused by the American presence and policies. At stake were the bases, with their troops as well
as naval and air assets, and the reliance on MAAG. Eisenhower needed to
decide what to do about Girard, the number of GIs and their dependents
abroad, and the existing SOFAs and similar agreements. Somehow, Eisenhower had to simultaneously placate both allies, who demanded jurisdiction
over U.S. troops in an effort to recover sovereignty, and American politicians

and their constituents, who opposed SOFAs and tried to push amendments through Congress to ensure that GIs would not be tried in foreign courts. A wrong decision could mean a weakening, if not the destruction, of America's entire containment policy.

13

Defending the American Bases of Hegemony

The immediate reaction of the Eisenhower administration to the Reynolds riot and the Girard case was to consider troop reductions as a way of lessening tensions and the chances of more incidents. The day after Black Friday, Dulles told his staff that, together, the cases suggested the need to review the U.S. policy of "stationing of troops abroad but in particular in Oriental countries." At a press conference on May 29, Dulles pointed to the number of U.S. soldiers on Taiwan as "the basic cause of the trouble." He remembered that in 1919 the U.S. delegation to the Paris Peace Conference took over a number of French homes around their hotel. One night, an old woman confronted a U.S. Marine guarding one of these structures, waving a cane and shouting, "This is my home." This was just weeks after the armistice and if there had been a crowd, people would have sympathized. As for the Taiwan riots, Dulles denied that the ROC had any active involvement, but did question its handling of the mob. He also admitted that China had a history of anti-foreign outbreaks and resented anything resembling extraterritoriality.[1]

Meanwhile, Eisenhower felt strongly that "prompt and radical steps had to be taken to cut down the number of our armed forces in foreign countries. . . . It was inevitable that they would sooner or later produce strong anti-American feeling."[2] He told a group of U.S. lawmakers that the Reynolds and Girard cases underscored the need to review "the desirability of maintaining U.S. forces in the Far East."[3] In early June, Ike expressed astonishment over the Reynolds riot, which raised the issue of the "undesirability of having troops stationed in a foreign country—something that should only be done when impossible to avoid it." Although he thought that U.S. troops had been well-behaved since 1942, he had worried about the issue of GI behavior since 1945. He wanted to withdraw them, "but of course it would be risking the collapse of our position in the Far East if we were to pull out of Formosa and Korea."[4]

Obviously, the judgment that troop numbers were behind the problems confronting the United States in Asia oversimplified all of the events that happened in Taiwan and Japan. The idea certainly allowed Democrats to criticize the administration. Senators, like Albert Gore (D-TN) and Lyndon Johnson (D-TX), complained about the large number of Americans living abroad and the huge sums of money appropriated to agencies like USIA and foreign aid programs.[5] Senator Allen Ellender (D-LA), who traveled throughout Asia, including Taiwan, in the mid-1950s, argued that too many Americans traveled to poor areas of the world to live like kings. In Taiwan, Americans lived in the finest homes, drove the finest cars, and wore the best clothes. Until they stopped flaunting their wealth, such riots would occur again.[6] Senator Mike Mansfield (D-MT) complained of the "snowballing of American personnel" followed by "post exchanges, American automobiles, American salaries, American high schools, American standards of living." Thus, the "anti-American riots . . . in a country considered to be a staunch ally" pointed to an "underlying resentment that must have been simmering beneath the surface for some time."[7] Even if such comments were made by the opposition party, many in the administration nevertheless believed that troop reductions would go a long way toward preventing future similar incidents. Two days after the protests, Walter McConaughy suggested that since MAAG operated under the embassy, the number of advisors should be held to an "absolute minimum" and be handpicked on the basis of "high character, sound judgment, and emotional stability."[8]

In addition to considering troop reduction abroad, Ike approved a plan by the Operations Coordinating Board (OCB) to determine how many U.S. citizens, including dependents, were stationed or residing abroad and to find ways to improve the foreign perception of Americans living overseas. To his amazement, Eisenhower learned that the number was approximately 1 million, including an increase in U.S. personnel in countries like France and Germany. In July, the OCB recommended that U.S. personnel be kept at a minimum. Part of the problem was that the facilities made available by the United States and/or its allies attracted dependents to live overseas. Defense Secretary Wilson noted that one reason why Washington was reducing its troop levels in Korea was because the United States did not want dependents to travel there. Otherwise, if the United States built "better swimming pools for dependents overseas we would never get our forces back home." Eisenhower thought it a huge mistake "to make overseas quarters too luxurious." In areas like the Philippines, he could see establishing such quarters because the United States planned to stay a long time, but not in countries like West Germany, where the United States "might withdraw." Eisenhower issued a directive that all agencies report the number of Americans abroad to the OCB, which would note major increases and decreases in the number of Americans overseas, highlight trouble spots where the country might want to keep personnel levels at a minimum, and look for ways to improve attitudes toward Americans, including orientation programs and language training.[9]

In the meantime, plans were made to reduce GI numbers in Taiwan and Japan. In May 1957, the Defense Department called for a 25 percent decrease in the number of U.S. military personnel in Taiwan and an across-the-board reduction of 12 percent throughout Asia. Rankin told Admiral Stump that he supported the reduction of American personnel "since our problems seem to increase roughly as the square of the number of official Americans." In June, Eisenhower even called for a 60 percent reduction in troops in Japan. By October 1957, ground forces in Japan were reduced to eighty-two thousand, with plans to maintain a force of sixty-three thousand by June 1958.[10]

One idea apparently considered was to deploy more tactical nuclear weapons to compensate for the troop reductions. After the Reynolds riot, Wilson told the press that "Americans could be forced to 'go home' anywhere 'if enough people don't like us.'" Reducing the number of troops in places like Taiwan could have a negative impact on an ally's security, so Wilson looked at using modern weapons to replace the troops.[11]

From the point of view of the State Department, the option of greater reliance on technology and less on troops was not feasible. Walter Robertson and Marshall Green, who participated in the Nash Mission, argued that over the next several years "the physical security of the United States and the maintenance of its position and influence in the world will continue to depend on the existence of a well-positioned and well-dispersed system of overseas military bases and operating facilities," especially in Asia, where U.S. allies were far away and on the periphery of the PRC. Overseas bases permitted the United States to launch a counteroffensive, to deploy forces quickly to deal with "local aggression," and to "promote U.S. political objectives." Until the development of intercontinental ballistic missiles, the United States relied on manned atomic bombers supplemented by intermediate-range ballistic missiles. Besides the general irritations and incidents created by U.S. forces abroad, the United States could expect opposition from allied and American public opinion to greater reliance on atomic weapons. U.S. allies did not gain security from the presence of such weapons. (Indeed, when Washington tried to remove a nonnuclear combat wing of F-86s from Taiwan in 1958, Chiang Kai-shek balked. The combat wing provided more assurance of an American commitment to defend ROC territory than the nuclear-capable Matadors.[12]) Allies also feared that not only would their country become a nuclear target, but that the United States would use such weapons "in all situations, however small and limited." Increasingly, U.S. allies wanted a say in the decision to use atomic weapons.[13]

Troop reductions and greater reliance on technology to ensure U.S. security and lower tensions with allies were long-term solutions to an immediate problem. Neither solved the problem of Girard, the question of Asian jurisdiction over U.S. troops, or the stakes in Asia. On the morning of May 24, Dulles phoned Eisenhower to discuss Black Friday just hours after the worst of the protests occurred but while the situation remained volatile. Both Eisenhower and Dulles were confounded by the riots because they did not fully understand the facts of the killing of Liu Ziran. Eisenhower thought that Reynolds had chased Liu before shooting him. Dulles could not understand why the man was acquitted, and mistakenly believed that Reynolds was on duty when the shooting occurred. Eisenhower thought the court-martial should have been held in the United States to avoid such an incident.[14]

In light of what had just happened, the secretary of state wondered if Girard should be handed over to the Japanese. Despite the Taiwan protests, Ike did not think so. Using words that could have described Robert Reynolds, Ike declared that he knew "the American army" and that "American forces will not let one of their own people be tried in foreign court if they can help it. (We are up against the same thing here at home too.)" Dulles, though, worried that the Taipei riot would cause a "chain reaction also in Japan. The issues at stake are tremendous." In Taiwan, it was a "question of sentence, not jurisdiction." However, if the United States did not hand Girard over to Japan, "as Defense originally agreed we might as well write Japan off." With the uproar from American congressional leaders and public opinion, Ike wondered if Japan could already be written off. The Defense Department realized that it had made a mistake by agreeing to waive jurisdiction, but the deal was done. "Now Japan says are your agreements any good?" Eisenhower feared for "our status of forces in Europe and everywhere else," and he wanted to take a hard look "at these Asiatic countries, and decide whether we can stay there. It does not seem wise if they hate us so much." The two also agreed that the SOFAs "were unclear" and in need of modification so that a U.S. soldier "should be tried by US court martial when committing a crime 'when on duty' and *not* 'in performance of duty.' (Indeed, if it is in performance of duty it is not a crime.)" After hanging up the phone, Dulles told his people that the president opposed handing Girard over to Japan.[15]

The next day, upon further reflection, Eisenhower changed his mind. The Reynolds riot clearly had an impact. He told Dulles that the United States should indeed hand Girard over to Japan, and it had to be done in such a manner that Congress understood that this was not some special case and would not set a precedent. The United States would not hand over any more GIs who got into an accident or did something wrong while on duty.

Ike also wanted to forestall "a stream of criticism" of the SOFAs with Japan and other countries.[16]

On May 28, Eisenhower met with Dulles, Wilson, and a number of officials and generals. In a phone call before the meeting, Wilson told Dulles that he wanted to hold onto Girard until the attorney general agreed that granting Japan jurisdiction accorded with previous agreements or until the president ordered him to give Girard up. Dulles replied that Eisenhower was prepared to do just that, but that the president "should not be put into that position."[17] At the White House meeting, the idea of approaching the attorney general was shot down, as was the idea that Japan "conduct a trial in absentia." The United States had made a deal, and "serious adverse consequences" would "ensue should the United States refuse to honor that agreement." That morning, Eisenhower told congressional leaders that since procedures had been followed and the government had ceded jurisdiction, "a mistake, the President thought," the United States could not back out of the agreement. Eisenhower believed that the "word of the U.S. Government was at stake." He added: "It is awfully hard . . . for a great nation to turn around and say it didn't mean what it said in the first instance."[18] Likewise, Dulles told several congressmen that there was no way to retract the deal "without throwing doubt upon the value of agreements and raising a storm which might sweep us out of all the Western Pacific." The secretary of state then notified Ambassador MacArthur of Eisenhower's decision, and warned him to "expect intense public and congressional reaction." On June 4, 1957, Dulles and Wilson issued their joint statement that the Girard case had "far-reaching implications, involving as it does the good faith of the United States" in carrying out the decision reached by the Joint Commission. After reviewing the facts of the case, the two agreed that Girard should be tried in Japan "in order to preserve the integrity of our pledges."[19]

The result was a political firestorm in which congressmen, journalists, and the American people were outraged that the U.S. government would hand over to a former enemy for trial a U.S. soldier who had been drafted and was on duty protecting U.S. property. Foreign Legion chapters, city mayors, and citizens from all over the country demanded that Girard be tried in a military court. Vince Genovese, who lived in Dallas, Texas, claimed that he lost family members in the Pacific during World War II and called the U.S. decision "disgraceful." Americans lashed out against what they described as "political expediency," saying Washington had caved in to a country known for brutality during the war. Some called this appeasement, and after "all the bloodshed that it took to bring these people in line, DOLLARS AND APPEASEMENT won't make or build a lasting friendship." Dorris Smith, of Jacksonville, Florida, and thousands of others were appalled that their political leaders had forgotten Pearl Harbor. Like Ronald Haber, of Queens, New York, citizens wondered how the administration could hand an American "to a group of biased and prejudiced defeated peoples." J. J. del Castillo, of Rockville Centre, New York, called the decision "one of the prime examples of cowardice and lack of manhood that is becoming typical of the Administration." One individual asked Dulles, "How yellow and cowardly can you, Wilson and Ike get?" Americans would have agreed with the Philip Rossi family of Mount Vernon, New York, who attacked the concept of the SOFA, describing it as "not only unconstitutional, but un-American, unjust, and without precedent in American history."[20] Newspapers across the country condemned the NATO SOFA for violating American rights.[21] Two retired Marine Corps generals, P. A. Del Valle and Merritt B. Curtis, headed an organization called Defenders of the American Constitution, Inc., that devoted itself to the elimination of SOFAs and ensuring that all U.S. troops retained their U.S. constitutional rights.[22]

Members of Congress received numerous letters of protest from their constituents, many of whom were veterans of World War II or had children who fought and/or died in the Korean War. The criticisms of the government, especially Dulles, Wilson, and the Senate, were scathing. George Mahon (D-TX) told Dulles, "I am getting some pretty violent reaction in regard to the Girard case in Japan." Joe Evins (D-TN) reported that "protests continue to mount from mothers of servicemen and citizens generally over unwarranted and unprecedented action of State Department in acquiescing to Japanese demands for trial of . . . Girard."[23] Senator Knowland admitted to Dulles that he had never seen such a negative reaction as he had in the Girard case.[24] One woman told Page Belcher (R-OK), "Anyone who had anything to do with passing the Status-of-Forces Treaty should be taken out and hung." Mrs. A. B. Carley asked Senator Robert Kerr (D-OK), "Have you and the other *servants* and *representatives* of the American people, forgotten, 'Pearl Harbor, The Bataan Death March,' the way those Japs starved and mistreated our soldiers and civilians. Who is responsible for such a treaty?" A telegram to Kerr stated simply, "Bring Girard and the other military home and let the Japs go to hell."[25]

Politicians and newspaper editors also used Black Friday to criticize the administration along several different lines. Some correctly saw a connection between the Taiwan protests and Ike's decision to allow Girard to be tried by Japan. Noah Mason (R-IL) described the U.S. decision to hand Girard over to Japan as "appeasement" intended to "head off another international incident, such as the Formosa riots."[26] An *Austin Statesman* editorial insisted that

Girard had been handed over in order to forestall "anti-American, mob-like hysteria. . . . The value of an American soldier apparently is less important than appeasing a Japanese mob."[27]

Others saw Taiwan as a warning that GIs could not be tried in Asian courts. Arthur L. Miller (R-NE) argued that in Japan there is no jury system and there could be a "certain tension and prejudice against our troops and civilian personnel." He added that this was demonstrated in supposedly "friendly" Taiwan, where people rioted because they did not like the court-martial verdict.[28] Gordon Scherer (R-OH) agreed, saying that local "hatreds and prejudices," as evidenced by what happened on Taiwan, made it "impossible to get normal safeguards" to give a GI a fair trial.[29] In the Senate, Paul Douglas (D-IL) claimed that Black Friday led the administration to make the mistake of allowing a GI to be tried in a Japanese court and not by court-martial.[30]

While there were opponents to allowing Taiwan to have a SOFA, others believed that the United States showed disrespect to its ally by not allowing it one. Journalists such as John O'Donnell and Alistair Cooke wrote that the riots occurred in Taiwan because there was no SOFA, playing into the hands of communist propaganda.[31] Supporters of Chiang Kai-shek believed that Americans would have reacted as the Chinese had if the shoe had been on the other foot.[32] John Henderson (R-OH) spoke of how men like Sergeant Reynolds defended "the principles of Americanism, including rights to American type of justice," and thought that a SOFA with Taiwan would have deprived Reynolds of such justice. He added that the riots occurred because the ROC could not try a man who committed a crime while off duty.[33] The *Camden Chronicle* called the Reynolds court-martial a "white-wash" and said the riots would have been avoided by having a SOFA.[34] Senator Jenner, a longtime critic of SOFAs, declared that two wrongs had been committed: someone had made Girard, who killed someone while on duty, an international pawn by giving him to Japan. In Taiwan, the United States had treated the ROC unfairly by not allowing it to try Reynolds.[35] Proponents and opponents of a SOFA for the ROC failed to understand, though, that Reynolds had diplomatic immunity. Even if there had been a SOFA, it would have been on U.S. terms, meaning exclusive jurisdiction. Events would have unfolded much as they already had, with people in Taiwan condemning it for being an unequal treaty. Yet, all of this was part and parcel of the domestic uproar facing Eisenhower.

Eisenhower had his supporters, few though they were. Teddy de Nolasco defended the decision to hand over Girard as "the only course to take in the light of the circumstances surrounding the case." He did not agree with congressmen and veterans groups who were outraged, and he believed that anything else would make the United States "guilty of hypocrisy." A citizen of Wilmington, North Carolina, asserted that the decision would "stop the unfriendly trend against U.S. in all places where we have troops."[36] Several newspapers around the country claimed that Eisenhower had no other choice. A *Christian Science Monitor* editorial warned congressmen that attempts to add constitutional amendments that would place GIs above foreign law would "revive hated 'extraterritoriality' in the Orient" and open the United States to the "charge of imperialism."[37] In a letter to the editor of the *Elmira Star Gazette,* Richard Murphy, a former GI, declared that "our military interest and Japanese sovereignty must be reconciled" and that the United States had to abide by the Administrative Agreement.[38] Charles Gubser (R-CA) attacked extraterritoriality as a "threat to the security of the United States." Until it possessed an ICBM, the United States needed overseas bases to maintain security and needed SOFAs to maintain mutual respect.[39] Senator Jacob Javits (R-NY) worried about the impact the Reynolds case and the Girard case "would have on public opinion and the possible demand for unrealistic and unjustifiable changes in our Status of Forces agreements." To eliminate them would jeopardize overseas bases.[40] The *Galesburg Register–Mail* editorialized that "in all fairness we can hardly demand as a price for this defensive assistance the abandonment by our friends of their sovereign right to adjudicate crimes committed on their soil. We would not do this for them."[41]

On June 5, Eisenhower gave a press conference in which he felt he had been "pushed pretty hard" on the Girard case "fallout" and other issues. At that moment, Prime Minister Kishi wanted to visit the United States. People like Sam Rayburn (D-TX) thought the timing inopportune. Eisenhower suggested postponement, but "pointed out that we had been trying desperately to save the friendship of 95 million people, and cannot run the risk of hurting their feelings now."[42] Dulles informed MacArthur of the "anti-Japanese sentiment" sweeping the country, but added that he would have expected anti-American demonstrations in Japan if the United States had not turned over Girard.[43]

In Japan, the news that the United States would indeed allow Girard to be tried in the Japanese court system was received with "deep satisfaction." Although Kishi shared his appreciation of the decision, MacArthur warned him to expect outbursts of anti-Japanese sentiment during his upcoming visit to the United States. Throughout June, various Japanese newspapers expressed the view that most Americans did not have a full understanding of the case, did not know that Girard's actions exceeded his orders, and were not aware of the fair and impartial hearings given to U.S. troops.[44]

In an effort to educate the American people, the State Department issued a document explaining the origins of the NATO SOFA and how SOFAs worked in Europe and Japan. The document pointed to how U.S. security during the Cold War relied heavily on the establishment of overseas bases and the stationing of "large land, naval and air forces abroad in time of peace." To allow local U.S. commanders to "retain maximum authority over their troops" and help foreign governments maintain law and order, reciprocal agreements like SOFAs were necessary. Likewise, around ten thousand foreign troops were on U.S. soil every year, so Washington sought "the maximum protection for its own servicemen that it was willing to accord" to allied troops. U.S. troops would only be tried by foreign governments for off-duty offenses, but those nations could waive jurisdiction. In 1956, out of 14,394 offenses committed in Europe, foreign governments waived jurisdiction for 66 percent of the cases and dropped over three hundred cases. In Japan, 98.6 percent of all cases were tried by the United States. Sentences imposed by foreign governments were lighter. A U.S. court-martial normally gave a man eleven years for rape; the average sentence imposed by foreign governments was 4.6 years. (The document did not comment on prison conditions in the United States versus those of Europe, Japan, or other countries.) The NATO SOFA also gave troops more safeguards than international law.[45]

Such efforts to better inform Americans seemed to fall on deaf ears, and in the meantime the Girard case took a surprising turn. Regardless of what the State Department or anyone had to say about the leniency of foreign courts, William Girard was not about to allow himself to be subjected to Japanese justice. He hired lawyers, who filed a motion in Washington, D.C.'s U.S. District Court and subpoenaed John Foster Dulles and Charles Wilson. The lawyers asked that the Girard case be brought before the court to determine if the Joint Committee's waiver of jurisdiction was legal. U.S. attorney general Herbert Brownell filed a series of briefs and gave an oral argument in opposition, but Judge Joseph McGarraghy ruled that Girard's constitutional rights had been violated.[46]

This defeat in the U.S. District Court forced the administration to go to the Supreme Court. Brownell believed that the District Court failed to recognize that when the Senate ratified the peace treaty with Japan, it agreed to the Administrative Agreement too. He intended to appeal, but suggested to Dulles that since this was a foreign relations matter, Eisenhower should use presidential prerogative and ignore it. Brownell added that although "we cannot show a critical emergency . . . there is involved an important point of Presidential power that would have worldwide repercussions." Dulles agreed, saying that the decision affected America's "whole defense posture and collective security arrangements all over the world."[47] In a situation where the

United States wanted to permanently station troops abroad, the host state needed to waive jurisdiction. Otherwise, if the host nation demanded 100 percent jurisdiction, the United States could not put troops there.[48]

In a meeting of State Department and Pentagon civilian and military legal experts, the assistant judge advocate general warned that the U.S. District Court's decision would have "serious repercussions" because "waivers could no longer be obtained for American troops" and "they would be put in foreign jails all of the time." The deputy attorney general also worried that a presidential decision, approving the action of both the secretary of state and the secretary of defense, "could be held up for months, with grave potentiality of injury to United States interests throughout the world" by a U.S. district judge. The group agreed that speedy consideration by the Supreme Court was in order, even if the justices preferred to go on summer vacation. In the meantime, the Japanese were informed that they should move Girard's trial date to August. Until the Supreme Court ruled on the issue, the administration could do nothing to lift the restraining order.[49]

Besides the district court decision, another threat to presidential power and SOFAs emanated from the House of Representatives. For several years, Frank Bow had criticized administrative agreements and SOFAs for giving host nations jurisdiction in a manner that damaged American prestige. For example, he argued that the SOFA with Japan caused the United States to lose face. He continued to tout his Bow Resolution or constitutional amendment to place GIs under the exclusive jurisdiction of the United States. On May 20, when Congress took up a resolution that would allow the loan or sale of forty-nine warships to European, Latin American, and Asian countries, including Taiwan, Bow used the opportunity to condemn the handing over of Girard as a "giving away of sovereignty." He questioned giving U.S. property to so-called friendly nations while the United States would not protect American soldiers sent to those countries. Bow's statements evoked similar anti-SOFA comments and observations from numerous representatives who opposed allowing Girard and others like him to be tried in foreign courts.[50] When discussing a civil rights bill, Bow claimed that GIs left the shores of the United States only to lose their civil rights, leading George Miller (D-CA) to argue that Girard had been "sold down the river" for "international political expediency."[51]

The State Department naturally opposed the Bow Amendment, and it caught the attention of some U.S. allies. The French embassy expressed concern about the "possible implications" of the amendment. The State Department argued that the principal reason why U.S. troops served overseas was to "protect the United States." By sending troops abroad, the United States and its allies received "more total protection by combining our strength with that of other nations than standing alone." Together, they stopped war "before it starts." SOFAs went to "the very heart of American foreign policy." America's "worldwide series of defensive alliances" were "vital to world peace and the survival of freedom," and the United States had to work with its allies "on the basis of equality and mutual respect." The communist powers wanted American troops out of Europe and Asia, and the Bow Resolution would only succeed in fulfilling their wish.[52] Despite the State Department's opposition, the House Committee on Foreign Affairs voted on June 27 in favor of the resolution by a margin of 18–8.

Days later, the battle over SOFAs and the fate of Girard shifted to the U.S. Supreme Court. On July 2, lawyers for both sides submitted briefs. Girard's lawyers wanted McGarraghy's ruling affirmed, but they also wanted the court to overturn his decision refusing to issue a habeas corpus writ that would lead to Girard's release. They called his continued incarceration illegal. Brownell and J. Lee Rankin argued that the shooting occurred on sovereign Japanese territory, where its government could claim exclusive jurisdiction. Both countries possessed agreements that allowed the United States to waive jurisdiction, making this a matter for the "executive branch," not the courts. Girard no longer had immunity from Japanese prosecution because of the waiver. Even if the treaties were somehow invalidated or the United States did not live up to its bargain, Japan could still assert its territorial right to try Girard. During oral arguments on July 8, Rankin added to this reasoning by declaring, "The Government has not been able to find any sovereign country in the world that recognizes the right of immunity under international law."[53] On July 11, the Supreme Court voted 8–0 to overturn McGarraghy's decision. The court ruled that since the U.S. Senate ratified the NATO SOFA and the Administrative Agreement as well as the amendment of 1953, there was no "constitutional or statutory barrier" that prevented the United States from waiving jurisdiction.[54]

The Supreme Court's decision proved to offer relief for the Japanese. Newspapers expressed gratification for what the *Mainichi* called the clearing away of the "dark clouds" in U.S.-Japanese relations.[55] By contrast, American outrage against the Supreme Court was palpable. Americans, in some cases teenagers as young as fourteen, told their congressmen that the Supreme Court justices should be impeached, and called the decision a "betrayal" and "one of the blackest decisions reached by any court."[56] A *Wilkes-Barre Times-Leader* editorial declared, "What gripes the American people is that assorted reds, pinks, punks, and racketeers have full protection under the Constitution of the United States, but a defender of our country has none. This does not make sense." The *Nashville Tennessean* called the decision an "ugly prec-edent" in which a GI was "traded off to a foreign nation for an uncertain good will." The *Omaha World Herald* described the decision as a "sellout" of GI constitutional rights. Newspapers called Girard a "sacrificial lamb" and a "martyr." George Sokolsky described the court as "small men who in pursuit of doctrinaire legalism are creating disorder throughout the country." The *Wall Street Journal* noted that "the Supreme Court again placed treaties and executive agreements above the individual rights of citizens that are embod-ied in the United States Constitution."[57]

In Congress, politicians were incensed. Wint Smith (R-KS) called the Supreme Court "'guardians' of Communists' liberty."[58] Philip Philbin (D-MA) warned that the decision would nullify the Uniform Code of Mili-tary Justice.[59] In the Senate, Bricker, Spessard Holland (D-FL), Strom Thur-mond (D-SC), and George Smathers (D-FL) wanted the upper house to go on the record in favor of resolutions that kept GIs out of foreign courts or announced that the United States would not waive primary jurisdiction over GIs for acts of commission and omission while on duty.[60] In the lower house, congressmen now tried to use the Bow Resolution against Eisenhower's $3.2 billion Mutual Security bill.

These threats from Congress forced Eisenhower to pressure Republicans to hold the line. Even before the Supreme Court decision, he was told that Democrats supported the Bow Resolution as a way of "embarrassing Repub-licans," and that its passage would "force American troops out of overseas bases." Knowland wanted an executive order stating that any GI accused of a crime committed on a military post or on duty would be tried by U.S. court-martial. The senator opposed allowing a "young man drafted in peace-time, sent overseas against his will, assigned to a duty" to be "turned over and tried." Robert Dechert countered that such an executive order would establish "no waivers of jurisdiction." Moreover, the Bow Resolution would negate every treaty signed by the United States in which it waived jurisdic-tion. When told that Congress might override a veto of the amendment, Ike threw down the gauntlet: he was "ready to fight it all the way."[61] Now the Bow Resolution threatened the Mutual Security bill. Ike told legislators that "he could not express how strongly he felt about the Bow Amendment and for-eign aid." The United States had to deal with other sovereign powers. "There might be a few countries that would accept the presence of our troops on the basis of extraterritoriality," Eisenhower added, "but he felt sure that nearly all, if not all, would refuse to do so." He warned that "if the Republicans in Congress deserted him on this matter, he would be more disappointed than for any other thing that has happened in his presidency."[62]

At a news conference held on July 17, the day that the House considered the bill, a *New York Times* reporter asked Eisenhower what he thought of the Bow Amendment. Ike answered that SOFAs were "absolutely essential to the system of alliances we have now, and without them those alliances will fall to pieces, because we would be compelled to bring our soldiers home." Furthermore, the United States dealt with sovereign nations with which it sought friendly relations: "We are not trying to dominate. We are not trying to establish a new system of international imperialism of some kind."[63]

In the meantime, the entire House of Representatives convened as a committee to discuss the Mutual Security Act of 1957. Although Charlie Halleck (R-IN) talked Bow out of attaching his resolution to the bill, other opponents of SOFAs tried to add their own amendments that eliminated or modified Article VII of the NATO and Japan SOFAs to give the United States exclusive jurisdiction over its troops.[64] For some representatives, it was an opportunity to send a message that Congress was displeased with the other two branches of government. Representatives from both sides of the aisle, though, came out in opposition. A resolution similar to Bow's was defeated by a vote of 134–134.[65] Although Congress still cut Ike's foreign aid bill (some of which earmarked money to Taiwan) by nearly one-third, the president won the fight to defend SOFAs.[66]

Academics who studied presidential leadership style later spoke of Eisenhower's "hidden hand," in which controversial decisions were made behind the scenes by Ike. Eisenhower revealed the hand if he felt he needed to take an issue head-on, such as the Bricker Amendment.[67] In dealing with the fallout from the Reynolds protests and the Girard case, the hand was there for all to see as the president made one crucial decision after another. In each instance, Eisenhower looked at the broader picture. The negative Asian reactions made him fear for the entire security structure that the United States had built since the late 1940s. Months later, when Frank Nash issued his report on overseas bases to Eisenhower, he argued that the overseas base system was a "major instrument of our foreign policy." It was proof that the United States would back its allies against communism, and gave Washington "leverage" to promote its political objectives. Nash concluded, "Our base system is key to our survival as a nation."[68] Yet, he worried that the whole question of criminal jurisdiction "has seeds of serious danger to the ability of the US to continue effectively its operations abroad, and to the support and cooperation of allied peoples and governments for the Free World alliance."[69]

Nash's report really reflected the views of Eisenhower. In a letter to a friend written shortly after the defeat of the House resolutions, the president expressed chagrin at the "serious attempt made to force me to denounce our Status of Forces treaties. These treaties . . . are fair and just to Americans serving abroad and are the only means by which we retain jurisdiction in most offenses committed. . . . To denounce them would make us completely isolationist and force us to abandon practically every base we have abroad." Eisenhower was astounded by the congressional reaction that reflected "either abysmal ignorance or a far greater concern for local political sentiment than for the welfare of the United States." All politicians thought of themselves as "intensely patriotic," but in the end "it does not take the average member long to conclude that his first duty to his country is to get himself re-elected." The fundamental "lack of understanding of America's national position and obligations" explained why Americans wanted to "make a national hero out of a man who shot a woman—in the back at something like ten to fifteen yards." Although many Americans believed that the United States could be both secure and prosperous "by withdrawing into a fanciful 'Fortress America,'" Eisenhower thought "there can be no such thing as security in isolation, no matter if our armed forces were multiplied three-fold." The president viewed the mutual security program as representing "America's best investment." "Through them," he added, "we are able to keep down the direct costs of our own military establishment. More than this, we are increasing the consuming power of many friendly nations and helping to build up future markets for our rapidly expanding productive capacity." In 1956, the United States exported $9 billion in goods, and subtracting all the money spent on military aid, the United States still had a "comfortable surplus." Ike envisioned the United States "expanding markets" around the world. All of this resulted from a mutual security program that strengthened freedom and exhausted communism.[70]

In answering a letter from another friend who complained about the Girard case, Eisenhower recalled that when he took command of NATO he dealt with the "question of offenses committed by our soldiers on foreign soil." He argued that the "forward air bases are absolutely essential for our defense" and the United States had sought permission to put GIs in those areas. As a former officer serving in foreign lands, he worked to ensure that the men under his command received "fair and just treatment." He added: "I do not believe I should, by implication, be accused of failing to recognize and defend their rights as American soldiers." Nevertheless, Ike asked a rhetorical question in regard to a foreign soldier being trained in the United States: "Suppose one of these men while on leave in your community should burn your house. Would you be willing to send him for trial to a group of officers of his own nationality at the base where he may be training?" Eisenhower noted that a number of allies gave Americans a lot of leeway, "far more than I think we would be willing to give in like circumstances." True, the United States provided security to these countries, "but in some cases at least they feel that we are making of them targets which they otherwise might not be."[71]

Ike's consideration for U.S. allies proved to be wise. In the case of Japan, Ike's effort may have gone a long way to forestall increased Japanese hostility toward the U.S. presence there. In June 1957, just after the announcement that Girard would be handed over to the Japanese courts, the USIA asked nearly two thousand Japanese for their opinion of U.S. troops and bases in Japan. The USIA noted that from January 1956 to July 1957, Japanese perceptions of U.S. troops had deteriorated only slightly since the last poll, taken in late 1955. The percentage of Japanese who believed that relations between the general population and the American forces were poor increased from 15 to 23 percent. When asked why relations were not good, 13 percent believed that Japan remained "under American jurisdiction," 12 percent blamed different cultural and living standards, and 8 percent faulted lack of trust and understanding. Although a separate poll found that 20 percent of Japanese blamed the Girard case for unfavorable views of the United States, the USIA found no evidence of increased animosity toward U.S. forces. Forty-five percent believed that U.S. troops had more rights and privileges than they should. Thirty-four percent wanted the United States to withdraw immediately, while another 23 percent wanted a later withdrawal. Of nearly nine hundred Japanese interviewed, 22 percent wanted a withdrawal within a year or two, 16 percent in three to five years, and 4 percent in six to ten years. Fifty-six percent did not believe the bases were good for Japan, 19 percent feared that Japan would be dragged into a war or even be the victim of a nuclear attack, 14 percent opposed the requisition of land for the bases, 9 percent believed the bases undermined Japanese independence, and 7 percent believed the bases were for the defense of the United States, not Japan. Of the 53 percent of Japanese who knew of the U.S.-Japan Security Treaty, only 5 percent expressed satisfaction with it, while 17 percent expressed dissatisfaction. Five percent opposed the treaty because Japan was treated as an unequal, and 4 percent opposed the construction of U.S. bases.[72]

The animosity did not increase significantly even though statements elicited from Japanese civilians showed that U.S. soldiers often encouraged them to pick up shells and did fire on them from time to time. One Japanese woman said that soldiers would either give them shells or toss them into the bushes, making fun of the Japanese, "like feeding chickens." Others said that U.S. troops, much like William Girard, made a game of firing spent cartridges from their grenade launchers.[73]

The Girard trial, which got under way on August 29, lessened hostility

as well. It lasted into November, and by then Americans were already losing interest in the case. The events at Little Rock, Arkansas, in September
involving the fight over civil rights and desegregation distracted the nation.
The Soviet launch of *Sputnik,* the first manmade satellite, shocked the United
States to its core, and a failed attempt by the latter to launch its own satellite
only further humiliated the superpower. Some Americans seemed to come to
their senses about Girard after cooler reflection and realized that he did not
quite fit their portrayal of a hero. The *Houston Post* editorialized that the case
"has been a sorry affair from the beginning, full of sound and fury, signify-
ing nothing but human folly, irrationality and emotionalism rampant." As for
Girard, here was someone "barely on the threshold of manhood, and with a
mentality approaching the vacuous, he could scarcely be regarded by the Japanese . . . as representative of the forces that smashed them."[74] Even in Japan
people lost interest in the case. Few attended the court proceedings, where
the media outnumbered the spectators.[75]

In the final days of the trial, the chief justice told Girard that the "court
does not feel that you fired this . . . fatal shot with any intent to hit anyone." Leading questions from the chief justice prompted the soldier to say, "I
am sorry for what happened."[76] On November 19, the Japanese court found
Girard guilty and gave him a three-year suspended sentence. The court ruled
that the shell pickers shared some blame for the incident because they will-
ingly entered an area where live-fire military exercises were held, but it also
criticized the U.S. government for not doing a better job of disposing of the
spent cartridges. It further ruled that by luring the shell pickers and then
firing at them, Girard went beyond official duty out of "excessive mischief"
and for the "sole purpose of satisfying momentary caprice." The court found
no evidence that Girard despised the shell pickers.[77] With no appeal coming from Japanese prosecutors, Girard and Candy, now his wife, left Japan in
December, and he was discharged from the U.S. Army. Although he neither
confirmed nor denied the rumor, a source close to the Girard family claimed
that he received a less than honorable discharge. Over the next two years
Girard struggled to find work, especially after Candy gave birth to a child.[78]

Newspapers in the United States received the verdict with mixed reactions. Some acknowledged that the trial had been fair and that the Japanese
court had been very merciful, more so than a court-martial would have been.
Right-wing newspapers like the *New York Journal-American* and the *Pitts-
burgh Post-Gazette* agreed that the trial had been fair, but still insisted that
Girard should have been tried by court-martial. The *Baltimore Sun* remained
dissatisfied because the issue of SOFAs had not been settled, and the *Washington Post* warned that "the provincialism that has come to the surface dur-

ing the Girard controversy is a dangerous sign of weakness in a country that relies upon alliances for its security."[79]

In Japan there was opposition to the light sentence. If a Japanese citizen had committed the same offense, he or she would have received five years' imprisonment. Japanese were also surprised to learn that Girard earned almost as much money as the chief justice, who received hate mail, one of which declared, "Go home to America." The British embassy agreed that the trial had been fair, but that if there had been any bias, it was to let Girard off lightly. Interestingly, a week after the Girard verdict, two U.S. Air Force personnel were sentenced to three years' hard labor for punching a taxi driver and not paying a fare of 230 yen ($16 in 2015 American dollars).[80] Even if Japanese disagreed with the sentence, USIA detected a reversal in the negative trend toward the U.S. troop presence and believed that the American handling of the Girard case played a role in tempering Japanese anger. Likewise, State Department officials thought the trial resulted in an easing of tensions between the United States and Japan over jurisdiction.[81]

Yet, none of this resolved the issues that lay at the core of the events that had occurred in Taiwan since March. Asians still demanded a retrial of Sergeant Reynolds. They wanted an end to diplomatic immunity and a reduction in the number of military personnel and dependents on their soil who enjoyed the privilege. The ROC wanted a SOFA that gave it some jurisdiction. In the fight to hand Girard over to the Japanese, the Eisenhower administration spoke of how Japan should have jurisdiction and that nations did not recognize immunity from the law. These were the very arguments that lay at the heart of the Reynolds case, in which the United States refused to allow Reynolds to be tried in the Chinese judicial system. In light of Black Friday, would there be a significant change in American policy toward the ROC and the PRC? Would Washington reduce the number of advisors, provide them only limited diplomatic immunity, and sign a SOFA that gave the ROC broader jurisdiction? Would Americans learn their lesson and seek to change their attitudes and cast off their image as "snobs"?

14

Status Quo

Despite the tensions surrounding Black Friday, representatives from both the ROC and the United States did what they could to show that they were still Cold War allies. There were signs of goodwill. Numerous individuals paid their respects to those Americans injured and expressed condolences. A Chinese Boy Scout troop gave Ambassador Rankin a new American flag. Fruit baskets were given to Americans during the Dragon Boat Festival. In June, Defense Minister Yu Dawei visited U.S. installations on Guam. A team of American atomic scientists held conferences in Taiwan to discuss U.S.-ROC cooperation on the "peaceful uses of atomic energy." The U.S. Air Force band played for a crowd of seven thousand Chinese, including Chiang Kai-shek and his wife. General Bowen attended graduation ceremonies for the Chinese Military Academy.[1]

On September 9, 1957, the U.S. embassy staff moved back into the now refurbished building to great fanfare. Nearly four months had passed since the May 24 riots that wreaked so much destruction. Chinese and American bands played "The Star-Spangled Banner" as the Stars and Stripes was raised to the spot from which it had been ripped down on Black Friday. With the exception of Chiang Kai-shek, many ROC officials, including Chiang Ching-kuo, were in attendance. The ceremony passed with little concern on the part of the locals, lending credence to Andrew Franklin's belief that "there never has been any real or widespread anti-American feeling" in Taiwan.[2]

Beneath the open displays of mutual goodwill, however, resentment and fear on the American side persisted. Maurine Rankin, wife of the ambassador, found the riots "shocking . . . in view of what the U.S. have done for Taipei and the Nationalists for so many years and the money and help of every kind that has been so generously given." American morale in Taiwan plummeted, especially among those who directly experienced the riots. The embassy offered to allow female personnel and families of embassy staff to travel to Okinawa to get away from the strain caused by the riots.[3] Two months after Black Friday, Alexander Boase observed that he would "be happy" if he never saw "any part of the Far East again."[4] MAAG advisors engaged in a good deal of grumbling, and some may have been perturbed when an order went out stating that off-duty personnel could not carry a sidearm.[5] Before the riots, Frank Nesci, who was injured during the attack on the embassy, spoke with a number of MAAG personnel who had a low opinion of Sergeant Reynolds's character and believed that, for a man who had served in the army for so many years, he "used extremely poor judgment in killing Liu." They rued an action that brought discredit to all U.S. soldiers. After the riots, MAAG soldiers were so embittered with the Chinese that they regretted that Reynolds killed only one. Likewise, embassy personnel were "hardened toward the Chinese."[6]

Soon, both sides accused the other of acts of revenge. When the head of the U.S. Naval Auxiliary Communication Center eliminated a section of Chinese workers in an effort to downsize, the Chinese claimed that it was in retaliation for the riots.[7] In late July, an argument broke out between Americans and Chinese trying to share a small beach in Tamsui, a fenced-in area given exclusively to Americans by the ROC in 1952 known as MAAG Beach. Although top ROC officials could use the beach, a campaign by the Chinese press forced the ROC to open the area to the general public. The local Chinese populace suddenly resented this special privilege afforded to Americans and began throwing seaweed at American beachgoers. One U.S. officer commented, "Maybe we are imagining things. You can't put your finger on it but the Chinese seem to be pushing in on us."[8] An American woman also beat three Chinese soldiers "who resented the fact that her dog wanted to bite them." U.S. authorities shipped the woman off the island, but Chinese troops occupied the beach anyway and kept the Americans out. Once again, Americans blamed the so-called evil Chiang Ching-kuo for creating a mini version of Black Friday. When Admiral Ingersoll ordered the beach off-limits for twenty-four hours, the Chinese press accused the Americans of preferring racial segregation at the beach. Andrew Franklin called the charges absurd. Before the incident, Europeans and Chinese alike shared the beach, as long as they had passes.[9]

Even the issue of providing Ao Tehua with compensation remained contentious. On May 24, U.S. and Chinese officials in Taiwan were supposed to meet to discuss the matter. The riots not only prevented the meeting from occurring but, according to Rankin, "stiffened opposition among American officials here to any kind of payment as reflecting on court-martial, condoning riot and establishing bad precedent." Because of the American refusal to retry Reynolds, the ROC embassy in Washington suggested that Ao Tehua file a civil claim against Reynolds before a U.S.-ROC Joint Committee in Taipei. If the claim was denied, she could hire a lawyer and file a suit in the Court of Claims in Washington, D.C. If rejected there, she could sue Reynolds in U.S. courts and potentially win $10,000.[10]

As days passed, both the State Department and the ROC Foreign Ministry saw the political expediency of providing compensation, but there were complications. The ROC wanted the matter to disappear, and was prepared to quietly pay Ao Tehua NT$50,000–NT$100,000. Chinese newspapers in Manila, however, led a campaign to raise funds for the woman.[11] The Chinese press in Taiwan opposed Liu's widow taking "blood money" from the United States. John Foster Dulles argued that, since the Chinese would inevitably link compensation with the verdict, payment was preferable to not settling a claim that "has caused widespread resentment against the United States."[12] Likewise, others in the State Department viewed an ex gratia payment as a way of healing the political wounds caused by the riots.[13] In August, James Pilcher and the MAAG judge advocate general agreed that Ao Tehua should receive US$10,000, and proposed establishing a fund to which all U.S. government agencies could contribute money.[14] In October, Robertson told the Pentagon that, politically, payment to Ao Tehua was advisable. Although William Girard had yet to be convicted, compensation had already been offered to the husband of Sakai Naka. To not make payment would set a bad precedent, but payment would be an "act of grace and compassion" that would heal relations between the United States and the ROC. The ROC Foreign Ministry, however, advised Rankin that since the widow received US$4,000 from various Chinese associations, compensation would be "unwise" because the woman might refuse it "with unfortunate results for our public relations in Taiwan."[15]

Within nearly four months after the riots, Karl Rankin spoke with all the members of the country team to assess relations with their ROC counterparts. In a report to John Foster Dulles, he claimed that relations were "in a generally healthy state." Problems that existed before the riots remained, but there was progress, as measured by ROC willingness to take MAAG's and others' advice on matters. Ralph Powell, director of USIS, observed that "the Chinese wish to forget the May 24 incident . . . and that they desire to return to a *status quo ante*."[16] If that is truly what the Chinese wanted, they may have gotten more "status quo" than they bargained for.

In light of the events that had occurred just a few months before, one would think the United States would have made significant changes in either its policies or its practices and that Americans on Taiwan would have changed their attitudes and behavior. In September, President Eisenhower sent the Herter-Richards Mission, led by Christian Herter and James P. Richards. Richards warned Chiang Kai-shek that Washington was deeply concerned about the riots, and told the generalissimo point-blank that Americans wanted lower taxes and were increasingly opposed to foreign aid. (Indeed, a small number of Americans complained to their congressmen about the millions in foreign aid handed out each year that underpinned the anti-Americanism, including one who blamed people in Taiwan for using the protests "to air their hatred of this country."[17]) He further warned that congressmen were saying that if Chiang could not control a riot, how could he retake something as huge as mainland China? Overall, he saw Chiang Kai-shek as a dictator with good health and mind and Taiwan as economically stable, but Chinese morale was deteriorating and "latent anti-American feeling" existed. Richards concurred with one Chinese who suggested that Chiang Ching-kuo should go to the United States to get "thoroughly 'brain washed,'" meaning he should "have a thorough course in democratic institutions." Upon returning to Washington, Richards told Eisenhower and Dulles that any change in U.S. policy toward Taiwan would be "disastrous." The ROC claimed that armed intervention against the PRC could occur if discontent arose from within, a view that Richards did not discount. Moreover, he worried about the impact on the rest of Asia if the United States broke ties with the ROC.[18]

There actually was no need for concern. From the outset, U.S. officials, politicians, and political operatives took a number of steps to reassure Chiang Kai-shek that the American policy would remain unchanged. When the riots first occurred, White House Chief of Staff James Hagerty assured the ROC embassy that the White House deemed its government's "immediate and prompt actions [apologies] to be satisfactory," while Senator Knowland and House Minority Leader Joseph Martin (R-MA) promised to limit the riots' impact on U.S. aid for Taiwan. Although Senator John Sparkman (D-AL) blamed the stationing of troops in Taiwan for the riots, he told ROC diplomats not to be "too upset about it." Simply lay low, and "people would naturally forget it."[19] As early as June 8, Chiang Kai-shek concluded that while the riots had possessed the potential to turn the United States against the Chiang clique and push Washington to recognize the PRC, his apology of June 1 had had a profound effect because U.S. anger and talk about him and his son had diminished. This was in part because Edwin Plitt was satisfied that there was no ROC conspiracy and Karl Rankin admitted that he had been misled by rumors regarding Chiang Ching-kuo. In order to reassure allies that the United States would remain true to its policy, Dulles gave a speech in late June insisting Washington would not accord political recognition to Beijing.[20] To do so would undermine the hopes of millions of overseas Chinese and those on the mainland opposed to the communist regime, demoralize the ROC, and weaken communist resistance in Asia.[21]

As for Ike, in anger he often questioned why the United States kept troops in Asia, but he had no intention of abandoning the region. Even after the Reynolds riot, Eisenhower remained steadfast in his belief that if Taiwan fell to communism, dominoes would fall. In August 1957 he had a conversation with Senator Richard Russell (D-GA), who questioned Taiwan's value to the United States. Eisenhower answered that there was sure to be fallout in the Far East if Taiwan fell to the PRC. In 1958, during the second offshore crisis, in which the PRC opened fire on Jinmen and Mazu, Ike told Senator Theodore Green (D-RI), chairman of the Senate Foreign Relations Committee, who argued that the American people would never support military action to defend Jinmen, that the "whole Formosa Straits situation is intimately connected with the security of the United States and the free world." Eisenhower also reiterated to Britain's foreign minister his belief that "if Formosa were lost, then a hole would result in the very middle of the island chain of defense. Should the Reds eventually control Formosa, that . . . would be a real Munich."[22]

In September, the NSC proposed modifying NSC-5503, which could be interpreted as supporting ROC offensive operations against the PRC, so that the ROC military mission became a purely defensive one. The NSC planning board suggested that the notion that the ROC could launch such operations ran "counter to prudent U.S. advice and inhibits the attainment of other U.S. objectives with respect to Taiwan such as progress toward self-support." Because of fears that the ROC would build up its military and launch an attack, the NSC wanted to make clear to the ROC that, barring changes in the PRC or in the world generally, U.S. military and economic assistance would not be "premised on the assumption of the GRC's return to power on the mainland."[23]

When Eisenhower learned of these proposed changes, he emphatically disagreed, saying that ROC hope of returning was the only thing sustaining morale. Dulles agreed, believing that any change in policy with regard to ROC military missions would be a "major disaster." Although Chiang Kai-shek believed that discontent within the PRC would open the door to military intervention, the chances of the PRC experiencing a situation akin to Hungary or Poland were slim. Nevertheless, the "series of small islands and peninsula countries," like the ROC, in Asia relied on the hope that the PRC would "one day blow up." Dulles declared that if military missions in Taiwan were changed in a manner that destroyed ROC hopes, "the United States would lose the whole show in the Far East. We simply could not afford to permit the Chinese Nationalists to think we believe that a Communist China was a permanent fixture of history." Yet, Eisenhower made it clear that if there was such a blowup, the U.S. response would be limited, such as providing amphibious landing craft. The president wanted military assistance to be focused on "defensive equipment." Although he and Dulles remained committed to defending the island chain, Ike opposed any type of military buildup that suggested that the United States supported an offensive.[24]

Thus, in the opinion of Andrew Franklin, the United States and the ROC persisted in their contradictory policies regarding the offshore islands. The United States protected them for defensive purposes, but the ROC retained them for offensive ones. In late 1957, ROC officials claimed that there was enough discontent in the PRC that all one had to do was invade and the people would be with them. For years, the government maintained Mainland Recovery Committees that planned for "the return." At one point, Paul Meyer told the British that if a Hungary-type scenario occurred in the PRC, "neither the Nationalists nor the Americans would necessarily stand by." Nevertheless, in the aftermath of the 1958 offshore crisis, in which U.S. public opinion and Western allies spoke out against going to war with the PRC over Jinmen and Mazu, Dulles prevailed on Chiang Kai-shek to publicly renounce the use of force in recovering the mainland. Although Chiang and other government officials later reinterpreted the statement to mean that force was not the only option and continued to hold out the hope of a Hungary-type uprising occurring in the PRC, Eisenhower still refused to sanction an attack for fear of a general war and possibly the collapse of the ROC.[25]

One change that occurred in the aftermath of the riots pertained to personnel. Richards blamed Karl Rankin for being in Hong Kong "without permission" during the protests. The implication was that Rankin was not at his post to help his people deal with a crisis. Richards was also annoyed with Rankin's attitude of treating the riots "as 'one of those things' that might happen anywhere" and for agreeing with Chiang Kai-shek on every matter regardless. As a result, Richards recommended that Rankin be recalled. Arguably, Karl Rankin should have been in Taiwan dealing with top ROC leaders in the hours prior to the riots, trying to find a solution satisfying to both sides before events got out of hand. His idea of separating the verdict from the embassy by being out of the country clearly failed. Walter Robertson agreed that, after seven years in Taiwan, Rankin should be transferred, but he insisted this was no reflection on Rankin's performance, which he judged as "outstanding." The next month, Rankin was offered the post to Yugoslavia. In January 1958, the State Department reassigned him to Belgrade. Even this change reflected continuity: he was replaced by Everett Drumright, another staunch supporter of Chiang Kai-shek.[26]

Although the United States did not change high policy, it could have modified the agreements that legalized the status of U.S. military personnel and gave them diplomatic immunity. The protests could have been an impetus to sign a SOFA with Taiwan. ROC officials watched the Girard case with interest. Chinese legislators believed that their agreements with the United States allowed them to demand that Reynolds be tried in Chinese courts. He was not on duty when he killed Liu Ziran. He shot a man he claimed was a peeping tom, making it a "private matter."[27] During the debate over SOFAs, the U.S. government spoke of sovereignty, nations exercising jurisdiction when crimes were committed on their soil, and world opposition to diplomatic immunity. Time and again, the Eisenhower administration and members of Congress argued that extraterritoriality could no longer remain the order of the day. All of the arguments made to justify allowing Japan to try Girard applied equally to Taiwan. Ike promised that the United States did not intend to impose a new imperialist system. This was a golden opportunity to win Chinese support by giving the ROC greater jurisdiction and to end the abuse of diplomatic immunity.

Instead, the Reynolds riot undercut any interest in a SOFA. In July 1957, the NSC's Progress Report for Taiwan declared that Black Friday had "seriously impaired the relations of mutual confidence that had previously existed between Chinese and Americans in Taiwan" and made it "very much more difficult to conclude negotiation of a status of forces agreement." It added, "there is an atmosphere of restraint where before close and cordial relations were common."[28]

The Americans showed little interest because the light sentences passed down by the Chinese courts against the rioters did not reassure them that justice could be found in the Chinese legal system. U.S. embassy officials were already upset with O. K. Yui's report, which essentially called Reynolds a murderer and criticized the court-martial. Rankin pointed out that ROC authorities originally insisted that sending Reynolds outside of Taiwan would cause more anger than a not guilty verdict. Now they lamented that the trial was held "on Chinese soil, since it recalled the days of extraterritoriality." Americans still believed that the ROC looked upon the riots with a degree of satisfaction, and that the light sentences were "an effort to cover up" and protect those at the top who were responsible. The U.S. embassy's portrayal of the Chinese courts-martial as a "cover up for more important persons" and for questioning the "good faith and integrity of the Chinese Government's serious effort to bring to justice all persons responsible for the destructive acts" incensed the ROC Foreign Ministry.[29]

Regardless, the riots raised for Rankin "a doubt as to whether an American could be assured of a fair trial in a Chinese court if politics became involved."[30] He explained to Frank Nash that if there was a certainty of guilt and a Chinese promise not to punish an individual more severely than would occur under U.S. law, only then would he consider giving the ROC criminal jurisdiction. Rankin admitted later that there was "no absolute assurance of justice in any court, including our own," and, maybe after cooler reflection, observed that in nearly all cases, "Chinese courts undoubtedly would treat an American serviceman fairly." Yet, in those exceptional cases, the United States had to convince the ROC to waive jurisdiction.[31] The Reynolds case most certainly would have fallen into such an exceptional category. He thought that a Chinese court, looking at the same evidence, would have sentenced Reynolds to "30 to 90 days in prison to save face for a Chinese official, albeit a minor one, who was caught in an embarrassing situation and paid with his life. That is not our idea of justice." In his report to Eisenhower, Nash concluded that "until the question of adequacy is resolved by some authoritative determination, such as a comprehensive study of Chinese judicial procedures and practices, the US position should be that any status of forces agreement should provide, in practice at least, for exclusive US jurisdiction over US personnel covered by the agreement."[32]

American officials recognized, though, that after an event like Black Friday, the ROC would not only refuse to waive its right of jurisdiction, but would demand a new agreement to restrict diplomatic immunity. In this respect, they were very right. In July, Foreign Minister George Yeh told a Chinese reporter that SOFA talks were on hold because of the whole question of "jurisdiction," and that the people did not welcome foreigners with diplomatic immunity.[33] One Chinese legislator asked, "Do we have to give their pet dogs diplomatic immunity too?"[34] Some ROC officials wanted immunity limited to colonels and above. When Yeh proposed to Rankin that diplomatic immunity apply only to MAAG officers, the ambassador made it clear that, with congressional anger over the Girard case and the pending U.S. Supreme Court decision, it was "premature to advance new proposals on criminal jurisdiction." The higher echelons of the ROC government likewise recognized the American fear that if they allowed the Chinese to try one U.S. soldier, the Chinese would want to try all GIs who committed a crime.[35]

In the face of what Nash described as "Chinese repeated insistence that they cannot accept a status of forces agreement having jurisdiction provisions less favorable to China than those with Japan and the NATO countries," Rankin understood the need to find a solution that allowed the ROC to save face. He proposed that, in an exchange of letters that would accompany the new SOFA, there should be language that gave the United States "the initiative in seeking a waiver of jurisdiction in any case which seemed to be to us of 'particular importance.'" In other words, the United States would determine what cases were of "particular importance." Rankin added that if Washington had treated the Reynolds case as such and quickly made an ex gratia payment to Liu Ziran's widow, the ROC, "in view of their dependence on United States support," would have waived jurisdiction and Black Friday would have been avoided.[36]

The State Department demurred. Walter Robertson pointed out that "adoption of your proposed formula in the case of Taiwan would create an undesirable precedent in our negotiations with other countries." He was still prepared to give the ROC a SOFA that contained the NATO-Netherlands formula, which, by virtue of the secret minute, had worked well in Japan, where U.S. troops were given more lenient sentences than a U.S. court-martial would have meted out. The State Department had already assured Frank Bow that it would seek a SOFA with Taiwan that contained "jurisdictional provisions as favorable to the United States" as those found in similar agreements with U.S. allies. Rankin questioned the NATO-Netherlands formula's "appropriateness in this part of the world," but he thought that Taiwan would demand no less than that formula and expected it would work in Taiwan.[37] Even if the United States granted Taiwan a SOFA, the ROC knew that MAAG advisors, the bulk of U.S. military personnel in Taiwan, retained diplomatic immunity.[38]

As a result, there was no movement on either side to reach an agreement. As an official in the ROC Foreign Ministry explained, "things have not been the same since May 24 and it is necessary to proceed slowly and meticulously in view of public opinion and criticism of the Executive by the Legislative Yuan." In particular, ROC politicians demanded an investigation as to why Taiwan should accord diplomatic immunity to U.S. soldiers and why it could not get a SOFA similar to the ones signed with Japan and NATO. Another, commenting about a corruption case in Taiwan, argued that the ROC "could scarcely conduct successful negotiations with the U.S. on a status of forces agreement unless the dignity of Chinese law is upheld and freed of corruption."[39] In 1958, when the Chinese showed interest in restarting SOFA talks, they still demanded jurisdiction in matters that went beyond "security offenses," including "causing the death of a human being, or rape, or smuggling, or illicit traffic of narcotics."[40]

In the meantime, both sides took actions to prevent another riot. The ROC declared that its education would now emphasize citizenship and not nationalism. Just days after the riots, Chiang Kai-shek gave a speech in which he praised Americans for their "scientific management" and exhorted his people to emulate the American administrative management style of taking personal responsibility. He also pointed to the failure to show initiative when dealing with an event like Black Friday and the failure to use force. Americans observed Chinese police undergoing riot control training. The ROC also tried to educate its people on why U.S. advisors were in Taiwan and had diplomatic immunity. It issued a pamphlet entitled "Strengthen Chinese-American Cooperation, Destroy the Common Enemy" that declared that the May 24 riots gave the impression "that our nation is uncivilized and ignorant of international law and diplomatic knowledge." The pamphlet noted that when the Defense Department in Washington turned down the ROC's request for a retrial of Sergeant Reynolds, "it was nevertheless another stab at our feelings." Yet, it quoted the Fifth Amendment of the U.S. Constitution and articles from the UCMJ, which greatly differed from Chinese law, to show that retrial was impossible because Reynolds would be placed in double jeopardy. It went on to discuss how diplomatic immunity was an international courtesy, and should not be equated to extraterritoriality. MAAG personnel all over the world enjoyed the same privilege—in Spain, Turkey, Iran, Greece, Japan, and elsewhere. Finally, the pamphlet explained that even if the ROC had had a SOFA with the United States prior to March 20, Reynolds would still have had immunity.[41]

Concurrently, the United States worked to ensure that its officials in Taiwan were "indoctrinated in Chinese customs." It encouraged U.S. agencies in Taiwan to reduce their personnel, stressed the importance of U.S.-ROC mutual interests, and provided better orientation for Americans traveling to Taiwan. It further established a more expeditious process of paying off claims against U.S. personnel, and ensured that Americans carried liability insurance if they drove their own cars. Finally, the United States attempted to reduce the size of MAAG by the end of 1958, tried to tighten control of the black market, and established a procedure that expedited ex gratia payments. This latter procedure was put to the test in 1958 when a U.S. Air Force sergeant, for reasons not made clear, injured a Chinese officer. The Americans quickly expressed condolences and offered compensation. Although ultimately rejected, the offer, in American judgment, showed a greater sensitivity that resulted in "smooth settlement."[42]

These measures were necessary because American attitudes had not changed. Two months after the riots, constant complaints were made about Americans' driving. The situation was so bad that the U.S. embassy distributed a letter written by a MAAG captain in the TDC calling on compatriots to show more courtesy on the road. The letter noted that nearly all automobiles in Taiwan were U.S.-made and most had been issued a diplomatic license plate. Americans assumed that they had "special privileges" that made them superior to all other traffic, including pedestrian, and allowed them to use the car's horn to demand the right of way at all times. The letter emphasized, *"A horn is not intended as an instrument to blast obstacles from the path."* The captain asked, "if you 'drive with your horn,' you are proclaiming to the public: 'I am demanding special privilege for myself; I have power and armour to overcome lesser persons.' Is this the spirit of a 'good American?' DOES IT MAKE FRIENDS?"[43]

Accidents continued to occur. Nearly a year after Black Friday, a U.S. Air Force captain accidentally knocked down a Chinese man while driving his car. The man's friend followed the American, busted out a rear window with his fist, and then slapped the officer twice after he stopped and got out of his car. A crowd gathered, but the officer did not retaliate and Chinese policemen arrested the assailant, who was drunk.[44]

The United States still had the opportunity to do something about diplomatic immunity and the number of Americans living in Taiwan. Nearly a month after Black Friday, Rankin wrote that the large population of Americans robbed diplomatic immunity of its original meaning. In November, Nash provided Eisenhower with analysis of the riots. He observed that "the Asian wave of nationalism has not missed Taiwan, and considering the concentration of official Americans in and around Taipei, resentment of their special immunities is bound to exist."[45] This nationalism was "potentially anti-American, not because of a basic dislike of America and Americans, but because of a deep-seated objection to special privileges enjoyed by foreigners on their soil."[46] It was imperative that the United States reduce to a minimum those personnel that enjoyed diplomatic immunity because "last May's attack on our Embassy in Taipei brought . . . a realization that the mere presence of large numbers of Americans, in privileged position as compared to the local citizenry, can stir the resentment of the inhabitants even though there are no large areas of land taken over by the United States for military bases." Over a year after Black Friday, U.S. military intelligence detected that the tensions that led to the riots remained, "although abating, and probably will again become latent."[47]

Despite the administration wanting to reduce the number of U.S. personnel in places like Taiwan, there were actually over 11,200 Americans there in March 1958 as opposed to 9,903 on May 1, 1957. Over one thousand personnel were sent to Taiwan to help with the Matador missile installation. From Belgrade, Rankin continued to decry the thousands of Americans and the overlapping missions that he claimed cost American taxpayers "$50 million annually for overhead in Free China, to carry out our programs." More importantly, he asked, "Why are more official Americans needed to operate an aid program in a sovereign state than formerly were required to govern a colony of equivalent size? Such neo-colonialism gives substance to Red charges of American 'occupation.'"[48]

With the increase in U.S. military personnel in 1958, what the U.S. government believed to be the underlying causes of the Reynolds riot persisted. There also seemed to be a growing breakdown in discipline among U.S. advisors that became alarming to military leaders. General Leander L. Doan, who now headed MAAG-Taiwan, issued a standing order against lax discipline, because of the "appalling" increase in the number of vehicular accidents involving U.S. military personnel, and the growing number of reports of "drunkenness, disorderliness, and disregard of the rights and feelings of others in public places." The general also complained about soldiers "instigating violence in public . . . using disrespectful, profane, and obscene language; public displays of affection, which are an insult to the Chinese people; and non-payment of pedicab drivers, small merchants and bar owners for services or goods rendered." Soldiers also tended to be sloppy in their salutes if they gave them at all. Doan insisted, "Our conduct and appearance in public are important factors in obtaining the respect of the Chinese people."[49]

The potential for incidents was not limited to Americans. In one instance, a Chinese sentry chased and pointed a loaded pistol, "ready to fire," at a MAAG sergeant's wife as she tried to drive the housegirl of a U.S. Marine sergeant to his compound home. Fortunately, the man did not fire and later apologized to the American woman. In another case, a Chinese navy sentry refused to allow two Chinese housegirls to enter an American compound and even slapped one despite their holding passes. In a third instance, two young American boys, whose fathers were MAAG officers, discovered a group of Chinese marines going through their picnic lunch. When they tried to retake possession, a marine punched one of the boys, a twelve year old, in the eye, leaving "a sizable bruise and egg above and behind his right eye." The commandant for the ROC Marine Corps apologized for the incident and ordered that the man responsible be detained for one month.[50]

Although the situation remained ripe for an incident, SOFA talks dragged on. On August 12, 1958, the ROC Foreign Ministry submitted a draft SOFA that borrowed heavily from the NATO one. A meeting was held, but the offshore crisis of 1958 interrupted the talks. The crisis led to the "rapid influx of non-MAAG United States units," and Washington wanted to provide an "umbrella" of legal coverage for them. In November, Washington gave the ROC a draft of the interim agreement in which the United States refused to budge from its original position of demanding exclusive jurisdiction. The drawdown in tensions led the Chinese to ignore the interim agreement and to push for a Japan-like SOFA because of pressure from the Legislative Yuan.[51] Then, in February 1959, a prominent Chinese lawmaker was killed in a car accident involving a GI. This led to increased demands by the Legislative Yuan and Chinese in general to seek a "speedy conclusion" of negotiations, but the ROC Foreign Ministry was also "emphatic" in its refusal to grant exclusive jurisdiction and spoke again of limiting diplomatic immunity for MAAG advisors.[52]

Thus, the protests of May 24 that devolved into angry riots brought about no appreciable changes. The agreements according diplomatic immunity remained in place, and the majority of Americans there remained beyond Chinese justice. On Black Friday, Chinese and Taiwanese wielded the only weapons they possessed to express their outrage against perceived American injustice and diplomatic immunity for a GI who took an Asian man's life. If the riots achieved anything, it was as an outlet, maybe a necessary safety valve, to release pent-up anger and frustration that came from being in close proximity with a Little America and all of the privileges and attitudes that came with it.

Epilogue

Warnings Unheeded

In 1960, President Eisenhower visited Taiwan, becoming the first and only Cold War president to do so. The people greeted him warmly. The shouts of "Kill the Westerners" from that day in May 1957 had long since faded. (By contrast, Ike cancelled his visit to Japan, where violent mass protests broke out against the U.S.-Japan Security Treaty and American use of Japan to launch U-2 spy planes.) The offshore crisis of 1958, the last major crisis to affect the alliance until its demise in 1980, solidified relations once more. Yet, Americans grew tired of the tensions that led to threats of the use of nuclear weapons by the United States over the offshore islands. They increasingly leaned toward supporting measures to reduce tensions with the PRC.[1] It is possible that the riots created for some Americans an image of Chiang Kai-shek as an ungrateful ally not worth a World War III or nuclear Armageddon.

In the meantime, the issue of diplomatic immunity for U.S. military advisors faded away. After touring Asia in early 1958, John Foster Dulles expressed more concern with how communist propaganda used every official statement to prove that the United States was "militaristic." There were also comments from the Senate Foreign Relations Committee that U.S. military assistance "helped to create abroad a militaristic image of the United States which is a distortion of our national character." This led to the formation of yet another presidential committee, led by William H. Draper. The Draper Committee ultimately concluded that Asian nations, which received 27 percent of U.S. military assistance, did not perceive the United States as militaristic because they depended so heavily on American aid in the face of potential Chinese Communist aggression.[2]

Eisenhower still worried about the problem of too many U.S. troops and dependents abroad. In 1960, he ordered that 200,000 of the 484,000 U.S. dependents overseas be called back home, but the chief targets were the United Kingdom, Japan, West Germany, and France. Taiwan was not affected. In the final days of his presidency, Eisenhower recommended cuts in military personnel abroad, including MAAG, but this was in reaction to a gold crisis, not diplomatic immunity and hostile foreign reaction to it. When he met with President-elect John F. Kennedy, Eisenhower explained that although dependents were being brought home, he faced resistance from the

State Department and worried about the morale of U.S. troops abroad that were impacted by this policy.[3]

Although the Kennedy administration paid attention to the overall problem, it continued to use MAAG to fulfill U.S. foreign policy goals, expanding its presence in Laos, Cambodia, Thailand, and, of course, South Vietnam, where it was increasingly used to train and engage in counterinsurgency warfare. In fact, Eisenhower recommended that Kennedy send a MAAG unit to Laos because "if Laos fell, then Thailand, the Philippines, and of course Chiang Kai-shek would go." The MAAG units were seen as preferable to ground forces because of potential local hostility. In 1961, Vice President Lyndon Johnson visited Southeast Asia, including Taiwan. He argued that without the island outposts of Japan, the Philippines, and Taiwan, "the vast Pacific becomes a Red Sea." With a prescience that he later ignored, Johnson warned Kennedy: "Asian leaders—at this time—do not want American troops involved in Southeast Asia other than on training missions. American combat troop involvement is not only not required, it is not desirable. Possibly Americans fail to appreciate fully the subtlety that recently-colonial peoples would not look with favor upon governments which invited or accepted the return this soon of Western troops." He concluded: "I consider the key here is to get our best MAAG people to control, plan, direct and exact results from our military aid program" in Southeast Asia.[4]

The Reynolds riot could have provided some warning of what could happen through the introduction of Americans into cultures very different from that of the United States. As the chief of MAAG for Cambodia would explain, "Few occidentals really understand Cambodia and Cambodians, and even fewer Cambodians really understand us." It certainly provided fodder for books like *The Ugly American*, which John F. Kennedy read. Published in 1958, William Lederer and Eugene Burdick's fictional account spoke of an "ugly American" who succeeded in dealing with Asians whereas others stumbled and bumbled while battling communism in Asia. Those characters became synonymous with what many believed to be "ugly Americans": people who, as representatives of the United States, were racist, ignorant of foreign cultures, and undercut American prestige and policy. In closing their novel with a factual overview of Asia, Lederer and Burdick noted that "there is a rising tide of anti-Americanism" among nations allied with the United States.[5]

The Kennedy administration consciously tried to find a better caliber of men to send as part of MAAG units throughout the world, presumably to avoid further outbursts. As with Taiwan, the administration and MAAG found themselves at odds with local governments. Political clashes led to MAAG withdrawal from Cambodia, where the U.S. embassy saw two instances of government-supported mob riots against it in 1964 and 1965, though the damage fell far short of Black Friday. In South Vietnam, the administration further violated the Geneva Accords by increasing the number of advisors there.[6] In a year, the number jumped from 3,205 to over 9,000. By 1963, there were nearly 17,000 U.S. advisors in South Vietnam.[7] The few thousand MAAG advisors sent to Taiwan that caused so much consternation in the 1950s paled in comparison. Long before then, some of the patterns from the Taiwan experience began to emerge. In 1961, while the Kennedy administration heatedly debated a proposal to deploy eight thousand troops there, Ngo Dinh Diem, South Vietnam's leader, opposed the introduction of U.S. ground forces. When the Americans suggested that their advisors participate in some of South Vietnam's "administrative organs," he refused, saying it would cause "nationalistic resentment" among the Vietnamese that the Viet Cong could capitalize upon. He further complained that "Americans got frustrated when things were not done 'their way,' causing resentment among Vietnamese" and that he did "not wish to build up situation like that which resulted in anti-American blow-out in Taiwan some time ago." He only wanted "certain Americans, on selective basis and on request."[8] Within two years, Diem would be overthrown with American acquiescence and executed by his own people. In 1965, Johnson escalated U.S. involvement there. By 1968, the approximately 550,000 troops deployed in South Vietnam, augmented by forces throughout Southeast Asia, represented an avalanche in terms of the exportation of U.S. systems and culture and the number of Americans abroad. The crimes committed by U.S. soldiers, not to mention the deaths caused by combat and war crimes on both sides, including My Lai, overwhelmingly diminished the significance of the shooting of Liu Ziran.

Despite the expansion of U.S. power in Southeast Asia and a greater presence of American personnel in Taiwan, the United States and the ROC still could not agree to a SOFA. Talks did not resume until June 1959, and remained stalled into both the Kennedy and Johnson administrations despite more incidents. In 1962, two MAAG enlisted men got drunk and beat Chinese men, women, and children at an intersection in Taipei. Chinese police had to use force to restrain both, one of whom cursed the arresting officers and threatened to assault another. There were also two allegations of rape. The first involved a MAAG sergeant who was charged for sexual assault after he allegedly forced a fifteen-year-old deaf-mute bar girl into his room and assaulted her twice. He denied knowing that she was a minor and said that he had paid her NT$200 for sex. There was evidence that the Chinese bar owner lied to the American, and the woman's father withdrew the complaint, but MAAG insisted that the man be transferred back to the United States. In the second instance, a twenty-year-old woman alleged rape against another MAAG sergeant and provided much detail. A medical examination showed that the woman's hymen had been penetrated for the first time in the previous forty-eight hours, which fit her accusation that she had been raped the previous day. Two days later, the sergeant handed NT$4,000 over to the woman's grandmother. The rape allegation was not pursued and the case was closed.[9]

In January 1963, SOFA negotiations restarted after a three-year hiatus, but after sixteen sessions, talks still could not overcome the obstacle of jurisdiction. By 1964, the State Department felt no "sense of urgency . . . to conclude an agreement just for the sake of an agreement." That is, until J. R. Harrod, an American civilian with the U.S. Air Force and father of two, was shot and killed by his American-Japanese wife because she discovered that he had a girlfriend in Japan. ROC and U.S. officials now had a reason to expedite talks.[10] The woman could not be tried under Chinese law, and the U.S. Supreme Court had ruled in 1957 (*Reid vs. Covert*) that U.S. citizens could not be court-martialed for capital crimes committed against their spouses who just happened to be in the military or worked for a military branch.[11] Within a few weeks there was a reported incident in which three GIs attacked a Chinese woman in Changhua, angering legislators and citizens once again.[12]

On August 31, 1965, both sides signed a SOFA similar to NATO's, but the jurisdiction clause was modeled after the one contained in the agreement with West Germany. The ROC waived its rights to jurisdiction except in cases involving "security offenses against the Republic of China, offenses causing the death of a human being, narcotics offenses, robbery, rape and arson." U.S. military personnel were protected from the ROC's Special Laws, which were derived from martial law, and could not be tried in a Chinese military court. Any that found themselves accused would be placed in U.S. custody until a trial handed down a verdict, and the ROC agreed to provide "comprehensive trial safeguards."[13]

After ten years of on-again, off-again talks, the ROC finally possessed an agreement that met most of its demands while assuring Americans that they would be treated well under the Chinese system of justice. The agreement exceeded the provisions of the SOFA signed with the Philippines that same month and that with South Korea in 1967.[14] In Taiwan, the agreement received mixed reviews. Although the ROC praised it, some legislators noted that MAAG personnel still enjoyed immunity. They criticized the SOFA for falling short by not placing all U.S. soldiers under Chinese jurisdiction or for being another "unequal treaty." The ROC legislature ratified the agreement by a vote of 134–22, but nearly one hundred legislators boycotted the session, and over two hundred walked out of the Legislative Yuan prior to the vote. Nevertheless, even if limited, the SOFA proved wise. By 1968, not only were there nine thousand military and civilian personnel with seventy-five hundred dependents living in Taiwan, but three thousand U.S. servicemen visited the island every month for "rest and recuperation" (in other words, spending time hooking up with girls in bars and at hot spring baths). Of those stationed in Taiwan with dependents, it was estimated that three thousand soldiers enjoyed diplomatic immunity.[15]

Incidents continued to occur. In 1966, a GI on R & R got drunk and set a fire in a hotel that killed several guests. Although the ROC demanded jurisdiction in this case, it never went to trial for reasons never explained. That same year, a drunken U.S. soldier struck and dragged a Chinese woman six hundred yards with his car while driving at a high rate of speed, killing her instantly. He stopped only because he hit another pedestrian. He then left the scene. His wife, who had tried to drive them both home until he complained of her slow driving and took over the wheel, turned him in to authorities. The ROC demanded jurisdiction and he was sentenced to twenty months in prison for manslaughter. After appeal, the Taiwan High Court reduced the sentence to six months or payment of a fine in lieu of a prison stay. The over-turning of the original verdict angered a number of Taiwan jurists because the High Court ignored ROC laws in an effort to be lenient toward someone who had to come to Taiwan to defend it.[16]

If the United States had not demanded diplomatic immunity for advisors like Reynolds, but rather had agreed to limited immunity or a SOFA umbrella for MAAG advisors, the ROC judicial system might have treated Reynolds in a similar fashion. Possibly either a Chinese judge or the High Court, assuming Reynolds filed an appeal, would have shown similar leniency toward him. Both sides could claim that the process worked. Of course, Rankin might have complained that this was not justice. Americans and Chinese would have agreed with him whether they truly thought Reynolds guilty or innocent. Politics, though, superseded justice, and justice was often a casualty of the Cold War.

Looking back more than fifty years, the events surrounding Robert Reynolds, as well as William Girard, seem to be a historical "much ado about nothing." The U.S.-ROC alliance was resilient enough to survive what was indeed a serious crisis. Those who hoped that America would recognize the PRC, sought U.N. trusteeship over Taiwan, or wanted to see the United States thrown out of Taiwan were disappointed. The Taiwan protests of 1957 provide little encouragement to those who seek to modify the behavior or practices of a hegemon, ally or not.

From a broader perspective, the Taiwan protests need to be seen as part of the growing resistance or backlash to U.S. hegemony by its allies prior to the Vietnam War. American attitudes toward Asians seemed rather callous. GIs could kill Asians and be set free, and in their defense of their troops some Americans were not very mindful of those who lost their lives. During the heated debate over Girard, William Harpham, the British minister to Japan, wrote, "it is difficult to avoid the impression that in Japan the interests of Girard's victims do not count beside the political capital to be made out of his alleged crime, while in the United States amid all the shouts for rights and justice for Girard, no one seems to have stopped to remember that his victim's children, too, were 'mother's sons.'" Similar callousness toward blacks protesting segregation at Little Rock, Arkansas, in 1957 and Birmingham, Alabama, in 1963 only heightened for allies, neutrals, and enemies alike the sense of American racial prejudice. Incidents involving U.S. troops continued to occur, including two in the Philippines in 1964 that were similar to the Girard case. They led to anti-American demonstrations as well as anti-base and anti-nuclear demonstrations that evolved into anti–Vietnam War protests in Japan and elsewhere.[17]

The Taiwan protests were a warning then and now of the inherent dangers of putting U.S. soldiers into other countries that are immune to local justice. In the context of the Cold War and decolonization in Asia, the reliance on thousands of advisors (as opposed to dozens) who were protected by diplomatic immunity or demanding exclusive jurisdiction for U.S. forces was a form of playing with political fire. Even in the twenty-first century, incidents involving individuals who are beyond local laws can still create a great deal of resentment, particularly when foreign hosts find that U.S. military justice operates differently from their own and from American criminal trials. U.S. officials seethed at the newspaper reporting of the 1950s that helped to fan Chinese anger during the Reynolds case. Today, they face a new world in which average citizens relying on the Internet can send texts, tweets, videos, and photos to expose alleged crimes, share information, rally protestors, and even launch cyber attacks against the United States in retaliation or as a form of protest.

If the United States does not want to face future backlashes like the Taiwan protests or like those in Cambodia that led to the expulsion of the MAAG there, it needs to give host nations more jurisdictional voice. In some respects, Washington has been willing to demand exclusive jurisdiction while allowing the host nation the opportunity to request that the United States waive *its* jurisdictional rights in cases involving offenses against local laws committed while not on duty.[18] On the other hand, pilots operating

UAVs over Afghanistan, Pakistan, and elsewhere from within the continental United States or outside the affected area are protected from prosecution by foreign courts. Even supporters of reliance on UAVs in the War on Terror are worried that the United States will set "a troublesome precedent with regard to extrajudicial and extraterritorial killings."[19] In combat zones like Iraq (prior to the American withdrawal) or Afghanistan, exclusive jurisdiction made sense, but with time and more stability the United States could cede some jurisdiction. However, journalists have noted that one reason why the United States withdrew from Iraq in 2011 was because it failed to secure immunity for its troops from Iraqis, who saw immunity as an infringement of their sovereignty. In 2014, the United States threatened to do the same with regard to Afghanistan unless it secured exclusive jurisdiction.[20]

In situations in which there are thousands with immunity and not at war or engaged in combat on a significant basis, the privilege of diplomatic immunity or a SOFA that provides military immunity in the form of exclusive jurisdiction sends the wrong message. Threat of court-martial aside, putting U.S. troops beyond local laws does not encourage soldiers to abide by or respect the laws of a host nation. Rather, it promotes a contrary lack of discipline and prejudice against locals. The privilege makes allies essentially second-class citizens in their own country and creates the impression that they are occupied and hold a lower status internationally. It also undermines America's soft power, meaning its culture and values, not only in solidifying allied support but in winning friends from other nations. If the United States remains committed to pursuing a policy of mutual security, it must show that it is committed to the cause of justice, for its soldiers and its allies alike.

Notes

Introduction

1. Frank C. Nash, "United States Overseas Military Bases: Report to the President," December 1957, 3–4, Dwight David Eisenhower Papers, Dwight David Eisenhower Presidential Library, Abilene, Kansas (hereafter cited as Eisenhower Papers); "Report From Washington—Prescott Bush-Mansfield B. Sprague Radio Interview," June 14, 1957, Prescott Bush Papers, University of Connecticut Library, Thomas J. Dodd Research Center, Storrs, Connecticut.

2. See "Background of the Status of Forces Agreement," an attachment to "NATO Status of Forces Agreement, March 18, 1953," box 7, NATO Status of Forces, FE, 1953, Misc. Subject Files, RG 59, NA; for Article VII, see http://www.nato.int/cps/en/natolive/official_texts_17265.htm (accessed March 3, 2013).

3. Johnson, *Blowback*, 43; see also Johnson, *The Sorrows of Empire*, 5.

4. Nash, "United States Overseas Military Bases: Report to the President," Appendix, 71.

5. Mason, *Status of Forces Agreement (SOFA)*, http://www.fas.org/sgp/crs/natsec/RL34531.pdf (accessed March 5, 2013).

6. Johnson, *Blowback*, 34–37, 42–43; Johnson, *The Sorrows of Empire*, 92–93.

7. The concept of nations asking the United States to provide economic and military assistance in the face of a threat is discussed in Lundestad, "Empire by Invitation?," 263–277; Lundestad uses the terms empire and hegemony interchangeably, but his discussion of "America's position of strength in 1945" implies hegemony.

8. Reynolds, *Rich Relations*; see also Longmate, *The GIs*.

9. Eisenhower to Nash, October 15, 1956, in Nash, "United States Overseas Military Bases: Report to the President."

1. A Shooting on Grass Mountain

1. Reynolds Court-Martial File, RG 153, Records of the Office of the Judge Advocate General (Army) 1692–1981, NA, St. Louis, Missouri; Eighth United States Army Korea, Meritorious Unit Citation, May 26, 1951, *danghao* 425.2/0031, WJDA; Proceedings of a General Court-Martial, Taipei, Taiwan, May 20, 1957, box 9, CA, 1957, RG 59, NA.

2. Statement of Robert G. Reynolds, March 21, 1957, box 9, CA, 1957, RG 59, NA; Robert Reynolds Testimony, April 17, 1957, in Reynolds Court-Martial File.

2. Islands against the Red Tide

1. Jespersen, *American Images of China*, 59–81; Christensen, *Useful Adversaries*, 77–79, 93–97, 100–109; Department of State, *United States Relations with China*,

405; Blum, *Drawing the Line*, 165–177; Finkelstein, *Washington's Taiwan Dilemma, 1949–1950*, 207–250; Accinelli, *Crisis and Commitment*, 3–17.

2. Diary entry, June 22, 1951, V. K. Wellington Koo Papers, Butler Library, Columbia University, New York, New York (hereafter cited as Koo Papers); Qin, ed., *Zongtong*, 9:9, 10.

3. Phillips, *Between Assimilation and Independence*, 73–84; Lai, Myers, and Wei, *A Tragic Beginning*, 50–160. For an older account, see Kerr, *Formosa Betrayed*, 232–310.

4. Huebner, "The Abortive Liberation of Taiwan," 258; Phillips, *Between Assimilation and Independence*, 98–102.

5. Roy, *Taiwan*, 109–110; Craft, *V. K. Wellington Koo*, 223–235.

6. Accinelli, *Crisis and Commitment*, 17–34, 67; Christensen, *Useful Adversaries*, 133–137; President Truman's Special Message to Congress on the Mutual Security Program, May 24, 1951, http://www.mtholyoke.edu/acad/intrel/pentagon/ps3.htm (accessed May 8, 2012); Clough, *Island China*, 10.

7. Qin, ed., *Zongtong*, 9:222; Burns, Memorandum for Director, International Security Affairs, Department of State, March 26, 1951, box 7, FE, Records Relating to Economic Aid, 1948–1958, RG 59, NA.

8. Qin, ed., *Zongtong*, 9:233.

9. Burns, Memorandum for Director; Johnson to Clubb, March 13, 1951, Department of State, *Foreign Relations of the United States, 1951, Korea and China*, vol. 7, part 2, 1591–1596; Lin, "Taiwan's Secret Ally"; Tucker, *Uncertain Friendships*, 69.

10. Chase, *Front Line General*, 162–171, 184.

11. Barber, "Military Assistance Advisory Group Formosa," 53–59. For a brief overview of MAAG's history, see *U.S. MAAG-Taiwan*.

12. "Karl Rankin, 92, U.S. Diplomat in Europe and East for 34 Years," *New York Times*, February 9, 1991; Rankin, *China Assignment*, 29, 159; Foreign Office Records (hereafter cited as FO) 371/127472/FCN10345/56, Franklin to Dalton, December 16, 1957, Public Records Office, National Archives, Kew, UK (hereafter cited as PRO).

13. Rankin, *China Assignment*, 262, 330; Cullather, "The U.S. and Taiwanese Industrial Policy," 5–12.

14. Rankin, *China Assignment*, 260–261.

15. Ibid., 262, 330. A brief biography of Powell is found in U.S. Congress, House of Representatives, *United States Policy in Asia: Hearings Before the Subcommittee of the Far East and the Pacific of the Committee on Foreign Relations*, 7; Belmonte, *Selling the American Way*, 57–58, 71–72; Kerr, *Formosa Betrayed*, 146–147; Tucker, *Uncertain Friendships*, 77; interview with Seymour I. Nadler, November 21, 1989, Association for Diplomatic Studies and Training Foreign Affairs Oral History Project Information Series, Library of Congress, http://memory.loc.gov/service/mss/mssmisc/mfdip/2005%20txt%20files/2004nad01.txt. (accessed May 8, 2012).

16. Rankin, *China Assignment*, 260; Cull, *The Cold War and the United States Information Agency*, 103.

17. "Formosa," box 6, CA, Mutual Defense Assistance Act, 1951, RG 59, NA;

Chase to Chiang, June 15, 1951, *Zhongmei junshi baogao yu jianyi* (Report and recommendations regarding ROC-U.S. military matters), *danghao* 427/0006, WJDA.

18. Debriefing of Lieutenant Colonel A. Bets, U.S. Air Attaché, "Formosa," box 2, CA, Formosa Military, RG 59, NA; views of Major General William C. Chase, February 18, 1952, ibid.; Department of Defense, *Taiwan*, 42; U.S. Department of the Army, General Staff, G-2, "The Chinese Nationalist Armed Forces," *Intelligence Review* (August 1951): 53.

19. Questions and Answers on Title III Program-Formosa, June 1951, box 7, FE, Records Relating to Economic Aid, 1948–1958, RG 59, NA; Webb to Lawton, April 17, 1951, ibid.; Review of Far Eastern Programs, NSC 135, November 18, 1952, ibid.

20. Garver, *The Sino-American Alliance*, 66, 235; Chase to multiple recipients, December 8, 1952, box 2, CA, Formosa Military, RG 59, NA; Yeh to Radford, August 6, 1953, *danghao* 427/0006, WJDA; 231st Meeting of the National Security Council, Washington, January 13, 1955, Department of State, *Foreign Relations of the United States, 1955–1957, China*, 2:18.

21. Garver, *The Sino-American Alliance*, 67; U.S. Military Assistance and Advisory Group-Formosa, Country Statement on MAP, December 1957, U.S. Army Military History Institute, Army War College, Carlisle Barracks, Pennsylvania (hereafter cited as MHI).

22. Tucker, *The China Threat*, 73–87.

23. Eisenhower to Churchill, February 18, 1955, Department of State, *Foreign Relations of the United States, 1955–1957, China*, 2:293.

24. Eisenhower to Churchill, March 22, 1955, box 10, Diary Series, Eisenhower Papers; Eisenhower to Churchill, March 29, 1955, ibid.; Eisenhower to Douglas, March 29, 1955, ibid.

25. Nash, "United States Overseas Military Bases: Report to the President," 34.

26. 240th Meeting of the National Security Council, March 10, 1955, Department of State, *Foreign Relations of the United States, 1955–1957, China*, 2:348; Eisenhower to Dulles, April 5, 1955, ibid., 2:447; National Intelligence Estimate, April 16, 1955, ibid., 2:480.

27. Diary entry, June 23, 1951, Koo Papers.

28. Robertson to Dulles, April 25, 1955, Department of State, *Foreign Relations of the United States, 1955–1957, China*, 2:512; Eisenhower-Radford telephone conversation, February 1, 1955, Eisenhower Papers.

29. Stump to Carney, January 28, 1956, Department of State, *Foreign Relations of the United States, 1955–1957, China*, 3:283–284; Robertson to Gray, July 23, 1956, ibid., 3:406.

30. Joint Agreement Pertaining to Matador Unit, March 23, 1957, *Mei tuniushi feidan budui zhuTai* (U.S. Matador missile unit deployed to Taiwan), *danghao* 426.2/0006, WJDA; chronology of events related to Matador, box 2, FE, Top Secret Files Relating to the Republic of China, 1954–1965, RG 59, NA; Robertson to Dulles, March 6, 1957, ibid.; Mindling and Bolton, *U.S. Air Force Tactical Missiles 1949–1969*, 134–135.

31. See Chinese and Western newspaper clippings in *danghao* 426.2/0006, WJDA; 611.93/5–1557, Johnson to Dulles, Confidential U.S. State Department Central Files, *China, People's Republic of China 1955–59, Foreign Affairs* (Frederick, Md.: University Publications of America, 1987), reel 5 (cited hereafter as *China, People's Republic of China 1955–59, Foreign Affairs*).

32. Country Statement on MAP, December 1957, MHI; Gaddis, *Strategies of Containment*, 146–154; Aliano, *American Defense Policy from Eisenhower to Kennedy*, 37–38.

33. McConnell to LeMay, February 9, 1954, Curtis E. LeMay Papers, Library of Congress, Washington, D.C.

34. Eisenhower-Dulles conversation, March 6, 1955, Department of State, *Foreign Relations of the United States, 1955–1957, China*, 2:336–337.

3. Advice and Dissent

1. For hegemony, see Hunt, *The American Ascendancy*, 308–314. For the argument that U.S. wars in Asia represented phases of dominance until defeat in Vietnam, see Hunt and Levine, *Arc of Empire*, 1–8. Hunt and Levine define empire as control of territory through coercion and use of native collaborators and military force. They prefer the term hegemony and claim that empire is not "interference." They also take issue with Jeremy Friedman, who, in a review of their work, does equate interference with empire. For this debate, see Friedman, "Review by Jeremy Friedman," 8; and Hunt and Levine, "Author's Response," 25–26.

2. Lin, "U.S.-Taiwan Military Diplomacy Revisited," 975–976, 977–978, 981, 989–990.

3. U.S. Policy toward Formosa and the Government of the Republic of China, January 15, 1955, Department of State, *Foreign Relations of the United States, 1955–1957, China*, 2:31–33.

4. John Thomson, e-mail to the author, June 24, 2012; diary entry, February 19, 1948, Koo Papers.

5. Craft, *V. K. Wellington Koo*, 228, 232; Radford-Chiang conversation, June 3, 1953, *yingxiang hao* 11-NAA-02720, WJDA.

6. Department of Defense, *Taiwan*, 39; "Estimate of Chinese Nationalist and Communist Capabilities with Reference to Formosa and the Offshore Islands, December 1, 1954," U.S. Department of the Army, General Staff G-2, Intelligence Estimate of Chinese Nationalist and Communist Capabilities with Reference to Formosa and The Offshore Islands," Report (1954), MHI.

7. Marks, *Counterrevolution in China*, 128–129, 134; Liu, "Indoctrinating the Youth," 114, 149, 163; Wang, "A Bastion Created," 323; diary entry, May 7, 1954, Koo Papers.

8. Wang, "A Bastion Created," 330. See also Tsang, "Chiang Kai-shek and the Kuomintang's Policy to Reconquer the Chinese Mainland," 59–60, 67–68.

9. Dean Rusk, future secretary of state under John F. Kennedy, opposed either Chiang Ching-kuo or his brother, Chiang Wei-kuo, becoming leader of the ROC.

See diary entry, May 11, 1951, Koo Papers; "U.S. Is Uneasy About Chiang's Ruthless Heir," *Miami News,* November 13, 1954, 18.

10. Roy, *Taiwan,* 90; diary entry, April 27, 1954, Koo Papers.

11. Li, *Madame Chiang Kai-shek,* 363. See also Tucker, ed., *China Confidential,* 119–120; Yeh-Rankin conversation, May 29, 1957, box 8, folder 4, Karl Rankin Papers, Seeley Mudd Manuscript Library, Princeton, Princeton University, New Jersey (hereafter cited as Rankin Papers); William Miller, "Long Taut Taipeh Tensions Explode into Violent Outburst," *World Journal,* May 27, 1957.

12. 793.13/8–1955, Sebald to Murphy, *China, People's Republic of China 1955–59, Foreign Affairs,* reel 2; FO 371/114987/FC1015/18, Hermann to Far Eastern Department, August 31, 1955, PRO.

13. Shi, "Jiang Jingguo yu Mei guwen tuan," 6; Qin, ed., *Zongtong,* 10:16, 23, 59, 125; Taylor, *The Generalissimo's Son,* 216, 231; FO 371/114987/FC 1015/19, Crowe to Joy, September 28, 1955, PRO.

14. Diary entry, April 22, 1951, Koo Papers; Qin, ed., *Zongtong,* 11:34.

15. Diary entry, April 13, 1953, Koo Papers; Jones to Yeh, July 29, 1952, *MAAG nipai guwen shaozhu zhi baoan silingbu* (MAAG proposal to send advisors to the Taiwan Garrison Command), *danghao* 426.1/0002, WJDA.

16. Jones-Yeh conversation, July 26, 1952, *danghao* 426.1/0002, WJDA.

17. Jones-Chase-Yeh conversation, August 1, 1952, *danghao* 426.1/0002, WJDA; Jones-Yeh conversation, September 23, 1952, ibid.; Qin, ed., *Zongtong,* 11:222.

18. Radford-Chiang conversation, June 3, 1953; Radford-Chiang conversation, June 4, 1953, both in *yingxiang hao* 11-NAA-02720, WJDA.

19. Diary entries, September 20, 29, and 30, 1953; October 12, 1953; October 15, 1957, Koo Papers.

20. Qin, ed., *Zongtong,* 10:271, 11:9–10.

21. Shi, "Jiang Jingguo yu Mei guwen tuan," 6.

22. Taylor, *The Generalissimo's Son,* 216–217.

23. FO 371/127472/FCN 1015/12, Franklin to Lloyd, October 22, 1957, PRO; FO 371/127472/FCN 1015/16, Franklin to Far East Department, November 13, 1957, PRO.

24. Yeh to Koo, March 24, 1954, *Zhongmei junshi baogao yu jianyi* (Report and recommendations regarding ROC-U.S. military matters), *danghao* 427/0006, WJDA; Wang, "A Bastion Created," 330; Tucker, *Uncertain Friendships,* 73; Kerr, *Formosa Betrayed,* 423.

25. FO 371/114987/FC 1015/16, U.S. Summary, July 21, 1955, PRO; Cochran to McConaughy, September 14, 1955, box 7, folder 3, Rankin Papers.

26. FO 371/114987/FC 1015/20, Audland-Osborn conversation, October 10, 1955, in Joy to Crowe, October 17, 1955, PRO; Taylor, *The Generalissimo,* 483–484.

27. Howard to Yeh, September 21, 1955, *yingxiang hao* 11-NAA-01657, WJDA; diary entry, August 20, 1955, Koo Papers.

28. FO 371/114987/FC 1015/20, Audland-Osborn conversation, October 10, 1955, in Joy to Crowe, October 17, 1955, PRO.

29. Boyle to Gruin, September 16, 1955, enclosing letter written by John Osborne, September 12, 1955, *yingxiang hao* 11-NAA-01657, WJDA; Radford quote from diary entry, October 3, 1955, Koo Papers.

30. Report by the Commission of Enquiry on the Case of General Sun Li-Jen Relative to the Communist Spy Kuo Ting-Liang, *yingxiang hao* 11-NAA-01657, WJDA; FO 371/114987/FC 1015/21, Tamsui to Foreign Office, October 21, 1955, PRO.

31. See enclosures in FO 371/114987/FC 1015/27, M. Mackay to Foreign Office, November 30, 1955, PRO.

32. FO 371/114987/FC 1015/25, Crowe Foreign Office Minute, PRO; 611.93/10–2155, Cochran to State, October 21, 1955, *China, People's Republic of China 1955–59, Foreign Affairs*, reel 3.

33. Liu, "Indoctrinating the Youth," 161–162; FO 371/127542/FCN 1015/3, Franklin to Far Eastern Department, January 29, 1957, PRO.

34. Qin, ed., *Zongtong*, 9:197, 200, 214, 220, 245, 248, 10:118.

35. Ibid., 11:210.

36. Chase to Chow, January 17, 1952, *danghao* 427/0006, WJDA; Schaller, *The United States and China*, 78–80; Chase to Chiang, October 19, 1953, *danghao* 427/0006, WJDA; "Proposal and Comments as Studied and Drafted by SS-5, MND on the 'Recommendations on Reorganizations of Ground Forces into Two Type Field Armies' by Gen. Chase," ibid.

37. Record of Conversation on Army Reorganization at Residence of the Chief of the General Staff, February 1, 1952, *danghao* 427/0006, WJDA.

38. Yeh to Radford, March 23, 1954, *danghao* 427/0006, WJDA; Radford to Yeh, May 4, 1954, ibid.; Chase to Chow, April 27, 1954, ibid.; Chow to Chase, May 4, 1954, ibid.; Qin, ed., *Zongtong*, 11:90, 92, 99, 100.

39. Craft, *V.K. Wellington Koo*, 248; Garver, *The Sino-American Alliance*, 76–77; Country Statement on MAP, December 1957, MHI; Eisenhower to Churchill, February 10, 1955, box 4, Dulles-Herter Series, Eisenhower Papers.

40. Diary entry by president's press secretary (Hagerty), Department of State, *Foreign Relations of the United States, 1955–1957, China*, 2:305–306.

41. FO 405/285, 188, MacMillan-Dulles conversation, June 20, 1955, PRO.

42. Robertson to Dulles, April 25, 1955, Department of State, *Foreign Relations of the United States, 1955–1957, China*, 2:509; Robertson to Dulles, April 25, 1955, ibid., 2:510–517.

43. Eisenhower-Eden conversation, January 31, 1956, Department of State, *Foreign Relations of the United States, 1955–57, China*, 3:293–294.

44. Tucker, *The China Threat*, 89–92.

45. Young, *Negotiating with the Chinese Communists*, 44–53; 611.93/10–2155, Cochran to State, October 21, 1955, *China, People's Republic of China 1955–59, Foreign Affairs*, reel 3; Cochran to Rankin, August 25, 1955, box 7, folder 3, Rankin Papers; Cochran to Rankin, August 8, 1955, ibid.; Cochran to Drumright, August 8, 1955, ibid.; FO 371/114987/FC1015/18, Hermann to Far Eastern Department, August 31, 1955, PRO.

46. Young, *Negotiating with the Chinese Communists*, 91–109; FO 405/286, 245, Franklin to Lloyd, May 14, 1956, PRO; Yeh-Rankin conversation, November 15, 1955, enclosed in Rankin to McConaughy, November 17, 1955, box 7, folder 4, Rankin Papers; Rankin to Bowden, November 4, 1955, box 7, folder 4, Rankin Papers.

47. Qin, ed., *Zongtong*, 10:77.

48. Ibid., 10:235, 241.

49. Diary entry, April 22, 1951, Koo Papers; Qin, ed., *Zongtong*, 10:257, 259.

50. Qin, ed., *Zongtong*, 10:290, quote at 10:397.

51. U.S. Policy toward Formosa and the Government of the Republic of China, January 15, 1955, Department of State, *Foreign Relations of the United States, 1955–1957, China*, 2:31–33.

52. "Interdepartmental Committee on Certain U.S. Aid Programs, Taiwan," July 6, 1956, box 1, FE, Top Secret Files Relating to the Republic of China, 1954–1965, RG 59, NA; Progress Report (July 3, 1957) on U.S. Policy toward Taiwan and the Government of the Republic of China by the Operations Coordinating Board, box 58, National Security Council Staff, Disaster File, Nationalist China (10), Eisenhower Papers; Department of Defense, *Taiwan*, 41–42.

53. "Summary of the Revised Direct Military Support Requirements of the 'Kai Plan' (Code Name: 'Hsieh Plan')," 1955 *nian junxie yusuan* (Military assistance budget for 1955), *danghao* 427/0001, WJDA; Brant to Wong, February 21, 1955, ibid.; Wong to Yeh, February 22, 1955, ibid.

54. Cochran to McConaughy, September 14, 1955, box 7, folder 3, Rankin Papers.

55. Rankin to Hsu, November 8, 1955, enclosed in Rankin to McConaughy, November 17, 1955, box 7, folder 4, Rankin Papers; Rankin-Chen conversation, November 16, 1955, box 7, folder 4, Rankin Papers.

56. Cochran to Department of State, June 28, 1955, Department of State, *Foreign Relations of the United States, 1955–1957, China*, 2:615–616; 611.93/8–1155, Cochran to Rankin, *China, People's Republic of China 1955–59, Foreign Affairs*, reel 2.

57. 611.93/10–2155, Cochran to State, October 21, 1955, *China, People's Republic of China 1955–59, Foreign Affairs*, reel 3.

58. Ibid.; Yeh-Rankin conversation, November 15, 1955, enclosed in Rankin to McConaughy, November 17, 1955, box 7, folder 4, Rankin Papers.

59. 611.93/8-1155, Cochran to Rankin, *China, People's Republic of China 1955–59, Foreign Affairs*, reel 2; Cochran to Rankin, August 25, 1955, box 7, folder 3, Rankin Papers; Cochran to Department of State, August 15, 1955, Department of State, *Foreign Relations of the United States, 1955–1957, China*, 3:47–49.

60. 611.93/8-1155, Cochran to Rankin, *China, People's Republic of China 1955–59, Foreign Affairs*, reel 2; 611.93/10–2155, Cochran to State, October 21, 1955, *China, People's Republic of China 1955–59, Foreign Affairs*, reel 3.

61. 611.93/10–2155, Cochran to State, October 21, 1955, *China, People's Republic of China 1955–59, Foreign Affairs*, reel 3; 611.93/8–1155, Cochran to Rankin, August 11, 1955, ibid., reel 2.

62. Rankin to Department of State, October 21, 1955, Department of State, *Foreign Relations of the United States, 1955–1957, China,* 3:139–143; Smythe to Stump, September 18, 1955, ibid., 3:91–92.

63. *New York Times,* November 2, 1993, B1; Rankin to McConaughy, November 17, 1955, box 7, folder 4, Rankin Papers.

64. Rankin-Chiang Kai-shek conversation, November 21, 1955, Department of State, *Foreign Relations of the United States, 1955–1957, China,* 3:180–181n2; Hedding to Radford, February 24, 1956, ibid., 3:315. See also ibid., 3:315n2.

65. Report by the Interdepartmental Committee on Certain U.S. Aid Programs, Department of State, *Foreign Relations of the United States, 1955–1957, China,* 3:389, 392, 393; FO 405/286, 245, Franklin to Lloyd, May 14, 1956, PRO, 245; Country Statement on MAP, December 1957, MHI.

66. United States Policy and Attitudes toward Chinese Communists and Republic of China, March 5, 1956, box 7, folder 6, Rankin Papers.

67. Rankin to Smith, June 13, 1957, box 17, CA, 1957, RG 59, NA.

68. FO 371/120868/FC 1019/5, Davis-Scott conversation, June 16, 1956, PRO.

69. Conroy to Meyer, June 25, 1956, box 8, folder 1, Rankin Papers.

70. Taylor, *The Generalissimo's Son,* 240; Chiang-Dulles conversation, March 16, 1956, Department of State, *Foreign Relations of the United States, 1955–1957, China,* 3:327–329; Chiang-Robertson conversation, March 17, 1956, ibid., 3:331–332.

71. Chiang to Eisenhower, April 16, 1956, Department of State, *Foreign Relations of the United States, 1955–1957, China,* 3:346–348; Chiang-Radford conversation, August 1, 1956, ibid., 3:411–415.

72. Chiang to Eisenhower, December 11, 1956, Department of State, *Foreign Relations of the United States, 1955–1957, China,* 3:446–448; Chiang-Pilcher conversation, December 17, 1956, ibid., 3:455.

73. Observations of Editor Cheng on the Overseas Chinese, Morale on Taiwan and the May 24 Riot, July 22, 1957, box 8, CA, 1957, RG 59, NA; Payne Templeton, May 24 Riots in Taipei, August 7, 1957, ibid.

74. Rawls Knox, "Washington Shifts Policy in Pacific," *Hong Kong Standard,* March 10, 1957; *Mei duiHua zhengce* (U.S. Policy toward China), *danghao* 411.2/0055, WJDA; "Meiguo kongzhi le ziyo zhongguo ma?" (Does America control Free China?) *Gongshang Ribao* (Commercial Times), April 5, 1957, *danghao* 411.2/0055, WJDA.

75. Chiang-Rankin conversation, January 9, 1957, box 8, folder 3, Rankin Papers.

76. Formosa 13th Air Force, 1957, Office of Special Investigations, Inspector General, Headquarters Pacific Air Force, U.S. Air Force Historical Research Agency, Maxwell Air Force Base, Montgomery, Alabama (hereafter cited as USAFHRA).

77. Diary entry, December 9, 1955, Koo Papers.

78. FO 405/286, 245, Franklin to Lloyd, May 14, 1956, PRO, 246; FO 405/286, 264, 265, Franklin to Lloyd, October 21, 1956, PRO, quote from 264.

4. Little America on Taiwan

1. Diary entry, June 25, 1952, Koo Papers.

2. Rankin, *China Assignment,* 105; Rankin to Perkins, February 16, 1952, box 5, folder 5, Rankin Papers.

3. *New York Times,* September 6, 1952, 2. For a modern-day description of these former military residences, see "The US Military's Cold War Housing in Shanzihou and Tianmu," March 23, 2010, http://english.gov.taipei/ct.asp?xItem=1130982&ct Node=27687&mp=100002 (accessed January 6, 2011).

4. Sino-American Relationships, June 19, 1945, box 3, CA, U.S. Armed Forces in China (January–June 1945), RG 59, NA.

5. Tucker, *Uncertain Friendships,* 36–38; Movement to Formosa of Dependents of MAAG Personnel, December 16, 1952, box 2, CA, Records Relating to Economic Aid, 1948–1958, RG 59, NA.

6. FO 405/286, 233, Franklin to Lloyd, March 9, 1956, PRO; FO 405/285, 193, Hermann to MacMillan, October 26, 1955, PRO.

7. Comiskey, U.S. Military Program on Taiwan—Background Information, October 4, 1956, box 18, CA, 1956, RG 59, NA; Comiskey to Clough, January 15, 1957, box 4, CA, 1957, RG 59, NA; Comiskey to McConaughy, January 28, 1957, ibid.; Comiskey to Clough, December 9, 1957, ibid.; "US to Build 25-Million-Dollar Strategic Bomber Base on Formosa," *Chinese World Journal,* January 4, 1957, 1.

8. Nash, "United States Overseas Military Bases: Report to the President," 34; Rankin to Nash, June 17, 1957, box 8, folder 5, Rankin Papers; Rankin to Henderson, April 25, 1956, box 7, folder 6, Rankin Papers; Memorandum to Minister Edwin A. Plitt, June 21, 1957, box 8, folder 5, Rankin Papers.

9. Greater Responsibility for the Chinese in Economic Fields, July 30, 1957, box 8, folder 5, Rankin Papers.

10. Rankin to Radford, January 3, 1956, box 7, folder 5, Rankin Papers.

11. Rankin to Henderson, April 25, 1956, box 7, folder 6, Rankin Papers.

12. Greater Responsibility for the Chinese in Economic Fields, July 30, 1957, box 8, folder 5, Rankin Papers.

13. Rankin to Powell, October 12, 1956, box 8, folder 1, Rankin Papers.

14. Rankin to Nash, June 17, 1957, box 8, folder 5, Rankin Papers; Green, Holdridge, and Stokes, *War and Peace with China,* 44.

15. "Parkinson's Law," *Economist* (November 19, 1955), http://www.economist .com/node/14116121?story_id=14116121 (accessed January 30, 2013).

16. 240th Meeting of the National Security Council, March 10, 1955, Department of State, *Foreign Relations of the United States, 1955–1957, China,* 2:348; FO 371/114987/FC 1015/14, Hermann to Far Eastern Department, July 1955, PRO; FO 371/114987/FC 1015/22, Hermann to Far Eastern Department, October 18, 1955, PRO.

17. [Dulles, Radford, and Wilson], Memorandum of Conversation, March 26, 1955, Department of State, *Foreign Relations of the United States, 1955–1957, China,* 2:403, 542n.

18. Jurika, ed., *From Pearl Harbor to Vietnam,* 327–330; Eisenhower-Radford telephone conversation, February 1, 1955, Eisenhower Papers.

19. Department of State, *Foreign Relations of the United States, 1955–1957, China,* 2:553nn2, 3; Stump to Carney, January 28, 1956, ibid., 3:283–284.

20. Chiang-Rankin conversation, July 7, 1956, Department of State, *Foreign Relations of the United States, 1955–1957, China,* 3:395–397; State-Joint Chiefs of Staff Meeting, August 31, 1956, ibid., 3:425–426.

21. Jacobs, *Cold War Mandarin,* 96; Nash, "United States Overseas Military Bases: Report to the President," 167, 187, 190.

22. 290th Meeting of the National Security Council, July 12, 1956, Department of State, *Foreign Relations of the United States, 1955–1957, Foreign Aid and Economic Defense Policy,* 10:79–82.

23. Wu Cheng-jin, "Interview with a Former A-ma," May 22, 2011, Yangming-shan Historical Building–Eco Village Preservation and Education Alliance, http://en.yeswecan.org.tw/?page_id=2 (accessed July 20, 2014); Glenn Jones, e-mail to author, October 25, 2012; Proceedings of a General Court-Martial, Taipei, Taiwan, May 20, 1957, box 9, CA, 1957, RG 59, NA; William Dawson, e-mail to author, August 12, 2010; John Hart, letter to the editor, *New York Times,* August 3, 1958, E8.

24. Vincent Kramer, e-mails to author, September 17, 18, 2012.

25. Alvah, *Unofficial Ambassadors.* In the late 1960s, the author's grandmother-in-law lost her home to a typhoon. American military or civilian personnel rebuilt her one-floor home, which stood until the 1990s, when it was torn down to allow for expansion of a local middle school.

26. Szonyi, *Cold War Island,* 134–146; Wu, "Interview with a Former A-ma."

27. William Dawson, e-mail to author, August 12, 2010.

28. Clough to Rankin, October 22, 1957, box 2, CA, 1957, RG 59, NA. The article by Fred Sparks, "United States Hurt by Black Market in Formosa," *Washington Daily News,* October 16, 1957, was enclosed in Clough's letter.

29. Qin, ed., *Zongtong,* 10:45–46; Accinelli, *Crisis and Commitment,* 65–66, 138–139. See also Rawnsley, "Taiwan's Propaganda Cold War," 86, 92–93; Taylor, *The Generalissimo's Son,* 239.

30. Diary entries, March 16, 1953; September 2, 1953, Koo Papers; Qin, ed., *Zongtong,* 10:96, 118.

31. "Formosa Fraud Charged; Black Market Operations Laid to 'Foreign Service Personnel,'" *New York Times,* October 27, 1953.

32. Importation and Sale of Merchandise, Including Sale of Commissary and Post Exchange Items, October 16, 1956, Headquarters, Military Assistance Advisory Group, Taiwan, October 16, 1956, box 2, CA, 1957, RG 59, NA.

33. Rankin to Clough, November 14, 1957, box 2, CA, 1957, RG 59, NA.

34. Chaille to Rankin, August 28, 1957, box 2, CA, 1957, RG 59, NA.

35. Chaille to Clough, November 18, 1957, box 2, CA, 1957, RG 59, NA.

36. William Dawson, e-mail to author, August 12, 2010.

37. Chaille to Pilcher, October 16, 1957, box 2, CA, 1957, RG 59, NA.

38. Fred Sparks, "U.S. Is Seen Responsible in Part for Formosa Riot," *El Paso Herald-Post*, May 28, 1957, 18.

39. Fred Sparks, "Snobs Sent by America into Asia Make Unpretty Picture," *Fort Worth Press*, October 31, 1957, in Rankin to Roy Howard, November 27, 1957, box 8, folder 3, Rankin Papers.

40. Vincent Kramer, e-mail to author, July 18, 2012.

41. FO 371/127471/FCN 10345/3, Franklin to Lloyd, February 21, 1957, PRO; Ambassador William Gleysteen Jr., Interview, June 10, 1997, Association for Diplomatic Studies and Training Foreign Affairs Oral History Project, accessed May 5, 2014, http://adst.org/OH%20TOCs/Gleysteen,%20William%20H.,%20Jr.toc.pdf.

42. Rankin to Roy Howard, November 27, 1957, box 8, folder 3, Rankin Papers.

43. "'Isolation Living' Hits U.S. in East; Americans and Families Often Fail to Get Acquainted with the Southeast Asians," *New York Times*, August 21, 1955, 12.

44. Rankin to McConaughy, August 20, 1956, box 8, folder 1, Rankin Papers. Smythe was a West Point graduate who commanded infantry divisions in Europe and Korea. See Joseph Kennedy, "Norristown Fielded Winning WWII General George Smythe and His 47th Infantry Fought in Two Major Battles in the European Theater," *Inquirer*, November 5, 1995, http://articles.philly.com/1995-11-05/news/25682581_1_norristown-resident-john-smythe-german-army (accessed May 26, 2014).

45. Masaru Ogawa, "Taiwan and the United States," (1958), *Mei duiHua zhengce* (U.S. Policy toward China), *danghao* 411.2/0055, WJDA.

46. FO 405/285, 193, Hermann to MacMillan, October 26, 1955, PRO.

47. "Riot Scars Fading on Formosa," *Daytona Beach News Journal*, June 20, 1957, 4, http://news.google.com/newspapers?nid=1873&dat=19570620&id=_oUeAAAAIBAJ&sjid=hMsEAAAAIBAJ&pg=1078,3241129 (accessed September 24, 2013).

48. FO 371/127472/FCN10345/53, Kibling-Wright conversation, November 13, 1957, PRO.

49. Jones to Clough, July 18, 1957, box 17, CA, 1957, RG 59, NA.

50. Statement of Ardith H. Miller, secretary at the embassy, May 31, 1957, box 8, folder 4, Rankin Papers.

51. Jones to Clough, July 18, 1957, box 17, CA, 1957, RG 59, NA.

52. Diary entry, August 7, 1951, Koo Papers.

53. Harrington to Twining, May 27, 1957, box 17, CA, 1957, RG 59, NA.

54. Sparks, "U.S. Is Seen Responsible in Part for Formosa Riot," 18.

55. FO 405/285, 193, Hermann to MacMillan, October 26, 1955, PRO; FO 371/127452/FNC 1015/1, Franklin's Brief for "Eden Hall Conference," December 4, 1956, PRO; Observations of Editor Cheng on the Overseas Chinese, Morale on Taiwan and the May 24 Riot, July 22, 1957, box 8, CA, 1957, RG 59, NA.

56. Miller, "Long Taut Taipeh Tensions Explode into Violent Outburst," 1.

57. Hua Mingyi, "Taibei shijian jingwei" (The scope of the Taibei Incident), *Ziyou ren* (The Freeman), June 1, 1957, 2.

58. FO 371/127471/FCN 10345/3, Franklin to Lloyd, February 21, 1957, PRO.

59. Rankin to Dulles, May 26, 1957, Department of State, *Foreign Relations of the United States, 1955–1957, China,* 3:536.

60. FO 371/127471/FCN 10345/3, Franklin to Lloyd, February 21, 1957, PRO.

61. Reynolds, *Rich Relations,* 143–144, 241–261.

62. FO 371/127471/FCN 10345/4, Franklin to Lloyd, February 23, 1957, PRO.

5. A Law unto Themselves

1. Chiu, "The United States Status of Forces Agreement with the Republic of China," 69.

2. Congress, House of Representatives, *Status of Forces Agreements: Hearings before the Committee on Foreign Affairs, House of Representatives,* 353.

3. Nash, "United States Overseas Military Bases: Report to the President," 59; "The Question of the Special Status of U.S. Military Assistance and Advisory Group," in *524 shi jian youguan jigou baogao* (Report from relevant organizations on the May 24th Incident), *danghao* 425.2/0004, WJDA; Lieutenant Colonel Ross R. Condit, Investigating Officer's Report, May 6, 1957, in Reynolds Court-Martial file (hereafter Condit, Investigating Officer's Report).

4. "NATO Status of Forces Agreement, March 15, 1953, attachment, Background of the Status of Forces Agreement," box 7, NATO Status of Forces, FE, 1953, Misc. Subject Files, RG 59, NA.

5. Acheson and Lovett to Truman, January 8, 1952, Department of State, *Foreign Relations of the United States, 1952–1954, China and Japan,* vol. 14, part 2, 1098–1100.

6. Longmate, *The GIs,* 160–161; Reynolds, *Rich Relations,* 144–148; Department of State, *Foreign Relations of the United States, 1943, China,* 699–700.

7. Marshall and Wedemeyer to War Department, Chief of Staff, January 21, 1946; Acheson to Marshall, May 1, 1946, both in box 39, RG 334, Records of the Joint U.S. Military Advisory Group to the Republic of China, NA.

8. For discussion of the history of diplomatic immunity and how it was abused during the late Cold War years, see Farhangi, "Insuring against Abuse of Diplomatic Immunity," 1518–1526; also see Ross, "Rethinking Diplomatic Immunity," 173–180; Langhorne, "The Regulation of Diplomatic Practice," 13.

9. A traditional view of the Terranova Incident being an accident is discussed in Hunt, *The Making of a Special Relationship,* 1–2. A more recent study reveals that the action was deliberate. See Joseph Askew, "Revisiting New Territory: The Terranova Incident Revisited," 351–371; Scully, *Bargaining with the State from Afar,* 68, 127–131, 151–152.

10. "The Question of the Special Status of U.S. Military Assistance and Advisory Group," *danghao* 425.2/0004, WJDA; diary entry, July 22, 1954, Koo Papers.

11. Becker to Dechert, June 24, 1958, box 1, FE, Top Secret Files Relating to the Republic of China, 1954–1965, RG 59, NA.

12. Department of State, *Foreign Relations of the United States, 1955–1957, China,* 2:552n6.

13. Dulles to Rankin, June 22, 1955, Department of State, *Foreign Relations*

of the United States, 1955–1957, China, 2:607–610; see also 2:607–609nn2, 3; "The Question of the Special Status of U.S. Military Assistance and Advisory Group," *danghao* 425.2/0004, WJDA; *China News,* June 5, 1963, in *Meijun diwei xieding an ziliao (jianbao)* (Newspaper clippings and documents regarding the ROC-U.S. Status of Forces Agreement), *danghao* 426.1/0026, WJDA.

14. For a fuller discussion of these points and the issues that arose in Europe as a result of legal differences, see Snee and Pyle, *Status of Forces Agreements and Criminal Jurisdictions.*

15. "Meijun diwei xieding an ziliao" (Documents regarding Status of Forces Agreements), *danghao* 426.1/0026, WJDA; Discussion of Jurisdiction Article in Status of Forces Agreement with Foreign Minister Yeh at Your Luncheon February 28, February 27, 1957, box 1, FE, Top Secret Files Relating to the Republic of China, 1954–1965, RG 59, NA.

16. *Amendment of Article XVII of the Administrative Agreement under Article III of the Security Treaty.*

17. Huebner, "Chinese Anti-Americanism, 1946–48," 117–118; Pepper, *Civil War in China,* 52–58; Stuart to Byrnes, April 22, 1947, Department of State, *Foreign Relations of the United States, 1947, The Far East: China,* 7:105–106; Stuart to Byrnes, May 16, 1947, ibid., 7:121; Stuart to Byrnes, May 27, 1947, ibid., 7:147.

18. Qin, ed., *Zongtong,* 11:224.

19. Comiskey, U.S. Military Program on Taiwan—Background Information, October 4, 1956, box 18, CA, 1956, RG 59, NA; Nash, "United States Overseas Military Bases: Report to the President," 5, 6.

20. Negotiating Chronology, *Meijun diwei xieding duian* (Counterproposals to the U.S.-ROC Status of Forces Agreement), *danghao* 426.1/0037, WJDA; Rankin to State, January 26, 1956, Department of State, *Foreign Relations of the United States, 1955–1957, China,* 3:282–283.

21. Grant, "The Bricker Amendment Controversy," 572–582; "Bricker Denounces NATO Troops Treaty," *Albuquerque Journal,* May 8, 1953, 15; "Votes with Majority," *Anderson Herald,* July 13, 1953, 15.

22. "NATO Status of Forces Agreement, March 15, 1953, attachment, Background of the Status of Forces Agreement," box 7, NATO Status of Forces, FE, 1953, Misc. Subject Files, RG 59, NA; Jenner to Johnston, June 7, 1957, box 59, Olin DeWitt Talmadge Johnston Papers, South Carolina Political Collections, University of South Carolina, Columbia, South Carolina (hereafter cited as Johnston Papers).

23. Discussion of Jurisdiction Article in Status of Forces Agreement with Foreign Minister Yeh at Your Luncheon February 28, February 27, 1957, box 1, FE, Top Secret Files Relating to the Republic of China, 1954–1965, RG 59, NA.

24. Allison to Dulles, November 14, 1956, Department of State Central Decimal File, 1955–1959, box 3966, NA; Robertson to Phleger, January 3, 1957, ibid.; Comparison of Jurisdictional Provisions in Japanese, Netherlands and Proposed Chinese Agreement, box 1, FE, Top Secret Files Relating to the Republic of China, 1954–1965, RG 59, NA; Horsey to Abbott, October 17, 1958, ibid.

25. T. C. Tang, "The Sino-American Status of Forces Agreement," *Central News Agency,* June 14, 1957, box 8, CA, 1957, RG 59, NA.

26. Stump to Burke, February 18, 1956, box 18, 430.1 Status of Forces, CA, 1956, RG 59, NA.

27. Stump to Burke, January 14, 1956, box 18, 430.1 Status of Forces, CA, 1956, RG 59, NA.

28. Cochran to McConaughy, March 19, 1956, box 18, 430.1 Status of Forces, CA, 1956, RG 59, NA.

29. McConaughy, Clough, and Comiskey, Status of Forces Negotiations, March 5, 1956, box 18, 430.1 Status of Forces, CA, 1956, RG 59, NA; McConaughy, Clough and Comiskey, Status of Forces Negotiations, May 9, 1956, ibid.; Robertson, Clough, Status of Forces Negotiations with GRC, May 18, 1956, ibid.

30. Trials of American Servicemen in Japan and Japanese War Criminals, Lot File no. 61D68, box 8, Subject Files Relating to Japan, 1954–59, RG 59, NA.

31. Status of Forces Negotiations, March 9, 1956, box 18, 430.1 Status of Forces, CA, 1956, RG 59, NA.

32. Jurisdiction Provisions in SOF Agreement being Negotiated with GRC, box 18, 430.1 Status of Forces, CA, 1956, RG 59, NA

33. Negotiating Chronology, *Meijun diwei xieding duian* (Counterproposals to the U.S.-ROC Status of Forces Agreement), *danghao* 426.1/0037, WJDA; Position Paper, n.d., box 1, FE, Top Secret Files Relating to the Republic of China, 1954–1965, RG 59, NA; Clough to Robertson, January 17, 1957, box 8, CA, 1957, RG 59, NA.

34. Clough to Rankin, March 14, 1957, box 8, CA, 1957, RG 59, NA.

35. Comparison of Jurisdictional Provisions in Japanese, Netherlands and Proposed Chinese Agreement, box 1, FE, Top Secret Files Relating to the Republic of China, 1954–1965, RG 59, NA; Clough to Rankin, March 14, 1957, box 8, CA, 1957, RG 59, NA.

36. Comiskey to McConaughy, April 2, 1957, box 8, CA, 1957, RG 59, NA.

37. Becker to Dechert, June 24, 1958, box 1, FE, Top Secret Files Relating to the Republic of China, 1954–1965, RG 59, NA.

38. 611.93/1–2258, Dechert to Becker, *China, People's Republic of China 1955–59, Foreign Affairs,* reel 6.

39. Masaru Ogawa, "Taiwan and the United States," (1958), *Mei duiHua zhengce* (U.S. Policy toward China), *danghao* 411.2/0055, WJDA.

40. The Warsaw Pact: Its Role in Soviet Bloc Affairs from Its Origin to the Present Day, May 6, 1966, CIA Directorate of Intelligence, CIA-RDP79T00826A000600010056-8, NA; Soviet Military Forces in Eastern Europe, June 29, 1966, ibid.

41. Clough to Wilson, August 15, 1957, box 8, CA, 1957, RG 59, NA. Examples of such courts-martial can be found in RG 334, United States Pacific Command, MAAG-Taiwan, 1957, NA.

42. Rankin to Reinhardt, April 18, 1957, enclosed in 711.551/12–1957, Comiskey to Rankin, December 26, 1957, RG 59, NA.

6. A Tale of Two Criminal Investigations

1. Condit, Investigating Officer's Report.

2. Statement of Robert G. Reynolds, March 21, 1957, box 9, CA, 1957, RG 59, NA; statement of Eugene McJunkins, March 22, 1957, ibid.

3. Proceedings of a General Court-Martial, Taipei, Taiwan, May 20, 1957, box 9, CA, 1957, RG 59, NA; Condit, Investigating Officer's Report.

4. "Guanyu May 24 Taibei shi buxin shijian jiantao baogao huibian" (Assembled reports regarding the May 24th Taibei incident," *524 shijian zhuanan jiantao* (Review of the May 24th Incident investigation), *danghao* 425.2/0013, WJDA.

5. Condit, Investigating Officer's Report.

6. Ibid.; Report of Investigation, April 12, 1957, box 9, CA, 1957, RG 59, NA; Report of Interview with M/Sgt Reynolds' Maid, April 6, 1957, ibid.

7. Master Sergeant Billie R. Chaney, Report of Investigation, March 29, 1957, box 9, CA, 1957, RG 59, NA (hereafter Chaney, Report of Investigation, March 29, 1957).

8. Rankin-Plitt-Yeh conversation, June 8, 1957, *524 shijian duiMei jiaoshe* (U.S.-ROC discussions regarding the May 24th Incident), *danghao* 425.2/0016, WJDA.

9. Lieutenant Colonel James F. Fewster, Report of Proceedings by Investigating Officer, April 17, 1957, in Reynolds Court-Martial File; Condit, Investigating Officer's Report; Chaney, Report of Investigation, March 29, 1957; Joseph L. Salonick, Cooperation of Chinese Agencies in the Reynolds Case, June 26, 1957, in 711.551/7–557, Meyer to Department of State, Department of State, Central Decimal File, 1955-1959, box 2838, RG 59, NA.

10. Qin, ed., *Zongtong*, 7:332.

11. Ibid., 9:217; diary, July 24, 1954, Koo Papers. One recent work describes the school as providing reindoctrination to civilians only. See Marks, *Counterrevolution in China*, 135, 136.

12. Tsang, "Chiang Kai-shek and the Kuomintang's Policy to Reconquer the Chinese Mainland," 64–66; Chao and Myers, "A New Kind of Party."

13. FO 371/127471/FCN10345/18, Franklin to Foreign Office, May 30, 1957, PRO.

14. Meyer-Yeh conversation, July 24, 1957, box 17, CA, 1957, RG 59, NA; Rankin to State, May 26, 1957, Department of State, *Foreign Relations of the United States, 1955–1957, China,* 3:536–537.

15. Phillips, "Taiwan's Intelligence Reform," 173.

16. Observations on the Taipeh Incident, June 13, 1957, box 8, CA, 1957, RG 59, NA; Report, July 16, 1957, *524 shijian zhuanan jiantao* (Review of the May 24th Incident investigation), *danghao* 425.2/0014, WJDA; letter to the editor, *Japan Times,* May 31, 1957, *524 shijian zhuwai geguan jianbao ji zhuanti baogao* (Newspaper clippings and special reports from overseas consulates and embassies regarding the May 24th Incident), *danghao* 425.2/0026, WJDA; Rankin-Plitt-Yeh conversation, June 8, 1957, *524 shijian duiMei jiaoshe* (U.S.-ROC discussions regarding the May 24th Incident), *danghao* 425.2/0016, WJDA; memorandum, *danghao* 425.2/0014, WJDA.

17. Statement of Robert Reynolds, March 21, 1957, in Reynolds Court-Martial File; Ottawa Liu to Bowen, March 22, 1957, box 9, CA, 1957, RG 59, NA. Bowen was a West Point graduate who served with distinction as the Eighth Army's G-3, during World War II and led airborne operations during the Korean War. See McDaniel, *The Major*, 169; Smith, *Triumph in the Philippines*, 230n; Wright and Greenwood, *Airborne Forces at War*, 115–119

18. Chaney, Report of Investigation, March 29, 1957.

19. Harrington to Twining, May 27, 1957, box 17, CA, 1957, RG 59, NA.

20. "Liu Ziran an jueyi" (Suspicions behind the Liu Ziran case), *Lianhe bao* (United Daily), March 25, 1957, 2.

21. Condit, Investigating Officer's Report.

22. "Yangmingshan Shooting Case Has Behind-the-Scene Story, Reynolds Kills Liu Because of Anger," *National Evening News*, March 27, 1957, box 9, CA, 1957, RG 59, NA; "Murder of Liu Tzu-Jan Not Because of Peeping Bathing but of Other Arguments, Reynolds Killed in Emotional Indignance," *Min Chu Wan Bao*, box 8, CA, 1957, RG 59, NA; "Comments on the Liu Tzu-Ran Shooting Case," *Cheng Hsin Hsin Wen*, April 1, 1957, ibid.

23. Tang T'ien, "Yangmingshan Shooting Case," *Niu Ssu* (News), April 6, 1957, box 8, CA, 1957, RG 59, NA; Chen Musheng to the editor, *Lianhe bao* (United Daily), March 24, 1957, 2.

24. May 24 Riots in Taipei, July 31, 1957, box 8, CA, 1957, RG 59, NA; 711.551/7–557, Meyer to Dulles, box 2838, RG 59, NA; "Guanyu May 24 Taibei shi buxin shijian jiantao baogao huibian" (Assembled reports regarding the May 24th Taibei incident), *524 shijian zhuanan jiantao* (Review of the May 24th Incident investigation), *danghao* 425.2/0013, WJDA.

25. Jang, "A History of Newspapers in Taiwan," 100; "Changsha Liu Ziran an: Jiangfu junfa shenpan" (The case of Liu Ziran: Letting a court-martial decide the verdict), *Lianhe bao* (United Daily), May 5, 1957, 3.

26. *Lianhe bao* (United Daily), May 22, 1957, 3.

27. *Lianhe bao* (United Daily), May 20, 1957, 3; Cheney, Report of Investigation, March 29, 1957; Master Sergeant Billie F. Chaney, Report of Investigation, April 12, 1957, box 9, CA, 1957, RG 59, NA (hereafter Chaney, Report of Investigation, April 12, 1957).

28. Answering Questions Raised by the U.S. Embassy with Regard to the Legislative Yuan's Report on the May 24th Riot, July 9, 1957, in *danghao* 425.2/0014, WJDA; "Guanyu May 24 Taibei shi buxin shijian jiantao baogao huibian" (Assembled reports regarding the May 24th Taibei incident), *524 shijian zhuanan jiantao* (Review of the May 24th Incident investigation), *danghao* 425.2/0013, WJDA.

29. Bowen to Stump, May 27, 1957, enclosed in Stump to Dulles, May 29, 1957, box 8, CA, 1957, RG 59, NA.

30. McConaughy to Robertson, June 6, 1957, box 8, CA, 1957, RG 59, NA.

31. Headquarters, Military Assistance Advisory Group, Taiwan, Special Court

Martial Order, July 2, 1957, RG 334, United States Pacific Command, MAAG, Taiwan, 1957, NA; *China News,* April 8, 1957, in *Liu Ziran beisha* (The Killing of Liu Ziran), *danghao* 425.2/0032, WJDA.

32. "Guanyu May 24 Taibei shi buxin shijian jiantao baogao huibian" (Assembled reports regarding the May 24th Taibei incident), *524 shijian zhuanan jiantao* (Review of the May 24th Incident investigation), *danghao* 425.2/0013, WJDA.

33. "Guanyu liexi baogao meijun Lei Nuo qiangsha Liu Ziran an jingguo ji dafu zhi zhixun fayan jilu shifu qingqia zhaoyou" (Record of a meeting to answer questions regarding events surrounding the killing of Liu Ziran by Robert Reynolds), May 27, 1957, *524 shijian duinei yiban wenjian* (Internal documents related to the May 24th Incident), *danghao* 425.2/0015, WJDA; FO 371/127472/FCN10345/37, "Report by Mr. O. K. Yui, President of the Executive Yuan, on Actions Taken by the Government Regarding the Incident on May 24, 1957, in Taipei," PRO (cited hereafter as Report by Mr. O. K. Yui).

34. Chaney, Report of Investigation, March 29, 1957.

35. Clark B. Williams and Samuel McClatchie, Report of Autopsy, March 30, 1957, box 9, CA, 1957, RG 59, NA; Li Pao-chu, Report of Chemical Test, ibid.; Li Pao-chu and Tao Ming-hai, Ballistic Test Report, March 24, 1957, ibid.

36. Chang Pang-Liang to Ministry of Foreign Affairs, April 10, 1957, box 8, CA, 1957, RG 59, NA.

37. On March 23, Ao Tehua provided a signed statement that her husband did not know Reynolds. See *Lifa yuan gongbao* (Proceedings of the Legislative Yuan) 19, no. 8 (1957): 114.

38. Statement of Robert G. Reynolds, March 21, 1957, in Reynolds, Court-Martial File; Chaney, Report of Investigation, April 12, 1957; Master Sergeant Billie F. Chaney, Report of Investigation, May 4, 1957, box 9, CA, 1957, RG 59, NA (hereafter Chaney, Report of Investigation, May 4, 1957).

39. Lieutenant Colonel Collins Wight, letter of reference, March 22, 1957; Colonel Clark Williams, letter of reference, March 22, 1957, both in Reynolds Court-Martial File.

40. Report of Proceedings by Investigating Officer, April 17, 1957, in Reynolds Court-Martial File.

41. Pilcher Memorandum, March 21, 1957, box 9, CA, 1957, RG 59, NA; Condit, Investigating Officer's Report; *China Post,* April 7, 1957, box 9, CA, 1957, RG 59, NA. I have put the exchange rate at NT$25 to US$1 based on information provided by the embassy regarding an accident involving a GI that killed a Chinese pedestrian in June 1957 and the amount of compensation provided to the dead man's family.

42. McConaughy to Robertson, May 24, 1957, Department of State, *Foreign Relations of the United States, 1955–1957, China,* 3:525; *Lifa yuan gongbao* 19, no. 8 (1957): 105.

43. Obituary, Ross R. Condit Sr., http://www.arlingtoncemetery.net/rrcondit.htm (accessed February 2, 2013).

44. The following paragraphs are based on Condit, Investigating Officer's Report.

45. Record of Police Interrogation, March 27, 1957, *Liu Ziran beisha* (The Killing of Liu Ziran), *danghao* 425.2/0033, WJDA.

46. Reynolds Court-Martial File.

47. Reynolds Court-Martial File; Department of Defense, *Manual for Courts-Martial U.S. Army 1949*, 233.

48. Thorpe to Bowen, May 7, 1957, Reynolds Court-Martial File; Bowen to Stump, May 29, 1957, box 8, CA, 1957, RG 59, NA.

49. Rankin-Plitt-Yeh conversation, June 8, 1957, *524 shijian duiMei jiaoshe* (U.S.-ROC discussions regarding the May 24th Incident), *danghao* 425.2/0016, WJDA; memorandum, July 1, 1957, box 8, folder 5, Rankin Papers.

50. May 24 Riots in Taipei, July 31, 1957, box 8, CA, 1957, RG 59, NA.

51. "Let Justice Be Done," *China Post*, May 20, 1957, in *Lei Nuozi qiangsha Liu Ziran* (The shooting death of Liu Ziran by Robert Reynolds), *danghao* 425.2/0030, WJDA.

7. The Court-Martial of Sergeant Robert Reynolds

1. Unless otherwise noted, the following is based on Proceedings of a General Court-Martial, Taipei, Taiwan, May 20, 1957, box 9, CA, 1957, RG 59, NA.

2. Department of Defense, *Report to Honorable Wilber M. Brucker*, 252.

3. For a brief overview, see Allison, *Military Justice in Vietnam*, 1–20; Department of Defense, *Manual for Courts-Martial U.S. Army 1949*, 3.

4. Department of Defense, *Manual for Courts-Martial U.S. Army 1949*, 33–34.

5. "Xianchang diaocha yu shenxun ceji" (Reporting from the court room) *Zhengxin xinwen* (Reliable News), May 22, 1957, 4; *Zhonghua minguo shishi jiyao*, 532, 533.

6. Reynolds Court-Martial File.

7. "U.S. Court-Martial Finds Reynolds Not Guilty in Killing Liu Tze-Jan," *China Post*, May 24, 1957; Thorniley to the Department of the Army, June 6, 1957, in Reynolds Court-Martial File.

8. Justice of a Different Culture

1. Letter to Yeh, May 27, 1957, *524 shijian gefang laihan* (Incoming correspondence regarding the May 24th Incident), *danghao* 425.2/0003, WJDA; *Zhonghua minguo shishi jiyao*, 558–559; "Guanyu liexi baogao meijun Lei Nuo qiangsha Liu Ziran an jingguo ji dafu zhi zhixun fayan jilu shifu qingqia zhaoyou" (Record of a meeting to answer questions regarding events surrounding the killing of Liu Ziran by Robert Reynolds), May 27, 1957, *524 shijian duinei yiban wenjian* (Internal documents related to the May 24th Incident), *danghao* 425.2/0015, WJDA.

2. *Lifa yuan gongbao* 19, no. 8 (1957): 103; "Guanyu May 24 Taibei shi buxin shijian jiantao baogao huibian" (Assembled reports regarding the May 24th Taibei incident," *524 shijian zhuanan jiantao* (Review of the May 24th Incident investigation), *danghao* 425.2/0013, WJDA.

3. "Justice Ministry Spokesman Says Reynolds' Trial Unfair," *China Post*, May 24, 1957, in box 8, CA, 1957, RG 59, NA.

4. "Taiwan yulun yiban" (A segment of Taiwan public opinion), *Guanghua wan-bao* (Kwong Wah Evening News), May 29, 1957, *524 shijian zhuMei geguan jianbao ji zhuanti baogao* (Newspaper clippings and special reports from Chinese consulates in the United States regarding the May 24th Incident), *danghao* 425.2/0027, WJDA.

5. Memorandum of conversation, May 24 Riots in Taipei, August 7, 1957, box 8, CA, 1957, RG 59, NA; memorandum of conversation, May 24 Riots in Taipei, July 31, 1957, ibid. The incident at Tunghai University was described by a Chinese newspaper as occurring the day after the riots. See "Zhongshi shudao deyi, buhui fasheng yiwai" (Appropriate measures make incidents in Taichung City unlikely), *Lianhe bao* (United Daily), May 26, 1957, 3.

6. "Lei Nuo yingpan wuzui ma?" (Is Reynolds really not guilty?), *Zhengxin xin-wen* (Reliable News), May 24, 1957, 4; Zi Jian, "Lei Nuozi qiangsha liu yidian" (Six doubtful points about the Reynolds shooting), *Zili wanbao* (Independence Evening), May 21, 1957, 4; "Kan Lei Nuo ande panjue" (Looking at the verdict in the Reynolds case), *Gongshang ribao* (Commercial Times), May 29, 1957, in *Lei Nuozi qiangsha Liu Ziran* (The shooting death of Liu Ziran by Robert Reynolds), *danghao* 425.2/0030, WJDA.

7. "Lei Nuo de yishi" (Reynolds's awareness), *Zhengxin xinwen* (Reliable News), May 24, 1957, 1; "Leian kaiting huaxu" (The Reynolds trial sidelights), *Lianhe bao* (United Daily), May 23, 1957, 3; *Lifa yuan gongbao* 19, no. 8 (1957): 105.

8. Chiu, "The United States Status of Forces Agreement with the Republic of China," 72–74; Tao, "The Sino-American Status of Forces Agreement," 4n28. An early description of this process, prior to the reforms of the 1930s, is found in Bryant, "Extraterritoriality and the Mixed Court," 30.

9. "Guanyu liexi baogao meijun Lei Nuo qiangsha Liu Ziran an jingguo ji dafu zhi zhixun fayan jilu shifu qingqia zhaoyou" (Record of a meeting to answer questions regarding events surrounding the killing of Liu Ziran by Robert Reynolds), May 27, 1957, *524 shijian duinei yiban wenjian* (Internal documents related to the May 24th Incident), *danghao* 425.2/0015, WJDA; Bodde and Morris, *Law in Imperial China*, 182–183.

10. *Lifa yuan gongbao* 19, no. 8 (1957): 103, 129.

11. FO 371/127472/FCN10345/26, Franklin to Lloyd, June 4, 1957, PRO; Chiu, "The United States Status of Forces Agreement with the Republic of China," 78 and note 102.

12. *Xingzheng waijiaobu Guo buzhang Gongchao sifa xingzhengbu Guo buzhang Fengxiang baogao: Meijun Lei Nuo shangshi changsha Liu Ziran an jingguo qingxing quanwen* (Foreign Minister Yeh Gongchao-Justice Minister Guo Fengxiang report on recent developments regarding the Liu Ziran Case), May 24, 1957, *Lifa yuan gongbao* 19, no. 7 (July 16, 1957): 93 (hereafter cited as Yeh-Guo Report).

13. The pamphlet was called "Strengthen Chinese-American Cooperation, Destroy the Common Enemy."

14. FO 371/127472/FCN10345/26, Franklin to Lloyd, June 4, 1957, PRO.

15. "Taiwan yulun yiban" (A segment of Taiwan public opinion), *Guanghua wan-*

bao, May 29, 1957, *524 shijian zhuMei geguan jianbao ji zhuanti baogao* (Newspaper clippings and special reports from Chinese consulates in the United States regarding the May 24th Incident), *danghao* 425.2/0027, WJDA; Luo Bote, "Leinuo qiangsha Liu Ziran an xiju shide zhunshi panjue zunshi shenpan" (The Robert Reynolds court-martial trial theatrics), *Xinwen tiandi,* June 1957, 4–5, in *Zhonghua minguo shishi jiyao,* 560.

16. *Xin wanbao* (New Evening Post), May 24, 1957, *danghao* 425.2/0003, WJDA.

17. *Zili wanbao* (Independence Evening Post), May 24, 1957, 1; "Kangyi meijun mieshi renquan" (Protesting GI contempt for human rights), *Lianhe bao* (United Daily), May 24, 1957, 1.

18. "Leinuo an jiejue le ma?" (Has the Reynolds case been resolved?), *Zili wanbao* (Independence Evening Post), May 26, 1957, 4; "Lei Nuo de yishi" (Reynolds's awareness), *Zhengxin xinwen,* May 24, 1957, 1; "Taiwan yulun yiban" (A segment of Taiwan public opinion), *Guanghua wanbao,* May 29, 1957, *524 shijian zhuMei geguan jianbao ji zhuanti baogao* (Newspaper clippings and special reports from Chinese consulates in the United States regarding the May 24th Incident), *danghao* 425.2/0027, WJDA.

19. "Letter to the Editor, May 23, 1957," *China Post,* May 24, 1957.

20. "Kepa de shengli zhangsheng! Liu Ziran chenyuan ruhe?" (The Horrible victory applause! What about Liu Ziran's profound injustice?"), *Gongshang ribao* (Kang Sheung Daily), May 24, 1957, 3; "Frustration Triggers 'Black Friday' Riot," *Post-Standard,* June 2, 1957, 12; "Taiwan dui Mei kangzheng xingdong" (Taiwan Takes a Stand Against America), *Gongshang ribao* (Kung Sheung Daily News), May 25, 1957, 3.

21. Zhu Fuhua to the editor, *Lianhe bao* (United Daily), May 24, 1957, 3; "Sharen wuzui: Zhengshi peishenzhi bulixiang" (A killer is not guilty: Confirms that jury system is not desirable), ibid.; Yeh-Guo Report, 93; Jones to Clough, July 18, 1957, box 17, CA, 1957, RG 59, NA.

22. Brent to Moyer, June 6, 1957, box 17, CA, 1957, RG 59, NA; "Guanyu Liu Ziran an xinwen chuli zhi jiancha ji jihou gaijian yijian" (Some ideas regarding the press's handling of the Liu Ziran case and proposed improvements), *524 shijian zhuanan jiantao* (Review of the May 24th Incident investigation), *danghao* 425.2/0013, WJDA. Actually, the *Zhengxin xinwen* provided a brief overview of the jury composition and stated that the jury would issue a verdict. The *Zili Wanbao* also provided a fairly accurate outline of procedures, including telling readers that if found not guilty, there would be no retrial. See "Lei Neidi sha Liu Ziran an" (The case of Robert Reynolds killing Liu Ziran), *Zhengxin xinwen* (Reliable News), May 18, 1957, 4; *Zili wanbao* (*Independence Evening Post*), May 18, 1957, 4.

23. Jones to Clough, July 18, 1957, box 17, CA, 1957, RG 59, NA.

24. Diary entry, June 10, 1957, box 66, Chiang Kai-shek Diaries, Hoover Institution Archives, Stanford, California (hereafter cited as Chiang Diaries).

25. Bowen to Stump, May 29, 1957, box 8, CA, 1957, RG 59, NA.

26. Rankin to Smith, June 13, 1957, box 17, CA, 1957, RG 59, NA.

27. Rankin-Chiang conversation, May 27, 1957, Department of State, *Foreign Relations of the United States, 1955–1957, China*, 3:538–539.

28. Transcript of Radio Panel Discussion on the May 24, 1957, Incident in Taipei, Taiwan, *524 shijian jianbao ji yiban ziliao* (Newspaper clippings and documents regarding the May 24th Incident), *danghao* 425.2/0012, WJDA.

29. Pilcher to Hsu, June 24, 1957, box 17, CA, 1957, RG 59, NA.

30. "Leinuo wuzui" (Reynolds not guilty!") *Zhonghua ribao* (China Daily News), May 24, 1957, 2; "Wulun dongji ruhe, sharen fa suo burong" (Whatever the motive, a killer is guilty before the law), *Lianhe bao* (United Daily), May 24, 1957, 3.

31. Letter to the editor, *Lianhe bao* (United Daily), May 24, 1957, 3.

32. "Chenmo de guanzhu" (Unspoken concern), *Lianhe bao* (United Daily), May 23, 1957, 3.

33. "Di liudian jihua?" (A six-point plan?), *Lianhe bao* (United Daily), May 24, 1957, 3.

34. Transcript of Radio Panel Discussion on the May 24, 1957, Incident in Taipei, Taiwan, *524 shijian jianbao ji yiban ziliao* (Newspaper clippings and documents regarding the May 24th Incident), *danghao* 425.2/0012, WJDA.

35. Supplemental Data, box 17, CA, 1957, RG 59, NA.

36. FO 371/127472/FCN10345/26, Franklin to Lloyd, June 4, 1957, PRO; Jones to Clough, July 18, 1957, box 8, CA, 1957, RG 59, NA.

37. *Guanghua zaobao* (Guanghua Daily), May 29, 1957, *danghao* 425.2/0027, WJDA; Observations on the Taipeh Incident, June 13, 1957, box 8, CA, 1957, RG 59, NA.

38. Diary entry, May 27, 1957, Tsiang Tingfu Diaries, 1956–1961, reel 3.

39. *Lifa yuan gongbao* 19, no. 8 (1957): 115. An editorial published in a San Francisco newspaper "conceded that Liu was a 'peeping tom,' but such action does not deserve death." See Lee Dai-ming, "Anti-American Riots in Taipeh," *Chinese World Journal*, May 25, 1957, 1.

40. Robertson to Rankin, August 2, 1957, box 8, CA, 1957, RG 59, NA.

41. Wang Tong, "Tingshang fang weiwangren" (Interviewing the widow in the courtroom), *Zhengxin xinwen* (Reliable News), May 21, 1957, 4.

42. Steele to Bowen, April 29, May 16, 1957, both in Reynolds Court-Martial File.

43. Reynolds Court-Martial File.

44. "Bufen mei renshi ren shenjue bugong" (Some Americans believe the verdict to be unfair), *Lianhe bao* (United Daily), May 24, 1957, 3; *Zhonghua minguo shishi jiyao*, 556–557.

45. *Lifa yuan gongbao* 19, no. 7 (1957): 93; "A Question of Justice," *Time* (June 3, 1957), 17.

46. Lamb, "The Court-Martial Panel Selection Process," 103–166.

47. See Articles 32 and 37 of the 1961 Vienna Convention on Diplomatic Relations, http://legal.un.org/ilc/texts/instruments/english/conventions/9_1_1961.pdf.

48. "Reynolds Should Have Been Punished, Says General Van Fleet," *China Post*,

June 12, 1957, *danghao* 425.2/0030, WJDA; "Formosan Mob Action," *San Francisco News,* May 25, 1957, *524 shijian zhuwai geguan jianbao ji zhuanti baogao* (Newspaper clippings and special reports from overseas consulates and embassies regarding the May 24th Incident), *danghao* 425.2/0026, WJDA.

49. 711.551/6–457, Hocking to Dulles, box 2838, RG 59, NA; 711.551/6–1857, Yingling to Dulles, ibid.; 711.551/7–1557, Denlinger to Dulles, ibid.; 711.551/5–2557, Carl Yingling to Robertson, May 25, 1957, RG 59, NA

50. Letter to the editor, *Ventura County News,* May 31, 1957, *danghao* 425.2/0003, WJDA.

51. Gamer to Wilson, June 4, 1957, in Reynolds Court-Martial File; Carpenter to Wilson, May 25, 1957, ibid.; Crutcher to Wilson, May 25, 1957, ibid.

52. Holt to Gamer, June 19, 1957, Reynolds Court-Martial File; Report by Mr. O. K. Yui.

53. Pilcher memorandum, May 23, 1957, box 9, CA, 1957, RG 59, NA.

54. McConaughy to Robertson, June 6, 1957, box 8, CA, 1957, RG 59, NA; Ingersoll to Stump, May 29, 1957, box 17, CA, 1957, RG 59, NA.

9. Black Friday

1. Riots Injuring American Employees and Destruction of Contents of United States Embassy and United States Information Service Building at Taipei, May 24, 1957, box 17, CA, 1957, RG 59, NA (cited hereafter as Riots Injuring American Employees); "Strengthen Chinese-American Cooperation, Destroy the Common Enemy," *524 shijian duiMei jiaoshe* (U.S.-ROC discussions regarding the May 24th Incident), *danghao* 425.2/0017, WJDA.

2. *China Post,* May 25, 1957, 4.

3. Rankin to Henderson, October 23, 1957, box 8, folder 6, Rankin Papers; Karl Rankin, memorandum to Minister Edwin A. Plitt, June 10, 1957, box 17, CA, 1957, RG 59, NA.

4. Lieutenant Colonel George Chow, Memorandum for Record, June 24, 1957, box 17, CA, 1957, RG 59, NA.

5. Yeh-Guo Report, 91; Pilcher-Yeh conversation, May 24, 1957, *524 shijian duiMei jiaoshe* (U.S.-ROC discussions regarding the May 24th Incident), *danghao* 425.2/0016, WJDA; Department of State, *Foreign Relations of the United States, 1955–1957, China,* 3:531.

6. "Zi Lei Nuozi shenpan wuzui hou zhi May 24 shangban shishi zhi chuli qingxing" (Timeline of measures taken from the Reynolds acquittal until May 24th 10:00 A.M.), *524 shijian zhuanan jiantao* (Review of the May 24th Incident investigation), *danghao* 425.2/0013, WJDA.

7. Statement by Howard E. Chaille, First Secretary of the Embassy, box 17, CA, 1957, RG 59, NA (cited hereafter as Statement by Howard E. Chaille); statement by Alexander C. Boase regarding the Seige [*sic*] on the American Embassy, ibid. (cited hereafter as Statement by Alexander C. Boase); Chronology of Mob Attack on U.S. Embassy and USIS at Taipei, ibid. (cited hereafter as Chronology of Mob Attack).

8. "May 24 shangban shishi hou zai zhian fangmian chuli qingxing" (Timeline of security measures taken after 10:00 A.M. on May 24th), *danghao* 425.2/0013, WJDA.

9. Riots Injuring American Employees.

10. "Lei Nuo an yinqi xuanrandabo" (Reynolds's case stirs up tempest), *Lianhe bao* (United Daily), May 25, 1957, 3.

11. The official report issued by the ROC stated that a man, Hong Jinceng, from the BCC, was on scene with a tape recorder, but Wang Ta-kung, also with the BCC, was arrested as well for recording Ao Tehhua. See Report by Mr. O. K. Yui; *Chinese World Journal*, May 27, 1957, 1.

12. Statement of Riot by C. J. Stanley, box 8, folder 4, Rankin Papers; Report by Mr. O. K. Yui.

13. 711.551/5–3157, Rankin to Dulles, Department of State, Central Files, 1955–1957, box 2837, RG 59, NA. This report was prepared on May 24, but not sent until days later because of the events that followed.

14. Statement by Alexander C. Boase.

15. Captain H. R. McKibbin Memorandum for the Record, June 24, 1957, box 17, CA, 1957, RG 59, NA.

16. "Sifa xingzheng bu diaocha ju diaocha qingbao baogao: Liu Ziran zhi qifu mei dashiguan kangyi yinqichunzhong saodong shibian xiangqing" (Ministry of Justice's Bureau of Investigation's Intelligence Report: Details of the protest by Liu Ziran's wife at the U.S. embassy and the subsequent riots), May 25, 1957, *524 shijian duinei yiban wenjian* (Internal documents related to the May 24th Incident), *danghao* 425.2/0015, WJDA.

17. 711.551/5–3157, Rankin to Dulles, Department of State, Central Files, 1955–1957, box 2837, RG 59, NA.

18. Riots Injuring American Employees.

19. "Lei Nuo an yinqi xuanrandabo" (Reynolds's case stirs up tempest), *Lianhe bao* (United Daily), May 25, 1957, 3.

20. "Liu Ziran zhi Qifu mei dashiguan kangyi."

21. Riots Injuring American Employees; *Shijie Ribao* (World Journal), May 25, 1957, *524 shijian zhuMei geguan jianbao ji zhuanti baogao* (Newspaper clippings and special reports from Chinese consulates and embassy in the United States regarding the May 24th Incident), *danghao* 425.2/0027, WJDA.

22. Statement of Riot by C. J. Stanley, box 8, folder 4, Rankin Papers.

23. Statement of Ardith H. Miller, secretary at the embassy, May 31, 1957, box 8, folder 4, Rankin Papers (hereafter cited as Statement of Ardith H. Miller).

24. Report by Mr. O. K. Yui.

25. Summarized Report on Investigation by the Taipei Garrison Command of Persons Arrested on May 24, 1957, *524 shijian zhuanan jiantao* (Review of the May 24th Incident investigation), *danghao* 425.2/0014, WJDA; "Lei Nuo an yinqi xuanrandabo," *Lianhe bao* (United Daily), May 25, 1957, 3.

26. Riots Injuring American Employees; Report by Mr. O. K. Yui.

27. Statement by Alexander C. Boase; Riots Injuring American Employees.

28. Meyer to Clough, July 22, 1957, box 8, CA, 1957, RG 59, NA.

29. Report by Mr. O. K. Yui.

30. Statement by James B. Pilcher, Department of State, *Foreign Relations of the United States, 1955–1957, China*, 3:532–533; FO 371/127472/FCN10345/26, Franklin to Lloyd, June 4, 1957, PRO.

31. Statement of Paul Meyer on May 25, 1957, box 17, CA, 1957, RG 59, NA (hereafter cited as Statement of Paul Meyer); statement by Howard E. Chaille.

32. Statement by Alexander C. Boase; Riots Injuring American Employees.

33. "Lei Nuo an yinqi xuanrandabo" (Reynolds's case stirs up tempest), *Lianhe bao* (United Daily), May 25, 1957, 3; Summarized Report on Investigation by the Taipei Garrison Command of Persons Arrested on May 24, 1957, *524 shijian zhuanan jiantao* (Review of the May 24th Incident investigation), *danghao* 425.2/0014, WJDA.

34. Report by Mr. O. K. Yui; Chronology of Mob Attack.

35. Statement by William H. Gleysteen, box 17, CA, 1957, RG 59, NA.

36. Riots in Taipei, May 24, 1957; statement by Henry Bonner, box 17, CA, 1957, RG 59, NA (hereafter cited as Statement by Henry Bonner); statement by John J. Conroy, First Secretary of the Embassy, ibid.

37. Summarized Report on Investigation by the Taipei Garrison Command of Persons Arrested on May 24, 1957, *524 shijian zhuanan jiantao* (Review of the May 24th Incident investigation), *danghao* 425.2/0014, WJDA.

38. Statement of Paul Meyer; statement by Howard E. Chaille; statement by Alexander C. Boase; Chronology of Mob Attack.

39. 711.551/6–457, Meyer to Dulles, Department of State, Central Files, 1955–1957, box 2838, RG 59, NA.

40. Lieutenant Colonel George Chow, Memorandum for Record, June 24, 1957, box 17, CA, 1957, RG 59, NA.

41. 711.551/6–457, Meyer to Dulles, Department of State, Central Files, 1955–1957, box 2838, RG 59, NA.

42. "Formosa-Riot GI Lands Here," *San Francisco Chronicle*, May 27, 1957, *524 shijian zhuwai geguan jianbao ji zhuanti baogao* (Newspaper clippings and special reports from overseas embassies regarding the May 24th Incident), *danghao* 425.2/0026, WJDA; "Riot Sergeant Tells Story," *San Francisco Examiner*, May 27, 1957, ibid.

43. "GI Who Sparked China Riot Arrives," *Oakland Tribune*, May 27, 1957, 3. When and where Reynolds served in Vietnam is unknown because his military records were destroyed in the famous 1973 fire in St. Louis, Missouri. When Reynolds died in 1986, his obituary mentioned that he served in Vietnam. His wife, Clare, passed away in 1979. Both were buried in Reynolds's hometown of Colora, Maryland. See http://www.idreamof.com/cemetery/md/cecil/nottingham/nottingham-p-z.html.

44. Report by Mr. O. K. Yui; statement by Howard Jones, Second Secretary of the Embassy, box 17, CA, 1957, RG 59, NA (hereafter cited as Statement of Howard Jones).

45. Brent to Moyer, June 6, 1957, box 17, CA, 1957, RG 59, NA.

46. Statement by Howard E. Chaille; statement by Norma Platter, box 17, CA, 1957, RG 59, NA (hereafter cited as Statement by Norma Platter).

47. Chronology of Mob Attack; statement by Alexander C. Boase; statement of Paul Meyer.

48. Statement of Karl D. Ackerman, Second Secretary and Vice Consul and Security Officer, box 17, CA, 1957, RG 59, NA; statement by Norma Platter; May 24 Riots in Taipei, August 5, 1957, box 17, CA, 1957, RG 59, NA; Chronology of Mob Attack.

49. Statement by Francis C. Prescott, Second Secretary of the Embassy, box 17, CA, 1957, RG 59, NA.

50. "Bentuan guanyu Liu Ziran bei Lei Nuo qiangsha an, shudao xuexiao xuesheng ji shehui tuanyuan qingxing ruci" (Report on the Liu Ziran Incident and efforts to enlighten students and association members), n.d., *524 shi jian youguan jigou baogao* (Report from relevant organizations regarding the May 24th Incident), *danghao* 425.2/0004, WJDA.

51. Chronology of Mob Attack.

52. Captain H. R. McKibbin Memorandum for the Record, June 24, 1957, box 17, CA, 1957, RG 59, NA; Osborn to Jones, August 23, 1957, box 8, CA, 1957, RG 59, NA; Jones to Clough, July 18, 1957, ibid.

53. Brent to Moyer, June 6, 1957, box 17, CA, 1957, RG 59, NA; Chronology of Mob Attack.

54. Lieutenant Colonel George Chow, Memorandum for Record, June 24, 1957, box 17, CA, 1957, RG 59, NA.

55. *China Post,* May 27, 1957, in FO 371/127472/FCN 10345/31, PRO; Chronology of Mob Attack; Riots Injuring American Employees; Report by Mr. O. K. Yui; "USIS Still a Shambles, Moving to New Office," *China News,* May 29, 1957, *524 shijian jianbao ji yiban ziliao* (Newspaper clippings and documents regarding the May 24th Incident), *danghao* 425.2/0011, WJDA.

56. Brent to Moyer, June 6, 1957, box 17, CA, 1957, RG 59, NA.

57. Report by Mr. O. K. Yui; Summarized Report on Investigation by the Taipei Garrison Command of Persons Arrested on May 24, 1957, *524 shijian zhuanan jiantao* (Review of the May 24th Incident investigation), *danghao* 425.2/0014, WJDA; Rankin to State Department, June 23, 1957, box 8, folder 5, Rankin Papers.

58. Report by Mr. O. K. Yui; Chronology of Mob Attack.

59. K. L. Rankin, Memorandum on Events of May 24, 1957, box 17, CA, 1957, RG 59, NA; Chronology of Mob Attack.

60. Statement by Henry Bonner.

61. Chronology of Mob Attack; Karl Rankin, memorandum to Minister Edwin A. Plitt, June 10, 1957, box 17, CA, 1957, RG 59, NA (cited hereafter as Rankin, Memorandum to Plitt).

62. Rankin, Memorandum to Plitt; Chronology of Mob Attack; Barker to the Department of the Army, May 25, 1957, Department of State, *Foreign Relations of*

the United States, 1955–1957, China, 3:530; Ingersoll to Dulles, May 24, 1957, box 8, Dulles-Herter Papers.

63. "Statement of Activities During May 24 Incident by Donald L. Whittaker," box 17, CA, 1957, RG 59, NA; Rankin, Memorandum to Plitt.

64. Chronology of Mob Attack; Rankin, Memorandum to Plitt.

10. Accusations

1. FO 371/127471/FCN10345/18, Franklin to Foreign Office, May 30, 1957, PRO; Ingersoll to Stump, May 29, 1957, box 17, CA, 1957, RG 59, NA.

2. Pre-May 24 Reports from Embassy Taipei Regarding Public Feeling on Reynolds' Case, June 6, 1957, box 8, CA, 1957, RG 59, NA.

3. FO 371/127472/FCN 10345/26, Franklin to Lloyd, June 4, 1957, PRO.

4. Lieutenant Colonel George Chow, Memorandum for Record, June 24, 1957, box 17, CA, 1957, RG 59, NA; Memorandum of conversation, May 24 Riots in Taipei, August 7, 1957, box 8, CA, 1957, RG 59, NA; Barker to Brucker, May 26, 1957, box 17, CA, 1957, RG 59, NA.

5. "Zhongshi shudao deyi, buhui fasheng yiwai" (Appropriate measures make incidents in Taichung City unlikely), *Lianhe bao* (United Daily), May 26, 1957, 3; "Taibei shi buxin de saoluan" (Taibei's unfortunate riot), *Lianhe bao* (United Daily), May 27, 1957, 3; memorandum, July 1, 1957, box 8, folder 5, Rankin Papers.

6. Rankin-Yeh conversation, May 29, 1957, *524 shijian duiMei jiaoshe* (U.S.-ROC discussions regarding the May 24th Incident), *danghao* 425.2/0016, WJDA.

7. Pilcher Memorandum, May 31, 1957, box 4, CA, 1957, RG 59, NA; Glenn Jones, e-mail to author, October 25, 2012; Vincent Kramer, e-mail to author, September 17, 2012.

8. Taiwan Provincial Government Notice, May 17, 1957, *China Post,* May 28, 1957, 4; Taiwan Garrison Command Notice, May 28, 1957, in *China Post,* May 29, 1957, 3; Barker to Brucker, May 26, 1957, box 17, CA, 1957, RG 59, NA.

9. Excerpts of letter written by Father Richard Downey, Tung Hsih, Taiwan, June 6, 1957, box 8, CA, 1957, RG 59, NA; Osborn to Jones, August 29, 1957, ibid., box 4.

10. Clough to Robertson, June 12, 1957, box 8, CA, 1957, RG 59, NA.

11. FO 371/127471/FCN 10345/19, Franklin to Foreign Office, May 30, 1957, PRO.

12. Chronology of Mob Attack; Supplemental Data, box 17, CA, 1957, RG 59, NA; Pilcher to Jones, June 24, 1957, box 17, CA, 1957, RG 59, NA.

13. FO 371/127472/FCN 10345/26, Franklin to Lloyd, June 4, 1957, PRO.

14. FO 371/127472/FCN 10345/29, Franklin to Dalton, May 30, 1957, PRO.

15. Statement by Pilcher, Department of State, *Foreign Relations of the United States, 1955–1957, China,* 3:533; Memorandum of a Conversation, May 24, 1957, box 17, CA, 1957, RG 59, NA; Chronology of Mob Attack.

16. Robertson to Pilcher, July 16, 1957, box 17, CA, 1957, RG 59, NA.

17. USIS-London to Washington, May 27, 1957, box 9, CA, 1957, RG 59, NA.

18. Taipei Incident of May 24: Points You May Wish to Make to the Foreign Affairs Subcommittee, May 26, 1957, box 8, CA, 1957, RG 59, NA; Kusnitz, *Public Opinion and Foreign Policy*, 78.

19. Ku to Yeh, May 30, 1957, *524 shijian zhuMei geguan laiwang wendian* (Telegrams between the Foreign Ministry and ROC consulates and embassy in the United States regarding the May 24th Incident), *danghao* 425.2/0028, WJDA; FO 371/127471/FCN 10345/22, Caccia to Foreign Office, May 31, 1957, PRO.

20. Ku to Yeh, May 30, 1957, *524 shijian zhuMei geguan laiwang wendian* (Telegrams between the Foreign Ministry and ROC consulates and embassy in the United States regarding the May 24th Incident), *danghao* 425.2/0028, WJDA; "Riots Raise Question of Basic Policy," *Hong Kong Standard*, May 31, 1957, *524 shijian jianbao ji yiban ziliao* (Newspaper clippings and documents regarding the May 24th Incident), *danghao* 425.2/0011, WJDA; untitled article written by Spencer Davis, ibid.

21. "Wrecking of American Embassy Occasion for Serious Thought," *Houston Chronicle*, May 27, 1957, *524 shijian zhuwai geguan jianbao ji zhuanti baogao* (Newspaper clippings and special reports from overseas embassies regarding the May 24th Incident), *danghao* 425.2/0026, WJDA; "We Can't Buy Friends," *San Francisco News*, May 27, 1957, ibid.; *Honolulu Advertiser*, May 25, 1957, ibid.; "How Secure Are We on Formosa?," *San Francisco Chronicle*, May 27, 1957, ibid.; "Yanks 'High Living' Called Factor in Formosa Attack," *San Francisco Chronicle*, May 27, 1957, ibid.; "Taipei Violence Awakens Us to Fact Nationalists Too Are Asians," *Houston Post*, May 26, 1957, ibid.

22. C. L. Sulzberger, "Logic, Love and American Understanding of China," *New York Times*, May 29, 1957, 20; Thomas Hamilton, "U.S. Far East Policies Due for a Reappraisal," *New York Times*, June 2, 1957, 179.

23. O. Edmund Clubb, "Formosa: The Dream Dissolves," *The Nation* (June 8, 1957), 491–493; Nathaniel Peffer, "Do We Need Formosa?," *New Republic* 136 (June 24, 1957), 15–17; "Global Indigestion," *Wheeling Intelligencer*, May 28, 1957, in Appendix, *Congressional Record*, June 7, 1957, A4466.

24. Diary entries, May 24–25, 1957, Chiang Diaries.

25. Chronology of Mob Attack; diary entry, May 26, 1957, Chiang Diaries.

26. Rankin-Chiang conversation, May 27, 1957, Department of State, *Foreign Relations of the United States, 1955–1957, China*, 3:538; Progress Report (July 3, 1957) on U.S. Policy toward Taiwan and the Government of the Republic of China, box 58, Disaster File, NSC Council Staff, Eisenhower Papers; Chronology of Mob Attack.

27. Memorandum for Captain B. A. Robbins, June 3, 1957, box 8, CA, 1957, RG 59, NA.

28. Chiang Kai-shek, "Mob Violence Brings Dishonor to the Nation," June 1, 1957, *Vital Speeches of the Day* 23 (June 15, 1957): 517–518; diary entry, June 1, 1957, Chiang Diaries.

29. Rankin-Chiang conversation, May 27, 1957, Department of State, *Foreign Relations of the United States, 1955–1957, China*, 3:538–539; diary entry, May 27, 1957, Chiang Diaries.

30. Chronology of Mob Attack; Department of State, *Foreign Relations of the United States, 1955–1957, China,* 3:530n; Ingersoll to Stump, May 29, 1957, box 17, CA, 1957, RG 59, NA.

31. FO 371/127472/FCN 10345/26, Franklin to Lloyd, June 4, 1957, PRO; Interim Assessment of Riots of May 24 in Taipei, in Progress Report (July 3, 1957) on U.S. Policy toward Taiwan and the Government of the Republic of China, box 58, Disaster File, NSC Council Staff, Eisenhower Papers; McClure to Twining, May 25, 1957, box 17, CA, 1957, RG 59, NA.

32. FO 371/127472/FCN 10345/26, Franklin to Lloyd, June 4, 1957, PRO.

33. Memorandum of conversation, May 24 Riots in Taipei, July 31, 1957, box 8, CA, 1957, RG 59, NA; 711.551/5-2557, Ingersoll to Dulles, box 2837, RG 59, NA.

34. *Zhonghua minguo shishi jiyao,* 575; McConaughy to Robertson, May 24, 1957, Department of State, *Foreign Relations of the United States, 1955–1957, China,* 3:525; Memorandum for Minister Plitt, June 19, 1957, box 17, CA, 1957, RG 59, NA.

35. Statement by Henry Bonner, box 17, CA, 1957, RG 59, NA; memorandum, July 1, 1957, box 8, folder 5, Rankin Papers.

36. "Signs of 'Organization' Revealed in Formosa Riot," *San Francisco Chronicle,* May 27, 1957, *danghao* 425.2/0026, WJDA; Barker to Brucker, May 25, 1957, Department of State, *Foreign Relations of the United States, 1955–1957, China,* 3:530–531; Keyes Beech, "Things Will Never Be the Same between U.S., China," *Honolulu Star Bulletin,* June 5, 1957, *danghao* 425.2/0028, WJDA; Memorandum of Conversation, May 24 Riots in Taipei, August 7, 1957, box 8, CA, 1957, RG 59, NA; Lederer, *A Nation of Sheep,* 54.

37. McConaughy to Robertson, May 26, 1957, Department of State, *Foreign Relations of the United States, 1955–1957, China,* 3:534–535; FO 371/127471/FCN10345/18, Franklin to Foreign Office, May 30, 1957, PRO; statement by Henry Bonner.

38. Richards to Dulles, October 9, 1957, Department of State, *Foreign Relations of the United States, 1955–1957, China,* 3:626.

39. Statement by Howard Jones.

40. Barker to the Department of the Army, May 25, 1957; Jones to Clough, July 18, 1957, box 8, CA, 1957, RG 59, NA; Memorandum of conversation, May 24 Riots in Taipei, July 31, 1957, box 8, CA, 1957, RG 59, NA.

41. Statement by Henry Bonner.

42. *The Public Papers of the Presidents of the United States: Dwight D. Eisenhower, 1957,* 441.

43. Rankin-Plitt-Yeh conversation, June 8, 1957, *524 shijian duiMei jiaoshe* (U.S.-ROC discussions regarding the May 24th Incident), *danghao* 425.2/0016, WJDA.

44. Ku to Yeh, May 30, 1957, *524 shijian zhuMei geguan laiwang wendian* (Telegrams between the Foreign Ministry and ROC consulates and embassy in the United States regarding the May 24th Incident), *danghao* 425.2/0028, WJDA.

45. David Lawrence, "Formosa Riot Was Cold War Battle," *Cedar Rapids Gazette,* May 29, 1957, 6; transcript of radio broadcast by Fulton Lewis, May 24,

1957, *danghao* 425.2/0028, WJDA; "Formosa Riot an Old Chinese Custom," *San Antonio Light*, May 31, 1957, 46.

46. 611.93/2–1957, Dulles to Johnson, *China, People's Republic of China 1955–59, Foreign Affairs*, reel 5; Qing, *From Allies to Enemies*, 283.

47. Harold C. Hinton, "Farewell to Formosa?" *Commonweal* 66 (June 28, 1957), 319–321.

48. Rankin-Shen conversation, May 25, 1957, *danghao* 425.2/0016, WJDA; 711.551/5–3157, Rankin to Dulles, Department of State, Central Files, 1955–1957, box 2837, RG 59, NA.

49. 711.551/5–3157, Rankin to Dulles, Department of State, Central Files, 1955–1957, box 2837, RG 59, NA; FO 371/127471/FCN 10345/18, Franklin to Foreign Office, May 30, 1957, PRO; Meyer-Yeh conversation, July 24, 1957, box 17, CA, 1957, RG 59, NA.

50. Tucker, *The China Threat*, 236n15; Dorsey to Clough, October 5, 1957, box 1, CA, 1957, RG 59, NA; 611.93/8–257, Lei Chan-Hsu-Stanley-O'Grady conversation, *China, People's Republic of China 1955–59, Foreign Affairs*, reel 5; Taylor, *The Generalissimo*, 491.

51. Lemnitzer to Multiple Recipients, June 13, 1957, box 9, CA, 1957, RG 59, NA; diary entries, July 15, 1957, and July 22, 1957, Tsiang Tingfu Diaries, reel 3; Richards to Dulles, October 9, 1957, Department of State, *Foreign Relations of the United States, 1955–1957, China*, 3:626.

52. FO 371/127472/FCN 10345/26, Franklin to Lloyd, June 4, 1957, PRO; Ma-Webster conversations, May 25, 1957, and June 9, 1957, box 8, CA, 1957, RG 59, NA; 711.551/5–3157, Rankin to Dulles, Department of State, Central Files, 1955–1957, box 2837, RG 59, NA.

53. FO 371/127472/FCN 10345/26, Franklin to Lloyd, June 4, 1957, PRO; FO 371/127472/FCN 10345/40, Franklin to Dalton, July 16, 1957, PRO; Tucker, *The China Threat*, 236n16.

54. 711.551/5–3157, Rankin to Dulles, Department of State, Central Files, 1955–1957, box 2837, RG 59, NA; Paraphrase of Taipei's Telegram to Department, June 23, 1957, box 8, folder 5, Rankin Papers; Bowen to Stump, May 29, 1957, box 8, CA, 1957, RG 59, NA.

55. Ingersoll to Stump, May 29, 1957, box 17, CA, 1957, RG 59, NA; Brent to Moyer, June 6, 1957, box 17, CA, 1957, RG 59, NA; FO 371/127472/FCN 10345/26, Franklin to Lloyd, June 4, 1957, PRO; Brent to Moyer, June 6, 1957, box 17, CA, 1957, RG 59, NA; Lederer, *A Nation of Sheep*, 55–56; Department of State, *Foreign Relations of the United States, 1955–1957, China*, 3:541.

56. Cumming to Acting Secretary, May 30, 1957, box 8, CA, 1957, RG 59, NA.

11. To the Chinese Heart of the Matter

1. Diary entry, May 27, 1957, Chiang Diaries

2. Diary entry, May 26, 1957, Chiang Diaries; Rankin-Yeh conversation, May 29, 1957, *524 shijian duiMei jiaoshe* (U.S.-ROC discussions regarding the May 24th Incident), *danghao* 425.2/0016, WJDA.

3. Diary entry, June 4, 1957, Chiang Diaries.

4. Unless otherwise noted, much of the following is based on Report by Mr. O. K. Yui.

5. Summarized Report on Investigation by the Taipei Garrison Command of Persons Arrested on May 24, 1957, *524 shijian zhuanan jiantao* (Review of the May 24th Incident investigation), *danghao* 425.2/0014, WJDA.

6. "Zi Lei Nuozi shenpan wuzui hou zhi May 24 shangban shishi zhi chuli qingxing" (Timeline of measures taken from the Reynolds acquittal until May 24th 10:00 A.M.), *524 shijian zhuanan jiantao* (Review of the May 24th Incident investigation), *danghao* 425.2/0013, WJDA.

7. "May 24 shangban shishi hou zai qingyun sheyun fangmian chuli qingxing" (Timeline of measures taken after 10:00 A.M. on May 24th to control youth and social groups), *524 shijian zhuanan jiantao* (Review of the May 24th Incident investigation), *danghao* 425.2/0013, WJDA.

8. Robert G. Reynolds Incident, November 14, 2010, *An Ordinary Chinese*, http://anordinarychinese.blogspot.com/2010/11/robert-g-reynolds-incident.html (accessed March 2, 2013); Emergency Notice of the China Youth Anti-Communists National Salvation Corp [*sic*] General Headquarters, May 24, 1957, box 8, CA, 1957, RG 59, NA.

9. Lin Jiaqun, "Liu Ziran shijian" (The Liu Ziran incident), *Zhongguo shibao* (China Times), May 25, 2010, A9, http://blog.udn.com/tel2366/4063223 (accessed March, 15, 2014).

10. Chen Hanqiang, "524 Liu Ziran shijian" (The May 24 Liu Ziran incident), February 15, 2006, http://blog.xuite.net/hanchiang/education/5647640-524 (accessed March 15, 2014).

11. *Shijie ribao* (World Journal), May 25, 1957, *524 shijian zhuwai geguan jianbao ji zhuanti baogao* (Newspaper clippings and special reports from overseas embassies regarding the May 24th Incident), *danghao* 425.2/0027, WJDA.

12. Lieutenant Colonel George Chow, Memorandum for Record, June 24, 1957, box 17, CA, 1957, RG 59, NA; Clough to Robertson, June 12, 1957, box 8, CA, 1957, RG 59, NA; Barker to Taylor, May 25, 1957, box 17, CA, 1957, RG 59, NA.

13. Brent to Moyer, June 6, 1957, box 17, CA, 1957, RG 59, NA; FO 371/127471/FCN 10345/18, Franklin to Foreign Office, May 30, 1957, PRO; FO 371/127472/FCN 10345/26, Franklin to Lloyd, June 4, 1957, PRO.

14. Yeh-Meyer conversation, July 22, 1957, box 17, CA, 1957, RG 59, NA.

15. Dikotter, *The Tragedy of Liberation*, 124.

16. Progress Report (July 3, 1957) on U.S. Policy toward Taiwan and the Government of the Republic of China by the Operations Coordinating Board, box 58, National Security Council Staff, Disaster File, Nationalist China (10), Eisenhower Papers (hereafter cited as Progress Report, July 3, 1957).

17. Diary entry, June 30, 1957, Chiang Diaries.

18. Diary entry, June 28, 1957, Chiang Diaries.

19. Brent to Moyer, June 6, 1957, box 17, CA, 1957, RG 59, NA.

20. Memorandum of conversation, May 24 Riots in Taipei, July 31, 1957, box 8, CA, 1957, RG 59, NA.

21. Brent to Moyer, June 6, 1957, box 17, CA, 1957, RG 59, NA; Meyer to Clough, July 22, 1957, box 8, CA, 1957, RG 59, NA.

22. Diary entries, June 10–11, 1957, Chiang Diaries.

23. Ku to Yeh, May 25, 1957, *danghao* 425.2/0028, WJDA; Yeh-Meyer conversation, July 22, 1957, box 17, CA, 1957, RG 59, NA.; Country Statement on MAP, December 1957, MHI.

24. Transcript of Radio Panel Discussion on the May 24, 1957, Incident in Taipei, Taiwan, *524 shijian jianbao ji yiban ziliao* (Newspaper clippings and documents regarding the May 24th Incident), *danghao* 425.2/0012, WJDA; statement of Ardith H. Miller; Wang, *A Memoir*; "Statement by Wang Dezhen," *524 shijian duinei yiban wenjian* (Internal documents related to the May 24th Incident), *danghao* 425.2/0015, WJDA.

25. "Guanyu Liu Ziran an xinwen chuli zhi jiancha ji jihou gaijian yijian," (Some ideas regarding the press's handling of the Liu Ziran case and proposed improvements), *524 shijian zhuanan jiantao* (Review of the May 24th Incident investigation), *danghao* 425.2/0013, WJDA.

26. "Dui Lei Nuozi changsha Liu Ziran an ji May 24 Taibei shi buxin shijian xinwen yizhuan chuli jiantao baogao" (Report on the case of Reynolds killing Liu Ziran and the management of press reports of the May 24th Incident), *danghao* 425.2/0013, WJDA.

27. Ibid.; "Guanyu Liu Ziran an xinwen chuli zhi jiancha ji jihou gaijian yijian," (Some ideas regarding the press's handling of the Liu Ziran case and proposed improvements), *524 shijian zhuanan jiantao* (Review of the May 24th Incident investigation), *danghao* 425.2/0013, WJDA.

28. Paraphrase of Taipei's Telegram to Department, June 23, 1957, box 8, folder 5, Rankin Papers; Richards to Dulles, October 9, 1957, Department of State, *Foreign Relations of the United States, 1955–1957, China*, 3:626; diary entry, June 25, 1957, Chiang Diaries.

29. Progress Report, July 3, 1957.

30. See diary entries for May 21–25, 27, 28, 1957, *Wang Shuming jiangjun riji* (The diary of General Wang Shuming), Institute of Modern History, Academia Sinica, Nangang, Taiwan; diary entries for May 24–26, 1957, *Zhao Hengti xinsheng riji* (The Diary of Zhao Hengti), Institute of Modern History, Academia Sinica, Nangang, Taiwan; diary entries for May 24–25, 1957, Xu Yongchang, *Xu Yongchang riji* (The diary of Xu Yongchang), 12:172.

31. *Zhonghua minguo shishi jiyao*, 577.

32. Richards to Dulles, October 9, 1957, Department of State, *Foreign Relations of the United States, 1955–1957, China*, 3:626; Taylor, *The Generalissimo's Son*, 237; quote from Liu, "Indoctrinating the Youth," 207–208.

33. Summarized Report on Investigation by the Taipei Garrison Command of Persons Arrested on May 24, 1957, *524 shijian zhuanan jiantao* (Review of the May

24th Incident investigation), *danghao* 425.2/0014, WJDA; "Weicheng songdui Tai-bei shi buxin shijian chuli jingguo baogao shu jianqi" (Report on Handling the May 24 Riots' Aftermath), June 13, 1957, *524 shijian shenxun zuifan* (The May 24th Incident criminal trials), *danghao* 425.2/0018, WJDA.

34. "Court Martial Trial of 40 Black Friday Rioters Begins," *China News*, June 10, 1957, *danghao* 425.2/0018, WJDA; "Spotlight Falls on Young Boy," *Hong Kong Tiger Standard*, June 20, 1957, 3, ibid.

35. "Court Martial to Hand Down Riot Sentences in Five Days," *China News*, June 20, 1957, *danghao* 425.2/0018, WJDA; Supplemental Data, box 17, CA, 1957, RG 59, NA.

36. "Yesterday's Court Verdicts," *China News*, June 27, 1957, *danghao* 425.2/0018, WJDA.

37. Hsu-Meyer conversation, July 9, 1957, box 8, CA, 1957, RG 59, NA; comments on Mr. Meyer's memorandum of July 9, 1957, July 12, 1957, ibid.

38. Clough to Lockhart, June 13, 1957, box 8, CA, 1957, RG 59, NA.

39. Rankin to Dulles, May 26, 1957, Department of State, *Foreign Relations of the United States, 1955–1957, China*, 3:536; Ingersoll to Stump, May 29, 1957, box 17, CA, 1957, RG 59, NA; Rankin-Chiang conversation, May 27, 1957, Department of State, *Foreign Relations of the United States, 1955–1957, China*, 3:540; Chiang to Smith, June 19, 1957, box 118, H. Alexander Smith Papers, Seeley Mudd Manuscript Library, Princeton University, Princeton, New Jersey (hereafter cited as H. Alexander Smith Papers).

40. Memorandum of conversation, May 24 Riots in Taipei, August 7, 1957, box 8, CA, 1957, RG 59, NA; Supplemental Data, box 17, CA, 1957, RG 59, NA; "How One Riot Was Prevented," *524 shijian jianbao ji yiban ziliao* (Newspaper clippings and documents regarding the May 24th Incident), *danghao* 425.2/0011, WJDA.

41. FO 371/127471/FCN 10345/10, Tamsui to Foreign Office, May 24, 1957, PRO; Hua Mingyi, "Taibei shijian jingwei" (The scope of the Taibei Incident), *Ziyou ren* (The Freeman), June 1, 1957, 2; *Shijie ribao* (World Journal), May 28, 1957, *524 shijian zhuwai geguan jianbao ji zhuanti baogao* (Newspaper clippings and special reports from overseas embassies regarding the May 24th Incident), *danghao* 425.2/0026, WJDA.

42. Pilcher to Powell, June 6, 1957, box 17, CA, 1957, RG 59, NA.

43. FO 371/127472/FCN 10345/26, Franklin to Lloyd, June 4, 1957, PRO; *Lianhe bao* (United Daily), May 28, 1957, 3.

44. FO 371/127471/FCN 10351/16, Tamsui to Foreign Office, May 28, 1957, PRO; Hoghland to Nixon, July 23, 1957, box 8, CA, 1957, RG 59, NA.

45. Pilcher to Powell, June 6, 1957, box 17, CA, 1957, RG 59, NA; Clough, *Island China*, 44; Tucker, *The China Threat*, 142.

46. "Shi meiguoren chayi de shiqing" (The matter of Americans being flabbergasted), *Shijie ribao* (World Journal), May 31, 1957, *danghao* 425.2/0027, WJDA; Moy to Judd, June 7, 1957, *danghao* 425.2/0003, WJDA.

47. "Taibei shijian yu meiyuan" (The Taipei incident and U.S. assistance), *Xingxian ribao* (Sing Sian Yer Pao Daily News), May 31, 1957, *danghao* 425.2/0027, WJDA.

48. *Guanghua zaobao* (Guanghua Daily), May 30, 1957, *danghao* 425.2/0027, WJDA.

49. *Neimu guancha bao* (Behind-the-Scenes News), May 25, 1957, *danghao* 425.2/0026, WJDA.

50. Li Qiusheng, "Wo dui meiguo de shiwang yu xiwang" (My disappointment and hope in America), *Ziyou Ren* (The Freeman), June 5, 1957, 1.

51. *Guanghua zaobao* (Guanghua Daily), May 26, 1957, *danghao* 425.2/0027, WJDA.

52. *Zhengxing xinwen* (Reliable News), May 27, 1957, 1; *Huanqiu shibao* (The World), May 26, 1957, *danghao* 425.2/0026, WJDA; *Xinsheng wanbao* (New Life Nightly), May 27, 1957, ibid.; "Women de taidu" (Our attitude), *Zili wanbao* (Independence Evening Post), May 24, 1957, 4; "Taiwan qunzhong de fennu" (The Taiwan mob's indignation), *Guanghua wanbao* (Kwong Wah Evening News), May 27, 1957, *danghao* 425.2/0027, WJDA; "Taibei de fanmei baodong," *Xingxian ribao* (Sing Sian Yer Pao Daily News), May 27, 1957, ibid.; *Chaoran bao*, May 27, 1957, *danghao* 425.2/0026, WJDA.

53. "Leinuo panjue wuzui yu Taibei saodong shijian zhi jiantao" (A look at the Reynolds not guilty verdict and the Taibei Incident), *Ziyou Zhongguo* (Free China), 16 (June 1, 1957): 467–468, *524 shijian jianbao ji yiban ziliao* (Newspaper clippings and documents regarding the May 24th Incident), *danghao* 425.2/0012, WJDA.

54. Lin Jiaqun, "Xunzhao ying zhongren' huanyuan Liu Ziran shijian dangju ceng saoshe" (The Liu Ziran Incident) *Zhongguo shibao* (China Times), May 24, 2010, http://blog.udn.com/tpa285/4061903.

55. Chen quote from "Taipei Policemen Contradict Each Other at Court-Martial," *Hong Kong Standard*, June 20, 1957, *danghao* 425.2/0018, WJDA; "Yin yiren lingshe fating, man liangwei qingle lushi" (Two defendants tried separately request lawyers), *Lianhe bao* (United Daily), June 19, 1957, 3.

56. Statement of Ardith H. Miller.

57. "Duiyu Taiwan Lei Nuo shijian de guangan" (Observations on the Reynolds Incident in Taiwan), *Shijie ribao* (World Journal), May 27, 1957, *danghao* 425.2/0027, WJDA.

58. *Sifa xingzheng bu diaocha ju diaocha qingbao baogao* (Intelligence Report, Bureau of Investigation, Ministry of Justice), "Taiwan daxue xuesheng dui Liu Ziran an zhi fanying" (Taiwan University Students' reaction to the Liu Ziran Case), May 24, 1957, *danghao* 425.2/0015, WJDA; "Taida faxueyuan xuesheng juxing Liu Ziran an zuotanhui qingxing" (Circumstance behind the National Taiwan University Law College student discussion of the Liu Ziran Case), ibid.

59. *Zili wanbao* (Independence Evening Post), May 26, 1957, 4.

60. "Damage to Sino-U.S. Relations," *China Post*, May 25, 1957, in FO 371/127471/FCN 10345/20, PRO; Lin, "Cong guojifa guandian lun Minguo 46 nian Meijun Lei Nuo sharen shijian" (A Study of the Reynolds Case of 1957 from the Viewpoint of International Law), 235.

61. "Liu Ziran an jing mei junfa shenjue" (The Liu Ziran case and the U.S. court-

martial verdict), *Lianhe bao* (United Daily), May 25, 1957, 1; see also *Zili wanbao* (Independence Evening Post), May 25, 1957, 4.

62. "Dui Taibei shijian de kanfa" (A view of the Taibei Incident), *Ziyou Ren* (The Freeman), May 29, 1957, 1; *Zhonghua ribao* (China Daily News), May 31, 1957, *danghao* 425.2/0027, WJDA; "Cimei zhi suoyi weidi ye" (This is why the United States has become an empire), *Chengbao* (Singbao Daily News), May 25, 1957, *danghao* 425.2/0026, WJDA; *Huaqiao ribao* (Overseas Daily), May 26, 1957, ibid.; "Quxiao meijun zaitai hengyou waijiao tequan" (Cancel diplomatic immunity for U.S. advisors in Taiwan), *Zhonghua bao* (China News), May 31, 1957, *danghao* 425.2/0027, WJDA.

63. Report of O. K. Yui.

64. FO 371/127471/FCN 10345/18, Franklin to Foreign Office, May 30, 1957, PRO; "Xinpingqihe hua leinuo an" (Calmly discuss the Reynolds case), *Zili wanbao* (Independence Evening Post), May 24, 1957, 1; "Tongbao men, xianzai bushi chen-gyi qi de shihou!" (Compatriots, this is not the time to do as one pleases in anger!), *Zhengxin xinwen* (Reliable News), May 25, 1957, 1; "Buxin de fazhan" (Development of the unfortunate incident), *Zhonghua ribao* (China Daily News), May 25, 1957, 2.

65. Brent to Moyer, June 6, 1957, box 17, CA, 1957, RG 59, NA.

66. *Guanghua wanbao* (Guanghua Evening), May 29, 1957, *danghao* 425.2/0027, WJDA; Memorandum, *524 shijian zhuanan jiantao* (Review of the May 24th Incident investigation), *danghao* 425.02/0014, WJDA.

67. Statement of Ardith H. Miller; *Gongshang wanbao* (Commercial Evening), May 25, 1957, *danghao* 425.2/0026, WJDA; "Tai yulun yizhi zhizhai Meifang shen-pan bugongping" (Taiwan public opinion unanimously criticizes verdict as unfair), *Gongshang ribao* (Kung Sheung Daily), May 25, 1957, 3.

68. Phillips, *Between Assimilation and Independence*, 137–138.

69. 611.93/6–2657, Caprio to State Department, June 26, 1957, *China, People's Republic of China 1955–59, Foreign Affairs*, reel 5.

12. Repercussions

1. East Asian Reactions to Taipei Riots Reveal Sharp Criticism of US, June 11, 1957, box 3, RG 306, Records of the United States Information Agency, Office of Research, Public Opinion, Far East 1955–1960, NA (cited hereafter as East Asian Reactions to Taipei Riots).

2. Nash, "United States Overseas Military Bases: Report to the President," Appendix, 36.

3. Ibid., 29–30 and Appendix, 81–82, 87, 140–142.

4. "U.S. Troop Withdrawal Sentiments in West Germany, France and Japan, May 28, 1956," RG 306, Records of the United States Information Agency, Office of Research, Special Reports, 1955–1959, NA.

5. Schaller, *Altered States*, 128–129; MacArthur to Dulles, May 24, 1957, Department of State, *Foreign Relations of the United States, 1955–1957, Japan*, 23:315–316.

6. Possible Japanese Agreement to Publicize Secret Jurisdiction Waiver, June

18, 1957, Lot File no. 61D68, box 19, Subject Files Related to Japan, RG 59, NA.

7. 711.551/3–2357, MacArthur to Dulles, Department of State, Central Decimal File, 1955–1959, box 2837, RG 59, NA.

8. "Specialist with Problem," *New York Times*, July 12, 1957.

9. U.S. Supreme Court, *Wilson v. Girard*, 1957; Quarles to Adams, June 1, 1957, box 2, White House Central Files, Name Series, Eisenhower Papers.

10. Draft Memorandum for the President Prepared in the Department of State, Department of State, *Foreign Relations of the United States, 1955–1957, Japan*, 23:324.

11. Ibid.

12. U.S. Supreme Court, *Wilson v. Girard*, 1957.

13. Horsey to Dulles, February 8, 1957, Department of State, *Foreign Relations of the United States, 1955–1957, Japan*, 23:261–262.

14. U.S. Supreme Court, *Wilson v. Girard*, 1957.

15. 711.551/2–1257, Horsey to Dulles, Department of State, Central Decimal File, 1955–1959, box 2837, RG 59, NA.

16. U.S. Supreme Court, *Wilson v. Girard*, 1957; MacArthur to Dulles, February 26, 1957, Department of State, *Foreign Relations of the United States, 1955–1957, Japan*, 23:272.

17. U.S. Supreme Court, *Wilson v. Girard*, 1957.

18. MacArthur to Dulles, April 25, 1957, Department of State, *Foreign Relations of the United States, 1955–1957, Japan*, 23:282; Herter to MacArthur, May 1, 1957, ibid., 23:284.

19. Brucker to Lemnitzer, April 26, 1957, Department of State, *Foreign Relations of the United States, 1955–1957, Japan*, 23:283; Robertson to Dulles, May 20, 1957, ibid., 23:294–295.

20. The controversy behind Hubbard's decision to allow Japan jurisdiction over Girard is found in Curtain, "'We Might As Well Write Japan Off,'" 119–121; Robertson to Dulles, May 20, 1957, Department of State, *Foreign Relations of the United States, 1955–1957, Japan*, 23:294–296

21. Dulles-Robertson telephone conversation, May 20, 1957, box 6, folder 3, May–June 1957, Telephone Calls Series, Eisenhower Papers.

22. 711.551/5–1757, Laishley to Dulles, Department of State, Central Decimal File, 1955–1959, box 2837, RG 59, NA; 711.551/5–2157, Chamblee et al. to Dulles, ibid.; 711.551/5–2457, Republican Women's Study Club of Glendale, California, ibid.; 711.551/5–2357, State of Illinois, Seventieth General Assembly, Senate Resolution No. 51, ibid.; 711.551/5–2857, State of Illinois, Seventieth General Assembly, House Resolution No. 83, ibid.; 711.551/5–2957, Los Angeles County Federation of Republican Women to Dulles, ibid.; 711.551/5–2057, E. Ross Adair to Dulles, ibid.

23. FO 371/127577/FJ 1642/1, De la Mare to Dalton, May 24, 1957, PRO; FO 371/127577/FJ 1642/2, De la Mare to Dalton, May 25, 1957, PRO.

24. Dulles-Snyder telephone conversation, May 20, 1957, box 6, folder 3, Telephone Calls Series, May–June 1957, Eisenhower Papers.

25. Legislative Leadership Meeting, May 21, 1957, box 24, Diary, Eisenhower Papers; Dulles to Eisenhower, May 21, 1957, box 5, John Foster Dulles White House Memorandum, White House Correspondence, General, 1957, Eisenhower Papers.

26. Dulles to Brucker, May 21, 1957, Department of State, *Foreign Relations of the United States, 1955–1957, Japan,* 23:306.

27. 711.551/5–2157, Dulles to MacArthur, Department of State, Central Decimal File, 1955–1959, box 2837, RG 59, NA; Dulles-Brucker telephone conversation, box 6, folder 3, Telephone Call Series, Eisenhower Papers.

28. Eisenhower-Dulles telephone conversation, May 21, 1957, Eisenhower Papers.

29. Dulles-Brucker telephone conversation, May 21, 1957, box 6, folder 3, May–June 1957, Telephone Calls Series, Eisenhower Papers; Memorandum of Meeting, May 21, 1957, Department of State, *Foreign Relations of the United States, 1955–1957, Japan,* 23:307–308; 711.551/5–2157, Dulles to MacArthur, Department of State, Central Decimal File, 1955–1959, box 2837, RG 59, NA, RG 59, NA.

30. MacArthur to Dulles, May 22, 1957, Department of State, *Foreign Relations of the United States, 1955–1957, Japan,* 23:309.

31. 711.551/5–2357, MacArthur to Dulles, Department of State, Central Decimal File, 1955–1959, box 2837, RG 59, NA; MacArthur to Dulles, May 23, 1957, Department of State, *Foreign Relations of the United States, 1955–1957, Japan,* 23:314.

32. MacArthur to Dulles, May 24, 1957, Department of State, *Foreign Relations of the United States, 1955–1957, Japan,* 23:315–316.

33. Lemnitzer to Brucker, May 28, 1957, box 9, CA, 1957, RG 59, NA.

34. 711.551/5–2957, MacArthur to Dulles, Department of State, Central Decimal File, 1955–1959, box 2837, RG 59, NA; 711.551/5–3157, Emery to Dulles, ibid.

35. Nash, "United States Overseas Military Bases: Report to the President," Appendix, 123, 126; Berry, *U.S. Bases in the Philippines,* 86–97; Burrows to Dulles, May 27, 1956, Department of State, *Foreign Relations of the United States, 1955–1957, Southeast Asia,* 22:651n2; Nufer to Dulles, August 27, 1956, ibid., 22:677.

36. Cochran, "Jurisdiction over American Military Personnel under the U.S.-Philippine Status of Forces Agreement," 1–13.

37. Nufer to Dulles, August 30, 1956, Department of State, *Foreign Relations of the United States, 1955–1957, Southeast Asia,* 22:682–683; 711.551/5–2857, Smith to Dulles, Department of State, Central Decimal File, 1955–1959, box 2837, RG 59, NA; Possible Japanese Agreement to Publicize Secret Jurisdiction Waiver, June 18, 1957, Lot File no. 61D68, box 19, Subject Files Related to Japan, RG 59, NA.

38. 711.551/5–2357, MacArthur to Dulles, Department of State, Central Decimal File, 1955–1959, box 2837, RG 59, NA; "Anti-U.S. Riots Feared in Manila," *Weirton Daily Times,* May 27, 1957, 1.

39. East Asian Reactions to Taipei Riots; "Status of Forces Agreements," *Stevens Point Daily Journal,* June 6, 1957, 10.

40. 794.0221/8–2657, Dulles to Wilson, Department of State, Central Decimal File, 1955–1959, box 3966, RG 59, NA.

41. Nash, "United States Overseas Military Bases: Report to the President," Appendix, 91, 96.

42. Sawyer, *Military Advisors in Korea,* 48; Nash, "United States Overseas Military Bases: Report to the President," 33.

43. 711.551/10–357, Ockey to Robertson, Department of State, Central Decimal File, 1955–1959, box 2838, RG 59, NA; 711.551/10–1557, Ockey to Robertson, Department of State, Central Decimal File, 1955–1959, ibid.

44. 711.551/4–2557, Weil to Dulles, Department of State, Central Decimal File, 1955–1959, box 2837, RG 59, NA; 711.551/5–3157, Weil to Dulles, Department of State, Central Decimal File, 1955–1959, ibid.

45. 711.551/7–357, Jones to Dulles, Department of State, Central Decimal File, 1955–1959, box 2837, RG 59, NA.

46. Lemnitzer to Brucker, May 28, 1957, box 9, CA, 1957, RG 59, NA.

47. 711.551/5–3157, Weil to Dulles, Department of State, Central Decimal File, 1955–1959, box 2837, RG 59, NA; "The Common Enemy," *Korean Republic,* May 28, 1957, 2, *524 shijian zhuwai geguan jianbao ji zhuanti baogao* (Newspaper clippings and special reports from overseas embassies regarding the May 24th Incident), *danghao* 425.2/0026, WJDA; East Asian Reactions to Taipei Riots.

48. *Zhonghua ribao* (China Daily News), May 26, 1957, *524 shijian zhuwai geguan jianbao ji zhuanti baogao* (Newspaper clippings and special reports from overseas embassies regarding the May 24th Incident), *danghao* 425.2/0027, WJDA.

49. "Taiguo renming you ruhe?" (What do the Thai people think?), *Guanghua zaobao* (Guanghua Daily), May 29, 1957, *danghao* 425.2/0027, WJDA; see also "Taibei minzhong fanmei shijian" (The anti-American incident in Taiwan), *Guanghua wanbao* (Guanghua Evening), May 27, 1957, ibid.

50. 711.551/6–757, McCarthy to Dulles, Department of State, Central Decimal File, 1955–1959, box 2838, RG 59, NA; East Asian Reactions to Taipei Riots.

51. Memorandum of conversation, May 9, 1957, Department of State, *Foreign Relations of the United States, 1955–1957, Vietnam,* 1:803–806 (also see note 2); "Taipei Riot Stories Censored out of Saigon Chinese Press," *Hong Kong Standard,* May 28, 1957, *524 shijian jianbao ji yiban ziliao* (Newspaper clippings and documents regarding the May 24th Incident), *danghao* 425.2/0011, WJDA; East Asian Reactions to Taipei Riots.

52. East Asian Reactions to Taipei Riots; Department of State, *Foreign Relations of the United States, 1955–1957, China,* 3:560.

53. Department of State, *Foreign Relations of the United States, 1955–1957, China,* 2:32–33; NSC-5723, October 4, 1957, ibid., 3:622.

54. FO 371/127471/FCN 10345/14, O'Neill to Foreign Office, May 25, 1957, PRO; FO 371/127471/FCN 10345/15, O'Neill to Foreign Office, May 27, 1957, PRO; FO 371/127472/FCN 10345/34, O'Neill to Lloyd, June 7, 1957, PRO; Progress Report, July 3, 1957.

55. East Asian Reactions to Taipei Riots; see newspaper clippings regarding communist reactions and propaganda in *danghao* 425/0027, WJDA.

13. Defending the American Bases of Hegemony

1. Department of State, *Foreign Relations of the United States, 1955–1957, Japan,* 23:317; Secretary's Press Conference, May 29, 1957, box 8, CA, 1957, RG 59, NA.

2. Drain to Herter, May 26, 1957, box 11, McComber-Drain Chronological File, May 1957, Eisenhower Papers.

3. Legislative Leadership Meeting, May 28, 1957, box 2, Legislative Meetings, Eisenhower Papers.

4. Legislative Leadership Meeting, June 4, 1957, box 2, Legislative Meetings, Eisenhower Papers.

5. Murphy to Sims, May 24, 1957, box 4, CA, 1957, RG 59, NA.

6. Congress, Senate, 85th Cong., 1st Sess., *Congressional Record,* May 29, 1957, 7951–7956.

7. Congress, Senate, 85th Cong., 1st Sess., *Congressional Record,* June 10, 1957, 8595, 8596.

8. Progress Report, July 3, 1957; McConaughy to Robertson, May 26, 1957, box 8, CA, 1957, RG 59, NA.

9. Discussion at the 331st Meeting of the National Security Council, July 18, 1957, box 9, Ann Whitman File, NSC, Eisenhower Papers; National Security Council Meeting, July 19, 1957, box 9, NSC Files, Eisenhower Papers.

10. Rankin to Stump, June 3, 1957, box 8, folder 5, Rankin Papers; Legislative Leadership Meeting, June 4, 1957, box 2, Legislative Meetings, Eisenhower Papers; U.S. Force Reduction in Japan, December 9, 1957, Lot File 61D68, box 19, Department of State, Subject Files Related to Japan, RG 59, NA.

11. J. M. Roberts, "The Outburst in Formosa: Was It Resentment or Spontaneity?" *Titusville Herald,* May 29, 1957, 1.

12. Doyle to Stump, January 9, 1958, box 3, 306.13 NSC Reports and Correspondence, FE, Top Secret Files Relating to the Republic of China, 1954–1965, RG 59, NA.

13. Nash Survey, August 12, 1957, Lot File 61D 68, box 19, Department of State, Subject Files Related to Japan, RG 59, NA.

14. Eisenhower-Dulles telephone conversation, May 24, 1957, Department of State, *Foreign Relations of the United States, 1955–1957, China,* 3:528; Rankin-Plitt-Yeh conversation, June 8, 1957, *524 shijian duiMei jiaoshe* (U.S.-ROC discussions regarding the May 24th Incident), *danghao* 425.2/0016, WJDA.

15. Eisenhower-Dulles telephone conversation, May 24, 1957, Department of State, *Foreign Relations of the United States, 1955–1957, China,* 3:527–528; Eisenhower-Dulles telephone conversation, Department of State, *Foreign Relations of the United States, 1955–1957, Japan,* 23:316–317; editorial note, ibid., 23:317.

16. Dulles-Robertson telephone conversation, May 25, 1957, Department of State, *Foreign Relations of the United States, 1955–1957, Japan,* 23:322.

17. Dulles-Wilson telephone conversation, May 28, 1957, Department of State, *Foreign Relations of the United States, 1955–1957, Japan,* 23:332.

18. Legislative Leadership Meeting, May 28, 1957, box 2, Legislative Meetings, Eisenhower Papers.

19. Dulles-Knowland conversation, May 28, 1957, Department of State, *Foreign Relations of the United States, 1955–1957, Japan,* 23:334; 711.551/5–2957, Dulles to MacArthur, Department of State, Central Decimal File, 1955–1959, box 2837, RG 59, NA; Joint Statement of Secretary of State John Foster Dulles and Secretary of Defense Charles E. Wilson, ibid.

20. For just a sample of American reactions to the Girard case, see 711.551/6–457, Bray to Dulles, Department of State, Central Decimal File, 1955–1959, box 2838, RG 59, NA; 711.551/6–457, Humphries to Eisenhower, ibid.; 711.551/6–457, Adair to Dulles, ibid.; 711.551/6–457, Ward to Dulles, ibid.; 711.551/6–457, Ellmann to Dulles, ibid.; 711.551/6–557, Genovese to Dulles, ibid.; 711.551/6–557, Weller and Desky to Knowland and Kuchel, ibid.; 711.551/6–557, Bennett to Wilson and Dulles, ibid.; 711.551/6–557, del Castillo to Dulles, ibid.; 711.551/6–557, Trihey to Dulles, ibid.; 711.551/6–557, Nimitz to Dulles, ibid.; 711.551/6–557, Haber to Eisenhower, ibid.; 711.551/6–557, Koscak to Dulles, ibid.; 711.551/6–657, Stout to Dulles, ibid.; 711.551/6–657, Karg to Dulles, ibid.; 711.551/6–757, Barr to Dulles, ibid.; 711.551/6–857, Disabled American Veterans Executive Committee, Oklahoma, ibid.; 711.551/6–957, Philip Rossi et al., ibid.; 711.551/6–1057, Resolution, American Legion Post No. 29, Florida, ibid.; 711.551/6–1057, Thompson to Dulles, ibid.

21. "A Treaty Evil Exposed," *The Tablet,* May 25, 1957.

22. Peter Edson, "Girard Case Tops Treaty," *Indiana Evening Gazette,* June 8, 1957, 2.

23. 711.551/6–657, Wilson to Dulles, Department of State, Central Decimal File, 1955–1959, box 2838, RG 59, NA; 711.551/6–657, Baldwin to Dulles, ibid.; 711.551/6–657, Mahon to Dulles, ibid.; 711.551/6–857, Evins to Dulles, June 8, 1957, ibid.

24. Dulles-Knowland telephone conversation, June 5, 1957, box 6, folder 2, Memoranda of Tel. Conv., May 7–June 27, 1957, Telephone Calls Series, John Foster Dulles Papers, Eisenhower Presidential Library, Abilene, Kansas (hereafter cited as Dulles Papers).

25. Young to Belcher, June 6, 1957, box 29, folder 40, Page Belcher Papers, Carl Albert Congressional Research and Studies Center, Congressional Archives, University of Oklahoma, Norman, Oklahoma; Carley to Kerr, June 5, 1957, box 11, folder 6, Topical Series, Robert Kerr Papers, Carl Albert Congressional Research and Studies Center, Congressional Archives, University of Oklahoma, Norman, Oklahoma (hereafter cited as Kerr Papers); Rodgers to Kerr, June 5, 1957, Kerr Papers; Case to Belcher, June 10, 1957, box 1, file folder "Cpl. William Girard Armed Services Committee," Francis Case Papers, McGovern Library, Dakota Wesleyan University, Mitchell, South Dakota; VFW Post #4674 to Case, June 10, 1957, ibid.; Case to VFW Post #4674, June 11, 1957, ibid.; Richmond to Case, June 8, 1957, ibid.; Case to Richmond, June 11, 1957, ibid.

26. Congress, House, 85th Cong., 1st Sess., *Congressional Record,* June 4, 1957, 8294.

27. "Have We Thrown a United States Soldier to the Wolves?," *Austin Statesman,* June 6, 1957, in *Congressional Record,* June 13, 1957, A4624.

28. Congress, House of Representatives, 85th Cong., 1st Sess., *Congressional Record,* June 7, 1957, 8543.

29. Ibid., 8542.

30. Congress, Senate, 85th Cong., 1st Session, *Congressional Record,* June 10, 1957, 8598.

31. John O'Donnell, "Capitol Stuff," May 27, 1957, in *Congressional Record,* May 28, 1957, A4121; Alistair Cooke, "The Lessons of Formosa," in *Congressional Record,* June 5, 1957, A4365. See also Peter Edson, "Girard Case Tops Treaty," *Indiana Evening Gazette,* June 8, 1957, 2.

32. Frederick Brown Harris, "The Saturday Sermon for Formosa," *Philadelphia Bulletin,* in *Congressional Record,* June 26, 1957, A5110.

33. Congress, House of Representatives, 85th Cong., 1st Sess., *Congressional Record,* June 10, 1957, 8718.

34. "Girard and Civil Rights," *Camden Chronicle,* June 12, 1957, in *Congressional Record,* June 18, 1957, A4813.

35. Congress, House of Representatives, 85th Cong., 1st Sess., *Congressional Record,* June 11, 1957, 8875.

36. 711.551/6–557, De Nolasco to Dulles, box 2838, RG 59, NA; 711.551/6–857, M. D. Colstles to Dulles, ibid.

37. "The Girard Case," *New York Herald Tribune,* June 6, 1957, 24; "American Soldier, Japanese Justice," *Christian Science Monitor,* June 6, 1957, box 126, folder Status of Forces, Girard, H. Alexander Smith Papers.

38. Extension of Remarks of Hon. Sterling Cole, *Congressional Record,* June 27, 1957, A5170.

39. Extension of Remarks of Hon. Charles S. Gubser, *Congressional Record,* May 28, 1957, A4933.

40. Congress, Senate, 85th Cong., 1st Sess., *Congressional Record,* July 2, 1957, 10778, 10779.

41. "Status of Forces Treaties Essential," *Galesburg Register-Mail,* July 15, 1957, in *Congressional Record,* July 18, 1957, A5785.

42. Eisenhower-Dulles telephone conversation, June 5, 1957, box 25, Diary, Eisenhower Papers.

43. Dulles to MacArthur, June 5, 1957, Department of State, *Foreign Relations of the United States, 1955–1957, Japan,* 23:342–343.

44. 711.551/6–557, MacArthur to Dulles, Department of State, Central Decimal File, 1955–1959, box 2838, RG 59, NA; 711.551/6–657, MacArthur to Dulles, ibid.; 711.551/6–1257, Horsey to Dulles, June 12, 1957, ibid.

45. 711.551/6–0757, Criminal Jurisdiction over United States Servicemen Abroad under the NATO Status of Forces and Similar Agreements, Department of State, Central Decimal File, 1955–1959, box 2838, RG 59, NA.

46. 711.551/6–657, Current Status of the Girard Case, June 7, 1957, Department of State, Central Decimal File, 1955–1959, box 2838, RG 59, NA.

47. Minutes of Cabinet Meetings, June 28, 1957, Cabinet Series, Eisenhower Papers; Dulles-Brownell telephone conversation, June 18, 1957, box 6, folder 3, Memoranda of Tel. Conv., May 7–June 27, 1957, Telephone Calls Series, Dulles Papers; Dulles-Brownell telephone conversation, June 19, 1957, ibid..

48. Dulles-Rankin telephone conversation, June 21, 1957, box 6, folder 3, Memoranda of Tel. Conv., May 7–June 27, 1957, Telephone Calls Series, Dulles Papers.

49. 711.551/6–1957, Appeal of the Girard Case, Department of State, Central Decimal File, 1955–1959, box 2838, RG 59, NA; 711.551/6–1957, Issue of Whether the Girard Case Should Be Taken Directly to the Supreme Court, ibid.

50. Congress, House of Representatives, 85th Cong., 1st Sess., *Congressional Record*, February 11, 1957, 1942; ibid., May 20, 1957, 7264, 7265, 7272.

51. Ibid., June 7, 1957, 8541.

52. 711.551/7–1257, Martin-Wolf conversation, Department of State, Central Decimal File, 1955–1959, box 2838, RG 59, NA; 711.551/6–2857, Herter to Gordon, ibid.

53. Robert K. Walsh, "Supreme Court Receives Brief," *Evening Star,* July 2, 1957, A5; Robert K. Walsh, "High Court May Rule This Week on Girard," *Evening Star,* July 9, 1957, A8.

54. U.S. Supreme Court, *Wilson v. Girard,* 1957.

55. 711.551/7–1557, MacArthur to Dulles, Department of State, Central Decimal File, 1955–1959, box 2838, RG 59, NA.

56. These comments are gleaned from letters sent to Robert Kerr. See Topical Series, box 11, folder 7, Kerr Papers.

57. "Pyrrhic Victory in Girard Case," *Wilkes-Barre Times-Leader,* July 12, 1957, in *Congressional Record,* July 19, 1957, A5830; "Court's Backing of Girard Deal Sets an Ugly Precedent," *Nashville Tennessean,* July 12, 1957, in *Congressional Record,* July 22, 1957, A5891; "Without Justice," *Omaha World Herald,* July 13, 1957, in *Congressional Record,* July 22, 1957, A5895; "Protective Responsibility," *Aiken Standard and Review,* July 15, 1957, in *Congressional Record,* July 24, 1957, A5972; "The Girard Case," July 14, 1957, in *Congressional Record,* July 29, 1957, A6118; "Remedies for Muddled Rights," *Wall Street Journal,* July 15, 1957, in *Congressional Record,* July 15, 1957, 11630.

58. "The Girard Case: Extension of Remarks of Hon. Wint Smith," *Congressional Record,* July 22, 1957, A5895.

59. "Military Justice and Foreign Jurisdiction," *Congressional Record,* July 2, 1957, 12765.

60. Robert K. Walsh, "Girard Decision Stirs Attacks in Congress," *Evening Star,* July 12, 1957, A4; Smathers to Smith, July 23, 1957, box 126, H. Alexander Smith Papers. See also Smather's Resolution No. 163, ibid.

61. Legislative Leadership Meeting, July 9, 1957, box 2, Eisenhower Papers.

62. Ibid.

63. *The Public Papers of the Presidents of the United States: Dwight D. Eisenhower, 1957,* 549–550.

64. Pre-Press Conference Briefing, July 17, 1957, Misc., Eisenhower Papers.

65. Mutual Security Act of 1957, *Congressional Record,* July 17, 1957, 12007–12021.

66. Jacobs, *Cold War Mandarin,* 105.

67. Greenstein, *The Hidden-Hand Presidency,* viii–xii.

68. Nash, "United States Overseas Military Bases: Report to the President," 12.

69. Ibid., 53.

70. Eisenhower to Haslett, July 22, 1957, Dictation, Eisenhower Papers.

71. Eisenhower to East, September 12, 1957, Dictation, Eisenhower Papers.

72. Trends in Japanese Attitudes toward U.S. Troops, Bases and the Role of Atomic Weapons, October 17, 1957, RG 306, Records of the United States Information Agency, Office of Research, Public Opinion, Far East 1955–1960, NA.

73. 711.551/9–957, MacArthur to Dulles, Department of State, Central Decimal File, 1955–1959, box 2838, RG 59, NA.

74. FO 371/127577/FJ 1642/8, De la Mare to Dalton, October 1, 1957, PRO; "Girard Not Fit Subject for 'Great Issue,'" *Houston Post,* September 28, 1957, ibid.

75. 711.551/9–957, MacArthur to Dulles, Department of State, Central Decimal File, 1955–1959, box 2838, RG 59, NA.

76. 711.551/10–2557, MacArthur to Dulles, Department of State, Central Decimal File, 1955–1959, box 2838, RG 59, NA.

77. Ibid.; FO 371/127577/FJ 1642/10, Lascelles to Lloyd, December 10, 1957, PRO.

78. Sid Ross and Ed Kiester, "Sergeant Girard One Year Later," *Parade,* July 13, 1958, 6–7.

79. FO 371/127577/FJ 1642/9, Chancery to Far Eastern Department, November 26, 1957, PRO.

80. FO 371/127577/FJ 1642/10, Lascelles to Lloyd, December 10, 1957, PRO.

81. A Note on Japanese Attitudes Toward U.S. Troops, Bases and Some Related Issues, July 1958, RG 306, Records of the United States Information Agency, Office of Research, Public Opinion, Far East 1955–1960, NA; "The Frank Nash Report to the President: 'United States Overseas Military Bases,' January 29, 1958," Department of State, Lot File 61D68, box 19, Subject Files Related to Japan, RG 59, NA.

14. Status Quo

1. Progress Report, July 3, 1957; Barker to the Department of the Army, May 25, 1957, Department of State, *Foreign Relations of the United States, 1955–1957, China,* 3:530; FO 371/127472/FCN 10345/26, Franklin to Lloyd, June 4, 1957, PRO; FO 371 /127471/ FCN 10345/16, Franklin to Foreign Office, May 28, 1957, PRO; FO 371/127472/ FCN 10345/36, Franklin to Lloyd, June 18, 1957, PRO.

2. FO 371/127472/FCN 10345/45, Franklin to Lloyd, September 10, 1957, PRO.

3. Maurine Rankin to Pauline, June 22, 1957, box 8, folder 5, Rankin Papers; Robert Trumbull, "Taipei Seeks Pact on Status of GIs," *New York Times,* May 30, 1957, 3.

4. Memorandum of conversation, May 24 Riots in Taipei, July 31, 1957, box 8, CA, 1957, RG 59, NA.

5. FO 371/127472/ FCN 10345/40, Franklin to Dalton, July 16, 1957, PRO.

6. Memorandum of conversation, May 24 Riots in Taipei, August 5, 1957, box 8, CA, 1957, RG 59, NA.

7. FO 371/127472/ FCN 10345/40, Franklin to Dalton, July 16, 1957, PRO.

8. "American Military Personnel Banned from Tamsui Beach, Ingersoll Orders," *China Post,* July 22, 1957, in box 4, CA, 1957, RG 59, NA.

9. Memorandum of conversation, May 24 Riots in Taipei, August 5, 1957, box 8, CA, 1957, RG 59, NA; FO 371/127472/FCN 10345/52, Franklin to Far Eastern Department, July 30, 1957, PRO.

10. 711.551/6–1257, Rankin to Dulles, Department of State, Central Decimal File, 1955–1959, box 2838, RG 59, NA; Ku to Yeh, May 29, 1957, *524 shijian zhuMei geguan laiwang wendian* (Telegrams between the Foreign Ministry and ROC consulates and embassy in the United States regarding the May 24th Incident), *danghao* 425.2/0028, WJDA.

11. Shen-Powell conversation, June 12, 1957, box 9, CA, 1957, RG 59, NA; Program Coordinating Committee, June 11, 1957, ibid.

12. 711.551/6–757, Herter to Rankin, Department of State, Central Decimal File, 1955–1959, box 2838, RG 59, NA; 711.551/6–1257, Dulles to Rankin, ibid.

13. Robertson to Sprague, June 19, 1957, box 9, CA, 1957, RG 59, NA.

14. Program Coordinating Committee, August 13, 1957, box 9, CA, 1957, RG 59, NA.

15. 711.551/10–857, Robertson to Sprague, Department of State, Central Decimal File, 1955–1959, box 2838, RG 59, NA; 711.551/10–2157, Robertson to Sprague, ibid.

16. 611.93/9–1757, Rankin to Dulles, *China, People's Republic of China 1955–59, Foreign Affairs,* reel 5.

17. Gallant to Johnston, June 13, 1957, box 59, Johnston Papers; Strom to Johnston, May 25, 1957, ibid.

18. Tong-Richards conversation, September 30, 1957, box 2, CA, 1957, RG 59, NA; Richards to Dulles, October 9, 1957, Department of State, *Foreign Relations of the United States, 1955–1957, China,* 3:628; Memorandum of Discussion at the 338th Meeting of the National Security Council, October 2, 1957, Department of State, *Foreign Relations of the United States, 1955–1957, China,* 3:612.

19. Ku to Yeh, May 25, 1957, *danghao* 425.2/0028, WJDA; Ku to Yeh, May 29, 1957, ibid.

20. Diary entries, June 8, 16, 1957, Chiang Diaries; Kusnitz, *Public Opinion and Foreign Policy,* 78; Qing, *From Allies to Enemies,* 198.

21. Discussion at the 338th Meeting of the National Security Council, October 2, 1957, Department of State, *Foreign Relations of the United States, 1955–1957, China,* 3:612.

22. Congressional Leaders Meeting, August 27, 1957, box 2, Legislative Meet-

ings Series, July–August 1957, Eisenhower Papers; Eisenhower to Green, October 2, 1958, box 36, Dictation, October 1958, ibid.; Eisenhower-Lloyd-Caccia conversation, September 21, 1958, Department of State, *Foreign Relations of the United States, 1958–1960, China,* 19:250–251.

23. Lay to the National Security Council, September 9, 1957, Department of State, *Foreign Relations of the United States, 1955–1957, China,* 3:593–599, quotes from 597, 599.

24. Department of State, *Foreign Relations of the United States, 1955–1957, China,* 3:612–613, 614–615.

25. FO 371/127472/ FCN 10345/40, Franklin to Dalton, July 16, 1957, PRO; Tucker, *The China Threat,* 152–153, 156–157; Gordon, "United States Opposition to Use of Force in the Taiwan Strait, 1954–1962," 651–654.

26. Richards to Dulles, October 9, 1957, Department of State, *Foreign Relations of the United States, 1955–1957, China,* 3:625, 629; ibid., 3:629nn3, 4; Rankin, *China Assignment,* 334; Tucker, *The China Threat,* 33.

27. *Lifa yuan gongbao* 19, no. 8 (1957): 107.

28. Progress Report, July 3, 1957.

29. Memorandum, July 1, 1957, box 8, folder 5, Rankin Papers; Memorandum, *524 shijian zhuanan jiantao* (Review of the May 24th Incident investigation), *danghao* 425.02/0014, WJDA.

30. Rankin to Smith, June 13, 1957, box 17, CA, 1957, RG 59, NA.

31. Rankin to Nash, June 17, 1957, box 8, folder 5, Rankin Papers; Rankin to Clough, August 5, 1957, box 8, folder 6, ibid.

32. Rankin to Robertson, August 9, 1957, box 8, folder 6, Rankin Papers; Nash, "United States Overseas Military Bases: Report to the President," 55.

33. Clough to Rankin, July 9, 1957, box 8, CA, 1957, RG 59, NA; *Lianhe bao* (United Daily), May 25, 1958, 3.

34. *Lifa yuan gongbao* 19, no. 8 (1957): 106.

35. Trumbull, "Taipei Seeks Pact on Status of GIs"; Rankin-Yeh conversation, July 3, 1957, box 1, FE, Top Secret Files Relating to the Republic of China, 1954–1965, RG 59, NA; "Weicheng songdui Taibei shi buxin shijian chuli jingguo baogao shu jianqi" (Report on Handling the May 24 Riots' Aftermath), June 13, 1957, *524 shijian shenxun zuifan* (The May 24th Incident criminal trials), *danghao* 425.2/0018, WJDA.

36. Nash, "United States Overseas Military Bases: Report to the President," Appendix, 164; Clough to Wilson, August 15, 1957, box 8, CA, 1957, RG 59, NA.

37. Robertson to Rankin, December 4, 1957, box 1, FE, Top Secret Files Relating to the Republic of China, 1954–1965, RG 59, NA; Hill to Bow, June 13, 1957, box 4, CA, 1957, RG 59, NA; Rankin to Robertson, November 7, 1957, box 8, folder 6, Rankin Papers; Becker to Dechert, December 16, 1957, box 8, CA, 1957, RG 59, NA.

38. Robertson to Becker, December 4, 1957, box 1, FE, Top Secret Files Relating to the Republic of China, 1954–1965, RG 59, NA.

39. Pilcher to Clough, October 23, 1957, box 8, CA, 1957, RG 59, NA; *Shijie ribao* (World Journal), May 25, 1957, *524 shijian zhuMei geguan jianbao ji zhuanti baogao* (Newspaper clippings and special reports from Chinese consulates and embassy in the United States regarding the May 24th Incident), *danghao* 425.2/0027, WJDA.

40. Becker to Dechert, June 24, 1958, box 1, FE, Top Secret Files Relating to the Republic of China, 1954–1965, RG 59, NA; "Draft Exchange of Notes or Agreed Minutes Regarding Article XIV (Jurisdiction) April 1960," *Meijun diwei xieding guonei ge jiguan huiyi jilu* (Record of meetings by government agencies regarding the U.S.-ROC Status of Forces Agreement), *danghao* 426.1/0035, WJDA.

41. "Government Launching Citizenship Education Program," *China News*, June 18, 1957, *524 shijian jianbao ji yiban ziliao* (Newspaper clippings and documents regarding the May 24th Incident), *danghao* 425.2/0012, WJDA; Zhang, ed., *Jiang zongtong ji* (Works of President Chiang Kai-shek), vol. 2, *1980–1981*, 1983; 611.93/9–1757, Rankin to Dulles, *China, People's Republic of China 1955–59, Foreign Affairs*, reel 5; "Strengthen Chinese-American Cooperation, Destroy the Common Enemy," *524 shijian duiMei jiaoshe* (U.S.-ROC discussions regarding the May 24th Incident), *danghao* 425.2/0017, WJDA.

42. Progress Report, July 3, 1957; Operations Coordinating Board Report (April 16, 1958) on U.S. Policy toward Taiwan and the Government of the Republic of China, box 58, National Security Council Staff, Disaster File, Nationalist China (11), Eisenhower Papers; 611.93/9–1558, Comments on OCB Report on Taiwan, *China, People's Republic of China 1955–59, Foreign Affairs*, reel 6.

43. Pilcher to American Residents in Taiwan, July 25, 1957, *524 shijian duiMei jiaoshe* (U.S.-ROC discussions regarding the May 24th Incident), *danghao* 425.2/0017, WJDA.

44. 711.551/5–358, Drumright to Dulles, Department of State, Central Decimal File, 1955–1959, box 2837, RG 59, NA.

45. Paraphrase of Taipei's Telegram to Department, June 23, 1957, box 8, folder 5, Rankin Papers; Nash, "United States Overseas Military Bases: Report to the President," Appendix, 164.

46. Nash, "United States Overseas Military Bases: Report to the President," Appendix, 165.

47. Nash, "United States Overseas Military Bases: Report to the President," 34; Office of Special Investigations, Inspector General Headquarters, Pacific Air Force, July 1, 1958, USAFHRA, K-717.6243–3.

48. Operations Coordinating Board Report on U.S. Policy toward Taiwan and the Government of the Republic of China, April 16, 1958, Nationalist China, Eisenhower Papers; Rankin to Robertson, Department of State, *Foreign Relations of the United States, 1958–1960, China*, 19:2.

49. Discipline of the Command, November 18, 1958, box 1, RG 334, MAAG Taiwan, 1959, NA.

50. Phillips to Chief, Navy Section, MAAG, August 15, 1958, box 1, RG 334,

MAAG Taiwan, 1959, NA; Gutheinz to Senior Marine Adviser, August 14, 1958, ibid.; Benge to Bowen, February 8, 1958, ibid.; Lo to Benge, February 6, 1958, ibid.

51. Negotiating Chronology, *Meijun diwei xieding duian* (Counterproposals to the U.S.-ROC Status of Forces Agreement), *danghao* 426.1/0037, WJDA; Martin-Hsu conversation, December 29, 1958, box 11, FE, Top Secret Files Relating to the Republic of China, 1954–1965, RG 59, NA; Boas to Agger, December 30, 1958, ibid.

52. Operations Coordinating Board Report on U.S. Policy toward Taiwan and the Government of the Republic of China, April 15, 1959, Nationalist China, Eisenhower Papers; Department of State, *Foreign Relations of the United States, 1958–1960, China*, 19:732–733.

Epilogue

1. Schaller, *Altered States*, 155–158; LaFeber, *The Clash*, 319–322; Foot, *The Practice of Power*, 91–96.

2. Cabinet Minutes, March 21, 1958, box 10, Cabinet Series, Eisenhower Papers; Draper to Dulles, December 23, 1958, box 9, folder 23, Draper Committee, ibid.; Herter to Draper, February 17, 1959, ibid.

3. *China Post*, November 20, 1960, *MAAG nipai guwen shaozhu zhi baoan silingbu* (MAAG proposal to send advisors to the Taiwan Garrison Command), *danghao* 426.1/0002, WJDA; Memorandum of conversation, November 9, 1960, Department of State, *Foreign Relations of the United States, 1958–1960, Foreign Economic Policy*, 4:133; Eisenhower-Kennedy conversation, January 19, 1961, Department of State, *Foreign Relations of the United States, 1961–1963, Foreign Economic Policy*, 9:1–2.

4. Kennedy to McNamara, January 11, 1962, Department of State, *Foreign Relations of the United States, 1961–1963, National Security Policy*, 8:235–236; Parrott to Kennedy, March 22, 1962, ibid., 709; Kennedy-Eisenhower conversation, January 19, 1961, Department of State, *Foreign Relations of the United States, 1961–1963, Laos Crisis*, 24:19–20; Johnson to Kennedy, May 23, 1961, Department of State, *Foreign Relations of the United States, 1961–1963, Southeast Asia*, 23:8, 9.

5. Scherrer to Felt, November 15, 1961, Department of State, *Foreign Relations of the United States, 1961–1963, Southeast Asia*, 23:175; Lederer and Burdick, *The Ugly American*, 283.

6. Clymer, "A Casualty of War," 198–219; Gilpatric to Lansdale, May 5, 1961, Department of State, *Foreign Relations of the United States, 1961–1963, Southeast Asia*, 23:850–851.

7. Herring, *America's Longest War*, 104; Hunt, *Lyndon Johnson's War*, 66.

8. Herring, *America's Longest War*, 98; Nolting to State, December 3, 1961, Department of State, *Foreign Relations of the United States, 1961–1963, Vietnam, 1961*, 1:709.

9. See court-martial documents in RG 334, MAAG China, 1961–63, box 3, NA.

10. Department of State, *Foreign Relations of the United States, 1961–1963, North-*

east Asia, 22:337; Bundy to Wright, September 17, 1964, box 2, Political Affairs, CA, 1964, RG 59, NA; "U.S. Civilian Shot to Death by His Own Wife in Tainan," *China Post,* September 19, 1964, *Meiren zaitai fenzui* (Crimes committed by Americans in Taiwan), *danghao* 410/21/0006, WJDA; conversation with Feldman, September 21, 1964, ibid.

11. A lengthy discourse on the ramifications of this decision is found in U.S. Military Jurisdiction over Civilians, November 17, 1958, CIA Current Intelligence Bulletin, CIA-RDP62-00631R0003000110016-1.

12. C. C. Fu to Editor, "On Status of Forces Agreement," November 23, 1964, *China News,* November 25, 1964, *Meijun diwei xieding cankao ziliao* (Reference materials regarding the U.S.-ROC Status of Forces Agreement), *danghao* 426.1/0031, WJDA.

13. A detailed examination of the negotiations using Chinese sources can be found in Lee, "1957 nian Taibei 'Liu Ziran shijian' ji 1965 nian 'meijun zai Hua diwei xieding' zhi qianding," 32–54; Bundy to Rusk, August 23, 1965, Department of State, *Foreign Relations of the United States, 1964–1968, China,* 30:194.

14. For discussion of the 1965 U.S.-Philippine SOFA, see Cochran, "Jurisdiction over American Military Personnel under the U.S.-Philippine Status of Forces Agreement," 16–19; for the SOFA with South Korea, see Cho, "Status of Forces Agreement between the Republic of Korea and the United States," 49–62.

15. Tao, "The Sino-American Status of Forces Agreement," 12–13; for the number of Americans enjoying diplomatic immunity, see ibid., 6n40; Sydney Gruson, "'R and R' Tours on Taiwan: American Servicemen Bring a Mixed Blessing to the Island," *New York Times,* February 14, 1958, 6.

16. Tao, "The Sino-American Status of Forces Agreement," 14; Chiu, "The United States Status of Forces Agreement with the Republic of China," 78–81.

17. FO 371/127577/FJ 1642/5, Harpham to Lloyd, June 18, 1957, PRO; Hunt, *The American Ascendancy,* 206; Berry, *U.S. Bases in the Philippines,* 102–105; Schaller, *Altered States,* 194.

18. One example of this is the SOFA with Mongolia. Mason, *Status of Forces Agreement.*

19. Byman, "Why Drones Work," 41.

20. Tim Arango and Michael S. Schmidt, "Despite Difficult Talks, U.S. and Iraq Had Expected Some American Troops to Stay," *New York Times,* October 21, 2011, http://www.nytimes.com/2011/10/22/world/middleeast/united-states-and-iraq-had-not-expected-troops-would-have-to-leave.html?ref=statusofforcesagreement (accessed March 2013); Kal Raustiala, "Are We Really Pulling Out of Afghanistan?" *World Post,* February 7, 2014, http://www.huffingtonpost.com/kal-raustiala/afghanistan-status-of-forces-agreement_b_2625907.html (accessed March 9, 2014).

Bibliography

Diaries and Manuscript Collections

Boise State University, Albertsons Library, Boise, Idaho
    Frank Church Papers

Columbia University, Butler Library, New York, New York
    V. K. Wellington Koo Papers

Dakota Wesleyan University, McGovern Library, Mitchell, South Dakota
    Francis Case Papers

Dwight David Eisenhower Presidential Library, Abilene, Kansas
    John Foster Dulles Papers
    Dwight D. Eisenhower Papers

Hoover Institution Library and Archives, Stanford University, Palo Alto, California
    Chiang Kai-shek Diaries

Institute of Modern History, Academia Sinica, Nangang, Taiwan
    Wang Shuming jiangjun riji (The diary of General Wang Shuming),
    Zhao Hengti xinsheng riji (The diary of Zhao Hengti)

Library of Congress, Washington, D.C.
    Curtis E. LeMay Papers

Princeton University, Seeley Mudd Manuscript Library, Princeton, New Jersey
    Karl Rankin Papers
    H. Alexander Smith Papers

University of Connecticut Library, Thomas J. Dodd Research Center, Storrs, Connecticut
    Prescott Bush Papers

University of Oklahoma, Carl Albert Congressional Research and Studies Center, Congressional Archives, Norman, Oklahoma
    Carl Albert Papers
    Page Belcher Papers
    Robert Kerr Papers

University of South Carolina, South Carolina Political Collections, Columbia, South Carolina
    Olin DeWitt Talmadge Johnston Papers

Official Files

Republic of China
    Institute of Modern History, Academia Sinica, Nangang
    Waijiao dangan (Diplomatic Archives)

United Kingdom
    Foreign Office Records, FO 371, Public Records Office, National Archives, Kew

United States
National Archives and Records Administration, St. Louis, Missouri
    Record Group 153, Records of the Office of the Judge Advocate General (Army) 1692–1981
National Archives and Records Administration, College Park, Maryland
    Record Group 59, General Records of the Department of State, Decimal File
    Record Group 306, Records of the United States Information Agency, Office of Research, Public Opinion, Far East 1955–1960
    Record Group 334, Records of the Joint U.S. Military Advisory Group to the Republic of China
U.S. Air Force Historical Research Agency, Maxwell Air Force Base, Montgomery, Alabama
U.S. Army Military History Institute, Army War College, Carlisle Barracks, Pennsylvania

Miscellaneous

Chao, Linda, and Ramon H. Myers. "A New Kind of Party: The Kuomintang of 1949–1952." *Centennial Symposium on Sun Yat-sen's Founding of the Kuomintang for Revolution,* November 19–23, 1994, Taipei, Taiwan.
Dawson, William. E-mail message to the author. August 12, 2010.
Jones, Glenn. E-mail message to the author. October 25, 2012.
Kramer, Vincent. E-mail messages to the author. September 12, 17, 18, 2012.
Thompson, John. E-mail message to the author. June 24, 2012.

Oral Histories

Gleysteen, William, Jr. Interview, June 10, 1997. The Association for Diplomatic Studies and Training Foreign Affairs Oral History Project. http://adst.org/OH%20TOCs/Gleysteen,%20William%20H.,%20Jr.toc.pdf. Accessed May 5, 2014.
Nadler, Seymour I. The Association for Diplomatic Studies and Training Foreign Affairs Oral History Project Information Series. Library of Congress, 1989.

Published Documents

Republic of China

Lifa yuan gongbao (Proceedings of the Legislative Yuan). Vol. 19. Taibei: Lifa yuan mishu chu, 1957.

Qin Xiaoyi, ed. *Zongtong Jianggong dashi changbian chugao* (Preliminary draft of the major events in the life of President Chiang Kai-shek). Vols. 1–8. Taibei: Guomindang Historical Commission, 1978.

————. *Zongtong Jianggong dashi changbian chugao* (Chronology of President Chiang Kai-shek). Vols. 9–11. Taibei: Zhongzheng wenjiao jijinhui, 2002–2004.

Zhonghua minguo shishi jiyao, April to June, 1957 (Historical accounts of important events in the Republic of China). Taibei: Academia Historica, 1991.

United States

Amendment of Article XVII of the Administrative Agreement under Article III of the Security Treaty: Protocol, and Official Minutes, between the United States of America and Japan. Washington, D.C.: U.S. Government Printing Office, 1953.

Confidential U.S. State Department Central Files. *China, People's Republic of China 1955–59, Foreign Affairs*. Frederick, Md.: Univ. Publications of America, 1987.

Congress. House of Representatives. *Status of Forces Agreements: Hearings before the Committee on Foreign Affairs, House of Representatives, 84th Congress, 1st Session on H.J. Res. 309 and Similar Measures*. Part 1. Washington, D.C.: Government Printing Office, 1955.

————. House of Representatives. 85th Cong., 1st Sess. *Congressional Record*. Washington, D.C.: Government Printing Office, 1957.

————. House of Representatives. 89th Cong., 2nd Sess. *United States Policy in Asia: Hearings before the Subcommittee of the Far East and the Pacific of the Committee on Foreign Relations*. Part 1. Washington, D.C.: Government Printing Office, 1966.

————. Senate. 85th Cong., 1st Sess. *Congressional Record*. Washington, D.C.: Government Printing Office, 1957.

Department of Defense. *Manual for Courts-Martial U.S. Army 1949*. Washington, D.C.: United States of America War Office, 1949.

————. *Report to Honorable Wilber M. Brucker, Secretary of the Army, by the Committee on the Uniform Code of Military Justice, Good Order and Discipline in the Army*. Washington, D.C.: Government Printing Office, 1960.

————. *Taiwan*. Washington, D.C.: U.S. Military Assistance Institute, 1959.

Department of State. *Foreign Relations of the United States, 1943, China*. Washington, D.C.: Government Printing Office, 1957.

————. *Foreign Relations of the United States, 1947, The Far East: China*. Vol. 7. Washington, D.C.: Government Printing Office, 1972.

————. *Foreign Relations of the United States, 1951, Korea and China*. Vol. 7, part 1. Washington, D.C.: Government Printing Office, 1983.

———. *Foreign Relations of the United States, 1952–1954, China and Japan.* Vol. 14, part 2. Washington, D.C.: Government Printing Office, 1985.

———. *Foreign Relations of the United States, 1955–1957, Vietnam.* Vol. 1. Washington, D.C.: Government Printing Office, 1985.

———. *Foreign Relations of the United States, 1955–1957, China.* Vol. 2. Washington, D.C.: Government Printing Office, 1986.

———. *Foreign Relations of the United States, 1955–1957, China.* Vol. 3. Washington, D.C.: Government Printing Office, 1986.

———. *Foreign Relations of the United States, 1955–1957, Foreign Aid and Economic Defense Policy.* Vol. 10. Washington, D.C.: Government Printing Office, 1989.

———. *Foreign Relations of the United States, 1955–1957, Southeast Asia.* Vol. 22. Washington, D.C.: Government Printing Office, 1989.

———. *Foreign Relations of the United States, 1955–1957, Japan.* Vol. 23. Washington, D.C.: Government Printing Office, 1991.

———. *Foreign Relations of the United States, 1958–1960, Foreign Economic Policy.* Vol. 4. Washington, D.C.: Government Printing Office, 1991.

———. *Foreign Relations of the United States, 1958–1960, China.* Vol. 19. Washington, D.C.: Government Printing Office, 1996.

———. *Foreign Relations of the United States, 1961–1963, Vietnam, 1961.* Vol. 1. Washington, D.C.: Government Printing Office, 1988.

———. *Foreign Relations of the United States, 1961–1963, National Security Policy.* Vol. 8. Washington, D.C.: Government Printing Office, 1996.

———. *Foreign Relations of the United States, 1961–1963, Foreign Economic Policy.* Vol. 9. Washington, D.C.: Government Printing Office, 1995.

———. *Foreign Relations of the United States, 1961–1963, Northeast Asia.* Vol. 22. Washington, D.C.: Government Printing Office, 1996.

———. *Foreign Relations of the United States, 1961–1963, Southeast Asia.* Vol. 23. Washington, D.C.: Government Printing Office, 1994.

———. *Foreign Relations of the United States, 1961–1963, Laos Crisis.* Vol. 24. Washington, D.C.: Government Printing Office, 1994.

———. *Foreign Relations of the United States, 1964–1968, China.* Vol. 30. Washington, D.C.: Government Printing Office, 1998.

———. *United States Relations with China: With Special Reference to the Period 1944–1949.* Washington, D.C.: Government Printing Office, 1949.

The Public Papers of the Presidents of the United States: Dwight D. Eisenhower, 1957. Washington, D.C.: Government Printing Office, 1958.

Books, Articles, and Dissertations

Accinelli, Robert. *Crisis and Commitment: United States Policy toward Taiwan, 1950–1955.* Chapel Hill: Univ. of North Carolina Press, 1996.

Aliano, Richard A. *American Defense Policy from Eisenhower to Kennedy: The Politics of Changing Military Requirements, 1957–1961.* Athens: Ohio Univ. Press, 1975.

Allison, Graham. *Essence of Decision: Explaining the Cuban Missile Crisis.* Boston: Little, Brown, 1971.

Allison, William Thomas. *Military Justice in Vietnam: The Rule of Law in an American War.* Lawrence: Univ. Press of Kansas, 2007.

Alvah, Donna. *Unofficial Ambassadors: American Military Families Overseas and the Cold War, 1946–1965.* New York: New York Univ. Press, 2007.

Askew, Joseph. "Revisiting New Territory: The Terranova Incident Revisited." *Asian Studies Review* 28 (2004): 351–371.

Barber, Charles H. "Military Assistance Advisory Group Formosa." *Military Review* (December 1954): 53–59.

Belmonte, Laura A. *Selling the American Way: U.S. Propaganda and the Cold War.* Philadelphia: Univ. of Pennsylvania Press, 2008.

Berry, William E. *U.S. Bases in the Philippines: The Evolution of the Special Relationship.* Boulder, Colo.: Westview Press, 1989.

Blum, Robert M. *Drawing the Line: The Origin of the American Containment Policy in East Asia.* New York: Norton, 1982.

Bodde, Derk, and Clarence Morris. *Law in Imperial China: Exemplified by 190 Ch'ing Dynasty Cases.* Philadelphia: Univ. of Pennsylvania Press, 1973.

Braim, Paul F. *The Will to Win: The Life of General James A. Van Fleet.* Annapolis, Md.: Naval Institute Press, 2001.

Bryant, Robert T. "Extraterritoriality and the Mixed Court." *Virginia Law Review* 13 (November 1926): 27–36.

Byman, Daniel. "Why Drones Work: The Case for Washington's Weapon of Choice." *Foreign Affairs* 92 (July/August 2013): 32–43.

Chase, William C. *Front Line General: The Commands of Maj. Gen. William C. Chase.* Houston: Pacesetter Press, 1975.

Chiu, Hungdah. "The United States Status of Forces Agreement with the Republic of China: Some Criminal Case Studies." *Boston College International and Comparative Law Review* 3 (December 1979): 67–88.

Cho, Soon Sung. "Status of Forces Agreement between the Republic of Korea and the United States: Problems of Due Process and Fair Trial of U.S. Military Personnel." In *U.S. Status of Forces Agreements with Asian Countries: Selected Studies,* ed. Charles L. Cochran and Hungdah Chiu, 49–62. Occasional Papers/Reprints Series in Contemporary Asian Studies. No. 7. University of Maryland, School of Law, 1979.

Christensen, Thomas J. *Useful Adversaries: Grand Strategy, Domestic Mobilization, and Sino-American Conflict, 1947–1958.* Princeton: Princeton Univ. Press, 1996.

Clarke, Jeffrey J. *Advice and Support: The Final Years, 1965–1973: The United States Army in Vietnam.* Washington, D.C.: Center of Military History, U.S. Army, 1988.

Clough, Ralph. *Island China.* Cambridge: Harvard Univ. Press, 1978.

Clubb, O. Edmund. "Formosa: The Dream Dissolves." *The Nation* (June 8, 1957): 491–493.

Clymer, Kenton J. "A Casualty of War: The Break in American Relations with Cambodia, 1965." In *A Companion to the Vietnam War,* ed. Marilyn B. Young and Robert Buzzanco, 198–219. Malden, Mass.: Blackwell, 2006.

Cochran, Charles L. "Jurisdiction over American Military Personnel under the U.S.-Philippine Status of Forces Agreement." In *U.S. Status of Forces Agreements with Asian Countries: Selected Studies*, ed. Charles L. Cochran and Hungdah Chiu, 1–30. Occasional Papers/Reprints Series in Contemporary Asian Studies. No. 7. University of Maryland, School of Law, 1979.

Copper, John. *Taiwan: Nation-State or Province?* 6th ed. Boulder: Westview Press, 2012.

Craft, Stephen G. *V. K. Wellington Koo and the Emergence of Modern China*. Lexington: Univ. Press of Kentucky, 2004.

Cull, Nicholas J. *The Cold War and the United States Information Agency: American Propaganda and Public Diplomacy, 1945–1989*. Cambridge: Cambridge Univ. Press, 2008.

Cullather, Nick. "The U.S. and Taiwanese Industrial Policy." *Diplomatic History* 20 (winter 1996): 1–25.

Curtain, Neil. "'We Might as Well Write Japan Off': The State Department Deals with the Girard Crisis of 1957." *Journal of American-East Asian Relations* 19, no. 2 (2012): 109–131.

Dikotter, Frank. *The Tragedy of Liberation: A History of the Chinese Revolution, 1945–1957*. London: Bloomsbury Press, 2013.

Farhangi, Leslie Shirin. "Insuring against Abuse of Diplomatic Immunity." *Stanford Law Review* 38 (July 1986): 1517–1547.

Finkelstein, David M. *Washington's Taiwan Dilemma, 1949–1950*. Fairfax, Va.: George Mason Univ. Press, 1993.

Foot, Rosemary. *The Practice of Power: U.S. Relations with China since 1949*. Oxford: Clarendon Press, 1997.

Friedman, Jeremy. "Review by Jeremy Friedman." *H-Diplo Roundtable Reviews* 14, no. 27 (April 8, 2013): 7–10. http://www.hnet.org/~diplo/roundtables/PDF/Roundtable-XIV-27.pdf. Accessed May 3, 2014.

Gaddis, John Lewis. *Strategies of Containment: A Critical Appraisal of Postwar American National Security Policy*. New York: Oxford Univ. Press, 1982.

Garver, John W. *The Sino-American Alliance: Nationalist China and American Cold War Strategy in Asia*. Armonk, N.Y.: Sharpe, 1997.

Gordon, Leonard H. D. "United States Opposition to Use of Force in the Taiwan Strait, 1954–1962." *Journal of American History* 72 (December 1985): 637–660.

Grant, Philip A. "The Bricker Amendment Controversy." *Presidential Studies Quarterly* 15 (summer 1985): 572–582.

Green, Marshall, John H. Holdridge, and William N. Stokes. *War and Peace with China: First-Hand Experiences in the Foreign Service of the United States*. Bethesda, Md.: Dacor Press, 1994.

Greenstein, Fred I. *The Hidden-Hand Presidency: Eisenhower as Leader*. Baltimore: Johns Hopkins Univ. Press, 1994.

Herring, George. *America's Longest War: The United States and Vietnam, 1950–1975*. 4th ed. New York: McGraw Hill, 2002.

Hillman, Elizabeth Lutes. *Defending America: Military Culture and the Cold War Court-Martial*. Princeton: Princeton Univ. Press, 2005.

Huebner, Jon W. "The Abortive Liberation of Taiwan." *China Quarterly* 110 (June 1987): 256–275.

———. "Chinese Anti-Americanism, 1946–48." *Australian Journal of Chinese Affairs* 17 (January 1987): 115–125.

Hunt, Michael H. *The American Ascendancy: How the United States Gained and Wielded Global Dominance*. Chapel Hill: Univ. of North Carolina Press, 2007.

———. *Lyndon Johnson's War: America's Cold War Crusade in Vietnam, 1945–1968*. New York: Hill and Wang, 1996.

———. *The Making of a Special Relationship: The United States and China to 1914*. New York: Columbia Univ. Press, 1983.

Hunt, Michael H., and Steven I. Levine. *Arc of Empire: America's Wars in Asia from the Philippines to Vietnam*. Chapel Hill: Univ. of North Carolina Press, 2012.

Hunt, Michael, and Steven Levine. "Author's Response." *H-Diplo Roundtable Reviews* 14, no. 27 (April 8, 2013): 23–27. http://www.h-net.org/~diplo/round-tables/PDF/Roundtable-XIV-27.pdf. Accessed May 3, 2014.

Jacobs, Seth. *Cold War Mandarin: Ngo Dinh Diem and the Origins of America's War in Vietnam, 1950–1963*. Lanham, Md.: Rowman and Littlefield, 2006.

Jang, John Lun. "A History of Newspapers in Taiwan." Ph.D. diss., Claremont Graduate University, ProQuest, UMI Dissertations Publishing, 1968.

Jespersen, T. Christopher. *American Images of China, 1931–1949*. Stanford: Stanford Univ. Press, 1996.

Johnson, Chalmers. *Blowback: The Costs and Consequences of American Empire*. New York: Holt, 2000.

———. *The Sorrows of Empire: Militarism, Secrecy, and the End of the Republic*. New York: Holt, 2004.

Jurika, Stephen, ed. *From Pearl Harbor to Vietnam: The Memoirs of Admiral Arthur W. Radford*. Standford, Calif.: Hoover Univ. Press, 1980.

Kerr, George H. *Formosa Betrayed*. Boston: Houghton Mifflin, 1965.

Kusnitz, Leonard A. *Public Opinion and Foreign Policy: America's China Policy, 1949–1979*. Westport, Conn.: Greenwood Press, 1984.

LaFeber, Walter. *The Clash: U.S.-Japanese Relations throughout History*. New York: Norton, 1997.

Lai Tse-han, Ramon H. Myers, and Wei Wou. *A Tragic Beginning: The Taiwan Uprising of February 28, 1947*. Stanford: Stanford Univ. Press, 1991.

Lamb, Stephen A. "The Court-Martial Panel Selection Process: A Critical Analysis." *Journal of Military Law Review* 137 (summer 1992): 103–166.

Langhorne, Richard. "The Regulation of Diplomatic Practice: The Beginnings to the Vienna Convention on Diplomatic Relations, 1961." *Review of International Studies* 18, no. 1 (1992): 3–17.

Lederer, William. *A Nation of Sheep*. New York: Norton, 1961.

Lederer, William, and Eugene Burdick. *The Ugly American*. 1958. Reprint, New York: Norton, 1999.

Lee Guocheng. "1957 nian Taibei 'Liu Ziran shijian' ji 1965 nian Meijun zaiHua diwei xieding zhi qianding" (The Liu Ziran Incident of 1957 and the Signing of the U.S.-Republic of China Status of Forces Agreement, 1965). *Dongwu zhengzhi xuebao* (Soochow Journal of Political Science) 24 (2006): 1–66.

Li, Laura Tyson. *Madame Chiang Kai-shek: China's Eternal First Lady.* New York: Grove Press, 2006.

Lin Hsiao-tung. "Taiwan's Secret Ally." *Hoover Digest* 2 (April 6, 2012). http://www. hoover.org/research/taiwans-secret-ally. Accessed April 6, 2012.

———. "U.S.-Taiwan Military Diplomacy Revisited: Chiang Kai-shek, *Baituan,* and the 1954 Mutual Defense Pact." *Diplomatic History* 37 (November 2013): 971–994.

Lin Zhengfeng. "Cong guojifa guandian lun Minguo 46 nian Meijun Leinuo sharen shijian." (A Study of the Reynolds Case of 1957 from the Viewpoint of International Law). *Zhengda faxue pinglun* (National Chengchi Law Review) 4 (1971): 223–242.

Liu, Jennifer. "Indoctrinating the Youth: Guomindang Policy on Secondary Education in Wartime China and Postwar Taiwan, 1937–1960." Ph.D. diss., University of California, Irvine, ProQuest, UMI Dissertations Publishing, 2010.

Longmate, Norman. *The GIs: The Americans in Britain.* New York: Charles Scribner's Sons, 1975.

Lundestad, Geir. "Empire by Invitation?: The United States and Western Europe, 1945–1952." *Journal of Peace Research* 23 (September 1986): 263–277.

Marks, Thomas A. *Counterrevolution in China: Wang Sheng and the Kuomintang.* London: Frank Cass, 1998.

Mason, R. Chuck. *Status of Forces Agreement (SOFA): What Is It, and How Has It Been Utilized?* Congressional Research Service (March 15, 2012). http://www. fas.org/sgp/crs/natsec/RL34531.pdf.

McDaniel, W. Thomas. *The Major: The Senior Officer in Charge: Commanding Fellow Prisoners of War.* N.p.: Xlibris, 2011.

Mindling, George, and Robert Bolton. *U.S. Air Force Tactical Missiles 1949–1969: The Pioneers.* N.p.: Lulu.com, 2008.

Peffer, Nathaniel. "Do We Need Formosa?" *New Republic* 136 (June 24, 1957): 15–17.

Pepper, Suzanne. *Civil War in China: The Political Struggle, 1945–1949.* Berkeley: Univ. of California Press, 1978.

Phillips, Steven E. *Between Assimilation and Independence: The Taiwanese Encounter Nationalist China, 1945–1950.* Stanford: Stanford Univ. Press, 2003.

———. "Taiwan's Intelligence Reform in an Age of Democratization." In *Reforming Intelligence: Obstacles to Democratic Control and Effectiveness,* ed. Thomas C. Bruneau and Steven C. Boraz, 170–194. Austin: Univ. of Texas Press, 2007.

Qing Simei. *From Allies to Enemies: Visions of Modernity, Identity, and U.S.-China Diplomacy, 1945–1960.* Cambridge: Harvard Univ. Press, 2007.

Rankin, Karl Lott. *China Assignment.* Seattle: Univ. of Washington Press, 1964.

Rawnsley, Gary D. "Taiwan's Propaganda Cold War: The Offshore Islands Crises of 1954 and 1958." In *The Clandestine Cold War in Asia, 1945–65: Western Intelli-*

gence, Propaganda and Special Operations, ed. Richard J. Aldrich, Gary D. Rawnsley, and Ming-Yeh T. Rawnsley, 82–101. London: Frank Cass, 2000.

Reynolds, David. *Rich Relations: The American Occupation of Britain, 1942–1945.* New York: Random House, 1995.

Ross, Mitchell S. "Rethinking Diplomatic Immunity: A Review of Remedial Approaches to Address the Abuses of Diplomatic Privileges and Immunities." *American University International Law Review* 4, no. 1 (1989): 173–205.

Roy, Denny. *Taiwan: A Political History.* Ithaca: Cornell Univ. Press, 2002.

Sawyer, Robert K. *Military Advisors in Korea: KMAG in Peace and War.* Washington, D.C.: Government Printing Office, 1962.

Schaller, Michael. *Altered States: The United States and Japan since the Occupation.* New York: Oxford Univ. Press, 1997.

———. *The United States and China in the Twentieth Century.* New York: Oxford Univ. Press, 1990.

Scully, Eileen P. *Bargaining with the State from Afar: American Citizenship in Treaty Port China, 1844–1942.* New York: Columbia Univ. Press, 2001.

Shi Yonggui. "Jiang Jingguo yu Mei guwen tuan jibian junzhong zhenggong zhidu" (Chiang Ching-kuo, the U.S. Military Assistance and Advisory Group and the Heated Debate over the Armed Forces' Political Work System). *Zhuanji wenxue* (Biographical Literature) 610 (March 2013): 4–8.

Smith, Robert Ross. *Triumph in the Philippines.* Washington, D.C.: Government Printing Office, 1963.

Snee, Joseph M., and A. Kenneth Pyle. *Status of Forces Agreements and Criminal Jurisdictions.* New York: Oceana Publications, 1957.

Spector, Ronald. *Advice and Support: The Early Years, 1941–1960: The United States Army in Vietnam.* Washington, D.C.: Center of Military History, U.S. Army, 1985.

Szonyi, Michael. *Cold War Island: Quemoy on the Front Line.* Cambridge: Cambridge Univ. Press, 2008.

Tao, Lung-sheng. "The Sino-American Status of Forces Agreement: Criminal Jurisdiction over American Soldiers on Nationalist Chinese Territory." *Boston University Law Review* 51 (1971): 1–30.

Taylor, Jay. *The Generalissimo: Chiang Kai-shek and the Struggle for Modern China.* Cambridge: Belknap Press of Harvard Univ. Press, 2009.

———. *The Generalissimo's Son: Chiang Ching-kuo and the Revolutions in China and Taiwan.* Cambridge: Belknap Press of Harvard Univ. Press, 2000.

Tsang, Steve. "Chiang Kai-shek and the Kuomintang's Policy to Reconquer the Chinese Mainland, 1949–1958." In *In the Shadow of China: Political Developments in Taiwan since 1949,* ed. Steve Tsang, 48–72. Honolulu: Univ. of Hawai'i Press, 1993.

Tsiang Tingfu. *Tsiang Tingfu Diaries, 1944–1965.* Ann Arbor, Mich.: University Microfilms International, 1990. 4 reels.

Tucker, Nancy Bernkopf, ed. *China Confidential: American Diplomats and Sino-American Relations, 1945–1996.* New York: Columbia Univ. Press, 2001.

————. *The China Threat: Memories, Myths, and Realities in the 1950s.* New York: Columbia Univ. Press, 2012.

————. *Uncertain Friendships: Taiwan, Hong Kong, and the United States, 1945–1992.* New York: Twayne, 1994.

U.S. MAAG-Taiwan: An Oral History. Taibei: Ministry of National Defense, Republic of China, 2008.

Wang, Elizabeth Te-chen. *A Memoir: From Mainland China to 43 Years as an MP in Taiwan.* Taipei: Self-published, 2006.

Wang, Peter Chen-main. "A Bastion Created, a Regime Reformed, an Economy Reengineered, 1949–1970." In *Taiwan: A New History,* ed. Murray Rubenstein, 321–338. Armonk, N.Y.: Sharpe, 1999.

Wright, Robert K., and John T. Greenwood. *Airborne Forces at War: From Parachute Test Platoon to the 21st Century.* Annapolis, Md.: Naval Institute Press, 2007.

Xu Yongchang. *Xu Yongchang riji* (The diary of Xu Yongchang). 12 vols. Nangang: Academia Sinica, Institute of Modern History, 1991.

Young, Kenneth T. *Negotiating with the Chinese Communists: The United States Experience, 1953–1967.* New York: McGraw-Hill, 1968.

Zhang Qiyun, ed. *Jiang zongtong ji* (Works of President Chiang Kai-shek). 2 vols. Taibei: National Defense Research Institute, 1968.

Index

STUDIES IN CONFLICT, DIPLOMACY, AND PEACE

SERIES EDITORS: George C. Herring, Andrew L. Johns, and Kathryn C. Statler

This series focuses on key moments of conflict, diplomacy, and peace from the eighteenth century to the present to explore their wider significance in the development of U.S. foreign relations. The series editors welcome new research in the form of original monographs, interpretive studies, biographies, and anthologies from historians, political scientists, journalists, and policymakers. A primary goal of the series is to examine the United States' engagement with the world, its evolving role in the international arena, and the ways in which the state, nonstate actors, individuals, and ideas have shaped and continue to influence history, both at home and abroad.

ADVISORY BOARD MEMBERS

David Anderson, California State University, Monterey Bay
Laura Belmonte, Oklahoma State University
Robert Brigham, Vassar College
Paul Chamberlin, University of Kentucky
Jessica Chapman, Williams College
Frank Costigliola, University of Connecticut
Michael C. Desch, University of Notre Dame
Kurk Dorsey, University of New Hampshire
John Ernst, Morehead State University
Joseph A. Fry, University of Nevada, Las Vegas
Ann Heiss, Kent State University
Sheyda Jahanbani, University of Kansas
Mark Lawrence, University of Texas
Mitchell Lerner, Ohio State University
Kyle Longley, Arizona State University
Robert McMahon, Ohio State University
Michaela Hoenicke Moore, University of Iowa
Lien-Hang T. Nguyen, University of Kentucky
Jason Parker, Texas A&M University
Andrew Preston, Cambridge University
Thomas Schwartz, Vanderbilt University
Salim Yaqub, University of California, Santa Barbara

BOOKS IN THE SERIES

Truman, Congress, and Korea: The Politics of America's First Undeclared War
Larry Blomstedt

The Gulf: The Bush Presidencies and the Middle East
Michael F. Cairo

American Justice in Taiwan: The 1957 Riots and Cold War Foreign Policy
Stephen G. Craft

Diplomatic Games: Sport, Statecraft, and International Relations since 1945
Edited by Heather L. Dichter and Andrew L. Johns

Nothing Less Than War: A New History of America's Entry into World War I
Justus D. Doenecke

Enemies to Allies: Cold War Germany and American Memory
Brian C. Etheridge

Grounded: The Case for Abolishing the United States Air Force
Robert M. Farley

The American South and the Vietnam War: Belligerence, Protest, and Agony in Dixie
Joseph A. Fry

Obama at War: Congress and the Imperial Presidency
Ryan C. Hendrickson

The Conversion of Senator Arthur H. Vandenberg: From Isolation to International Engagement
Lawrence S. Kaplan

The Currents of War: A New History of American-Japanese Relations, 1899–1941
Sidney Pash

So Much to Lose: John F. Kennedy and American Policy in Laos
William J. Rust

Lincoln Gordon: Architect of Cold War Foreign Policy
Bruce L. R. Smith